How To Build
Vintage Hot Rod
V-8 Engines

George McNicholl

How To Build
Vintage Hot Rod
V-8 Engines

George McNicholl

MOTORBOOKS
INTERNATIONAL

First published in 2005 by Motorbooks International, an imprint of MBI Publishing Company, Galtier Plaza, Suite 200, 380 Jackson Street, St. Paul, MN 55101-3885 USA

The information in this book is true and complete to the best of our knowledge. All recommendations are made without any guarantee on the part of the author or Publisher, who also disclaim any liability incurred in connection with the use of this data or specific details.

This publication has been prepared solely by MBI Publishing Company and is not approved or licensed by any other entity. We recognize that some words, model names, and designations mentioned herein are the property of the trademark holder. We use them for identification purposes only. This is not an official publication.

Motorbooks International titles are also available at discounts in bulk quantity for industrial or sales-promotional use. For details write to Special Sales Manager at Motorbooks International Wholesalers & Distributors, Galtier Plaza, Suite 200, 380 Jackson Street, St. Paul, MN 55101-3885 USA.

ISBN 0-7603-2084-5

Printed in China

On the front cover: This Corvette 350-ci engine was installed in a 1923 Ford Model T Roadster Pickup. The engine was initially fitted with a tunnel-ram intake manifold. This engine is covered in Chapter 11.

Front cover inset: The water jacket holes in this Chevrolet small-block are chamfered by hand in order to clean up the top edges.

On the frontis/title page: My 1969 Corvette coupe with a big-block Chevrolet 454-ci engine backed by a Muncie M-20 manual four-speed transmission and a Corvette 3.08-ratio Posi-Traction rear end. The engine is featured in Chapter 12.

On the back cover: A good front view of the 1956 Chrysler 354-ci Hemi engine.

About the author: George McNicholl was born in Vancouver, B.C., Canada, more than 50 years ago. He purchased his first automobile engine (a Ford flathead V-8) when he was 12 years old. He sailed on deep-sea ships for 15 years, with the last two years in the position of captain. He is still involved in the shipping business, although he has been ashore for 25 years. Car and engine building have always been hobbies for McNicholl, and he has the greatest affection for the Ford flathead V-8. Suitably, he is the author of the MBI publication *How To Build A Flathead Ford V-8.*

Edited by Lindsay Hitch
Designed by Brenda C. Canales

CONTENTS

FOREWORD

I have been an automotive enthusiast and hot rodder for more than 40 years. The first book I wrote, *How to Build a Flathead Ford V-8,* was published by MBI Publishing Company and released in April 2003. I do not intend to bore you to death by rewriting my biography in this book. If anyone is interested, which I highly doubt, kindly purchase my flathead book and read about my background in the Foreword of that publication. I can certainly use the revenue from my first book toward the extremely high overhead I have at home as a result of my family!

I have been compiling the complete buildup information of my own engines and vehicles for over 20 years, as well as doing this for all the engines I have assisted Luke's Custom Machine & Design (see Appendix B—Resources) in assembling. That is where I spend the time off from my profession helping with engine assembly, detailing, and parts ordering. I assisted with the complete assembly of the Cadillac engine, the Chevrolet 327-ci engine, and the early Chrysler Hemi engines described in this book. The other engines described are mine, and I built all of them. At the end of Chapters 9 through 18, I included a summary section that contains the complete buildup information, including clearances, part numbers, and prices. This data is extremely valuable when determining the appraised value of a vehicle for insurance purposes and serves as a quick reference source.

A number of readers of my flathead book were aware of the buildup information I have compiled for other types of engines, and it was suggested that I write a book containing this information. I decided to act upon the concept and share the information I have accumulated over the years. I particularly wanted to describe the engines available from the 1950s to the early 1970s. I believe this will be of considerable assistance to hot rod and custom car owners wanting to build a decent V-8 street performance OHV (overhead valve) engine. Some of the parts used in these engines have become obsolete or difficult to locate, which is why I have listed alternative parts and suggestions whenever possible. It was not my intention to list every piece of aftermarket speed equipment available for these engines. There is good information throughout the book applicable to all the engines described—read the entire book.

ACKNOWLEDGMENTS

I would like to thank my wife, Jillian, for allowing me the use of her camera (once again), which I used to take every photograph in this book. I am certain the loan of this camera is going to cost me dearly down the road. I would also like to thank my son, Tyler, and daughter, Kristina, for attempting to educate me with some computer knowledge. What an uphill struggle that is!

I would sincerely like to thank Peter Bodensteiner, my acquisitions editor at MBI Publishing Company, for his continuing support of my projects. Through his superb efforts, my first book was published and has become a great success. I have to use some restraint when praising Peter. If I get carried away, he might want a raise at the expense of my book royalties!

INTRODUCTION

Chapters 1 through 8 provide a general explanation of the parts, machining requirements, and assembly procedures carried out in building a performance street engine. These procedures apply to all the engines described, and they are necessary if the owner desires a premium-quality engine. There is a world of difference between an engine building shop that routinely rebuilds the average automobile engine and a high-performance engine building shop where strict tolerances are the rule. Do not try to cut corners—the result will be extremely disappointing and most likely a waste of hard-earned cash. Only very experienced engine builders should attempt to assemble their own engines. Avoid a lot of grief and leave that to a professional engine builder.

Chapters 9 through 18 are each dedicated to a specific engine. The "Components Description" section provides a detailed explanation of the parts used along with some recommendations for alternative parts. The "Engine Summary" sums up the assembly procedures. The part numbers listed were those available at the time the engines were built; these may have been revised by the manufacturers. The prices for the aftermarket parts reflect retail prices in effect as of December 2004. These prices do not include taxes or shipping and handling charges and are based on the assumption that the owner of the engine will purchase his own parts to avoid a markup (often nearly 20 percent) by the machine shop or engine building shop. Although it is not a common practice to include the prices in most automotive publications, I have done so in order to provide as accurate an indication as possible of the cost of building one of these engines. The engines described here are not cheap; however, they are reasonable considering the quality of the parts used.

Note: These prices are in U.S. dollars. The prices indicated may vary in different parts of North America and are subject to change without notice.

The majority of the engines described in this book have been installed in vehicles. I have not included details on the bell housing, flywheel and clutch assembly, or the flexplate and torque converter assembly. Anyone building similar types of engines will have their own ideas for the types of transmissions that will be installed. Besides, I had to stop somewhere!

Many engine owners do not research the buildup of an engine properly. All the parts of an engine must fit correctly, and they must all work together in order to obtain the maximum potential from the engine. Some people rush out and buy the first part that comes to mind, ignoring the fact that that part might not be the correct one for that particular engine. They end up spending unbelievable amounts of money and then wonder why the engines do not perform as expected. The engines described in this book are proven models that function superbly. A lot of research went into building each of them, which is why they work. Good luck with your own hot rod or custom car project. Remember to drive safely and sanely.

CHAPTER 1
ENGINE BLOCK

Purchase and Magnaflux

Some of the greatest sources of information for the older V-8 engines are the parts catalogs published by the automobile manufacturers. These publications contain model and serial numbers, technical data, specifications, and optional part numbers, just to name a few items. The manuals are very helpful when building a street performance engine.

The book on the left is Chevrolet Power (5th edition) and the publication on the right is Chevrolet Chassis and Body Parts Catalog, for the 1953 through 1980 Corvette, published by General Motors. These types of manuals are extremely valuable sources of information.

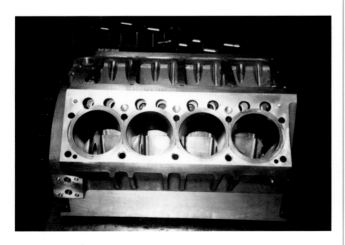

A Donovan aluminum early Chrysler Hemi engine block that is the basis for a 417-ci engine. It is a drag race engine block; there are no water jackets.

It is up to you whether you buy a complete engine or only the individual parts. If there is a source for the individual parts, it may prove to be more economical than buying a complete engine. A lot of the parts on a complete engine will not be used.

There are probably half a dozen companies that manufacture aftermarket small- and big-block Chevrolet engines. The engine blocks are available in cast iron or aluminum and range in retail price from about $2,000 and up for a cast-iron engine block (bare) to $4,000 and up for an aluminum engine block (bare). The (Ed) Donovan 417-ci aluminum drag racing engine block is the only early Chrysler Hemi aftermarket engine block manufactured (that I am aware of). Aside from wanting an engine with astronomical cubic inches, there is really no reason to purchase an aftermarket engine block as the basis for a street performance engine.

If you lack the necessary knowledge for inspecting the engine block, take someone along who is knowledgeable. The best way to have an engine block inspected is to take it to your local machine shop or engine building shop. A reasonable seller would most likely agree to the inspection.

Have the engine block thoroughly examined for cracks or damage. Visually examine the sides of the engine block, the oil pan

A World Products 081111 Merlin II CNC-machined cast-iron alloy tall deck (10.2 inches) Chevrolet engine block. This engine block comes with a 4.49-inch bore and four-bolt main bearing caps, and will accept all Chevrolet bolt-on parts.

rails, all the bolt holes, the cylinders, and the main bearing webs. The main bearing caps should be attached when purchasing an engine block. If they are missing, it is usually not difficult to locate replacements. However, the use of replacement main bearing caps will most likely require that the engine block be align honed or even align bored. This additional cost should definitely reduce the purchase price of an engine block.

Measure the cylinder bore size to ensure the engine block can be rebored. Most cast-iron V-8 engine blocks manufactured in the United States from the 1950s to the 1970s can be bored 0.030 inch oversize and many of them can be safely bored 0.060 inch oversize. If there is any question about how much material is left in the cylinder walls, have your local machine shop sonic test the cylinders.

The engine block, the main bearing caps, and the main bearing cap bolts should be Magnafluxed, technically known as "magnet particle testing." The estimated cost to Magnaflux an engine block and the main bearing caps and bolts is $45.

Cleaning

Remove all the bolts, the camshaft bearings, any bushings or retainers, the freeze plugs, and all the oil gallery line plugs. Have the engine block hot tanked prior to Magnafluxing in order to properly examine it.

Grind the valve lifter gallery smooth with a high-speed grinder with carbide bits and/or small sanding discs to assist with the oil return to the oil pan. This process can be performed after the engine block is hot tanked.

Redi-Strip Engine Block

Redi-Stripping (see Appendix B—Resources) is a non-acidic chemical process that completely removes all foreign matter from an engine block. The procedure ensures the water passages are absolutely clean, thus preventing overheating. A professional engine building shop will usually insist that an engine block is Redi-Stripped before the shop will work on it. It is absolutely amazing to see what has been living in an engine block, especially if the engine block is approaching the 50-year mark!

Detailing the Engine Block

After the engine block is Redi-Stripped, use a high-speed grinder with small sanding discs to remove all the rough areas from the outside of the engine block. The entire outside surface should be as smooth as possible.

Retap and Chamfer Bolt Holes

Run a tap through every bolt hole in the engine block to ensure each and every thread is in perfect shape and to obtain accurate torque readings when it is time to reassemble the engine. After the engine block is parallel decked, use a countersink bit in a drill and lightly chamfer all the cylinder head bolt holes to prevent those

The cylinder head bolt holes in this Chrysler 354-ci Hemi engine block are retapped. This engine block has been hot tanked, the exterior surface has been sanded and detailed, and the valve lifter gallery has been ground smooth and painted with Glyptal G-1228A medium-grey gloss enamel.

A World Products 081111 Merlin II Chevrolet big-block that has had the valve lifter gallery ground smooth and then painted with Glyptal G-1228A medium-grey gloss enamel. A Moroso 25001 oil gallery screen kit has been installed.

A small-block Ford 351W (Windsor) engine block undergoing a boring operation with a Rottler Boring Bar Company (model F2B) machine. This older type of boring bar still does an excellent job when an experienced machinist operates it.

An early Chrysler 392-ci Hemi racing engine block undergoing cylinder honing with a Sunnen Automatic Cylinder Resizing Machine (model CK-10). Notice the O-rings around the cylinders and the four-bolt main bearing cap conversion using splayed caps.

threads from being "pulled" when the cylinder head bolts, or studs, are torqued.

Glyptal is the paint used on electrical motors. This terrific paint will withstand very high temperatures and is almost impossible to chip. I prefer to purchase this paint in the spray can (rattle can) form for ease of application. As soon as the engine block is returned from being Redi-Stripped, paint the valve lifter gallery and the front of the engine block (behind the camshaft timing gear) with Glyptal. The paint is available from electrical repair outlets.

Purchase 16 plastic plugs (as close to the diameter of the valve lifter bosses as possible) from a local hardware store and insert them in the valve lifter bosses. You can wrap masking tape around the plugs to build up the diameter if they don't quite fit. You can also use a discarded set of valve lifters. Plug any other openings in the valve lifter gallery and mask off the rest of the engine block with newspaper. Glass bead the crankshaft oil slinger and the inside of the timing gear cover (unless it is aluminum), and paint them with Glyptal.

Machining

I have been using the services of High Performance Engines, British Columbia, Canada (see Appendix B—Resources), for my own engines over the past 30 years. The machine work for all the engines described in this book was performed at that shop. It is a superb engine building and machine shop where perfection and strict attention to detail are standard operating procedure. It may not be practical for people in other parts of North America to use that particular company, but it is imperative to locate a machine shop with similar high standards.

Cylinder Boring

Purchase the pistons and deliver them to the machine shop. The machine shop will then measure each piston with a micrometer and bore the cylinders accordingly to ensure there is adequate piston-to-bore clearance (after cylinder honing), measured below the bottom of the wrist pin perpendicular to the wrist pin. Ross Racing Pistons recommends a final piston clearance of 0.003 to 0.004 inch for an engine being fitted with its forged aluminum pistons. The company recommends a final piston clearance of 0.006 to 0.008 inch for an engine being fitted with its forged aluminum blower pistons. The engine block is usually bored within 0.003 to 0.004 inch of the final cylinder bore and then honed and deglazed, resulting in the final cylinder bore.

OHV (overhead valve) engines should be bored and the cylinders honed using a torque plate. The torque plate will simulate the distortion caused to the engine block when the cylinder heads are torqued in place. The same type of fastener used to bolt the cylinder heads in place should be used with the torque plate. Cylinder head studs place a different stress on the engine block than cylinder head bolts, even when these two types of fasteners are torqued to the same setting.

The main bearing caps must be installed and correctly torqued during the boring operation. The procedure places stress on the bottom end of the engine block and prevents the cylinders from distorting after they have been bored when the crankshaft is installed and torqued in position. The estimated cost for cylinder boring, honing, and deglazing is $125.

The cylinder boring is carried out using a Rottler Boring Bar Company model F2B boring bar or similar type of machine. The engine block is set up in the machine, the centerline of the crankshaft is located using a dial indicator, and the engine block is then clamped in position, ready for the actual cylinder boring operation.

The final stage of the boring operation is the cylinder honing and deglazing, which ensures the proper seating of the piston rings. The procedure can be performed using a Sunnen automatic cylinder resizing machine, Model CK-10, or similar piece of equipment. The honing machine removes the last 0.003 to 0.004 inch of material from the cylinder walls (using Sunnen 600 series 280-grit stones for cast-iron piston rings or Sunnen 800 series 400-grit stones for moly piston rings). The final result will be the finished bore. The finish on the cylinder walls will be a cross-hatch pattern.

Align Hone and Align Bore

The centerline of the crankshaft is the point from which all critical measurements are taken. The centerline of the crankshaft is used to ensure the engine block main bearing housing bores, with the main bearing caps attached, are exactly parallel.

The engine block main bearing housing bores must be measured with a dial indicator or inside micrometer to ensure they are in perfect alignment with each other and are not tapered. If this is not the case, the engine block will have to be align honed. If the main bearing caps are not those originally supplied with the engine block, align honing or possibly even align boring will have to be undertaken. Each time the align honing operation is performed, approximately 0.0005 inch of material is removed from the main bearing housing bores and the main bearing caps. This procedure is so critical it must only be done at a machine shop specializing in high-performance engine building. It costs approximately $200 to align hone and/or align bore an engine block.

Use a crankshaft that has been checked for alignment and is guaranteed to be straight as a means to check the main bearing housing bore alignment of the engine block. Install the correct main bearings for the crankshaft in the engine block, oil the main bearings well, install the crankshaft, and torque the main bearing cap bolts (or studs) correctly. The crankshaft should turn freely without any tight spots. If it does, the engine block is acceptable. If it does not, the engine block will have to be align honed.

Main bearing cap bolts create a different distortion in the bottom end of the engine block than do main bearing cap studs, even when these two types of fasteners are torqued to the same setting. If an engine block is align bored or honed with main bearing cap bolts in place, you cannot replace them with main bearing cap studs at any time thereafter. The reverse situation also applies. You must decide prior to align boring or honing which type of fasteners to use.

Use a Sunnen horizontal hone (model CH-100 align honing machine) or similar piece of equipment to align hone the engine block. Mill to remove approximately 0.005 inch from the mating surface of the main bearing caps and then proceed with the align

A small-block Dodge 360-ci engine block about to be align bored and honed on a Sunnen Horizontal Hone (Model CH-100) machine. Notice that splayed four-bolt main bearing caps have been installed.

A Dart Machinery 31384275 Iron Eagle small-block Ford engine block parallel decked with a Repco Automotive Company Type ASG machine. Even brand-new aftermarket engine blocks usually have to be parallel decked.

honing procedure. The engine block must be align bored when new custom-made main bearing caps are going to be installed and occasionally when stock main bearing caps (other than the original main bearing caps) are used. There are a number of align boring machines currently in use, including the Sunnen horizontal hone (model CH-100 with the Sunnen align bore attachment, model PLB-100) and the Torbin-Arp Manufacturing Company align boring machine (model TA15).

Parallel Deck

An engine block is parallel decked to ensure the deck height is the same for all the cylinders and to guarantee the deck is

The water jacket holes in this Chevrolet small-block are chamfered by hand in order to clean up the top edges.

A set of Chrysler Hemi 354-ci main bearing caps and bolts that have been shot peened to remove stress.

exactly perpendicular to the cylinder bores. The majority of engine blocks should be parallel decked; this requires the removal of approximately 0.005 to 0.015 inch of material from the deck surface. It costs approximately $110 to parallel deck an engine block.

Use a Repco Automotive Company Type ASG or similar machine to parallel deck the engine block. Use a dial indicator to locate the crankshaft centerline, clamp the engine block into position, and then parallel deck one side of the engine block, followed by the other side.

Shot Peen

The main bearing caps and the main bearing cap bolts can be shot peened while the engine block is at the machine shop being hot tanked and Magnafluxed. Shot peening will assist to remove any stress from those items.

Deglaze

Deglaze the valve lifter bosses with a wheel cylinder or ball hone. Hone the valve lifter bosses just enough to clean them up. Remove the absolute minimum of material in order to avoid excess valve lifter clearance, which will result in an oiling problem.

Cracks

If an engine block is cracked, it is best to take a pass on it. There are thousands of good used engine blocks available and all it takes is a little patience and perseverance to locate one. Search through Hemmings Motor News (www.hemmings.com), the local buy-and-sell newspaper, eBay (www.ebay.com), and good old "word of mouth." I purchase many items off eBay, but only from highly rated sellers.

Cleaning and Painting

After all the machining procedures described in this chapter have been performed, thoroughly clean the engine block with hot water and soap. Use long, thin engine brushes to reach as far into the oil passages as possible. Spend the time to do this job properly. The term "hospital clean" applies here!

Mask off the engine block with newspaper and use the cylinder head gaskets, timing gear cover gasket, oil pan gaskets, and water pump gaskets as templates for the masking. Polyurethane paint is the best paint to use for an engine block. The paint is extremely durable and nearly impervious to gasoline, lacquer thinner, antifreeze, oil, and brake fluid. There are a number of companies that produce polyurethane paint. I have found PPG polyurethane to be an excellent product and it is available in just about every imaginable color. You can purchase polyurethane paint at a local industrial supply store and even from your local body shop.

Polyurethane paint should be sprayed in a temperature-controlled paint booth by an experienced painter. I am one of the guilty parties that used to spray-paint engine blocks (and cars) in my alley and garage. This practice used to alienate most of the neighborhood and was a health hazard and a total environmental disaster. I now have all my engine blocks painted at a local body shop. Even some of us truly stubborn people have to change with the times.

After the engine block has been painted, install the freeze plugs in the engine block using Permatex aviation form-a-gasket. The most common type of freeze plug is the expansion plug manufactured by Pioneer and Dorman. Dorman also produces a copper bolt-in freeze plug for the early Chrysler Hemi engine blocks. Freeze plugs are very inexpensive and are available at your local automotive parts store.

O-rings

An engine block should be O-ringed if it is going to be equipped with a blower, although some engine builders believe this is only necessary if the boost is going to exceed 5 pounds. A groove is machined in the deck surface around the cylinders approximately 0.125 inch from the edge, after which a piece of stainless-steel wire is tapped into the groove. The groove is the same size as the diameter of the stainless-steel wire, usually 0.035 inch. A receiver groove is machined into the cylinder head in the exact position above the wire in the engine block. The wire in the engine block will press the cylinder head gasket into the receiver groove in the cylinder head, creating an excellent seal. It will cost approximately $100 to O-ring an engine block and receiver groove the cylinder heads.

A set of Dorman 568-010 quick-seal copper freeze plugs for the early Chrysler Hemi engine blocks.

An early-style Keith Black Chrysler 426-ci Hemi aluminum cylinder head that has been O-ringed for drag racing.

CHAPTER 2
CRANKSHAFT

The best crankshaft to use in a street performance engine is a forged steel unit. There is nothing wrong with cast steel crankshafts for mild street performance use—they are extremely durable and will run without problem for hundreds of thousands of miles. (The engines in most taxis and police vehicles are equipped with cast-iron crankshafts.) But for a top-quality, street performance engine, select only the best of parts, including a forged steel crankshaft. Forged steel crankshafts were available from the factory for all the engines described in this book with the exceptions of the Cadillac 500-ci engine and the Keith Black engine.

It is risky business to purchase a used crankshaft outright, not knowing whether it is cracked or the journals have been ground to the point that bearings are not available in the size required. I fully appreciate that it is becoming increasingly difficult to find a good used forged steel crankshaft, especially for early Chrysler Hemi engines. Do not let desperation cloud your thinking and buy the first crankshaft that appears on the scene. As a condition of purchase, have the crankshaft professionally examined by a quality machine shop of your choice. If the seller will not agree to this, walk away. As hard as it may be, there will always be another seller and another crankshaft.

There are many aftermarket crankshaft manufacturers offering

An early Chrysler 354-ci Hemi forged steel crankshaft (casting number 1619467) that has been shot peened, aligned, and Magnafluxed. The main and connecting rod journals have been ground 0.010-inch undersize, the oil holes chamfered, and the journals polished.

cast steel and forged steel crankshafts in all price ranges. Exotic crankshafts, such as "non-twist" forgings or billet steel, are readily available—there is only the simple matter of money! I am not aware of any company that offers a replacement crankshaft for the early Chrysler Hemi, although that situation will most likely be corrected in the near future by some enterprising party.

Magnaflux
The crankshaft must be Magnafluxed after the crankshaft is hot tanked and shot peened. The estimated cost to Magnaflux a crankshaft is $20.

Hot Tank and Shot Peen
The first thing to do with a crankshaft is to hot tank it, followed by shot peening. The shot peening will remove any stress within the crankshaft. Prior to hot tanking, remove the crankshaft timing gear with a gear puller.

Straightness, Chamfer, and Polish
Check the crankshaft for alignment and runout with the use of a dial indicator; have it straightened if necessary. Chamfer each oil hole by lightly grinding the sharp surfaces off around the oil holes. Do not create deep oval craters around the oil holes. The estimated cost to chamfer the oil holes is $20.

After the crankshaft has been ground and the oil holes chamfered, polish the journals to ensure an absolutely smooth bearing surface. The estimated cost of polishing the crankshaft journals is $30.

Regrinding and Cleaning
The crankshaft will most likely have to be reground, which will cost approximately $105. The maximum main bearing size for most OHV (overhead valve) V-8 engines is usually 0.030-inch oversize. The maximum connecting rod bearing size is usually 0.040-inch oversize.

If the main bearing or connecting rod journals are severely damaged or undersized to the point that bearings are not available, there are two methods of building up the journals. The first involves wire welding to build up the journal, after which the journal is ground in the usual fashion. This is a proven method of repair that a high-quality crankshaft grinding company can handle with ease. The estimated cost to wire weld a crankshaft journal is $140.

The second method of repair consists of spraying molten metal on the journal, after which the journal is ground in the usual fashion. The journal is then surface nitrided (casehardened) to 60 Rockwell C hardness. This procedure results in an extremely hard surface. The estimated cost to metal spray a journal is $140. After all the procedures mentioned in this chapter have been carried out, thoroughly clean the crankshaft with hot water and soap.

Main Bearings

Clevite 77 (Dana Corporation) and Federal Mogul manufacture top-quality engine bearings. The Clevite 77 bearings are a tri-metal construction with a soft alloy outer layer, copper-lead center, and steel backing. The standard-type Federal Mogul bearings are also a tri-metal construction with a steel backing, copper-lead center, thin nickel barrier, and lead-tin-copper outer layer. Main bearings and connecting rod bearings for the early Chrysler Hemi are becoming more difficult to locate. Fortunately, King Engine Bearings manufactures main bearings and connecting rod bearings in the most common sizes for the early Chrysler Hemi engines. These bimetal bearings are constructed with a steel backing and a bonded outer layer of Alecular material, which consists of an alloy of aluminum, tin, copper, and several other elements.

In order to check the main-bearing-to-crankshaft clearance, insert the main bearings in the engine block and the main bearing caps, and then torque the main bearing caps in position. Use an inside micrometer or a dial indicator to measure the inside diameter of the main bearings, and then use a micrometer to measure the main bearing journals on the crankshaft. The difference between these two measurements is the main bearing clearance. This clearance should be 0.0015 to 0.002 inch for a street performance engine.

Check the crankshaft end play by cleaning the main bearings with wax-and-grease remover and a clean lint-free cloth, installing the main bearings in the engine block and the main bearing caps, oiling the main bearings, installing the crankshaft, and correctly torquing the main bearing cap bolts or studs. Set up a dial indicator at the front of the engine block and attach it to the snout of the crankshaft or set the dial indicator up at the rear of the engine block and attach it to the flywheel flange on the rear of the crankshaft. Insert a pry bar against one of the crankshaft counterweights and then move the crankshaft forward and backward. The reading on the dial indicator is the crankshaft end play. Always refer to the engine manufacturer's shop manual for the recommended clearances and torque settings.

Have the shop that grinds your crankshaft provide the main and connecting rod bearings. This way you are guaranteed to have the correct bearings and not some that fit a World War I army tank. Clevite 77, Federal Mogul, and King Engine Bearings are available through local automotive parts outlets.

Timing Chains and Gear Drives

Install a new double-roller timing chain set in your street performance engine. Never contemplate installing a used timing chain set. Ertel Manufacturing Company and Cloyes produce excellent double-roller timing chain sets, each of which has a three-keyway crankshaft sprocket for advancing or retarding the camshaft timing. Double-roller timing chain sets are readily available at low cost from most automotive stores.

For those of you who want to go a step above the usual double-roller timing chain set installation, there are gear drives, available through local speed shops. The few companies that manufacture gear drives offer them at varying prices depending on whether the gear drive is for street use or competition use.

Harmonic Balancer

The small- and big-block Chevrolet engines were fitted with harmonic balancers; some were internally balanced, and others were externally balanced. The later Chrysler Hemi 331-ci and all the 354-ci Hemi engines use internally balanced harmonic balancers. The 1970 Cadillac 500-ci engine is equipped with an internally balanced harmonic balancer.

A set of Clevite 77 MS-1038P-10 main bearings (0.010-inch oversize) for a small-block Chevrolet 400-ci engine.

CHAPTER 3
CONNECTING RODS AND PISTONS

Purchase

All the engines described in this book were equipped at the factory with forged steel I-beam connecting rods, with the exception of the Keith Black engine. Factory forged steel I-beam connecting rods are designed for use with non-floating connecting rod bearings and are satisfactory for use in most street performance engines, even blown engines, provided the boost does not exceed 6 to 7 pounds.

The connecting rod bolts in any street performance engine should be upgraded. ARP (Automotive Racing Products) offers some of the best fasteners available today. Its high-performance-series connecting rod bolts are manufactured using 8740 chrome-moly steel rated at 190,000 psi, which is acceptable for most street performance engines, including mildly blown engines. If the engine is going to be a wild street machine or used for all-out competition, install ARP high-performance Wave-Loc connecting rod bolts, manufactured using 8740 chrome-moly steel rated at 210,000 psi, or the pro series Wave-Loc connecting rod bolts, manufactured using ARP2000 material rated at 220,000 psi. All the ARP bolts have rolled threads and the nuts are parallel ground. ARP products are available at your local performance outlet.

A number of companies manufacture connecting rods, although Cad Company (see Appendix B—Resources) is the only company I am aware of that supplies aftermarket steel billet connecting rods for the Cadillac 500-ci engine. Connecting rods are now available in I-beam or H-beam configurations and the prices vary greatly. Once again, the difference is only a matter of money. It is now cheaper to purchase certain models of new aftermarket connecting rods than it is to Magnaflux, shot peen, align, debeam, resize, rebush, and install new connecting rod bolts in used connecting rods. Adhere to the torque setting recommended by the manufacturer of the aftermarket connecting rods. The ultimate connecting rods are those supplied by Crower Cams & Equipment Company and Cunningham Rods (see Appendix B—Resources), although you can forget about any Christmas presents for the family if you purchase a set of those connecting rods!

A set of ARP 145-6002 high-performance-series connecting rod bolts manufactured using 8740 chrome-moly steel and rated at 190,000 psi. These bolts will be installed in a set of Chrysler 354-ci Hemi connecting rods.

The ultimate in connecting rods: Cunningham custom cross-grain flow pure 4340 chrome-moly steel, H-I beam connecting rods for a Chrysler 392-ci Hemi engine. The cap screw bolts are rated at 296,000 psi!

This connecting rod vise is the only type of fixture that a connecting rod should be clamped into.

A vintage set of Mickey Thompson aluminum connecting rods for an early Chrysler 392-ci Hemi engine. Do not use aluminum connecting rods in a street performance engine.

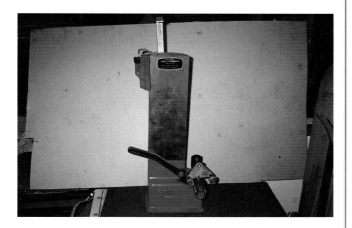

A Chevrolet 350-ci connecting rod is resized on a Sunnen Heavy-Duty Precision Honing Machine Powerstroker (Model LBB-1810).

A Sunnen (Model TN-111) connecting rod alignment tool, used to straighten bent or twisted connecting rods.

Aluminum connecting rods are designed for drag racing and should not be used in a street performance engine. Aluminum connecting rods have a tendency to stretch over time and eventually crack, which is why they are inspected after every race. They are also much bulkier than forged steel connecting rods, which means the engine block most likely has to be clearanced in order to fit those connecting rods.

Magnaflux and Shot Peen

The connecting rods must be Magnafluxed to ensure there are no hidden flaws. Shot peen the connecting rods to remove any stress points. The estimated cost to Magnaflux eight connecting rods is $30.

Align, Resize, and Rebush

Align the connecting rods with a Sunnen model TN-111 quick-check rod aligner tool, or similar instrument, and a connecting rod vise. Aligning ensures the connecting rods are vertically straight in both the front and side positions, not twisted or bent. Note: Never clamp the connecting rods in anything but a connecting rod vise.

The crankshaft end (the big end) of the connecting rod should be resized on a Sunnen Heavy-Duty Precision Honing Machine, Powerstroker model LBB-1810, or similar machine. This procedure will ensure the big ends are perfectly round and all the connecting rods are the same length, center to center (from the center of the big end to the center of the small end). The estimated cost to resize a set of eight connecting rods is $80.

Connecting rods with non-floating pistons are not fitted with wrist pin bushings; the wrist pin end (the small end) of the connecting rod is honed to fit the wrist pin. Some connecting rods

17

A Sunnen Heavy-Duty Precision Honing Machine (Model LBB-1499) honing the wrist pin end (the small end) of a Chevrolet 350-ci connecting rod.

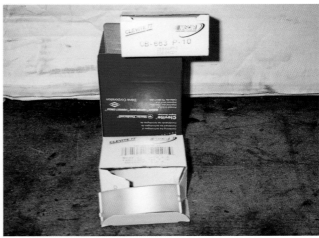

A set of Clevite 77 CB-663P-10 connecting rod bearings (0.010-inch oversize) for a small-block Chevrolet 350-ci engine.

with full-floating pistons are fitted with wrist pin bushings. New wrist pin bushings should be installed in connecting rods already fitted with wrist pin bushings if they are going to be used with full-floating pistons. The installation and honing of wrist pin bushings should only be done by a reliable machine shop. Clevite 77 and Federal Mogul manufacture quality wrist pin bushings, available from most automotive stores and some local machine shops.

Bring the pistons to the machine shop with the connecting rods. The machine shop can then hone the new wrist pin bushings allowing for 0.0015- to 0.002-inch clearance for the wrist pin. This is the accepted wrist pin clearance for a street performance engine.

The honing of the wrist pin end (the small end) of the connecting rod is carried out on a Sunnen Heavy-Duty Precision Honing Machine (model LBB-1499) or similar type of machine. The estimated cost of re-bushing and wrist pin fitting for a set of eight connecting rods is $120 (this does not include the cost of the wrist pin bushings).

Debeam and Boxing

All I-beam connecting rods should be debeamed to remove any hidden imperfections in the sides of the connecting rods that could lead to cracks and result in connecting rod failure. Use a high-speed grinder with a carbide bit and grind the sides to a smooth finish. Then sand the sides to a polished finish. The grinding and sanding must be done in a vertical direction (from top to bottom) with the flow of the grain in the connecting rod. Do not grind and sand across the grain.

It used to be a common practice to box the connecting rods used in serious street performance engines and especially in blown engines. It is far cheaper today to purchase new aftermarket connecting rods than it is to box a set of existing connecting rods. To box connecting rods, an insert is fabricated from 4130 chrome-moly steel plate (0.080-inch thickness) and welded to both sides of

an I-beam connecting rod. As soon as the welding is completed, the connecting rods are placed in a preheated 400-degree (Fahrenheit) oven for approximately eight hours. The oven is then turned off and the connecting rods are allowed to cool down overnight to room temperature. This process removes stress from the connecting rods. All the welds and the sides of the connecting rods are ground smooth (with the flow of the grain) and then sanded to a polished finish.

Connecting Rod Bearings

Clevite 77 and Federal Mogul manufacture good-quality connecting rod bearings for most automobile engines. As previously mentioned, it is becoming difficult to locate bearings for the early Chrysler Hemi engines, including connecting rod bearings. King Engine Bearings manufactures connecting rod bearings in the most common sizes for the early Chrysler Hemi engines.

It is extremely important to check the tang (tab) width of main bearings and connecting rod bearings to ensure they are the same width as the bearing notch in the main bearing housing bores and caps and the bearing notch in the connecting rods. It is not unusual to find bearings where the tang is too wide for the bearing notch in the main bearing housing bores and caps or in the connecting rods. On some rare occasions, the thickness of the tang is excessive, which will push the bearings outward and result in the immediate destruction of the bearings when the engine is initially started.

To correctly check the connecting rod bearing clearance, install the connecting rod bearings in the connecting rods, tighten the connecting rod nuts or bolts to the correct torque setting using a connecting rod vise, and then measure the connecting rod bearing bores with a dial indicator or inside micrometer. Measure the connecting rod journals of the crankshaft with a micrometer. The difference between these two measurements is the connecting rod bearing clearance.

Two Ross Racing Pistons custom blower pistons for a Chrysler 392-ci Hemi engine.

To correctly check the side clearance of a pair of connecting rods, use an inside micrometer and measure the distance across the connecting rod journal. Clamp the two connecting rods for that journal together in a connecting rod vise and use a micrometer to measure the thickness of the two connecting rods. The difference between these two measurements is the connecting rod side clearance per pair of connecting rods. Double-check the clearance with a feeler gauge when the connecting rods are installed on the crankshaft.

Pistons

The average passenger car engine manufactured in the United States is fitted with cast-aluminum pistons. This type of piston would probably last forever in most passenger cars, provided the oil and filter were changed on a regular basis. In the 1960s and the 1970s, a number of high-performance engines were equipped with forged aluminum pistons direct from the factory. Forged aluminum pistons are the only type of pistons to use in a street performance engine, especially if it is a blown engine. Forget about all the rumors that engines fitted with forged aluminum pistons burn oil and are noisy as a result of piston slap, due to forged pistons requiring more cylinder bore clearance.

I have been using Ross Racing Pistons' forged aluminum pistons for my own engines for a number of years. These high-quality pistons are available at a very reasonable price. The stocking pistons, which are off-the-shelf products, are readily available in the most common bore sizes for small-block and big-block Chevrolet engines. All the Ross Racing Pistons stocking pistons are manufactured using 2618 T-61 aluminum. They are fitted with aircraft-quality heat-treated wrist pins, and they are supplied with double Spiro-Lox retainers.

The Ross Racing Pistons custom flat top pistons can be used for a blown engine, provided the boost does not exceed 5 pounds. If more than 5 pounds of boost will be used, purchase the custom-forged aluminum blower pistons. Forged aluminum blower pistons have a thicker crown area, thicker ring lands, larger internal radii, and bigger wrist pin bosses in order to handle the higher operating temperatures and additional cylinder pressure. The top compression ring on a blower piston should be at least 0.250 inch below the top of the piston. The Ross Racing Pistons blower pistons are also manufactured using 2618 T-61 aluminum.

A street performance blown engine should have a compression ratio of approximately 7.5:1 to 8.0:1. This ratio is easily achieved when ordering custom blower pistons by providing Ross Racing Pistons with all the necessary information. This information should include the engine type, bore and stroke, connecting rod length, type of cylinder heads and cylinder head volume in cc's, camshaft specifications, valve size, type of fuel system, the type of blower, and the amount of blower boost.

Ross Racing Pistons has its own moly piston ring sets manufactured exclusively for its pistons, and they are the best piston rings to use in a street performance engine. Moly piston rings should be used in a blown engine due to the higher operating temperature and boost. The moly piston rings are much more flexible than cast-iron piston rings. The top piston rings are ductile SG iron and molybdenum inlaid, barrel lapped to ensure quick seating, and coated with zinc phosphate to add corrosion resistance. The second piston rings are cast iron and also zinc phosphate coated. The oil rings consist of a stainless-steel expander and chromium-plated carbon rails.

If the second compression ring gap is smaller than the top piston ring gap, there is less blowby; however, this could cause the top piston ring to flutter. Ross Racing Pistons recommends a larger second compression ring gap than the top compression ring gap in order to prevent piston flutter. The piston ring gap Ross Racing Pistons recommends for its moly piston ring sets is 0.004 inch by the cylinder bore for the top compression ring (plus 0.004 inch for blown engines) and 0.005 inch by the cylinder bore for the second compression ring (plus 0.004 inch for blown engines). Depending on the bore size, the oil ring gap is 0.014 to 0.018 inch. Always follow the manufacturer's instructions for piston ring gap.

To check the end gap of the piston rings, place a piston ring approximately 1 inch from the top of the cylinder in which it will be used. The piston ring must be perfectly square in the cylinder bore in order to obtain an accurate measurement. Use a feeler gauge to determine the end gap of the piston ring. If this end gap is in accordance with the end gap called for by the piston ring manufacturer, move on to the next piston ring and continue until you have checked all the piston rings for all the cylinders.

If the piston ring end gap is not wide enough, file the ends of the piston ring until the correct end gap is obtained. Use a rotary piston ring filing tool to ensure the ends of the piston ring remain parallel to each other.

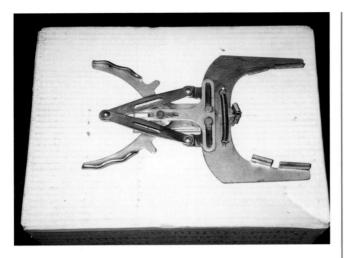

This piston ring expander must be used when installing piston rings on the pistons.

A set of big-block Chevrolet forged aluminum pistons installed on a set of Manley H-beam connecting rods at High Performance Engines. The piston rings are gapped and will soon be installed on the pistons.

Install the pistons on the connecting rods using a generous amount of oil on the wrist pin and the wrist pin bushing. Clamp the connecting rod in a connecting rod vise, place the piston over the connecting rod, insert the wrist pin, and spin the Spiro-Lox retainers into position using a small screwdriver. After stabbing your fingers a few times with the screwdriver, you will get the hang of installing Spiro-Lox retainers.

After the piston rings are correctly gapped, install them on the pistons using a piston ring installation tool. This tool expands the piston rings enough to install them on the pistons without scratching and gouging the aluminum pistons or breaking the piston rings. Prior to installing the piston assemblies in the engine block, turn the piston rings individually on the pistons within the piston ring manufacturer's recommended arc. This means that each

of the three piston rings on a piston are turned and positioned so the end gap is not in the same location for all three piston rings. This is also known as preferred ring gap location. Install the piston assemblies in the engine block using a piston ring compressor, which compresses the piston rings evenly around the piston. Then insert the piston in the cylinder bore by gently tapping the piston top with the handle of a rubber mallet or a piece of wood. Use plastic connecting rod bolt protectors when installing the piston assemblies so as not to nick the crankshaft connecting rod journals.

Check the valve-to-piston clearance prior to the final assembly of the engine. Rotate the crankshaft until one of the pistons is at TDC (top dead center), place some putty on the piston top, install one of the assembled cylinder heads (with or without the cylinder head gasket) using four cylinder head bolts (placed in the four corners), tighten the cylinder head bolts snugly, install the pushrods and rocker arms for that cylinder, adjust the valve lash, rotate the crankshaft at least two full turns, remove the cylinder head, and measure the valve depressions in the putty. The minimum intake-valve-to-piston clearance should be 0.100 inch and the minimum exhaust-valve-to-piston clearance should be 0.125 inch when using forged steel connecting rods.

Balancing

One of the most important steps in building a reliable engine is to have it professionally balanced. This is only a job for an experienced high-performance engine-building shop. Proper engine balancing is an art that should only be done by professionals. I have seen pistons and crankshafts that were supposedly balanced with great chunks out of the crankshaft counterweights and the wrist pin bosses in the pistons. It looked as though rats had been gnawing at them.

Use this piston ring compressor to install the pistons in the cylinder bores.

Checking the valve-to-piston clearance in a Chrysler 392-ci Hemi engine. The clearance must be checked prior to the final assembly of any engine.

A Ross Racing Pistons forged aluminum Chrysler 354-ci blower piston weighed on a Toledo Digital Scale.

A small-block Chevrolet 350-ci connecting rod weighed on a Toledo Digital Scale prior to balancing.

A small-block Chevrolet 350-ci connecting rod balanced on a Stewart-Warner Connecting Rod Balancer (Model 329738). This is a reciprocating balance.

Weigh the pistons on a Toledo Digital Scale or similar instrument to find the lightest-weight piston. Then lighten the other seven pistons to that weight by milling material from the bottom of the wrist pin bosses.

Weigh the connecting rods on a Stewart-Warner Connecting Rod Balancer, model 329738, or similar instrument to find the lightest connecting rod. Then lighten the other seven connecting rods to this weight by removing material from the area above the wrist pin bushing and the sides or bottom of the connecting rod cap using a belt sander. Balance each connecting rod by placing the crankshaft end (the big end) on the balancing machine with the

The same small-block Chevrolet 350-ci connecting rod undergoes a rotating balance.

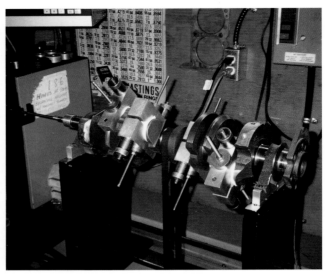

A small-block Chevrolet 350-ci crankshaft is balanced on a Hines Industries Digital Balancer. This is a critical step in the building of any street performance engine.

wrist pin end (the small end) suspended. This is called a rotating balance. Then place the wrist pin end (the small end) on the balancing machine with the crankshaft end (the big end) suspended. This is called a reciprocating balance. Balance the other connecting rods in the same manner. If the numbers on the sides of the connecting rods are sanded off, re-stamp them.

Balance the crankshaft with a Hines Industries Digital Balancer or similar machine. The pistons, wrist pins, wrist pin locks, piston rings, connecting rod bearings, connecting rods, connecting rod nuts, and even an estimated amount of lubricating oil are tallied up for a final weight. This exact amount of weight, in the form of an attachable bob weight, is bolted to each crankshaft connecting rod journal. The crankshaft is then spun on the balancing machine and additional weight is either removed by drilling material from the bottom edges of the crankshaft counterweights or weight is added by drilling and inserting heavy metal (Mallory metal) in the sides of the crankshaft counterweights to compensate for any imbalance.

The following is how bob weight is calculated:
Piston weight (each): _____ x 1 = _____ grams
Wrist pin (each): _____ x 1 = _____ grams
Wrist pin locks (pair/piston): _____ x 1 = _____ grams

Piston rings (set/piston): _____ x 1 = _____ grams
Reciprocating connecting rod (each): _____ x 1 = _____ grams
Rotating connecting rod (each): _____ x 2 = _____ grams
Connecting rod bearings (set/rod): _____ x 2 = _____ grams
Connecting rod nuts (pair): _____ x 2 = _____ grams
Oil (estimated): _____ x 1 = _____ grams
Total bob weight: _____ grams

(Thanks to Bud Child of High Performance Engines (see Appendix B—Resources) for this valuable information.)

Deliver the crankshaft pulley, the flywheel, the clutch disc, and the pressure plate to the machine shop for balancing if you intend to install a standard transmission. Deliver the crankshaft pulley and the flexplate if you plan to install an automatic transmission.

A professionally balanced engine will eliminate internal vibration, which in turn will guarantee the engine bearings enjoy a long and happy life. The estimated cost for a complete V-8 engine balance is $190.

Gaskets

Fel-Pro and Victor Reinz manufacture complete gasket sets for just about every V-8 engine ever built. The complete gasket sets can be purchased at local auto parts stores or speed product outlets.

CHAPTER 4
LUBRICATION SYSTEM

Purchase

Never install a used oil pump in a street performance engine. The oil pump is the heart of the oiling system in the engine, which dictates that only a new oil pump should be installed. New oil pumps are readily available for most V-8 engines and are inexpensive because many companies manufacture them. The oil pumps the factory supplied were excellent models and are still available as replacement parts. Remember: Just because an oil pump has a well-known speed equipment manufacturer's name on it, it is not necessarily any better than a factory oil pump.

Many engine builders believe a high-volume oil pump is a necessity for any street performance engine. This is simply not the case. All that a high-volume oil pump does is increase the supply of oil at the expense of extra horsepower used to deliver the extra volume of oil. Unless you intend to build a truly wild street performance engine, stay with a standard-volume oil pump. There is not much difference in price between a standard-volume and a high-volume oil pump.

Check the clearance between the top of the oil pump gears and the top cover of the oil pump. This clearance should be 0.00025 inch (without the top cover gasket) and is accomplished by sanding the top of the oil pump housing on a piece of thick glass if there is excessive clearance or by sanding the top of the oil pump gears on a thick piece of glass if the clearance is not adequate. After the oil pump is correctly clearanced, thoroughly clean it, apply motor oil to the gears, reinstall the top cover with the gasket using a dab of silicone sealant, and torque the bolts to 80 in-lb using Loctite.

The addition of pressure-balance grooves in the oil pump will actually stop the oil pump gears from chattering, which in turn will eliminate spark-scatter. This procedure is easy to carry out using

A new Milodon 31504 Chevrolet small-block oval track oil pan. This oil pan has a trapdoor system and windage tray installed.

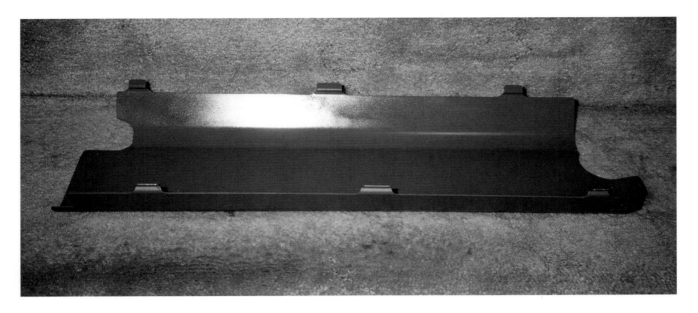

A GM 12555320 valve lifter gallery oil splash shield for a big-block Chevrolet engine, painted with Glyptal G-1228A medium-grey gloss enamel.

a high-speed grinder with a small grinding bit. Grind the pressure-balance grooves across the inside of the top cover, down the inside of the oil pump housing, and across the bottom of the inside of the oil pump housing. The pressure-balance grooves should be approximately 1/32 inch deep (0.03125 inch) and 1/16 inch (0.0625 inch) wide. Aftermarket oil pumps with pressure-balance grooves already in place are available, but it is cheaper to grind your own, provided you have a steady hand.

Oil Pan and Pickup

Some of the V-8 oil pans supplied at the factory had a limited oil capacity. There are a number of companies around today that manufacture stock replacement, street and strip, and drag racing oil pans in deep sump or low-profile models for most of the popular engines. The design of the vehicle frame and steering position will determine which oil pan is the most suitable for a particular vehicle. Many of the aftermarket oil pans have windage trays installed in them. A used oil pan will have to be cleaned, sandblasted or Redi-Stripped, have all the dents and scrapes removed, and painted. It is far more economical and easier to paint a new oil pan than go through all that. Install the oil pan with stainless-steel bolts, lockwashers, and AN flat washers using Loctite, and torque the bolts to 15 ft-lb. Install the oil pan gaskets and seals using silicone sealant.

Match the oil pump pickup to the oil pan. It is a good idea to purchase the oil pump pickup with the oil pan. The oil pump pickup should be tack-welded or brazed to the oil pump to prevent it from vibrating loose.

Check the height of the oil pump pickup from the bottom of the oil pan. Place a lump of putty on the oil pump pickup screen (or cover) and then place the oil pan in position on the engine block without using the oil pan gaskets. Press down on the oil pan and remove it. Then measure the thickness of the compressed putty. There should be 1/2- to 3/4-inch clearance between the oil pump pickup and the bottom of the oil pan. If there is not, adjust the height of the oil pump pickup accordingly.

Windage Trays

Windage trays, otherwise known as splash shields, are inexpensive and excellent items to install in street performance engines. They scavenge oil from the crankshaft rotation, reduce aeration of the oil, minimize oil slosh, and generally aid in oil control. Some windage trays are installed in oil pans and others consist of a semicircular design, flat tray, or louvered tray, which is bolted to the extended main bearing cap studs.

Valve Lifter Gallery Baffle

The valve lifter gallery baffle keeps hot oil off the underside of the intake manifold, thereby allowing for a cooler fuel/air mixture. One type of valve lifter gallery baffle is installed over the top of the valve lifters using spring steel clips positioned inside the valve lifter gallery to hold it in place. This type will not work with roller lifters and you should check to make certain it does not contact standard solid (mechanical) or hydraulic lifters. The better type of valve lifter gallery baffle sits on top of the engine block over the valve lifter gallery and is held in position by the intake manifold. Many intake manifolds that came out of the factory had a heat shield attached to the underside. Paint the valve lifter gallery baffle with Glyptal G-1228A medium-grey gloss enamel to assist with oil return.

CHAPTER 5
CAMSHAFT AND CYLINDER HEADS

Camshaft Bearings

The best camshaft bearings to install in a street performance engine are those manufactured by Clevite 77 or Federal Mogul. Remove the camshaft bearings with a camshaft bearing installation tool (also used to reinstall the bearings). This tool will prevent damage to the camshaft bearing housing bores and the camshaft bearings.

Camshaft

The camshaft is the heart of the engine and probably the most important part you will have to select. This is where research plays a key role. There are some very good camshaft manufacturers in the United States, and those companies can recommend exactly which camshaft to use. I prefer Crower Cams & Equipment Company for camshafts and related components. The company produces superior-quality products. You may well have your own preference for camshafts; that is fine, provided you choose the correct camshaft for your engine.

A basic understanding of camshaft technology is quite helpful, even to the novice engine enthusiast. Below is a brief explanation of the most common terms used when referring to camshafts. The catalogs distributed by most camshaft companies include a section on camshaft terminology and the mathematics associated with camshafts, if you would like a more in-depth explanation.

- Advertised Duration: Duration is the number of crankshaft degrees the intake and exhaust valves are held open. The advertised duration of a camshaft could mean anything. Years ago, camshaft

A set of Clevite 77 SH-616S camshaft bearings for a big-block Chevrolet 454-ci engine. Always use a camshaft bearing installation tool to install these bearings.

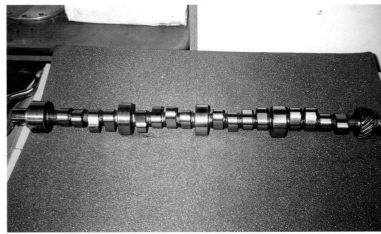

An Engle Cams TR-56 solid roller racing camshaft for a Chrysler 392-ci Hemi engine. The advertised duration is 308 degrees intake and exhaust, the duration at 0.050-inch lift is 260 degrees intake and exhaust, the valve lift is 0.531 inch intake and exhaust, and the lobe separation angle is 108 degrees.

A Cam-A-Go Company camshaft bearing installation tool, used to remove and install camshaft bearings.

manufacturers specified a camshaft had a duration of so many degrees; however, they did not specify at which point of tappet lift (camshaft lifter) that duration was calculated. The measurement could have been at 0.004-inch lift, 0.006-inch lift, 0.007-inch lift, 0.010-inch lift, 0.020-inch lift, or any lift imaginable. It seems as though none of the camshaft companies used a similar method to calculate the duration, making it nearly impossible to compare camshafts from different companies.

• Duration at 0.050-inch Lift: A number of years ago, camshaft manufacturers started to measure the duration at 0.050 inch of tappet lift (camshaft lifter). This is now the standard to use when comparing camshafts.

• Lobe Separation Angle: The lobe separation angle (or lobe centerline angle) is the angle between the intake and exhaust lobes at the maximum lift point, expressed in degrees. A large lobe separation angle (110 to 116 degrees) will result in a smoother idle and a greater power range. A smaller lobe separation angle (104 to 110 degrees) will result in a rougher idle and a narrower power range. The engines described in this book will be driven on the street, and thus should be equipped with a camshaft with a larger lobe separation angle to ensure the engine idles properly and has vacuum at idle.

• Overlap: Overlap is defined as the number of crankshaft degrees that the intake and exhaust valves are held open together. A camshaft with a lot of overlap creates a rough idle and is not recommended for a street performance engine.

• Valve Lift: This is the maximum net lift of the valve, expressed in decimals of an inch. The net valve lift is calculated in OHV (overhead valve) engines by multiplying the camshaft lobe lift by the rocker arm ratio and then subtracting the valve lash if solid (mechanical) lifters (tappets) are used. There is no valve lash when hydraulic lifters (tappets) are used.

Only use a new camshaft for a street performance engine. A used camshaft must have the lifters that were used with that camshaft matched exactly to the lobes on the camshaft, the same way they were installed in the engine. If the lifters are mixed up, the camshaft will be destroyed when the engine is started. Buying a used camshaft is a real gamble—it may well have been reground or one or more of the lobes might have gone flat. You can take a used camshaft to a reputable camshaft company for inspection, but why bother? New camshafts are not expensive and you know exactly what you are buying. Always install a new camshaft with new valve lifters. If you install new valve lifters with a used camshaft or used valve lifters with a new camshaft, camshaft failure is almost certainly guaranteed.

The main difference between a camshaft for a naturally aspirated street performance engine and a blown street performance engine is the lobe separation angle. A blown engine will usually have a larger lobe separation angle, something in the range of 112 to 116 degrees.

The major camshaft companies offer a wide variety of camshafts for most of today's popular engines. The best way to select a camshaft for an engine is to provide the camshaft manufacturer with all the relevant information for a particular vehicle. This should include the engine type, bore and stroke, type of cylinder heads and combustion chamber volume in cc's, compression ratio, size of valves, intended rocker arm ratio, type of intake system and carburetor cfm, type of transmission, rear end gear ratio, and the weight of the vehicle. An off-the-shelf camshaft might not be available for a specific engine, meaning a camshaft would have to be specifically ground. The cost of having a custom camshaft ground is about the same as purchasing an off-the-shelf camshaft. In many instances, I prefer to have a camshaft ground for a specific engine by Crower Cams & Equipment Company, using its latest state-of-the-art technology, to realize the engine's optimum output.

Degree Camshaft

The tools required to degree a camshaft are: 9-inch-diameter degree wheel, 1-inch travel dial indicator with a long stem, magnetic adjustable dial indicator stand, and heavy-gauge wire pointer (coat hanger-like material). Install the crankshaft, connecting rods and piston assemblies, the camshaft, and the intake and exhaust valve lifters for the No. 1 cylinder in order to degree the camshaft.

There are two accepted methods for degreeing a camshaft. The first one is referred to as the 0.050 lift method, described here.

Locate the TDC (top dead center) of the No. 1 piston with the dial indicator. Install the degree wheel on the nose of the crankshaft and attach the wire pointer to the engine block so it is as close as possible to the edge of the degree wheel. With the No. 1 piston at TDC, turn the degree wheel until the pointer is at the zero degree mark on the wheel, and then securely clamp the degree wheel in position so that it cannot move. Turn the crankshaft in one direction until the No. 1 piston reaches TDC; the wire pointer should be at the zero degree position on the degree wheel. Rotate the crankshaft in the opposite direction until the No. 1 piston reaches TDC; the wire pointer should be at the zero degree position on the degree wheel. The degree wheel is now perfectly positioned. Remove the dial indicator from the No. 1 piston.

Place the magnetic dial indicator stand on the deck of the engine block above the No. 1 intake valve lifter, and align the dial indicator so it passes through the deck and touches the top of the No. 1 intake valve lifter. The dial indicator must be at the same angle as the intake valve lifter in order to obtain an accurate reading.

Rotate the crankshaft until you locate the maximum lift point for the No. 1 intake valve lifter. Rotate the crankshaft one revolution past the maximum lift point. The intake valve lifter is now in the center of the base circle. Set the dial indicator to the zero position. Turn the crankshaft in the normal direction of rotation until it reaches a reading of 0.050 inch on the dial indicator. The degree wheel will now show the number of degrees BTC (before top center) for the No. 1 intake valve lifter. Rotate the crankshaft past the maximum lift point for the No. 1 intake valve lifter until the dial indicator again reaches 0.050 inch. The degree wheel will now show the number of degrees ABC (after bottom center) for the No. 1 intake valve lifter.

Remove the dial indicator and stand from the No. 1 intake valve lifter position and set them up above the No. 1 exhaust valve lifter. Align the dial indicator so it passes through the deck and touches the top of the No. 1 exhaust valve lifter. The dial indicator must be at the same angle as the exhaust valve lifter in order to obtain an accurate reading.

Rotate the crankshaft until you locate the maximum lift point for the No. 1 exhaust valve lifter. Rotate the crankshaft one revolution past the maximum lift point. The exhaust valve lifter is now in the center of the base circle. Set the dial indicator to the zero position. Turn the crankshaft in the normal direction of rotation until it reaches a reading of 0.050 inch on the dial indicator. The degree wheel will show the number of degrees BBC (before bottom center) for the No. 1 exhaust valve lifter. Rotate the crankshaft past the maximum lift point for the No. 1 exhaust valve lifter until the dial indicator again reaches 0.050 inch. The degree wheel will show the number of degrees ATC (after top center) for the No. 1 exhaust valve lifter.

All the readings from the degree wheel for BTC, ABC, BBC, and ATC should be in accordance with the manufacturer's camshaft specification card (timing tag). When the camshaft is degreed according to manufacturer specifications, your engine will reach its maximum performance.

The second accepted method for degreeing a camshaft is referred to as the intake centerline method. Use the same tools required for the previous method.

Locate the TDC (top dead enter) of the No. 1 piston with the dial indicator. Install the degree wheel on the nose of the crankshaft and attach the wire pointer to the engine block so it is as close as possible to the edge of the degree wheel. With the No. 1 piston at TDC, turn the degree wheel until the pointer is at the zero degree mark on the wheel and then securely clamp the degree wheel in position so it cannot move. Turn the crankshaft in one direction until the No. 1 piston reaches TDC; the wire pointer should be at the zero degree position on the degree wheel. Rotate the crankshaft in the opposite direction until the No. 1 piston reaches TDC; the wire pointer should be at the zero degree position on the degree wheel. The degree wheel is now perfectly positioned. Remove the dial indicator from the No. 1 piston.

Place the magnetic dial indicator stand on the deck of the engine block above the No. 1 intake valve lifter, and align the dial indicator so it passes through the deck and touches the top of the No. 1 intake valve lifter. The dial indicator must be at the same angle as the intake valve lifter in order to obtain an accurate reading.

Rotate the crankshaft in the normal direction of rotation until you locate the maximum lift point for the No. 1 intake valve lifter. Set the dial indicator to the zero position. Turn the crankshaft 0.100 inch in the opposite direction of rotation on the dial indicator. Turn

A set of Super Stock Industries (Performance Automotive Warehouse) 937 solid (mechanical) lifters for an early Chrysler 354-ci Hemi engine.

the crankshaft 0.050 inch in the normal direction of rotation. The reading on the dial indicator is 0.050 inch before the maximum valve lift. The degree wheel will now show the number of degrees BTC (before top center) for the No. 1 intake valve lifter. Rotate the crankshaft past the maximum lift point for the No. 1 intake valve lifter until the dial indicator again reaches 0.050 inch. The degree wheel will now show the number of degrees ABC (after bottom center) for the No. 1 intake valve lifter.

Add the number of degrees BTC to the number of degrees ABC and then divide the total by two. The result is the intake centerline. This should be the same as the intake centerline indicated on the manufacturer's camshaft specification card (timing tag). If it is not, adjust the camshaft timing gear until the correct result is obtained.

Valve Lifters

There are four basic types of valve lifters (also known as tappets or cam followers) used in today's OHV (overhead valve) V-8 street performance engines: the hydraulic lifter, the solid (mechanical) lifter, the solid (mechanical) roller lifter, and the hydraulic roller lifter. None of these lifters is adjustable; the valve adjustment is carried out at the rocker arm or by the use of adjustable pushrods. It is very important to match the camshaft and lifters with any camshaft. One manufacturer's camshaft should not be used with another company's lifters. In most instances this practice will void the camshaft manufacturer's warranty.

The most common type of valve lifter is the hydraulic lifter. The majority of engines delivered from the factory were equipped with hydraulic lifters. This type of valve lifter seldom causes a problem, provided the oil and filter are changed on a regular basis. The

A new set of Crower Cams & Equipment Company 66201 solid roller lifters for a Chevrolet 454-ci engine.

The two camshaft lifters shown are Schubeck Racing Engine Components 687RLG diamond-hard radius lifters for use in Chrysler engines.

installation of hydraulic valve lifters prevents the need to readjust the valve lash on a regular basis. The oil in the hydraulic lifters acts as a shock absorber for the valvetrain. The only negative aspect of hydraulic lifters is the potential for pump-up at higher engine speeds.

Solid (mechanical) lifters stabilize the valvetrain at higher engine speeds. Crower Cams & Equipment Company offers a coolface option for its Chevrolet solid lifters. This option consists of a 0.024-inch hole drilled in the center of the solid lifter face that provides oil to lubricate the camshaft lobe, ensuring a longer camshaft and lifter life. The coolface option does not result in a significant loss of oil pressure. The biggest drawback to using solid (mechanical) lifters is that they must be periodically adjusted.

Roller camshafts allow for more aggressive camshaft profiles. Solid roller lifters encounter less friction and thus less wear than solid (mechanical) lifters or hydraulic lifters. Most solid roller lifters are linked together with a moveable bar to prevent the lifter from rotating. Roller camshafts and lifters, however, are expensive.

Hydraulic roller lifters are excellent for use in street performance engines, even blown engines. The big advantage over solid roller lifters is that hydraulic roller lifters do not require periodic adjustment. This can be a real benefit for some engines where a lack of engine compartment space makes removing the valve covers for valve lash adjustment an almost impossible task. Hydraulic roller camshafts and lifters, however, are expensive.

The Crower Cams & Equipment Company 66274 groove-lock roller lifter is designed for Chevrolet V-8 engines; it is 0.842 inch in diameter and weighs 97 grams. This roller lifter is manufactured using heat-treated anodized aluminum and has two buttons on its side. A special jig cuts a vertical slot in the camshaft lifter bores in the engine block for the two camshaft lifter buttons to slide into, thereby preventing the camshaft lifter from rotating. This type of camshaft lifter was very popular in the 1960s for use with the Crower Cams & Equipment Company Imperial drag race roller camshafts, used in the early Chrysler Hemi engines. The current retail price for a set of the Crower Cams & Equipment Company 66274 groove-lock roller lifters is $650.

Schubeck Racing Engine Components 687RLG radius lifters are used with roller camshafts, although the lifters themselves do not have rollers. The material used in the manufacture of this camshaft lifter is referred to as diamond hard, and the weight of one of these lifters for use in a Chrysler engine is 43 grams. The current retail price for a set of these diamond-hard radius lifters is $900.

Follow the engine manufacturer's specifications for the camshaft end play and camshaft bearing clearance. The camshaft end play in some engines is controlled by a camshaft retaining plate and in other engines by a camshaft button attached to the front of the camshaft timing gear. The general practice is to allow 0.001- to 0.002-inch clearance between the camshaft and the camshaft bearings. Coat the camshaft journals with oil before installing the camshaft. Liberally coat the camshaft lobes and valve lifter bases with the camshaft lubricant supplied by the camshaft manufacturer.

Purchase the camshaft, valve lifters, valve springs, valve spring retainers, and valve stem locks as a package to guarantee the components will all work together.

Valves and Valve Seat Inserts

Stainless-steel valves are the best valves to use in a street performance engine. Stainless-steel valves are very durable and will last a lot longer

The installation of a camshaft retaining plate and the oil trough (used to lubricate the timing gear chain) installed in a 1958 Dodge Truck 354-ci Hemi engine block.

than factory-type valves. The most common valve stem sizes are 5/16 inch (0.3125 inch), 11/32 inch (0.34375 inch), and 3/8 inch (0.375 inch). There are a number of companies manufacturing stainless-steel valves in all price ranges. Some engine builders make the classic mistake of installing the biggest head diameter valves they can find, believing that bigger is better—not true! Unless an engine is being built for all-out racing, stay within the general size range of the valves provided by the factory for that particular cylinder head. The major automobile manufacturers have spent large sums of money to find the best valve sizes for their cylinder heads. Aftermarket cylinder heads usually have the optimum valve sizes installed.

The majority of today's automobile engines function on unleaded gasoline. The use of this fuel, or if the existing valve seat inserts are badly pitted, will most likely require the installation of hardened exhaust valve seat inserts. Only a competent machine shop should install valve seat inserts. The estimated cost of installing eight exhaust valve seat inserts is $100 (this does not include the cost of the actual exhaust valve seat inserts). Most aftermarket cylinder heads have hardened ductile iron exhaust valve seat inserts already installed.

Locate a machine shop that has a reputation for performing top-quality Serdi-machined multi-angle blueprint valve grinds. A multi-angle valve grind can comprise up to seven different angles, although the most common consists of three different angles. The Serdi valve-grinding machine is fitted with a boring bar that machines the valve seat inserts, rather than the old method of grinding the valve seat inserts with stones. The Serdi boring bar enables the valve seat inserts to be blended in with the intake and exhaust ports (referred to as pocket porting) and ensures all the valves are at equal depth in the valve seat inserts. The Serdi machine also guarantees the valves are perfectly centered in the valve seat inserts. No other valve-grinding machine does all these things.

Grind the valve seat inserts with a Serdi 60 Centering by Spherical and Flat Air Cushion valve-grinding machine. This Serdi machine is a top-of-the-line machine that performs outstanding valve seat insert grinding and is simply the best way to go for any street performance engine. The estimated cost for a Serdi-machined multi-angle blueprint valve grind is $135.

Grind the valves on a Sioux Tools Model 2075HP accu-chuck valve grinder or similar machine to obtain a quality multi-angle blueprint valve grind.

Valve Guides and Bushings

Most of the V-8 engines produced in the 1960s and the 1970s were fitted with cast-iron valve guides in the cylinder heads. These are not removable because they are part of the cylinder head casting. A street

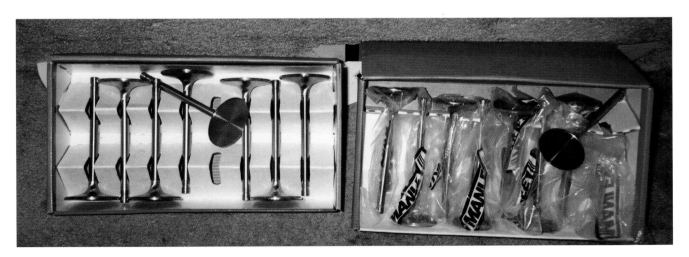

The valves on the left are Manley 11800-8 Pro Flow stainless steel (2.19-inch head diameter by 11/32-inch stem diameter). The valves on the right are Manley 11881-8 Race Master stainless steel (1.88-inch head diameter by 11/32-inch stem diameter). These are excellent valves for a performance street engine.

A World Products 030630 Merlin VR cast-iron Grumpy Jenkins cylinder head about to receive a superb valve grind using the Serdi 60 Centering by Spherical and Flat Air Cushion machine. The cylinder head is for a big-block Chevrolet and has large rectangular ports, 345-cc intake runner volume, and it is an open chamber model.

A stainless-steel valve is ground on a Kwik-Way multi-angle valve grinder. This type of valve grinder is an absolute necessity for a blueprint valve grind.

A set of Hot Heads Research & Racing 40044 bronze intake valve guides and 40046 bronze exhaust valve guides for the early Chrysler Hemi engines. They are designed for valves with an 11/32-inch stem diameter.

performance engine should have bronze valve guide liners installed due to their better endurance quality. The K-Line KL1842STA universal-length 3/8-inch (0.375-inch) bronze bullet valve guide liner is a good example. If you would like to replace the 3/8-inch (0.375-inch) stem diameter valves with 11/32-inch (0.34375-inch) stem diameter valves, install Manley Performance Parts 42158 bronze valve guide sleeves. These are simple procedures for a reliable machine shop.

The cast-iron valve guides in the early Chrysler Hemi cylinder heads can be removed and new bronze valve guides installed. Most aluminum aftermarket cylinder heads have phosphor bronze valve guides already installed; they should be knurled to ensure they stay permanently in place. The clearance between the valve and the valve guide bushing is critical, as it will affect oil control. This clearance should be approximately 0.002 inch in a street performance engine using today's unleaded gasoline.

Valve Springs and Spring Seat Cups

The lift of the camshaft, open spring seat height, and diameter of the valve spring seat in the cylinder head will determine the type of valve spring necessary. Always use the valve springs recommended by the camshaft manufacturer in order to avoid problems with valve spring coil bind and valve-spring-retainer-to-rocker-arm clearance. The majority of valve springs used in street performance engines are dual valve springs, dual valve springs with a damper, or triple valve springs, depending on the application. The most common types of performance valve springs are manufactured using chrome silicone steel, tungsalloy, or H-11 tool steel (Vasco Jet). Adhere to the manufacturer's recommendation for the installed valve spring height. Most performance valve springs are reasonably priced.

Use valve spring seat cups (or discs) with aluminum cylinder heads in order to protect the cylinder heads from galling and to prevent the valve springs from wandering. Quality spring seat cups (or discs) are manufactured using heat-treated chrome-moly steel and must be matched to the valve springs. These are not expensive.

Valve Spring Retainers, Locks, and Seals

The valve spring retainers must be matched to the valve springs, and the valve stem locks must be matched to the valve spring retainers as well as the valves. Street performance valve stem locks

Brand-new Crower Cams & Equipment Company 68932 spring seat cups and 68389 dual silicone valve springs for a Chevrolet 454-ci engine.

Some more trinkets from Crower Cams & Equipment Company. On the left are 86110-1 jumbo locks (10-degree by 11/32-inch valve stem diameter). On the right is a set of 87060 chrome-moly valve spring retainers (10-degree by 11/32-inch valve stem diameter).

are available in 7-degree or 10-degree styles. The 7-degree models are used for mild street performance engines, or stock engines, and are manufactured using heat-treated stamped alloy steel. These are a step above the factory valve stem locks. The 10-degree-style valve stem locks should be used for serious street performance engines. They are manufactured using heat-treated chrome-moly steel and are said to be twice the strength of the 7-degree valve stem locks. Performance valve spring retainers and valve stem locks are not expensive, although the 10-degree valve stem locks cost a whole lot more than the 7-degree valve stem locks.

Valve stem seals must be installed in any street performance engine for the important purpose of oil control, particularly with the intake valves. There are three basic types of valve stem seals. The first is the polyacrylate valve stem seal, used in the early Chrysler Hemi engines. These seals do not usually work with smaller diameter or dual valve springs. The second choice is the Hastings silver seal Teflon/steel valve stem seal, which requires the machining of

A rare Howard's finned aluminum timing gear cover for a Chrysler 331-ci or a Chrysler 354-ci Truck engine. It is fitted with a mechanical fuel pump boss and an opening for a fuel injection pump.

the valve guides for proper installation. This valve stem seal can be used in street performance engines but is more commonly used in race applications. The best choice for street performance use is the Enginetech viton positive-seal valve stem seal. The valve guides do not usually have to be machined to install these valve stem seals. The Enginetech valve stem seals are available at local performance outlets and are bargain priced at around $1 each.

Timing Gear Cover

A multitude of timing gear covers is available for street performance engines. The timing gear covers are manufactured using stamped steel or cast aluminum and are available in a chrome finish or polished aluminum. The small-block and big-block Chevrolet engines and early Chrysler Hemi engines all use a one-piece front oil seal. Note: Some aftermarket timing gear covers are so poorly manufactured that the oil seal in the front is not centered. This situation will most certainly lead to an oil leak. If you desire a chrome timing gear cover, have a factory cover chromed. The timing gear cover should be cleaned, glass beaded, and the inside painted with Glyptal G-1228A medium-grey gloss enamel to assist with oil return. Chrome timing gear covers are not expensive but aluminum timing gear covers are. Install the timing gear cover with polished stainless-steel bolts using Loctite, and torque the bolts to 20 ft-lb. Install the timing gear cover gasket using silicone sealant.

Cylinder Heads

Up to the early 1970s, the majority of cylinder heads manufactured in the United States for passenger vehicles consisted of one of two types of combustion chamber designs: the closed chamber and the open chamber. The closed chamber resembles a bathtub shape and the open chamber resembles a heart shape. The open chamber cylinder heads were introduced in the late 1960s to lower the

A 1956 Chrysler 1639273 timing gear cover for a 354-ci Hemi engine. The inside has been painted with Glyptal G-1128A medium-grey gloss enamel.

Cast-iron 1955 Chrysler 354-ci Hemi cylinder heads (casting number 1556157-1). They have been hot tanked, ported and polished, and gasket matched; the exterior surface has been sanded and detailed; and the area beneath the valve cover has been painted with Glyptal G-1228A medium-grey gloss enamel.

compression ratio in an engine and reduce emissions. The open chamber cylinder heads are better designed for the flow of the air/fuel mixture.

The hemispherical combustion chamber cylinder head probably has the most efficient combustion chamber design of all cylinder heads. Zora Arkus-Duntov (1909–1996) and Yuri Arkus-Duntov (1917–1980) introduced the Hemi cylinder heads to North America in 1947. The two brothers designed these cylinder heads as part of an overhead valve conversion kit for the Ford flathead V-8 engine. The name "Ardun" is derived from letters within their last name. Ardun cylinder heads were manufactured in England using 355 T-6 aluminum. The Ardun Engine Company, Inc., did not have much success with its product and, as a result, it is believed only 200 sets of the Ardun cylinder heads were ever produced. Zora Arkus-Duntov went on to become one of the most influential forces in the development of the Corvette. The famous small-block Chevrolet Duntov camshaft was named after him. The first Hemi cylinder heads manufactured for production passenger cars were introduced by Chrysler in 1951 for the Chrysler FirePower 331-ci engine.

From the start of the OHV (overhead valve) V-8 era in the early 1950s until the end of the big horsepower days in the early 1970s, the major automobile manufacturers in the United States equipped their engines with cast-iron cylinder heads. One exception was the 1960 small-block Chevrolet Corvette with aluminum cylinder heads, GM 3772894 and GM 3767468, casting number 3767466. These cylinder heads may have been installed on some of the earliest 1960 Corvettes equipped with fuel injection, although no one seems to know for certain. The famous race car driver and speed equipment manufacturer Mickey Thompson modified a few sets of those aluminum cylinder heads; two sets are rumored to still exist. Another exception was the big-block Chevrolet L88 and ZL-1 with rectangular port aluminum cylinder heads introduced in the late 1960s. The factory cast-iron cylinder heads came in all port shapes, all had different combustion chamber volumes, and only a few were suitable for street performance use. Today, the major automobile manufacturers market their own cast-iron or aluminum high-performance cylinder heads.

Currently, about a dozen manufacturers of aftermarket cylinder heads produce cast-iron and aluminum versions. The port volumes, combustion chamber designs and volumes, valve sizes, and prices vary greatly. Do not make the mistake of rushing off to your nearest speed equipment dealer and buying a set of cylinder heads with the biggest intake runner volume available. Intake volume is critical with relation to the displacement of the engine. A good example of this is the big-block Chevrolet 454-ci engine. This engine performs better on the street with oval port cylinder heads than with rectangular port cylinder heads. However, if the displacement of the engine is increased to 496 ci, rectangular port cylinder heads will increase performance.

If you plan to install used cast-iron cylinder heads on your engine, they should be hot tanked and Magnafluxed. If they have been lying in the bottom of a barnyard feed trough for a few years, the cylinder

A pair of first-design Ardun aluminum cylinder heads (309 and 310), the rocker arm assemblies, and the aluminum valve covers. These particular cylinder heads came off the famous Ardun/Mercury engine built by T. "Sooey" Suenega of Hawaii Motor Rebuilders. The engine was installed in a 1932 Ford five-window coupe that won the 1956 NHRA Nationals B/Altered class in Kansas City.

A pair of new GM 10051128 symmetrical port 356 T-6 aluminum cylinder heads. These Pro Stock cylinder heads for big-block Chevrolet engines were first introduced in 1987 and revised in 1992. They are a rectangular port, semi-open chamber design, have 68-cc combustion chamber volume, 400-cc intake runner volume, and 158-cc exhaust runner volume. They do not come with valve seat inserts installed.

heads may need to be Redi-Stripped to make certain they are clean. As soon as the cylinder heads are hot tanked or Redi-Stripped, mask off the outside, cover the valve guides with plastic caps, and paint the area beneath the valve covers with Glyptal G-1228A medium-grey gloss enamel. The enamel will greatly assist with oil return and will also help to prevent any rust from forming if moisture is present on the cylinder heads. For a great paint finish on the cylinder heads, use a high-speed drill and round sanding discs to smooth out the exterior surface. Retap all the bolt holes in the cylinder heads and do not forget to retap the spark plug holes. Aluminum cylinder heads should never be hot tanked. Most reputable machine shops have a cold tank for cleaning aluminum engine parts.

Have the combustion chambers cc'd after they have had rough areas removed or have been unshrouded (laying back) for bigger valves. Smear grease on the perimeter of the combustion chamber, and then place a plexiglass plate with a small hole in the top on top of the grease. Place a glass burette, capable of holding approximately 150 cc of water, and a stand above the combustion chamber. Drain the water through the hole in the plexiglass until the combustion chamber is filled. The burette will show the amount of water used. Perform this exercise for each combustion chamber. It will most likely be necessary to grind a small amount of material from some of the combustion chambers before they are all exactly the same volume. Patience, along with good humor, is a true virtue.

Match the intake and exhaust ports in the cylinder heads used for a street performance engine and smooth out the runners—better known as porting and polishing. Use blue machinist's dye around the intake and exhaust ports of the cylinder head, place the intake and exhaust manifold gaskets (that will be used with the cylinder head) in position, and then scribe around the intake and exhaust ports. Use a high-speed grinder with a carbide bit to remove

Rocker Arms and Pushrods

Two basic types of stud-mounted rocker arms are used in street performance engines. The first is made of stamped steel; the majority of those supplied by the factory did not have an accurate ratio. Aftermarket stamped steel rocker arms are manufactured with an accurate ratio and some have a roller tip, which reduces friction. Stamped steel rocker arms are not expensive to purchase and, as a general rule, they can be used in most street performance engines, provided the valve lift does not exceed 0.550 inch and the open valve spring pressure does not exceed 350 pounds. The second, and best, design is the roller rocker arm, which can handle large valve lifts and valve spring pressures as well as reduce friction within the valvetrain. Roller rocker arms are a lot more expensive than stamped steel rocker arms.

Two types of aftermarket aluminum roller rocker arms are commonly used: cast and extruded. The most economical are the cast-aluminum type, although they do not have the strength of the extruded aluminum roller rocker arms. Crower Cams & Equipment Company manufactures stainless-steel, heat-treated roller rocker arms. These are the ultimate stud-mounted rocker arms and they certainly are not cheap.

The best rocker arm assemblies for any type of engine are shaft-mounted rocker arms. The Ardun OHV (overhead valve) conversion kit came with shaft-mounted rocker arms, closely followed by the early Chrysler Hemi shaft-mounted rocker arms. Chrysler Corporation used to only offer adjustable rocker arms for its 300-series engines with solid lifter camshafts; the rest of its early Hemi engines were equipped with nonadjustable rocker arms for use with hydraulic camshafts. The early Chrysler Hemi engines were equipped with nonadjustable

An Ardun rocker arm assembly I rebuilt for Luke's Custom Machine & Design. It is a first-generation model that did not have end stands to support the rocker arm shafts. The two end stands were fabricated by Hawaii Motor Rebuilders in 1955 and are painted with Glyptal G-1228A medium-grey gloss enamel.

the material around the intake and exhaust ports until they match the gasket outline. Grind off all the rough areas in the intake and exhaust ports and generally smooth them out. Do not go "bananas" when you are doing this. Just remove the necessary amount of material; the result does not have to be a mirror-like finish. If you have never ported and polished cylinder heads, do not attempt it. Let your local machine shop handle this job. This way you will avoid striking water and destroying a set of cylinder heads. Finally, have the cylinder heads resurfaced to ensure they are flat for a perfect match for an engine block that has been parallel decked.

A set of Crower Cams & Equipment Company 70308-1 nonadjustable pushrods for a big-block Chevrolet 454-ci engine. The pushrods are manufactured using heat-treated, 4130 seamless chrome-moly steel and are 7/16 inch in diameter.

A set of Smith Brothers pushrods for the early Chrysler 354-ci Hemi engine. These 3/8-inch-diameter adjustable pushrods were custom made with 9.75-inch intake pushrod length and 11.225-inch exhaust pushrod length.

A set of Crower Cams & Equipment Company 88402L rocker arm studs with extended shanks for use in aluminum cylinder heads.

A set of Edelbrock 8551 (manufactured by ARP) cylinder head bolts for use with the Edelbrock big-block Chevrolet aluminum cylinder heads.

A set of Manley 42149 hardened-steel raised guide plates designed for use with 7/16-inch-diameter pushrods in big-block Chevrolet cylinder heads.

pushrods for use with the adjustable and nonadjustable rocker arms.

Shaft-mounted rocker arms do not flex under high-speed conditions, unlike stud-mounted rocker arms, which do. This is the reason stud girdles are installed on drag racing engines that use stud-mounted rocker arms. Cylinder head bolts, or studs, pass through the shaft-mounted rocker arm stands and the cylinder heads into the engine block, resulting in a very rigid fixture.

The early Chrysler Hemi rocker arm assemblies are amazing pieces of equipment—even with 50 years of wear and tear on them, it is rare to see a set that is worn out. I have rebuilt about a dozen sets of early Chrysler Hemi and Ardun rocker arm assemblies over the past couple of years. The only problems I have encountered with those assemblies are that the shafts are plugged with sludge, usually as a result of a lack of oil changes in the past, or that the assemblies are rusty from exposure to the elements. It is interesting to see all the lead (residue from the days before unleaded gasoline) wash out of the shafts when they are cleaned.

If you are not experienced with the disassembly and reassembly of shaft-mounted rocker arm assemblies, and the majority of people are

not, do not touch them. Find a first-class machine shop that is known for its expertise with these assemblies to do the job. If you insist on doing this task yourself, take some good photographs or make sketches as you disassemble the rocker arm assemblies. Take your time and do the job properly. Any mistake you make with the reassembly of shaft-mounted rocker arms will result in a painful and expensive situation.

Equip your street performance engine with 3/8-inch-diameter (0.375-inch) pushrods. The 7/16-inch-diameter (0.4375-inch) pushrods are heavier than the 3/8-inch-diameter (0.375-inch) pushrods and are generally used in racing engines with extremely high lift camshafts where strength is of the utmost importance, but they can be used in street engines.

Adjustable pushrods are used with shaft-mounted nonadjustable rocker arms, and nonadjustable pushrods are used with stud-mounted rocker arms or shaft-mounted adjustable rocker arms. Pushrods used with guide plates should be heat-treated. Some of the best pushrods available today are manufactured by Crower Cams & Equipment Company and Smith Brothers Pushrods (see Appendix B—Resources) using heat-treated 4130 seamless chrome-moly steel. The estimated cost of a set of these pushrods is $175.

Rocker Arm Studs and Guide Plates

The rocker arm studs used in most high-performance OHV (overhead valve) V-8 engines are threaded on both ends. One end is

A vintage pair of Weiand 7216 die-cast aluminum finned valve covers for the big-block Chevrolet engines. There are no dripper tabs in these valve covers.

A big-block Chevrolet 454-ci engine that was built by Luke's Custom Machine & Design. The valve covers are the Mickey Thompson 103R-48B polished finned aluminum model and have oil dripper tabs cast into them.

A pair of new Zip Products VC-207 chrome big-block Chevrolet 454-ci valve covers with oil dripper rails and baffled breather tube openings.

This big-block Corvette chrome valve cover is fitted with a Trans-Dapt 4998 rubber grommet and a Motorcraft EV-49-B PCV valve. The PCV valve is connected to the PCV fitting in a four-barrel carburetor.

screwed into the cylinder head and a rocker arm mounts on the other end. Many types of non-performance cylinder heads are fitted with pressed-in rocker arm studs, which should be changed to the screw-in type if the cylinder heads will be used on any engine other than a stock engine. This is an easy conversion for most machine shops and is not expensive. Small-block Chevrolet cylinder heads should be fitted with 3/8-inch-diameter (0.375-inch) rocker arm studs, and big-block Chevrolet cylinder heads should be fitted with 7/16-inch-diameter (0.4375-inch) rocker arm studs. The rocker arm studs used in aluminum cylinder heads have a longer shank to prevent the rocker arm stud from being pulled out of the cylinder head.

Crower Cams & Equipment Company and ARP manufacture some of the finest rocker arm studs from heat-treated 4340 chrome-moly steel. Rocker arm studs are not expensive. Tall poly lock rocker arm adjusting nuts, fitted with a setscrew, should be used with all types of stud-mounted rocker arms to ensure valve lash accuracy.

The top of the rocker arm stud must be ground flat when using these nuts. These are also inexpensive.

Use hardened, steel-raised pushrod guide plates on all cylinder heads equipped with stud-mounted rocker arms. The guide plates assist with the pushrod alignment. Manley Performance Products (see Appendix B—Resources) manufactures excellent guide plates at a very affordable price. The pushrod guide plates are mounted below the rocker arm studs. The rocker arm studs should be torqued to 50 ft-lb using Loctite for cast-iron cylinder heads and anti-seize compound for aluminum cylinder heads.

Cylinder Head Bolts and Studs

Use top-quality cylinder head bolts (manufactured by ARP or Milodon using 8740 chrome-moly steel, rated at 170,000 psi) in normally aspirated street performance engines. Use cylinder head studs rated at 190,000 psi in blown street performance engines to

A pair of Mooneyes USA MP1800 polished-aluminum valve cover breathers. They are the 90-degree-angle type and their width is 3 inches.

A small-block Chevrolet 350-ci engine fitted with Edelbrock 6073 Performer RPM aluminum cylinder heads and Crane Cams 11744-16 Energizer vacuum die-cast aluminum alloy roller rocker arms (1.50 ratio) for use with a 3/8-inch-diameter (0.375-inch) rocker arm stud. Those are poly lock rocker arm nuts.

ensure maximum gasket loading. The estimated cost of a set of cylinder head bolts is $55, and the estimated cost of a set of cylinder head studs is $140. Always follow the cylinder head manufacturer's recommendation for torquing cylinder heads.

Valve Adjustment

After the valvetrain in an engine is assembled, it must be properly adjusted. There is a very simple, easy, and quick method to do this. Rotate the crankshaft until an exhaust valve for a cylinder starts to open; adjust the intake valve for that cylinder. Rotate the crankshaft until the intake valve for that cylinder starts to close, and then adjust the exhaust valve for that cylinder. Adjust all the valves for each cylinder in the same manner.

Valve Covers, PCV Valves, and Breathers

Probably a hundred different types of valve covers are around today, ranging from rare vintage to NOS (new old stock), and they are manufactured using stamped steel, cast aluminum, or billet aluminum. The prices are in all ranges. In order to give your street performance engine the "uptown look" it deserves, have the valve covers chrome plated if they are stamped steel or polished if they are aluminum. Use stainless-steel studs, AN flat washers, lock-washers, and polished acorn nuts when installing the valve covers. Torque the valve cover acorn nuts (or bolts) to 15 ft-lb using Loctite in cast-iron heads and anti-seize compound in aluminum heads. Install the valve cover gaskets with silicone sealant.

Do not be in a rush to discard the factory valve covers for aftermarket valve covers—the automobile manufacturers sometimes offered very neat tricks with their equipment. The original cast-aluminum valve covers supplied with the Corvette LT-1 small-block Chevrolet engine (1970–1972) had rocker arm oil dripper tabs cast into them. The original stamped steel chrome valve covers supplied

with the Corvette L88 and ZL-1 big-block Chevrolet engines (1967–1969) had rocker arm oil dripper rails tack-welded to the inside. These oil dripper tabs and rails permit oil to be dripped onto the rocker arms. This is an excellent way to oil the stock-type, stud-mounted rocker arms, but it is not necessary for stud-mounted roller rocker arms or shaft-mounted rocker arms.

Install a PCV (positive crankcase ventilation) valve in any street performance engine in order to reduce emissions. PCV valves can be installed in valve covers, valley covers, or oil filler tubes. The stock right-side valve cover (passenger's side) for the 1970 to 1972 small-block Corvette LT-1 and the 1967 to 1969 big-block Corvette L88 and ZL-1 engines has an opening where a PCV valve with a rubber grommet can be fitted. The upper part of the oil filler tube for the 1967 small-block Corvette was fitted with a PCV valve. The early Chrysler Hemi engines have an opening at the rear of the valley cover where a PCV valve with a rubber grommet can be installed.

Some highly modified engines should have valve cover breathers installed in order to relieve crankcase pressure. Valve cover breathers can be used in conjunction with PCV valves. The early Chrysler Hemi valve covers did not have valve cover breathers or openings in them. This will limit the amount of breathing through a single crankcase breather/oil filler cap mounted on the valley cover, especially if the engine is equipped with a blower. Mooneyes USA (see Appendix B—Resources) sells great-looking polished-aluminum valve cover breathers for a reasonable amount of money, and the installation is a straightforward procedure.

You may decide to assemble your own cylinder heads, although you lack any real experience in this area. It is a much wiser decision to have someone like "T-Bone," the wizard of all cylinder heads, carry out the assembly at a premium shop like High Performance Engines. The potential for a stupid mistake, resulting in serious damage, is then avoided.

CHAPTER 6
INTAKE SYSTEM

Carburetors

Holley manufactures excellent carburetors, from stock replacement models to all-out high-performance gas-guzzling monsters. The classic-look Holley double-pumper carburetors are well suited for normally aspirated engines, and the silver finish blower carburetors are designed for supercharged engines. The double-pumper carburetors are available from 600 cfm to 850 cfm, but only in manual choke versions. The current retail price of these carburetors is $300 to $460.

Edelbrock manufactures the Performer carburetor, which is an excellent carburetor for street use and is available from 600 cfm to 800 cfm, with or without an electric choke. One of the best features of the Edelbrock Performer carburetors is there are no gaskets below the fuel level. The current retail price of these carburetors is $220 to $325.

The majority of hot rodders have a horrible tendency to charge off and buy the biggest-cfm carburetor they can lay their sweaty hands on. Each street performance engine is different, and the cfm required must be taken into consideration before deciding exactly which carburetor to purchase. The cfm requirement of a specific engine is calculated using the following formula:

$$\frac{\text{Cubic inches x Maximum rpm}}{3456} = \text{Carburetor cfm x 85 percent (volumetric efficiency)}$$

For example, consider a big-block Chevrolet 454-ci engine operating at a maximum of 6,500 rpm. Based on the above formula, the cfm requirement would be 853.9 at 100 percent volumetric efficiency. At 85 percent volumetric efficiency, which is used for high-performance engines, the actual requirement would be 725.8 cfm.

Many big-block Chevrolet 454-ci street performance engines are equipped with 850-cfm carburetors when, in fact, they could use a 750-cfm carburetor for daily street use. It is usually a good idea to go on the high side when selecting the cfm of a carburetor for a blown street performance engine. It is better to run rich with a blown engine than to have the engine lean out under boost, which will cause a very large engine explosion.

Fuel Pressure Regulator and Fuel Line

Install an electric fuel pump if the engine is equipped with a blower (in fact, an electric fuel pump is good for any engine) in order to ensure a constant and reliable fuel supply. Mount the electric fuel pump as close to the gas tank as possible so that it may push the fuel and not pull it. Install a fuel pressure regulator for each carburetor when using an electric fuel pump. Adjust the regulator(s) to 7 psi for modern Holley and Edelbrock four-barrel carburetors. The Holley 12-803 fuel pressure regulator is adjustable from 4 1/2 to 9 psi and has an almost chrome-like finish that may also be buffed. They are available from your local Holley dealer.

Install a fuel pressure gauge in the fuel inlet line or at the fuel pressure regulator. The V.D.O. 153-002 or the Holley 26-500 fuel pressure gauges (0 to 15 psi) are good models and have 1 1/2-inch-diameter faces. If the engine has a blower, the Auto Meter 4401 Pro Comp Ultra-Lite model (0-30 inch hg./0 to 20 psi, 2 5/8-inch-diameter face) is a very good gauge when installed below the blower. These gauges are available from your local speed equipment outlet.

Use stainless-steel 3/8-inch-diameter tubing for all fuel lines in a street performance vehicle; all steel fuel lines *must* be double

An Edelbrock 1405 Performer 600-cfm manual choke non-emission carburetor.

A Holley 26-500 fuel pressure gauge (0 to 15 psi) installed in a Holley 12-803 fuel pressure regulator, adjustable from 4 1/2 to 9 psi.

The tools required to fabricate stainless-steel fuel lines. On the left is a Sears 951252 tubing cutter. In the center is a Summit Racing Equipment 900310 double flaring toolkit. On the right is a Performance Tool W80675 precision tubing bender. All steel fuel lines must be double flared.

A 1961 Weiand CV6 Drag Star polished-aluminum, low-profile intake manifold with six Holley 94 carburetors for use on a small-block Chevrolet engine. "Tim, the polishing guy" did all the buffing, and it took me almost 100 hours to build this complete setup.

flared. Regular stainless-steel tubing will crack and split if it is double flared—double-annealed stainless-steel tubing will not. Summit Racing Equipment (see Appendix B—Resources) is the only source I am aware of that supplies double-annealed stainless-steel tubing. Fuel lines are fabricated using a tubing cutter, double-flaring tool, and a tubing bender. *Never*, and I repeat, *never*, use copper fuel or brake lines. Copper tubing will fatigue very easily and crack, causing a fire or brake failure, leading to the demise of the vehicle and possibly the driver as well.

Air Cleaners

In all likelihood, thousands of different types of air cleaners are on the market. Air cleaners are manufactured using stamped steel, cast aluminum, or billet aluminum, and they come in all price ranges.

A lot of air cleaners are sold with a paper-element air filter installed. Chuck this piece of garbage out and buy a quality air filter, such as a K&N element. K&N air filters are not cheap, but they are guaranteed for a million miles (good luck!) because they are reusable. K&N air filters are available at most automotive parts dealers.

Intake Manifolds

From the 1950s through the early 1970s, some of the best-known names in hot rodding manufactured aluminum intake manifolds for all the popular OHV (overhead valve) V-8 engines. Bruce Crower, Vic Edelbrock Sr., Frank McGurk, Fred Offenhauser, Mickey Thompson, and Phil Weiand are a few of the parties associated with the crossram, log, multi-carb, and tunnel-ram intake manifolds. Intake manifolds for 1x2-barrel, 2x2-barrel, 3x2-barrel, 4x2-barrel, 6x2-barrel, 8x2-barrel, 1x4-barrel, and 2x4-barrel carburetors have all been used on just about every type of OHV V-8 engine.

Intake manifolds are designed for specific applications and power ranges. There is no question that the best intake manifold for a street performance OHV engine is a dual-plane, single, four-barrel carburetor unit. This type of intake manifold usually has a power range from idle to 6,500 rpm, which is ideal for street use. A few single-plane intake manifolds have a power range from 1,500 to 6,500 rpm, which makes them suitable street candidates as well. Dual four-barrel carburetor crossram intake manifolds have been successfully used on the street, provided they are paired with the correct size carburetors. Although some hot rodders like the look of tunnel-ram intake manifolds on their engines, such intake manifolds should not be considered for street use because the power range is far too high, usually 3,200 to 9,000 rpm. Try sitting in rush hour traffic with a tunnel ram and 2 x 650-cfm double pumpers and you will know what I mean!

Edelbrock, Holley, Offenhauser, and Weiand (a division of Holley) manufacture some of the best street performance intake manifolds available, and those companies are great sources for advice when it comes to choosing the correct intake manifold for a specific application.

The automobile manufacturers have provided some very radical intake manifold designs of their own in the past. Chevrolet offered a dealer-installed crossram dual four-barrel carburetor aluminum intake manifold for the 1967 to 1969 Camaro Z-28. This wild two-piece unit consisted of the GM 3941126 (casting number) bottom section with the GM 3941130 (casting number) top section and two Holley 600-cfm double pumper carburetors. The Offenhauser 5893 base with the 5903 dual quad top is a replacement for the original Chevrolet crossram intake manifold. The 1969 Edelbrock 2560 (model STR-10) street crossram is also similar; although it is no longer manufactured, it can occasionally be found at swap meets and on eBay. Unless an intake manifold is a very rare item, it is always best to purchase a new intake manifold. New intake manifolds are not expensive and you will rest a lot easier knowing all the surfaces are true and the bolt holes are not stripped.

In 1972, Edelbrock introduced its 2850 (model SY-1) Smoke Ram crossram aluminum intake manifold. Smokey Yunick originally developed this two-piece unit for a small-block Chevrolet 302-ci engine to be used in Trans-Am racing. Smokey managed to pull 465 horsepower from his 302-ci engine—the Smoke Ram intake manifold was one of the reasons for those amazing results. A little-known fact about this intake manifold: it was the first true air gap intake manifold put into production. The power range is said to be 3,000 to 6,500 rpm, and it was designed to operate with a huge Holley 830-cfm double pumper carburetor (Smokey insists on this). This is probably the best single, four-barrel intake manifold ever produced for any of the earlier, non-emission, small-block Chevrolet engines. Good luck trying to locate one today!

Cadillac did not offer a performance intake manifold for its 500-ci engine. The Chrysler 300-series Hemi engines were equipped with a cast-iron intake manifold complete with 2x4-barrel carburetors. Chevrolet offered excellent single four-barrel carburetor aluminum dual-plane high-rise intake manifolds for its small-block 350-ci engine and its big-block 427-ci engine.

Regardless of the type of intake manifold you install, use polished stainless-steel bolts and AN flat washers when installing it. Use Loctite for cast-iron cylinder heads and anti-seize compound for aluminum cylinder heads when installing the bolts, and torque them to 25 ft-lb. Do not block off the heat riser passages in the intake manifold or the cylinder heads on an engine used for daily driving. In cooler climates, the engine would run horribly until it warmed up.

GMC 6-71 Blower

To the best of my knowledge, no one in the early 1970s produced a GMC 6-71 blower intake manifold for the Cadillac 500-ci engine. Cragar, Edelbrock, and Weiand all produced some of the first GMC 6-71 blower intake manifolds for the early Chrysler Hemi engines, as well as for the small-block and the big-block Chevrolet engines.

The GMC 6-71 supercharger (more commonly referred to as a blower) will be installed on three of the engines described in this book; therefore, I will limit my explanation and description of a blower to those particular models. The GMC 6-71 blower is a Roots type, named after the designers, the Roots brothers, circa 1850. This blower is fitted with two three-lobe helical rotors and gears, a front and rear bearing plate, a front cover, and the blower case. Although the GMC 6-71 blower consists of very few parts and is quite simple in design and construction, the proper clearances and assembly of the unit should be left strictly to an expert blower builder.

Bruce Crower, the founder of Crower Cams & Equipment Company, is credited with being the first person to top mount a GMC 6-71 blower on a modern OHV V-8 engine. In 1954, he set a record of 157 miles per hour at the Bonneville salt flats with his Chrysler Hemi-powered Hudson car. He had cast the five-belt blower pulleys in coffee cans using old pistons as the source of aluminum!

It is a common misperception that blowers are highly complex mechanical units found only on NHRA (National Hot Rod Association) Top Fuel, funny cars, or show cars. First of all, a GMC 6-71 blower is not complicated—only the two rotors turn. A blower forces a greater volume of the air/fuel mixture into the engine rather than drawing less of the mixture in, which occurs in a normally aspirated engine. The blower creates boost only when it can get enough air, which is usually at WOT (wide-open throttle), and this measurement

A 1970 Weiand 1984 high-ram aluminum dual-quad tunnel-ram intake manifold for a small-block Chevrolet 350-ci engine. This intake manifold has a chrome top and polished base and its power range is said to be from 2,800 to 8,000 rpm. Tunnel-ram intake manifolds should not be considered for street use.

A very rare 1972 Edelbrock 2850 (model SY-1) Smoke Ram crossram polished (by "Tim, the polishing guy") aluminum intake manifold. The famous Smokey Yunick developed it for the small-block Chevrolet 302-ci engine.

The underside of the Smoke Ram intake manifold; the air gap is visible at the end of the intake manifold. The underside is painted with V.H.T. SP-101 flat white high-temperature coating, an old drag racing trick. The theory behind it is that the white will reflect the heat from the underside of the intake manifold, thereby allowing for a cooler fuel/air mixture.

A rare Cragar 503 magnesium GMC 6-71 blower intake manifold for an early Chrysler 354-ci Hemi engine. The magnesium turns a grey-black color when exposed to the atmosphere and disintegrates when salt water contacts it.

is in pounds (pounds/square inch). Street performance engines rarely experience boost, at least among drivers who want to keep their drivers' licenses. The boost effectively raises the compression ratio of an engine, but it also raises the cylinder and exhaust temperatures and cylinder pressure. The blower is basically a very efficient and trouble-free mechanical device when it is properly set up.

The large bore GMC 6-71 blower cases have a horizontal inside diameter of 9 5/8 inches. The GM 5111715 and GM 5138725 blower cases are die cast, and the GM 5155866 blower case is sand cast. The bearing plates are interchangeable between the two models.

There are two front covers and bearing plates for the GMC 4-71 and GMC 6-71 blowers. The GM 5150233 front cover is the early sand-cast model, has smooth sides, and requires the use of 5/16-inch NC by 3 1/2-inch-long bolts to secure it to the blower case. The Blower Drive Service 671-1SG or the Mr. Gasket 770 front cover gasket and the GM 5150219 bearing plates are used with this cover. The GM 5114442 front cover is the later die-cast model, has ribbed sides, and requires the use of 5/16-inch NC by 2 1/4-inch-long bolts to secure it to the blower case. The Blower Drive Service 671-1DG front cover gasket and the GM 5122363 bearing plates are used with this cover. Incidentally, the bearing plates are interchangeable; they can be used for the front or the rear.

Luke's Custom Machine & Design has built complete GMC 6-71 blower setups for all types of engines over the years. The blower is completely disassembled and all the parts carefully inspected for cracks, score marks, or other damage. The blower case, rotors, front cover, and bearing plates are then thoroughly cleaned and glass

beaded. This is a tremendous amount of fun due to years' worth of diesel fuel and oil residue glued to the case and rotors. After cleaning one of these filthy beasts, I highly recommend you throw yourself in a hot tank for proper restoration. The front and rear bearing plates are machined for the installation of bearing support rings, and polished-aluminum end caps are attached over the rear bearings. The rear bearing plate is milled to half of the original thickness in order to assist with distributor clearance. The blower case, the front and rear bearing plates, and the front cover are then dispatched to "Tim, the polishing guy" for buffing. All new front and rear bearings, bearing seals, gaskets, and stainless-steel bolts are installed. A pressure relief valve, oil level sight gauge, oil filler, and oil drain plugs are fitted in the front cover. The blower is expertly clearanced and the rotors are double pinned. The current price for one of Luke's Custom Machine & Design GMC 6-71 show-polished blowers is $1,350 (without the snout).

Snout

Luke's Custom Machine & Design manufactures three types of blower snouts for the GMC 4-71 and GMC 6-71 blowers by CNC machining from 6061 aircraft-quality aluminum that is T-6 heat treated. The LS1000 short snout is most commonly used for small- and big-block Chevrolet engines, and it measures 3.875 inches long from the front of the blower case to the front of the flange on the snout. The LS1100 short shaft and the LS4100 gear coupler are used with this snout. The current price for the complete short snout is $340.

The LS2000 sculptured snout can be used on a variety of vehicles and truly is a work of art. I have one on my blown engine, and it is the immediate focal point of everyone's attention. This snout

A GMC 6-71 Roots-type blower disassembled: the blower case, the two rotors, front and rear bearing plate, and the front cover. The front and rear bearing plates have the bearings and seals installed.

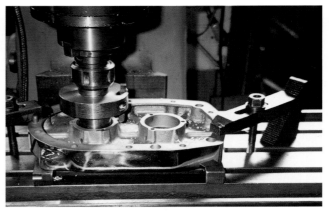

Luke's Custom Machine & Design machined the rear bearing plate. The bearing housings are milled in order to accept reinforcement rings.

Luke Balogh measures the rotor clearance in a GMC 6-71 blower equipped with one of his early Chrysler Hemi snouts. Luke did not pose for the photograph—he is actually measuring the rotor clearance.

Luke's Custom Machine & Design fabricated and installed the bearing support rings for this rear bearing plate.

The Luke's Custom Machine & Design blower snout shafts and gear couplers are CNC machined from 4140 chrome-moly heat-treated steel. All critical clearances are kept to within 0.0005 inch, and the splines on the snout shaft incorporate the largest depth presently offered in the industry. The male splines are cut on a gear hob and the female splines are cut on a gear shaper. Premium-grade double ball bearings and oil seals are installed. These blower snout shafts and couplers are designed to last.

Idler Pulley and Bracket

Luke's Custom Machine & Design fabricates idler pulleys using 6061 T-6 aluminum. The idler pulleys have a slight crown on the belt surface in order to keep the blower belt centered. The idler pulley bracket is also fabricated using 6061 T-6 aluminum.

Blower Drive Pulleys

The boost for a blown street performance engine is determined by adjusting the size of the blower drive pulleys. A crankshaft drive

measures 7.20 inches long from the front of the blower case to the front of the flange on the snout. The LS2200 sculptured shaft and the LS4100 gear coupler are used with this snout. The current price for a complete sculptured snout is $500.

The LS3000 medium snout is most commonly used for the early Chrysler Hemi engines and measures 5.00 inches long from the front of the blower case to the front of flange on the snout. The LS3300 medium shaft and the LS4100 gear coupler are used with this snout. The current price for the complete medium snout is $390. All the blower snouts are show polished.

A complete assortment of all Luke's Custom Machine & Design's blower snouts and snout shafts. The blown Chrysler Hemi 392-ci engine in the background is equipped with a complete blower drive setup.

A Luke's Custom Machine & Design polished aluminum idler pulley bracket installed on a big-block Chevrolet 454-ci engine. This idler pulley bracket permits the use of the stock alternator, power steering pump, and air conditioning brackets.

The Blower Drive Service 6927 pulley on the left has 27 teeth and is designed for use with a 13.9-millimeter pitch blower belt. The Blower Drive Service 6330 pulley on the right has 30 teeth and is designed for use with a 1/2-inch pitch (Gilmer) blower belt.

A Goodyear 14408M85 high-performance blower belt (8-millimeter pitch by 56.69-inch length by 3.35-inch width).

pulley that is smaller in diameter than the snout drive pulley diameter will result in an underdrive ratio. A crankshaft pulley that is larger in diameter than the snout drive pulley diameter will result in an overdrive ratio. Blower Drive Service offers blower drive belts and blower drive pulleys in 1/2-inch pitch (Gilmer), 8-millimeter pitch, 13.9-millimeter pitch, and 14-millimeter pitch sizes. The 1/2-inch pitch (Gilmer) blower drive belts come in the widest range of lengths, and a multitude of diameters are offered for all the blower drive pulleys.

The compression ratio of an engine increases when the engine experiences boost. For example, an engine with 8.0:1 compression ratio pistons and a boost of 10 pounds actually has a final compression ratio of 13.4:1. A final compression ratio exceeding 12.4:1 should not be considered for street use using today's highest octane, unleaded gasoline. Most street performance engines use anywhere from 5 to 10 pounds of boost. The Blower Drive Service (see Appendix B—Resources) catalog contains some very good blower information along with the tables required for calculating blower drive ratios and final compression ratios.

CHAPTER 7
IGNITION SYSTEM

Distributor

The ignition system is a very key part of any engine, particularly for a blown engine. It is mandatory to install a premium-quality distributor to prevent any ignition failure while a blown engine is experiencing boost. If ignition failure were to happen, some very serious damage would occur within the engine (and your wallet). An electronic distributor is the only type of distributor to consider for today's engines, blown or not.

The fuel mixture in a cylinder must be ignited before the piston reaches the top of the compression stroke to place the maximum pressure on the piston top for the power stroke. In order to do this, the timing must be controlled so there is more ignition advance at higher engine speeds than there is at lower engine speeds. The ignition advance increases as the engine accelerates. Any vacuum

A Mallory 609 magnetic breakerless module for converting factory-equipped or Mallory dual-point distributors.

advance is only a consideration at idle or low cruising speeds when the engine is not laboring. Most street performance engines should be equipped with vacuum advance distributors to reduce emissions, obtain better gas mileage, and avoid spark plug fouling.

The crankshaft makes two full revolutions for every camshaft revolution (count the number of teeth on the crankshaft and camshaft gears). If the mechanical advance of the distributor is 10 degrees, the actual advance is 20 degrees. If the crankshaft has 10 degrees of advance and the distributor has 20 degrees of actual advance, the result would be 30 degrees of total advance.

One of the best electronic distributors available today is the MSD Pro-Billet distributor, equipped with a maintenance-free magnetic pickup and machined from 6061 T-6 billet aluminum to within + or – of 1/1000 of an inch. There is an upper sealed ball bearing unit, and the shaft is polished and Tuftrided. These distributors will operate through 10,000 rpm—something a street performance engine will not and should not see. The MSD Pro-Billet distributors are available with or without vacuum advance and must be used with the MSD multiple-spark discharge ignition control box. The MSD distributors are available for most of the popular OHV V-8 engines at speed equipment stores and they are reasonably priced.

The Mallory (Mr. Gasket) Unilite model is another excellent distributor triggered by a self-contained, photo-optic infrared LED system. The Mallory magnetic breakerless ignition models are very popular as well. These distributors are machined from 6061 T-6 billet aluminum, there is an upper sealed ball bearing unit, and the shaft is heat treated and centerless ground. The Mallory Unilite and magnetic breakerless units are available with or without vacuum advance and will operate through 10,000 rpm. Mallory distributors are available for most of the popular OHV V-8 engines through Mr. Gasket outlets and their prices are reasonable.

The Mallory 501 Unilite conversion kit for factory equipped (Mallory dual-point distributor) is available for a current retail price of $100. The Mallory 605 Unilite module is $82, and the Mallory 609 magnetic breakerless module is $63.

Installing the Mopar Performance Parts (Chrysler) 2690430 distributor is currently a popular electronic distributor conversion for the early Chrysler Hemi engines. This distributor is used in the Chrysler 360-ci engines (non-Hemi). It used to be necessary to have the distributor shaft for this distributor extended in order to fit the

An older Mallory YC465HP dual-point mechanical advance distributor with a tachometer drive for use in a small-block Corvette 350-ci engine. Mallory converted this distributor to a Unilite infrared LED system. There is a Mallory 29426 aluminum/bronze drive gear installed for use with a billet steel roller camshaft.

early Chrysler Hemi engines. Hot Heads Research & Racing now offers extended oil pump intermediate driveshafts for the early Chrysler 354-ci and 392-ci Hemi engines that eliminate the requirement of extending the distributor shaft. Use the Mopar Performance Parts 3690430 distributor in conjunction with the Mopar Performance Parts 4007968 upgraded high-performance control unit, available from your local Chrysler dealer at a very economical price.

If an engine is equipped with a steel billet roller camshaft, the existing alloy steel or iron distributor drive gear must be replaced with an aluminum/bronze gear in order to be compatible. If this is not done, the alloy steel or iron gear will be slowly ground away, eventually resulting in the complete destruction of the engine. Mallory and MSD both offer aluminum/bronze distributor drive gears for a wide variety of distributors. The current retail price for these gears is $40 to $50.

Coil and Ignition Control

The Mallory 29440 Promaster ignition coil is an excellent ignition coil for street/strip use and, when used in conjunction with a Mallory Unilite distributor and the Mallory HyFire ignition control, it is effective up to 8,000 rpm. This ignition coil is larger than most ignition coils; however, the rugged case can withstand a

A Mallory 29440 Promaster ignition coil with a Mallory ballast resistor.

45

A set of Taylor/Vertex 70053 Pro Series black 8-millimeter Spiro-Pro spark plug wires with 135-degree boots for use in big-block Chevrolet 454-ci engines.

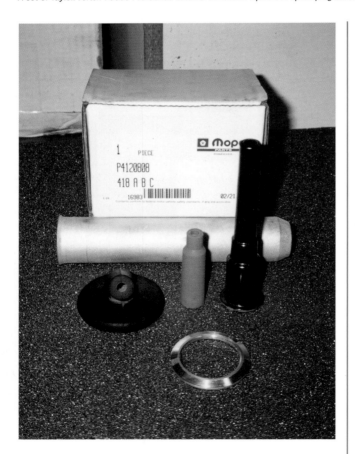

A Mopar Performance Parts (Chrysler) 4120808 Hemi spark plug tube and insulator kit with a Luke's Custom Machine & Design beveled spark plug tube ring.

lot of abuse. The current retail price for a Mallory 29440 ignition coil is $73.

The MSD 8200 Blaster 2 chrome ignition coil is a very good ignition coil to install on just about any street performance engine. It has an output of 45,000 volts and is compatible with ignition control boxes, unlike some aftermarket ignition coils that are not. The current retail price for an MSD 8200 coil is $34.

The Mallory 6852M HyFire VI-A microprocessor-controlled CD ignition system is a very good ignition control box. The Mallory 6853M HyFire VI-AL multi-spark CD ignition system with adjustable rev limiter is an excellent ignition control box for use with a blown street performance engine. The current retail price for the Mallory 6852M ignition control box is $115. The current retail price for the Mallory 6853M ignition control box is $170.

The MSD 6A (model 6200) ignition control box is another very good unit. The MSD 6AL (model 6420) ignition control box is equipped with rpm-limiter modules and is ideal for use on a blown street performance engine. The current retail price of an MSD 6A ignition control is $150, and the current retail price for the MSD 6AL ignition control is $196.

Spark Plug Wires

Taylor/Vertex manufactures top-quality spark plug wires for all types of automobile engines. They are available in a variety of colors and can be fitted with 90-degree, 145-degree, or 180-degree (straight) boots. The Taylor/Vertex Pro Series 8-millimeter Spiro-Pro high-performance spark plug wires are excellent for use in street

The chrome Chrysler alternator on the left is a Powermaster 17509 model, rated at 75 amps. The chrome GM alternator on the right is a Proform 66445 model, rated at 65 amps.

A TCI Automotive 351100 high-torque mini-starter, which draws 25 amps and produces 2.1 horsepower. This starting motor is designed for use on a big-block Chevrolet 454-ci engine.

engines. Mallory advises that copper-core or stainless-steel-wire-core spark plug wires should not be used with electronic ignitions. In addition to this advisory, there is no valid reason to use copper-core or stainless-steel-wire-core spark plug wires on a street performance engine. The Taylor/Vertex Spiro-Pro spark plug wire sets are currently available for a retail price of $55.

The early Chrysler Hemi engines can be nicely outfitted with the Mopar Performance 4120808 Hemi spark plug tube and insulator kit. Luke's Custom Machine & Design produces a beveled ring that fits at the top of the spark plug tube so the Hemi boots can be secured in position. The Hemi spark plug tube and insulator kit is a very inexpensive item, as are the spark plug tube rings. The Taylor/Vertex 35071 Spiro-Pro black 8-millimeter spark plug wire is available in 30-foot lengths (enough to do almost two engines) for use with the Hemi spark plug connectors.

For a nice detailing touch, install a set of Spectre 4245 chrome/plastic wire separators. These are low-cost items and they look good, as well as keeping the spark plug wires separated from each other.

Alternator

Install a chrome alternator on a street performance engine; the most common are the GM and Chrysler styles. Powermaster and Proform offer a wide variety of chrome alternators, ranging from 50 amps to 140 amps. The GM-style alternators are internally or externally regulated and are available with the standard or one-wire option. Chrysler-style alternators are externally regulated, although they are available with the standard or one-wire option. These chrome alternators vary in price from $95 to $200, depending on the amperage.

Starting Motor

A number of companies manufacture excellent high-torque mini-starters for all of today's popular OHV V-8 engines. Most mini-starters have twice the torque of the factory starting motors—a real benefit, especially in a blown street performance engine. The current retail price for a Powermaster mini-starter is $200. Chrome mini-starters are available for a little more money, but they are very difficult to polish if they are buried inside a vehicle with fenders.

CHAPTER 8
COOLING AND EXHAUST SYSTEMS

Water Pumps

Edelbrock, Flow Kooler, and Weiand manufacture some of the best aluminum water pumps available for OHV V-8 engines. Each water pump has a plate attached to the back of the impeller that increases the coolant by 20 to 30 percent and reduces the engine operating temperature by 15 to 30 degrees (Fahrenheit). The Edelbrock, Flow Kooler, and Weiand aluminum water pumps are available in polished or unpolished models and are competitively priced.

If you purchase an unpolished aluminum water pump, have it buffed to a show-quality finish. Luke's Custom Machine & Design contracts out with "Tim, the polishing guy" for any buffing requirements.

Your vehicle will be driven on the street; therefore, it should have a thermostat. Removing the thermostat will cause the coolant in the engine to move too fast for the heat to be dissipated.

Remember to use as little antifreeze as possible, or none at all, in the summer months and in hot climates. Antifreeze traps the heat in the engine cooling system and does not allow this heat to dissipate as quickly as it should, resulting in a much higher engine temperature than normal on hot days. Use only a minimal amount of antifreeze, or a suitable substitute, to lubricate the water pump.

You should not encounter any cooling problems with a street performance engine, provided there is a good clean engine block and radiator, mechanical or electric fan, and the water pump is in good working order. A fan shroud is often overlooked; however, it is an integral part of the cooling system and will aid in engine cooling.

Exhaust Headers

There are hundreds of exhaust headers manufactured for OHV V-8 engines by reputable companies. Exhaust headers are available in steel or stainless steel and in every shape imaginable with a variety of primary tube and collector sizes. Metallic-ceramic is one of the best coatings for steel exhaust headers. It is an extremely tough coating, very durable, and easy to keep clean. The major manufacturers of exhaust headers offer metallic-ceramic coating as an option. There are also a number of companies throughout North America that coat exhaust headers with metallic-ceramic for a reasonable price. If the exhaust headers are stainless steel, have them buffed.

The Trans-Dapt Stage 8 stainless-steel locking header bolts are the best fasteners to use to secure exhaust headers on an engine. The Stage 8 8911 bolts are designed for small-block Chevrolet engines, and the Stage 8 8912 bolts are designed for big-block Chevrolet engines. The bolts have a teardrop-shaped aluminum tab that fits over the head of the bolt and is held in position by a circlip. The teardrop is set against the header tube to prevent the bolt from coming loose. The Stage 8 bolt kits retail for about $35. Install the bolts in cast-iron cylinder heads using Loctite and in aluminum cylinder heads using anti-seize compound. Torque the exhaust header bolts to 25 ft-lb.

The early Chrysler Hemi engines used studs to secure the exhaust manifolds. If the studs are damaged or missing, Papco 264-048 engine studs (3/8x2-inch length) are available as replacements. Install the exhaust studs in the early Chrysler Hemi cylinder heads using Permatex aviation form-a-gasket since the stud holes are open to the water jackets.

A GM 3992071BE chrome water pump pulley bolted to an Edelbrock 8852 Victor Series polished-aluminum water pump. This setup is designed for a 1969 to 1972 Corvette big-block engine with power steering and air conditioning.

This pair of Hedman Hedders 68090 exhaust headers has been metallic-ceramic coated. These exhaust headers are designed for the 1968 to 1972 Corvette with a big-block engine, and they work in the models with air conditioning.

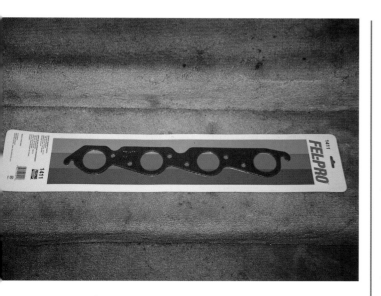

A pair of Fel-Pro 1411 exhaust header gaskets designed for use with the Edelbrock 6054 Performer RPM large rectangular port cylinder heads (bare) produced for the big-block Chevrolet 454-ci engines.

If you install aftermarket cylinder heads on a street performance engine, adhere to the recommendation of the cylinder head manufacturer when purchasing exhaust header gaskets. Fel-Pro and Mr. Gasket Ultra Seal exhaust manifold gaskets are very good products. Permatex ultra-copper high-temperature silicone is a good sealant for the exhaust header gaskets.

My Corvette 350-ci engine when it was installed in my 1923 Ford Model T Roadster Pickup. The engine was initially fitted with a tunnel-ram intake manifold. This engine is described in Chapter 11.

CHAPTER 9
1970 CADILLAC 500-ci ENGINE

The 1970 to 1976 Cadillac Fleetwood Eldorado was equipped with a 500-ci engine. The 1970 model was the most powerful of them all—its engine was advertised as having 400 horsepower at 4,400 rpm and 550 ft-lb torque at 3,000 rpm, and it was considered one of the non-smog motors. General Motors Corporation spared no expensive in using exotic metals for the manufacture of some of the internal engine parts.

Starting in 1972, the automotive industry changed from rating its engines using gross brake horsepower (bhp) to net brake horsepower. Gross brake horsepower was used to describe an engine without all the usual accessories installed, such as power steering, air conditioning pumps, and exhaust manifolds. Net brake horsepower included all the accessories usually installed on an engine. Pressure from the government, environmental groups, and the insurance industry spurred the change, as fuel consumption was becoming a major issue.

Many automotive enthusiasts have overlooked the Cadillac 500-ci engine as a good candidate for hot rods and custom cars, and lots of these engines are available for amazingly low prices. The

A 1970 Cadillac 500-ci engine block that has been hot tanked. The front of the engine block, along with the valve lifter gallery, has been painted with Glyptal G-1228A medium-grey gloss enamel.

engine described here was in excellent condition—it had obviously been well looked after—and it came out of a 1970 Cadillac Fleetwood Eldorado. The previous owner sold the complete running car for $500! Luke's Custom Machine & Design disassembled, thoroughly cleaned, and reassembled the engine with some new parts. This stock engine has been rebuilt and is technically not a street performance engine. I want to include a complete buildup description in my book because so little has been written about this engine. Luke Balogh installed this engine in his 1939 Ford COE (cab over engine) Truck, which will eventually be enclosed and used to haul one of his hot rods on long trips.

Cad Company (see Appendix B—Resources) is one of the best sources of engine parts for the Cadillac 500-ci engine. The company has been in business since 1984 and probably has every part for one these engines, as well as for all the other Cadillac engines, and every type of high-performance engine part available. They offer services such as cylinder head porting and polishing, rebuilding of rocker arm assemblies, and even supply complete running engines.

Components Description
Engine Block
The 1970 Cadillac Fleetwood Eldorado specifications are:
- 500-ci (8.2-liter) displacement
- 4.300-inch stock bore and 4.304-inch stock stroke
- Stock compression ratio: 10.0:1
- 400 horsepower at 4,400 rpm and 550 ft-lb torque at 3,000 rpm

The Cadillac 500-ci engine had the largest displacement of any passenger car engine manufactured in the United States in 1970. The last four digits of the casting number are 5200, which are the same last four digits of a 1970 Cadillac 472-ci engine. The only accurate way to determine if a Cadillac engine is the 500-ci model is to measure the stroke.

The Cadillac 500-ci engine block is fitted with five main bearing caps of the two-bolt design. The main bearing housing bore sizes are 3.438 to 3.439 inches. This engine block can safely be bored 0.060-inch oversize, provided there has not been any core shift (and there usually is not in this high-quality engine block). Refer to Chapter 1 for information regarding engine block preparation.

Pioneer PE120B brass freeze plug kits or Federal Mogul 1760 brass freeze plugs, used for the sides of the engine block, along with

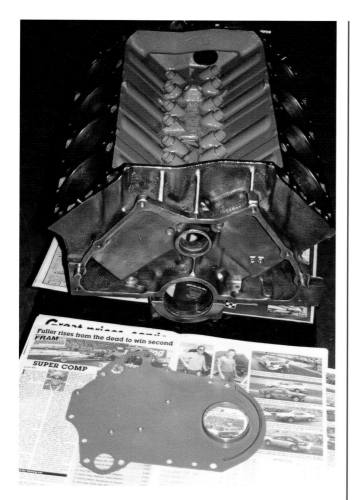

A rear view of the Cadillac 500-ci engine block. The valve lifter gallery and the inside of the GM 3633103 timing gear cover have been painted with Glyptal G-1228A medium-grey gloss enamel.

the Federal Mogul PS165 rear camshaft boss plug, are available at the bargain basement price of about $15.

Crankshaft

The GM 1496793 (casting number 1495094) crankshaft installed in the Cadillac 500-ci engine was manufactured using cast nodular iron and has six counterweights. The end thrust is taken by the No. 3 (center) main bearing. The casting number is usually located on the counterweight behind the fourth main bearing journal. The factory-recommended main bearing clearance is 0.0003 to 0.0026 inch, and the recommended crankshaft end play is 0.002 to 0.012 inch.

Clevite 77 MS-970-AL main bearings are available in standard size, 0.010-inch oversize, and 0.020-inch oversize. The current retail price for a set of these main bearings is $125. Federal Mogul 4906-MA main bearings are available in standard size, 0.010-, 0.020-, and 0.030-inch oversize. The current retail price for a set of these main bearings is $140.

The GM 3515077 harmonic balancer, with a triple-groove pulley, is secured to the crankshaft hub using four bolts. Cadillac no longer shows availability for this part; Cad Company is the only source I am aware of to purchase it. The company is offering a new viscous harmonic balancer for the current retail price of $349.

Connecting Rods and Pistons

The GM 3633111 forged steel I-beam connecting rods were used in the Cadillac 500-ci engine. The factory description of the material used in their manufacture was 84M Arma steel. These connecting rods are for pistons with pressed-in wrist pins. The size of the crankshaft end (the big end) is 2.624 to 2.625 inches. The factory-recommended connecting rod bearing clearance was 0.0005 to 0.0028 inch, and the recommended side clearance per pair of connecting rods was 0.008 to 0.016 inch. Cad Company offers billet steel connecting rods, with ARP 8740 chrome-moly steel bolts, for the Cadillac 500-ci engine at a current retail price of $699.

Clevite 77 CB-542-P connecting rod bearings are available in standard size, 0.001-, 0.002-inch oversize, 0.010-, 0.020-, 0.030-, and 0.040-inch oversize. The current retail price for a set of these connecting rod bearings is $80.

Federal Mogul 8-3345P connecting rod bearings are available in standard size, 0.001-, 0.010-, 0.020-, 0.030-, and 0.040-inch oversize. The current retail price for a set of these connecting rod bearings is $86.

The GM 3633466 pistons installed in the Cadillac 500-ci engine were manufactured using cast-aluminum alloy in a slipper-skirt design with pressed-in wrist pins. There were two types of piston domes with a unique swirl-chamber design. One was referred to as a binocular design, and some "experts" say this was the only type of piston used in the 1970 Cadillac 500-ci engine. The second piston was referred to as a flattened-peanut design and was supposedly only used in the 1968 to 1970 Cadillac 472-ci engine. In fact, this flattened-peanut piston was installed in the Cadillac 500-ci engine described in this chapter. The trough on the top of the piston was said to increase the turbulence in the combustion chamber, thereby promoting better combustion. The compression ratio was 10.0:1 with both pistons, and the combustion chamber volume was 76 cc. The factory-recommended piston skirt clearance was 0.0006 to 0.001 inch, measured perpendicular to the center of the wrist pin. The factory-recommended wrist pin clearance (in the piston) was 0.0002 to 0.0004 inch, and the recommended piston ring gap was 0.013 to 0.025 inch for the top compression ring, 0.013 to 0.025 inch for the second compression ring, and 0.015 to 0.055 inch for the oil ring.

Keith Black Performance markets the Silv-O-Lite cast-aluminum pistons for the Cadillac 500-ci engine. These pistons contain approximately 16 to 18 percent silicon hypereutectic alloy and also T-6 heat-treated aluminum. The Silv-O-Lite 353 cast-aluminum pistons have a flat top design with a compression ratio of 13.1:1 with a 76-cc combustion chamber volume and a compression ratio of 9.0:1

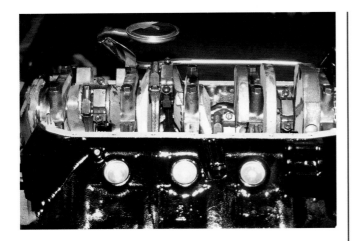

The GM 3633111 connecting rods have been installed and torqued. Notice the length of the GM 1495177 oil pump pickup tube. The oil pan is ready to be bolted in place.

with a 120-cc combustion chamber volume. The pistons are available in 0.030-, 0.040-, and 0.060-inch oversize. The current retail price for a set of these pistons with wrist pins is $375. The Silv-O-Lite 382 cast-aluminum pistons have a cup design with a compression ratio of 10.0:1 with a 76-cc combustion chamber volume and a compression ratio of 7.6:1 with a 120-cc combustion chamber volume. The pistons are available in 0.030-, 0.040-, and 0.060-inch oversize. The current retail price for a set of these pistons with wrist pins is $375. It would be wise to install a set of Ross Racing Pistons forged aluminum pistons with moly piston rings. The combination costs a few dollars more than the cast-aluminum pistons with cast-iron piston rings, but it is far superior for street performance use.

The Ertel Manufacturing Company 50850 cast-iron piston rings are stock replacement piston rings, and they are available in standard size, 0.010-, 0.020-, 0.030-, 0.040-, 0.050-, and 0.060-inch oversize. The current retail price for a set of these cast-iron piston rings is $45. Cad Company offers Childs & Albert moly top piston ring sets in standard size, 0.030-, 0.040-, and 0.060-inch oversize. The current retail price for a set of these moly piston rings is $115.

The Victor-Reinz FS3852 complete gasket set and the Victor-Reinz MS15943 valley pan/intake manifold gasket are designed for the Cadillac 500-ci engine. The current retail price for the gasket set is $75, and the valley pan/intake manifold gasket sells for $40.

Lubrication System

Unlike most OHV V-8 engines where the oil pump is mounted internally, the Cadillac 500-ci engine has an externally mounted oil pump that bolts to the right side (passenger's side) of the cast-iron water pump housing. The oil pump is equipped with spur (straight-cut) gears. If the oil pump gears are worn out or damaged, the Ertel Manufacturing Company DK-58F oil pump kit contains new gears. However, it is always best to install a new oil pump in any engine

that has been disassembled. The GM 1495177 oil pump pickup tube for this engine is about the longest one I have ever encountered—it must be 1.5 feet in length! The spin-on oil filter attaches directly to the oil pump.

The Melling M58F oil pump is a replacement model for the Cadillac 500-ci engine, and its current retail price is $75. The Clevite 611-1688 replacement oil pump is also available for this engine at a retail price of $67.

The Cadillac 500-ci engine was originally fitted with the GM 3514926 oil pan with a 5-quart capacity. The installation of the oil filter added another quart of oil. Luke's Custom Machine & Design decided a larger capacity oil pan was in order so the existing oil pan was modified. The Cadillac oil pan was cut horizontally about 2 inches below the oil pan rails, another section of approximately 2 inches was added, and the lower section was made up from the bottom half of an early Chrysler 354-ci Hemi truck oil pan. A vertical oil baffle was welded to the inside of the new oil pan, which now has a capacity of 7 quarts, plus 1 for the oil filter.

Understand that the oil pan modification just described might not work for many vehicles due to interference with the steering and/or frame. Luke Balogh mounted the engine mid-frame, behind the cab of his truck, where there is absolutely nothing below the oil pan except air. Specialty oil pans are available from Cad Company.

Camshaft and Cylinder Heads

Clevite 77 SH-530-S camshaft bearings are available for the Cadillac 500-ci engine. The current retail price for a set of these bearings is $48. Federal Mogul 1216M camshaft bearings are also available for the retail price of $53.

The GM 1486583 hydraulic lifter camshaft, for the Cadillac 500-ci engine, was manufactured using cast-iron alloy, described by the factory as 120M steel. Most of the camshaft specifications provided by the automobile manufacturers in the 1960s and early 1970s were less than helpful, and the specifications supplied by the factory for this engine are no exception. As usual, the advertised duration is given without any explanation as to what the camshaft lift was at that duration.

The Clevite 229-2299 hydraulic lifter camshaft is a replacement camshaft for the Cadillac 500-ci engine. The current retail price for this camshaft is $175, and a specification card showing duration at 0.050-inch lift is even included. The Crane Cams 1020571, 1020631, and 1020641 PowerMax hydraulic lifter camshafts are available with matching hydraulic valve lifters, valve springs, valve spring retainers, valve stem locks, and even valve stem seals. The Lunati (Holley) 34601, 34602, and 34603 hydraulic lifter camshafts are listed in the catalog. Matching camshaft kits are not shown in the catalog, although they should be available. Cad Company supplies its own camshafts and complete kits in a wide variety of grinds. The prices are competitive for the camshafts and kits from these three companies.

Luke's Custom Machine & Design fabricated this modified oil pan for the Cadillac 500-ci engine.

A few companies offer replacement hydraulic lifters for the Cadillac 500-ci engine. The Clevite 213-1685 hydraulic lifters retail for $52 a set. The Melling JB-969 hydraulic lifters cost $39 for a set. The Sealed Power (Federal Mogul) HT-969 hydraulic lifters are available at a retail price of $47 for a set. The Competition Cams 869-16 (for 350- to 455-ci Buicks) High Energy hydraulic lifters are available at $85 for a set. The Crane Cams 99284-16 (for 400- to 455-ci Buicks) anti-pump up hydraulic lifters cost $90 for a set. It is a good practice to purchase a camshaft with matching lifters; however, it is not always possible for some of the less-popular OHV V-8 engines. The GM 5232510 hydraulic lifters for the Cadillac 500-ci engine have a 2-inch overall length and a 0.840-inch diameter.

The GM 1487602 pushrods used in the Cadillac 500-ci engine are 11/32-inch diameter by 10.1875-inch length. The Clevite 215-4106 replacement pushrods retail for $57 a set. The Melling MPR-305 pushrods are available for $32 a set. The Sealed Power (Federal Mogul) RP-3178 pushrods cost $30 a set. Incidentally, all Clevite, Melling, and Sealed Power (Federal Mogul) products are available at most automotive parts stores. Cad Company sells chrome-moly steel pushrods with 5/16-inch and 3/8-inch diameters in different lengths, depending on the application.

Stock replacement timing chain sets are also available for the Cadillac 500-ci engine. The Clevite 9-3034 set is available for a retail price of $35. The Melling 3-498S set retails for $26. The Cloyes 20-3034 set costs $32. The Ertel Manufacturing Company 73034 timing chain set also costs $32. The Cloyes 9-3139 True Roller is the best timing chain set available for the Cadillac 500-ci engine. The crankshaft sprocket is multi-keyway manufactured from heat-treated SAE 1144 steel. The price for this model is $80.

The torque sequence for the timing gear cover is an item of major importance. Its two-piece design consists of a flat plate retaining the front one-piece oil seal and the timing gear cover/water pump housing. There are four bolts that are torqued to 22 ft-lb, three bolts that are torqued to 10 ft-lb, one bolt that is torqued to 10 ft-lb, and

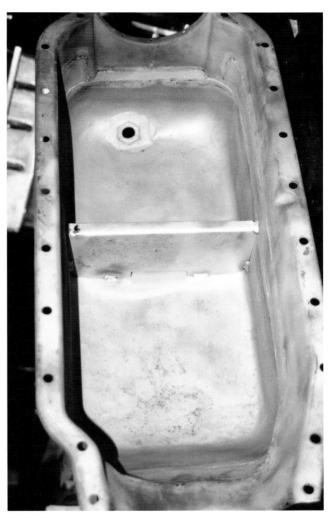

The inside of the oil pan fabricated by Luke's Custom Machine & Design. The vertical baffle is a nice touch.

two bolts that are torqued to 22 ft-lb. Refer to the Cadillac shop manual for the torque sequence of these bolts.

The last three digits of the 1970 Cadillac cylinder head casting numbers are commonly used when referring to these cast-iron cylinder heads. The GM 3633450 cylinder heads installed on the 1970 Cadillac 500-ci engine have a casting number that ended in 950, and they have a combustion chamber volume of 76 cc. The 950 cylinder heads were installed on the 1970 Cadillac 472-ci engine, as well as another cylinder head with a casting number of 250. The 250 cylinder heads also have a combustion chamber volume of 76 cc. These cylinder heads are similar and interchangeable, except that the 950 cylinder head does not have smog rails between the rocker arm stud pedestal support towers (rocker arm stud bosses), while the 250 cylinder head has these smog rails. Some "authorities" have stated only the 950 cylinder head was used on the 1970 Cadillac 500-ci engine; however, a set of the 250 cylinder heads were factory installed

The Cadillac 500-ci swirl chamber design (also known as the "flattened peanut" design) cast-aluminum pistons and the hydraulic valve lifters installed.

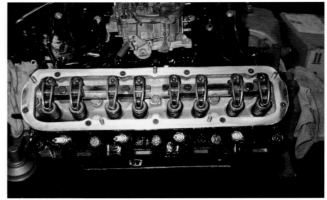

A GM 3633450 (casting number 1486250) cast-iron Cadillac cylinder head, better known as a "250" cylinder head. The smog rails are clearly shown between the rocker arms. The Luke's Custom Machine & Design aluminum valve cover spacer/adapter is used to install a 1969 Cal Custom 40-1018 polished-aluminum finned Ford FE valve cover.

on the 1970 Cadillac 500-ci engine described here. The 950 cylinder head weighs about 3 pounds less than the 250 cylinder head—another huge weight saving for all you racers out there.

The 1970 Cadillac cast-iron cylinder heads do not have the greatest design, and they are most definitely not high-performance cylinder heads. The factory did not provide a torque sequence for the cylinder heads; the only specification is that the cylinder head bolts are torqued to 115 ft-lb, working from the center outward. The five cylinder head bolts located under the valve cover are 4.36 inches long, four of the cylinder heads bolts between the exhaust ports are 4.77 inches long, one bolt next to an end exhaust port is 3.02 inches long, and one stud/bolt next an exhaust port is 4.77 inches long.

Cad Company has just released its new 355 T-6 aluminum cylinder heads for the Cadillac 500-ci engine. This excellent product weighs 50 pounds less than the Cadillac cast-iron cylinder heads. These aluminum cylinder heads are equipped with stainless-steel 2.19-inch head diameter intake valves and 1.90-inch head diameter exhaust valves, and they will flow better than any ported and polished Cadillac cast-iron cylinder heads. The cylinder heads can be fitted with shaft-mounted rocker arms or stud-mounted rocker arms, and roller rocker arms are available. The combustion chamber volume is 81 cc. The current retail price for a set of these fully assembled cylinder heads is $2,195, and they are well worth the money.

The GM 1486753 intake valves were manufactured using SAE (Society of Automotive Engineers) 1041 carbon-manganese steel; the valve head diameter is 2.00 inches, the valve stem diameter is 11/32 inch, and the overall valve length is 5.23 inches. The GM 5232537 exhaust valves were manufactured using 21-2 or GMR 241-M steel; the valve head diameter is 1.625 inches, the valve stem diameter is 11/32 inch, and the overall valve length is 5.245 inches. If the Cadillac 500-ci engine requires new valves, install a new set of stainless-steel intake and exhaust valves. Manley Performance Parts (see Appendix B—Resources) manufactures quality Race Master

and Race-Flo stainless-steel valves for street use. Cad Company also offers quality stainless-steel valves for most Cadillac engines.

The 1970 big-block Chevrolet 454-ci stock intake valves are the same overall length as the 1970 Cadillac 500-ci stock intake valves, and the 1970 big-block Chevrolet 454-ci stock exhaust valves are 0.100 inch longer than the 1970 Cadillac 500-ci stock exhaust valves. Once again, there is lots of potential for a variety of valvetrain modifications.

The 1970 Cadillac 500-ci engine was equipped with single valve springs. The installed height for the intake and exhaust valve springs was 60 to 65 pounds at 1.946 inches valves closed and 155 to 165 pounds at 1.496 inches valves open. Stock replacement valve springs are available from a few companies. The Clevite 212-1061 valve springs are available at a retail price of $28 for a set. The Melling VS-730 valve springs cost $27 for a set. The Sealed Power (Federal Mogul) VS-485 valve springs retail at $22 for a set.

The Sealed Power (Federal Mogul) VSR-7013 valve spring retainers retail at $48 for a set, and the Sealed Power (Federal Mogul) VK-115R valve stem locks are available at a retail price of $8 for a set. These are replacement parts for the 1970 Cadillac 500-ci engine. If you install an aftermarket street performance camshaft, purchase matching valve springs, valve spring retainers, and valve stem locks with the camshaft. The stock valvetrain components used with the Cadillac 500-ci engine are not suitable for anything other than a stock engine rebuild.

The 1970 Cadillac 500-ci engine was fitted with GM 9431676 rocker arm studs (7/16-inch diameter) and GM 1461986 and 1487268 stud-mounted rocker arms. The rocker arm ratio is 1:65. The rocker arm assembly was not designed for high-rpm use and was known to break apart if the owner attempted to race with it. Upgrade the entire valvetrain if you intend to use the Cadillac 500-ci engine for a street performance vehicle. Cad Company

The GM 3515328 (casting number 1495955) single-quad cast-iron intake manifold used on the Cadillac 500-ci engine. The GM 3515077 harmonic balancer and crankshaft pulley and GM 3633088 water pump were painted with Endura EX-2C black 160 high-gloss polyurethane.

An Offenhauser 3918 Pacesetter low-profile polished intake manifold with six Holley 94 carburetors for the 1949 to 1962 Cadillac 331-ci, 365-ci, and 390-ci engines. I built this setup for Marcus Edell, the owner of www.hotrodvintageparts.com, which is a great source for vintage Cadillac speed equipment.

markets improved rocker arm assemblies for various levels of performance use.

The stamped steel valve covers that the factory included with the 1970 Cadillac 500-ci engine look ridiculous—they are about half the width of the cylinder head and appear lost. Luke's Custom Machine & Design fabricated a pair of aluminum valve cover spacers/adapters in order to install a set of rare 1969 Cal Custom polished-aluminum finned Ford FE (Ford Edsel) valve covers. The result changes the outward appearance of the Cadillac engine, and it now looks like a 500-ci engine should.

Intake System

The 1970 Cadillac 500-ci engine was equipped with the GM 3515328 (casting number 1495955) dual-plane four-barrel carburetor cast-iron intake manifold. To say it is not the most efficient of intake manifolds is a gross understatement. A Rochester Quadrajet four-barrel carburetor was used with this intake manifold.

The Edelbrock 2115 Performer dual-plane aluminum intake manifold is an excellent product designed to operate from idle through 5,500 rpm. The plenum is dropped and the carburetor mounting pad is 3 inches higher than the carburetor mounting pad on the Cadillac 500-ci intake manifold. Edelbrock recommends its 1910 Performer RPM Q-Jet model (850 cfm), 1407 Performer manual-choke model (750 cfm), 1411 Performer electric-choke model (750 cfm), or its 1412 Performer manual-choke model (800 cfm). Even a stock Cadillac 500-ci engine will benefit from the installation of a new intake manifold and a carburetor. The current retail price for the Edelbrock 2115 intake manifold is $270, and the Edelbrock carburetors range in price from $240 to $490.

The AC-Delco N40966 mechanical fuel pump is a replacement fuel pump for the Cadillac 500-ci mechanical fuel pump. The AC-Delco model provides 5.25 to 6.50 psi of fuel pressure, and the current retail price is $40.

Ignition System

The Cadillac 500-ci engine was equipped with the GM 1111939 dual-point, 12-volt distributor. This distributor can be upgraded with a Mallory 501 Unilite conversion kit or a Pertronix Performance Products 1181 Ignitor electronic conversion kit. It is one thing to convert the stock dual-point distributor to an electronic distributor, but there are other parts in the distributor that should be thoroughly inspected and replaced as well. These include the shaft and bearing, the distributor cap and rotor, and the distributor drive gear. It is a much better idea to install a brand-new MSD 8363 Pro-Billet magnetic pickup distributor with vacuum advance. This distributor has a current retail price of $299.

The firing order for the 1970 Cadillac 500-ci engine is: 1, 5, 6, 3, 4, 2, 7, and 8. The right (passenger's side) bank from the front is: 1, 3, 5, and 7 cylinders. The left (driver's side) bank from the front is: 2, 4, 6, and 8 cylinders.

The 1970 Cadillac 500-ci engine was equipped with a 42-amp generator or a 55-amp generator for vehicles with air conditioning. Remember that if an engine is fitted with a generator and the distributor has been converted using a Mallory Unilite system, you should install the Mallory 29351 active power filter to protect the Unilite module against power surges. The active power filter is available for $35.

Cooling and Exhaust Systems

Instead of buying a new replacement or rebuilt water pump for the GM 3633088 water pump, purchase a new Flow Kooler 1778 aluminum water pump. The Flow Kooler water pump is currently available for $129.

The 1970 Cadillac 500-ci engine installed mid-frame, behind the cab of the truck. The AC-Delco N40966 mechanical fuel pump is visible.

Most of the major exhaust header companies do not manufacture off-the-shelf headers for the Cadillac 500-ci engine. Cad Company sells exhaust flange adapters that permit the installation of big-block Chevrolet or Ford headers on the Cadillac engine. These adapters sell for $70 and will drastically cut down the cost of an exhaust system.

Engine Summary

Note: The following prices for the engine block, crankshaft, connecting rods, pistons, harmonic balancer, pulleys, cylinder heads, valves, timing gear cover/water pump housing, water pump, and intake manifold are proportionally based on the entire engine's cost. This should explain why some of the prices appear low.

Engine Block

• 1970 Cadillac Fleetwood Eldorado 500-ci V-8 engine block; casting number 1495200; stock bore: 4.300 inches; stock stroke: 4.304 inches; two-bolt main bearing caps; 400 horsepower at 4,400 rpm and 550 ft-lb torque at 3,000 rpm; engine block weight (bare): 200 pounds; $200

• Engine block hot tanked, Magnafluxed, all threads retapped, and cylinder head bolt holes chamfered; main bearing caps and bolts Magnafluxed and shot peened; Federal Mogul 1760 brass freeze plugs (1 3/4-inch diameter) and Federal Mogul PS165 rear camshaft boss plug (2-inch diameter) installed using Permatex aviation form-a-gasket; valve lifter gallery expansion plugs (two) and front oil gallery expansion plugs (two) drilled, tapped, and stainless-steel 1/4-inch NPT (National Pipe Thread) plugs installed using Permatex aviation form-a-gasket; valve lifter bosses deglazed allowing for 0.002-inch valve lifter clearance; Weatherhead 31524-4 polished-brass engine block drain plugs (1/4-inch NPT) installed using pipe thread sealant; valve lifter gallery and front of engine block painted with Glyptal G-1228A medium-grey gloss enamel; exterior surface of engine block painted with Endura EX-2C black 160 high-gloss polyurethane; $400.56

A side view of the Cadillac 500-ci engine installed in the 1939 Ford C.O.E. Truck. This is an ideal position for the engine, as it greatly assists with weight distribution for the vehicle. Luke Balogh will fabricate stainless-steel exhaust headers for this engine—it is only a matter of time.

• Cylinders honed and deglazed using Sunnen 600 series 280-grit stones; final bore: 4.30 inches; piston-to-bore clearance: 0.002 inch, measured below the bottom of the wrist pin perpendicular to the wrist pin; $55

Engine block total: $655.56

Crankshaft

• GM 1496793 (casting number 1495094) cast nodular iron crankshaft; 4.304 inches stroke; main journal diameter: 3.250 inches; connecting rod journal diameter: 2.500 inches; internally balanced; crankshaft weight: 80 pounds; $100

• Crankshaft shot peened, Magnafluxed, aligned, oil holes chamfered, journals polished, and crankshaft balanced; GM 1486608 crankshaft oil slinger glassbeaded and painted with Glyptal G-1228A medium-grey gloss enamel; $163.33

• Clevite 77 MS-970-AL main bearings (standard size) installed, allowing for 0.002-inch crankshaft clearance and 0.007-inch end play; main bearing cap bolts torqued to 85 ft-lb using molykote; $125

• GM 3515077 harmonic balancer (6-inch diameter) with crankshaft hub and triple-groove crankshaft v-belt pulley (7 1/2-inch diameter) installed; crankshaft hub bolt installed using Loctite and torqued to 85 ft-lb; crankshaft pulley installed with Grade 8 bolts, lockwashers, and flat washers using Loctite and torqued to 30 ft-lb; crankshaft hub, harmonic balancer, and crankshaft pulley painted with Endura EX-2C black 160 high-gloss polyurethane; $168.83

Crankshaft total: $557.16

Connecting Rods and Pistons

• GM 3633111 (casting number 174) forged steel I-beam connecting rods with GM 1486553 connecting rod bolts (3/8-inch diameter) installed; length (center to center): 6.750 inches; weight:

818 grams each; connecting rod ratio: 1.57 (with 4.304 inches stroke); $80

• Connecting rods shot peened, Magnafluxed, aligned, resized, and balanced; $180

• Clevite 77 CB-542-P connecting rod bearings (standard size) installed with 0.002-inch connecting rod clearance and 0.012-inch side clearance per pair of connecting rods; connecting rod bolts installed using molykote and torqued to 50 ft-lb, allowing for 0.0055 inch stretch; $80

• GM 1495125 (casting number 1495125) cast-aluminum alloy slipper-skirt pistons, standard bore, 10.0:1 compression ratio, swirl-chamber design; weight: 723 grams each; pressed-in, heat-treated chrome-moly steel, straight-wall wrist pins; wrist pin diameter: 0.9999 inch; wrist pin length: 3.030 inches; Ertel Manufacturing Company 50850 cast-iron piston ring set, standard bore, 5/64-inch top compression ring width, 5/64-inch second compression ring width, and 3/16-inch oil ring width; piston rings installed within manufacturer's recommended arc; top compression ring gap: 0.017 inch, second compression ring gap: 0.016 inch, and oil ring gap: 0.017 inch; intake-valve-to-piston clearance: 0.200 inch, and exhaust-valve-to-piston clearance: 0.210 inch; $245

• Complete V-8 engine balance; Victor-Reinz FS3852 complete gasket set installed; $265

Connecting rods and pistons total: $850

Lubrication System

• Melling M58F standard volume oil pump installed and torqued to 20 ft-lb using Loctite; GM 1495177 oil pump pickup and screen installed; exterior surface of oil pump painted with Endura EX-2C black 160 high-gloss polyurethane; $101.67

• Rear oil seals installed using silicone sealant; GM 3514926 oil pan modified by Luke's Custom Machine & Design and painted with Endura EX-2C black 160 high-gloss polyurethane; oil pan gaskets installed using silicone sealant; oil pan installed with stainless-steel bolts, AN flat washers, and lockwashers, using Loctite and torqued to 15 ft-lb; AC-Delco PF-30 oil filter installed; engine lubricated with 8 quarts Pennzoil SAE HD-30-weight motor oil; $306

Lubrication system total: $407.67

Camshaft and Cylinder Heads

• Clevite 77 SH-530-S camshaft bearings installed with 0.002-inch camshaft clearance and 0.002-inch end play; No. 1, 2, 3, 4, and 5 camshaft bearings: SH-530; housing bore diameter: 1.8792 to 1.8802 inches; camshaft journal diameter: 1.75 inches; $48

• Clevite 229-2299 cast-iron alloy hydraulic lifter camshaft with advertised duration: 296 degrees intake and 310 degrees exhaust; duration at 0.050-inch lift: 218 degrees intake and 228 degrees exhaust; net valve lift: 0.505-inch intake and 0.512-inch exhaust (based on 1.65 ratio rocker arms); lobe separation angle: 110 degrees; valve lash (hot): zero; camshaft degreed; $175

A very nicely detailed Cadillac 500-ci engine built by Luke's Custom Machine & Design, completed in October 2002.

• Ertel Manufacturing Company 73034 timing chain set, steel gears, and Morse chain, installed with bolts torqued to 20 ft-lb, using Loctite; GM 3633103 timing gear cover and GM 1486784 water pump housing installed with Grade 8 bolts and lockwashers, using Loctite and torqued to 10 ft-lb and 22 ft-lb; timing gear cover and water pump housing gaskets installed using silicone sealant; $65.33

• Clevite 213-1685 hydraulic lifters, 2-inch length overall by 0.840-inch diameter, installed; $52

• GM 1487602 pushrods, 11/32-inch diameter by 10.1875-inch length, installed; $57

• GM 3633450 (casting number 1486250) cast-iron closed chamber, rectangular port cylinder heads, 76-cc combustion chamber volume, installed; cylinder heads hot tanked; area beneath valve covers painted with Glyptal G-1228A medium-grey gloss enamel, and exterior surface painted with Endura EX-2C black 160 high-gloss polyurethane; cylinder head weight (bare): 58 pounds; cylinder head bolts torqued to 115 ft-lb, using Permatex aviation form-a-gasket; $352

• GM 1486753 intake valves, SAE 1041 carbon-manganese steel, 2.00-inch valve head diameter, 11/32-inch valve stem diameter, 5.23-inch length overall; GM 5232537 exhaust valves, GMR 241-M steel, 1.625-inch valve head diameter, undercut stems, 11/32-inch valve stem diameter, 5.245-inch length overall, installed with Serdi-machined multi-angle blueprint valve grind; polyacrylate umbrella valve stem seals installed; $189

• Sealed Power (Federal Mogul) VS-485 single valve springs, 1.230-inch o.d. and 0.890-inch i.d., installed; installed height: 65 pounds at 1.946 inches valves closed and 165 pounds at 1.496 inches valves open; Sealed Power (Federal Mogul) VSR-7013 valve spring retainers and Sealed Power (Federal Mogul) VK-115R valve stem locks, 7-degree by 11/32-inch stem diameter, installed; $78

• GM 9431676 heat-treated steel rocker arm studs, 7/16-inch diameter, installed with GM 1461986 and GM 1487268 stamped steel rocker arms, 1.65 ratio; $60.99

• 1969 Cal Custom 40-1018 polished finned aluminum Ford FE valve covers installed with Luke's Custom Machine & Design polished aluminum 1/2-inch-thick valve cover spacer/adapter using polished stainless-steel bolts and lockwashers with Loctite and torqued to 75 in-lb; valve cover gaskets installed using silicone sealant; $318.66

Camshaft and cylinder heads total: $1,395.98

Intake System

• GM 3515328 (casting number 1495955) single-quad, cast-iron, low-profile intake manifold installed with Victor-Reinz MS15943 valley pan/intake manifold gasket, using silicone sealant with intake manifold bolts torqued to 25 ft-lb, using Loctite; underside of intake manifold painted with V.H.T. SP-101 white high-temperature coating, and exterior surface painted with Endura EX-2C black 160 high-gloss polyurethane; $170

• Rochester 40232-1999 Quadrajet (model 4MV) four-barrel carburetor, 800 cfm, 17/32-inch primary venturi, automatic choke, installed; $200

• AC-Delco N40966 mechanical fuel pump, 5.25 to 6.50 psi, installed with bolts torqued to 20 ft-lb, using Loctite; fuel pump gasket installed using silicone sealant; Summit Racing Equipment SUM-220238 polished stainless-steel 3/8-inch o.d. fuel line (fuel pump to carburetor) installed; $43.10

Intake system total: $413.10

Ignition System

• GM 1111939 dual-point distributor converted to breakerless system using Pertronix Performance Parts 1181 Ignitor electronic ignition; Standard Motor Products DR429 black distributor cap, DR311X rotor, and VC24A vacuum control installed; Pertronix Performance Products 40011 black Flame-Thrower high-performance ignition coil, 1.5 ohms, 40,000 volts, installed; $131.80

• Taylor/Vertex 70053 black Pro Series 8-millimeter high-performance Spiro-Pro spark plug wires, 135-degree boots, Kelvar resistor core, installed with Taylor 42700 black spark plug wire separators; NGK 7038 resistor-type spark plugs installed with 0.040-inch gap; $83.56

• Ford alternator, 12 volts, 100 amps, installed with GM 1401551 alternator brace and GM 1494838 generator mounting bracket; alternator brace and generator bracket painted with Endura EX-2C black 160 high-gloss polyurethane; Gates 11A1255 XL crankshaft/water pump/alternator v-belt, 7/16-inch by 49 1/2-inch length, installed; $250

• GM 1108552 rebuilt starting motor installed; $122.34

Ignition system total: $587.70

Cooling and Exhaust Systems

• 1970 Cadillac 3633088 (casting number) cast-iron water pump installed with Grade 8 bolts and lockwashers using Loctite and torqued to 22 ft-lb; water pump gasket installed using silicone sealant; GM 1601101 water pump pulley, double groove, 6 1/2-inch diameter, installed with Grade 8 bolts and lockwashers using Loctite and torqued to 20 ft-lb; GM 1486784 thermostat housing installed using Loctite on bolts and torqued to 20 ft-lb; thermostat housing gasket installed using silicone sealant; water pump, water pump pulley, and thermostat housing painted with Endura EX-2C black 160 high-gloss polyurethane; $83.33

Cooling and exhaust systems total: $83.33

Labor

• Labor for checking clearances, gapping piston rings, degree camshaft, valvetrain assembly, detailing, trial engine assembly, final engine assembly, and initial engine start-up; $800

Labor total: $800

Engine Grand Total: $5,750.50 (U.S.)

Note: The estimated output of this engine is 345 horsepower at 4,000 rpm and 517 ft-lb torque at 2,500 rpm (see Appendix A—Dyno Print-Outs).

CHAPTER 10
1967 CORVETTE 327-ci ENGINE (L79 CLONE)

The 1967 Corvette Sting Ray L79 high-performance small-block Chevrolet 327-ci engine was rated at 350 horsepower at 5,800 rpm and 360 ft-lb torque at 3,600 rpm. It is the most powerful 327-ci engine with a hydraulic lifter camshaft that Corvette ever offered. The most powerful Generation I small-block Chevrolet engine ever offered was the fuel-injected 1965 Corvette model with a 327-ci/375-horsepower engine.

A local pal of mine purchased a 1967 Corvette convertible at the end of 1995. The previous owner of this Corvette had discovered it, as a complete disaster, in Connecticut. The car was eventually trans-

The 1964 Chevrolet 327-ci engine block (casting number 3858180). The valve lifter gallery has been ground smooth and the engine block has been align honed, parallel decked, and bored and honed.

ported to Vancouver, British Columbia, Canada, where the frame, body, and interior were expertly refurbished from the ground up. By the time that work was completed, a so-called rebuilt small-block Chevrolet 327-ci engine had been installed. That engine turned out to be less than mediocre and soon became a great boat anchor. The original engine, transmission, and rear end had disappeared into the sunset years before; as a result, this vehicle would never be a "numbers matching" car. The plan was to build an engine that was similar to the original 1967 Corvette L79 model, although it proved impossible to locate a 1967 Chevrolet 327-ci engine block with a casting date of 1967. After a lot of foraging around and following up useless leads, we discovered a suitable candidate with a casting date of 1964 hidden away at High Performance Engines.

The engine described here was assembled with the assistance of some very talented people. High Performance Engines built the short block, and Luke's Custom Machine & Design completed the engine and installation. I assisted with the parts ordering, much of the cleaning, a lot of the assembly and detailing, and I also helped with the installation. The owner paid for everything. The result is a beautiful little small-block Chevrolet 327-ci engine that runs perfectly, sounds great, and has logged approximately 15,000 miles to date.

Components Description
Engine Block

The specifications for the 1967 Corvette L79 engine are:
- 327-ci (5.4-liter) displacement
- 4.001-inch stock bore and 3.250-inch stock stroke
- Stock compression ratio: 11.0:1
- 350 horsepower at 5,800 rpm and 360 ft-lb torque at 3,600 rpm

Chevrolet referred to its small-block engines built from 1955 to 1991 as Generation I. Chevrolet introduced its first 327-ci engine in 1962, and this was the first small block with a 4.00-inch bore. The 327-ci engines built from 1962 to 1967 were also referred to as the small-journal models, in reference to the 2.30-inch diameter of the main bearing crankshaft journals and the 2.00-inch diameter of the connecting rod crankshaft journals. The large-journal models were built in 1968 and 1969, and the name was in reference to the 2.45-inch diameter of the main bearing crankshaft journals and the 2.10-inch diameter of the connecting rod crankshaft journals. The large-

A truly rare NOS (new old stock) 1967 GM 3917265 (casting number 6764) small-journal forged steel crankshaft for a 1967 Chevrolet 302-ci engine with its original packing box. This crankshaft has a 3.00-inch stroke.

A GM 3838495 small-journal forged steel crankshaft. It has been shot peened, Magnafluxed, the main and connecting rod journals ground 0.010-inch undersize, the oil holes chamfered, the journals polished, and it has been balanced.

journal 327-ci engines have the same size main and connecting rod crankshaft journals as the small-block Chevrolet 350-ci engine.

The small-journal 327-ci engine blocks built for the Chevy II passenger cars are distinct from all the other 327-ci engine blocks. The oil filter boss is raised, the dip stick is in the right side (passenger's side) of the oil pan and not in the engine block on the left side (driver's side), and the clutch cross-shaft boss on the left side (driver's side) is not drilled and tapped.

The 1962 and 1963 Chevrolet 327-ci engines were fitted with a wider rear camshaft bearing than the rear camshaft bearing in the 1964 to 1967 engines. The earlier rear camshaft bearing is 0.200 inch wider than the later rear camshaft bearing and it has two small oil holes in it. The later model rear camshaft bearing can be installed in the early-model engine blocks, provided the rear camshaft bearing is placed far enough back in the rear camshaft journal. If this is not done, there will be a massive oil leak. Other than the differences just mentioned, all the small-journal 327-ci engine blocks are the same.

Here is a list of small-journal 327-ci engine block casting numbers (not including the Chevy II models):

3782870
3789817
3852174
3858174
3858180
3858190
3868657
3876132
3892657
3903352
3953512
3959512

These are the casting numbers I am aware of; there may well be others. The major concern for the engine block described in this chapter was to locate one in good condition and not worry about casting numbers and casting dates. A standard-bore engine block was eventually tracked down. There are some good books available

containing all the casting numbers and dates and VINs (vehicle identification numbers) for those readers who are looking for "numbers matching" engine blocks. Good luck with your search.

Refer to Chapter 1 for information pertaining to the preparation of the engine block. In keeping with the 1967 Corvette tradition, the engine block described in this chapter is going to be painted Chevrolet orange. It is a common practice for many engine builders to install valve lifter gallery plugs and screens to stop any debris in the valve lifter gallery from ending up in the oil pan. The Milodon 23150 lifter valley screen kit is available from your local speed shop for about $13. There are three valve lifter gallery oil line expansion plugs at the front of the engine block (behind the camshaft gear) that should be removed. Then drill and tap the three holes and install new stainless-steel 1/4-inch NPT plugs using Permatex aviation form-a-gasket.

The Chevrolet 327-ci engine blocks are all equipped with two-bolt main bearing caps. They are of sufficient strength for use in most street performance engines; however, these main bearing caps should be beefed up if you intend to build a wild street engine or install a blower. The Milodon 11050 splayed four-bolt main bearing cap conversion kit is available with bolts or studs. The current retail price for that kit is $197.95. The four-bolt main bearing caps should only be installed in the engine block by a very experienced machine shop, and the estimated cost to do so is $200. If a four-bolt main bearing cap conversion kit is installed, the engine block will have to be align bored and honed. The main bearing housing bore sizes are 2.490 to 2.491 inches.

The cylinders in the Chevrolet 327-ci engine block can be safely bored to 0.040-inch oversize, and some of the engine blocks have

A set of GM 3927145 forged steel connecting rods for the Chevrolet 327-ci engine. These connecting rods were shot peened, Magnafluxed, aligned, debeamed, resized, pin fitted, balanced, and new ARP 134-6001 bolts were installed.

A set of TRW L2166NF-30 power-forged aluminum racing pistons, the Clevite 77 bearings, and the ARP 134-6001 connecting rod bolts. The piston tops were painted with V.H.T. SP-101 white high-temperature coating, an old drag racing trick. The white paint will supposedly help to promote flame travel when the engine is initially started.

even been bored 0.060-inch oversize for racing. The cylinder boring of a 327-ci engine block to 0.060-inch oversize is risky business—the cylinder walls become very thin at that stage, and the chances of striking water are good. Have the cylinder walls sonic tested to determine if they can handle a 0.060-inch oversize bore and still have sufficient material left in the cylinder walls.

In order to obtain a perfectly true engine block, the Chevrolet 327-ci engine block should be align honed and parallel decked. The tolerances at the factory are not as strict as the standards set at a premium performance engine building shop. Refer to Chapter 1.

Crankshaft

All the Chevrolet 327-ci small-journal crankshafts were manufactured using forged steel, and the GM 3838495 crankshaft (casting number 4577) is the one to locate. This crankshaft was available from 1962 to 1967. This is a quality piece of equipment that will withstand a lot of abuse, even in a radical street performance engine. There are still a number of used small-journal crankshafts available on the open market, and the key is to find one in good condition where the main bearing journals or the connecting rod journals do not need to be ground in excess of 0.040-inch undersize. If the crankshaft journals are in excess of 0.040-inch undersize, there are no main bearings and connecting rod bearings currently available. The only solution to that problem is to have the crankshaft journal(s) built up using the wire weld or metal spray method, both of which would be costly propositions. Refer to Chapter 2 for an explanation of this matter.

The Clevite 77 MS-429-P main bearings are available in standard size, 0.001-, 0.010-, 0.020-, 0.030-, and 0.040-inch oversize.

The current retail price for a set of these main bearings is $65. The Federal Mogul 994M main bearings are available in standard size, 0.001-, 0.010-, 0.020-, 0.030-, and 0.040-inch oversize. The current retail price for a set of these main bearings is $75. These bearings are available at most automotive parts stores. The No. 5 main bearing is the thrust bearing. The factory-recommended main bearing clearance is 0.0008 to 0.0034 inch, and the recommended end play is 0.002 to 0.006 inch. Torque the main bearing cap bolts to 70 ft-lb using molykote.

Do not use the factory-installed harmonic balancer on a street performance engine. The Fluidampr 712430 harmonic balancer meets SFI specs 18.1, has a 7 1/4-inch o.d., and weighs 13.4 pounds. This harmonic balancer is designed for an internally balanced engine. The current retail price for the Fluidampr 712430 is $295, and it is available at speed performance shops. Use a quality crankshaft bolt and washer, such as an ARP 134-2501 (available for $18), to secure the harmonic balancer.

Connecting Rods and Pistons

The GM 3927145 forged steel I-beam connecting rod is the best Chevrolet connecting rod to install in a small-journal 327-ci engine. These connecting rods were heat treated and Magnafluxed at the factory and offered for use in the Corvette L79 and Camaro Z-28 engines. They have a teardrop shape below the wrist pin hole, their length (center to center) is 5.699 to 5.701 inches, and they weigh 567 grams each. The crankshaft end (the big end) is 2.124 to 2.125 inches, and the connecting rods have a pressed-in wrist pin. Replace

A Melling M55 standard-volume oil pump for use in all the small-block Chevrolet engines.

The Melling M55 standard-volume oil pump and the GM 3927136 windage tray installed. The Cloyes 93100 double-roller timing chain is visible just behind the crankshaft degree wheel.

the factory connecting rod bolts with ARP 134-6001 connecting rod bolts rated at 190,000 psi (11/32-inch diameter). The current retail price for these connecting rod bolts is $60, and they are available at any ARP dealer.

The Clevite 77 CB-745-P connecting rod bearings are available in standard size, 0.001-, 0.002-, 0.010-, 0.020-, 0.030-, and 0.040-inch oversize. The current retail price for a set of these connecting rod bearings is $38. The Federal Mogul 8-2020CP connecting rod bearings are available in standard size, 0.001-, 0.010-, 0.020-, 0.030-, and 0.040-inch oversize. The current retail price for a set of these connecting rod bearings is $45. The factory-recommended connecting rod bearing clearance is 0.0007 to 0.0028 inch, and the side clearance per pair of connecting rods is 0.009 to 0.013 inch. Torque the connecting rods bolts to 50 ft-lb using molykote and allowing for 0.006-inch stretch.

In order to be similar to the GM 3871208 pistons used in the Corvette L79 engine, a new set of TRW L2166NF-30 power forged aluminum racing pistons, 11.0:1 compression ratio (with 64-cc combustion chambers), 0.030-inch oversize, was installed in the Chevrolet 327-ci engine. The original purchase price for these pistons and wrist pins was $320, including a set of Sealed Power E251K-30 moly piston rings. These pistons and piston rings are available through most speed shops.

A compression ratio of 10.1:1 is usually the maximum that a street performance engine can operate at using high-octane, unleaded gasoline. Any compression ratio higher than this will most likely cause ignition pinging, leading to serious internal engine damage. The engine described here will have an 11.0:1 compression ratio. The solution is to add octane booster to each full tank of fuel.

The owner of this engine adds octane booster to each full tank of fuel and has never experienced any ignition pinging.

The Ross Racing Pistons 90251 forged aluminum racing pistons are excellent products for the Chevrolet 327-ci engine. These stocking pistons are intended for a 4.030-inch bore and 3.250-inch stroke, a 5.70-inch-long connecting rod. They have a 10.5:1 compression ratio with a 76-cc straight or angle-plug cylinder head combustion chamber, and they weigh 557 grams each. The aircraft-quality wrist pins have a 0.150-inch-thick wall, and double Spiro-Lox retainers are supplied along with them. The current retail price for a set of these pistons is $650. The Ross Racing Pistons forged aluminum racing pistons are available with cast-iron or moly piston rings.

The Fel-Pro 2802 complete gasket set is recommended for the assembly of the Chevrolet 327-ci engine. This gasket set retails for about $90.

Lubrication System

The Melling M55 standard-volume oil pump and the Melling M55HV high-volume oil pump are good choices to install in any small-block Chevrolet engine. These oil pumps are available for about $20 at most auto parts suppliers. If you desire a Chevrolet oil pump, the GM 3848907 oil pump originally used in the Corvette LT-1 and Camaro Z-28 engines is available for $90. Authenticity is not cheap. Have pressure balance grooves ground or milled into the new oil pump body, and check the oil pump for end clearance. Have the oil pump cavity in the rear main bearing cap polished using a high-speed grinder with a carbide bit. Check the oil pump passage from the rear main bearing cap into the engine block to ensure it is perfectly aligned. If it is not, use a high-speed grinder with a carbide bit and correct the situation. Torque the oil pump stud to 65 ft-lb using Loctite.

Install a new oil pump driveshaft in any street performance Chevrolet 327-ci engine. The ARP 134-7901 and the Moroso 22070 oil pump shafts are manufactured using heat-treated chrome-moly steel rated at 170,000 psi. Install a new oil pump stud as well. The ARP 230-7001, the Manley 42339, and the Milodon 17050 are all manufactured using heat-treated 8740 steel. The oil pump shafts retail for $11, and the oil pump studs retail for around $6.

The GM 359942 stamped steel oil pan was included on some of the 1963 to 1965 Corvette engines, and it had a rear sump with an internal oil baffle. This 6-quart-capacity oil pan (with the canister-type oil filter) is good for use with any Chevrolet 327-ci engine, provided there is sufficient steering clearance. This oil pan was installed on the engine described here in order to keep with the stock Corvette appearance. The GM 359942 oil pan is becoming a very scarce item these days, so the alternative is the Milodon 30900 low-profile oil pan with the left-side (driver's side) dip stick and a capacity of 6 quarts of oil. This is an excellent choice for any small-block Chevrolet engine using a rear sump oil pan. The Milodon 30910 is the chrome version for all you "uptown" people out there. The Milodon 30900 oil pan has a current retail price of $130, and the Milodon 30910 chrome oil pan has a current retail price of $170. Milodon products are available at most speed equipment suppliers.

If you purchase an aftermarket oil pan, buy the matching oil pump pickup screen (or tube) with the oil pan. This way you will not end up with one that fits an early Russian Lada. The Milodon 18311 oil pump pickup is used with the Melling M55 standard-volume oil pump and the Milodon 30900 or 30910 oil pans. The Milodon 18314 oil pump pickup is used with the Melling M55HV high-volume oil pump and the Milodon 30900 or 30910 oil pans. The current retail price for the Milodon oil pump pickups is $35.

The Milodon 32250 Diamond Stripper windage tray is recommended for use with the Milodon 30900 or 30910 oil pans and currently retails for $75. In order to install the windage tray, the Milodon 81148 adjustable windage tray studs (six) must be installed, and these are available for $48. The GM 3927136 windage tray was installed on the Corvette LT-1 and Camaro Z-28 engines, although it can be fitted to a Chevrolet 327-ci engine. The GM 3872718 windage tray studs (five) are required to mount the windage tray. The current retail price for the windage tray is $30, and the five studs are $45.

Do not leave the GM 3728502 crankcase ventilator out of a Chevrolet 327-ci street performance engine. This canister-type unit is 5 3/4 inches long and is secured in place to a breather port at the rear of the valve lifter gallery. An elbow is attached to the outside of the engine block above the breather port; the elbow is then connected by a rubber hose to the underside of the air cleaner base. The crankcase ventilator acts as an oil separator, preventing oil from being drawn out of the valve lifter gallery. The ventilator is also part

All the Competition Cams valvetrain components, including the 122102 High Energy hydraulic lifter camshaft. Always buy matched camshaft components.

of the 1967 Corvette 327-ci PCV (positive crankcase ventilation) system. The PCV valve is installed near the top of the oil filler tube in the 1967 Corvette L79 engine. From there, it is connected by a hose to the PCV fitting on the carburetor. The oil filler tube is located above the breather port at the front of the engine block.

The Chevrolet 327-ci engines were equipped with an oil filter canister and a replacement cartridge-type oil filter. The GM 5574535 (body) and GM 5573979 (valve) oil filter adapters are used with the canister-type oil filter. The Trans-Dapt 1024 oil filter adapter converts the canister-type oil filter to the post-1967 spin-on-type oil filter. This adapter uses a Fram PH-8A oil filter and currently retails for $10.

Camshaft and Cylinder Heads

The Clevite 77 SH-287S camshaft bearings for the 1962 and 1963 engines are available at a current retail price of $33. As a matter of interest, the Clevite 77 SH-289 is the rear camshaft bearing. The Federal Mogul 1145M camshaft bearings for the 1962 to 1963 engines are available at a current retail price of $39. The Clevite 77 SH-290S camshaft bearings for the 1964 to 1967 engines are available at a current retail price of $30. The Federal Mogul 1235M camshaft bearings for the 1964 to 1967 engines are available at a current retail price of $30. The 1964 to 1967 Chevrolet 327-ci engines use the same camshaft bearings as the small-block Chevrolet 350-ci engines.

The GM 3863151 hydraulic lifter camshaft for the 1967 Corvette L79 engine has not been manufactured for many years. As a result, an aftermarket replacement camshaft was required and the owner of the engine wanted one with specifications as close as possible to the L79 model. This left two choices: the Crane Cams 967601 Blueprint factory replacement hydraulic lifter camshaft at a retail price of $80 or the Competition Cams 122102 High Energy

The Competition Cams 122102 High Energy hydraulic lifter camshaft installed. The camshaft lobes are well lubricated.

A GM casting number 3890462 double hump cast-iron cylinder head that has been hot tanked and Magnafluxed. It is now ready for serious machining.

hydraulic lifter camshaft at a retail price of $95. The owner decided on the latter model. Crane Cams and Competition Cams products are available at most high-performance centers. Install a camshaft button on the front of the camshaft timing gear to prevent the camshaft from walking, thereby causing erratic timing. This item costs about $6.

Use the Competition Cams 812-16 High Energy hydraulic valve lifters, compatible with their camshaft. They have a current retail price of $90 for a set. The Competition Cams 7812-16 pushrods are 5/16-inch diameter, heat-treated for use with pushrod guide plates, and their current retail price is $30 for a set.

In the event that a stock-type engine is not required, or even desired, there are some excellent camshaft choices that will really wake up the Chevrolet 327-ci engine. If the Crower Cams & Equipment Company 00320 solid lifter camshaft, with a power range from 2,000 rpm to 6,000 rpm, was installed in the engine described here, the estimated output would be: 364 horsepower at 6,000 rpm and 384 ft-lb torque at 4,000 rpm. If the Crower Cams & Equipment Company 00321 solid lifter camshaft, with a power range from 2,400 rpm to 6,400 rpm, was installed in the engine described here, the estimated output would be: 370 horsepower at 6,000 rpm and 365 ft-lb torque at 4,500 rpm. The Crower Cams & Equipment 66900-980 solid lifters with the coolface option are great solid lifters to use with their camshafts. The current retail price for one of these camshafts is $135, and the solid lifters retail at $80 for a set or for $160 a set with the coolface option.

As mentioned earlier in this book, the Duntov camshaft was named after Zora Arkus-Duntov. This camshaft is GM 3736097 and was originally installed in the 1957 Corvette, although it was available for the 1957 to 1963 Corvettes. The Duntov camshaft was a solid (mechanical) lifter type and the Chevrolet specifications were: advertised duration: 287 degrees intake and 283 degrees exhaust; duration at 0.050-inch lift: 222 degrees intake and 221 degrees exhaust; valve lash (hot): 0.012 inch intake and 0.018 inch exhaust; lobe separation angle: 111 degrees; and the maximum lift with 1.5-ratio rocker arms was 0.381 inch intake and 0.380 inch exhaust. If the Duntov camshaft was installed in the engine described here, the estimated output would be: 349 horsepower at 6,000 rpm and 349 ft-lb torque at 4,500 rpm. In the late 1950s and early 1960s, the Duntov camshaft was considered a racing camshaft.

Install a decent double-roller timing chain set in the Chevrolet 327-ci engine. The Cloyes 93100 double-roller timing chain set has heat-treated sprockets and a multi-keyway crankshaft sprocket in order to advance or retard the camshaft timing. The current retail price for this timing chain set is $70. The GM 361925 timing gear cover is the model used on the 1967 Corvette L79 engine with the GM 3751232 harmonic balancer. There are numerous small-block Chevrolet timing gear covers with the timing tab installed in different positions on the timing gear covers. The tab must clear the harmonic balancer, and that is why the timing gear cover and the harmonic balancer must match. The small-block Chevrolet timing gear covers are still readily available at little or no cost, and the GM 3980267 one-piece oil seal is used with all of them.

The name "double hump" was given to some of the cylinder heads used on the Chevrolet 327-ci engines because the casting at the ends of the cylinder heads has a machined flat surface with two humps rising from it. Many people refer to all double hump cylinder heads as "fuelie" cylinder heads, which is a misnomer because only the GM casting 3782461 cylinder head was the original double hump cylinder head used on the 1961 Corvette equipped with fuel injection. The last three digits of the different double hump cylinder head casting numbers are 291, 461, and 462, and they have been installed on every type of Chevrolet 327-ci engine. None of the double hump cylinder heads had accessory bolt holes drilled into the ends of the cylinder heads, they did not have a temperature sending unit boss, they all used 14-millimeter by 3/8-inch reach spark plugs with a crush washer, and they all were manufactured using cast iron. I do not intend to list, or describe, every cylinder head casting number used on the Chevrolet 327-ci engine. I will, however, provide some information for the GM casting 3890462 cylinder head used on the engine described in this chapter.

The majority of the GM casting 3890462 double hump closed-chamber cylinder heads came from the factory with 1.94-inch-diameter intake valves and 1.50-inch-diameter exhaust valves. A few of these cylinder heads received the 2.02-inch-diameter intake valves and 1.60-inch-diameter exhaust valves. Some of the cylinder heads with the larger valves were installed on Corvette L79 and Camaro Z-28 engines. There is no way to tell what size valves are in a double hump cylinder head from the outward appearance; the cylinder head must be removed in order to determine the valve size. If the 2.02-inch/1.60-inch-diameter valves are going to be installed in a double hump cylinder head, have the area on the wall of the combustion chamber around the valves unshrouded (laying back). If this is not done, the air/fuel flow will be impeded and the cylinder heads will actually perform worse than if the stock 1.94-inch/1.50-inch-diameter valves had been left in. The GM casting 3890462 cylinder head has a 66-cc combustion chamber volume, a relief (flat spot) below the spark plug hole, and the intake runner volume is 160 cc.

The cylinder heads were delivered to "T-Bone," the wizard of all cylinder heads at High Performance Engines, where he performed his usual magic. They were pressure tested and Magnafluxed, which is a very good idea for older cylinder heads to ensure there are no hidden cracks. The intake and exhaust ports were mildly ported and polished and gasket matched. If you choose to do your own porting and polishing, just remove the rough spots in the runners. Do not get carried away grinding the ports—there is not a lot of material to play with and it is fairly easy to strike water in these early cylinder heads. The combustion chambers were ground smooth and equalized (cc'd) to 64 cc. Bronze valve guide liners were installed, the valves were unshrouded, new hardened exhaust valve seat inserts were installed, the cylinder heads were surfaced, and a Serdi-machined multi-angle blueprint valve grind was performed—the whole nine yards!

If you plan to install aftermarket valve springs in the camel hump cylinder heads and they have a larger outside diameter than the outside diameter of the stock Chevrolet valve springs, the valve spring seats will have to be enlarged to accommodate them. This is accomplished using a spring seat cutter and should only be performed by an experienced machine shop. The area beneath the valve spring seat is quite thin and it is very easy to penetrate into the water jacket. Do not try this at home.

The Competition Cams 981-16 single valve springs with damper were installed. These valve springs are 1.250 inches o.d. and 0.880 inch i.d.; the installed height is: 110 pounds at 1.70 inches valves

This GM casting number 3890462 double hump cylinder head will be installed on the engine. The bronze valve guide liners have been installed, and the intake ports are being gasket matched.

closed and 285 pounds at 1.25 inches valves open; coil bind: 1.13 inches. The Competition Cams 742-16 matched valve spring retainers (11/32-inch stem diameter) are manufactured using hardened alloy steel. The Competition Cams 601-16 stamped steel 7-degree valve stem locks (11/32-inch stem diameter) and the Competition Cams 501-16 valve stem seal O-rings were installed as well. The current retail price for a set of the valve springs, valve spring retainers, valve stem locks, and valve stem seals is $150. The valve springs in the Chevrolet 327-ci engine were fitted with the GM 3836755 valve stem oil shield. This oil shield was cup shaped and fitted over the top of the valve spring and assisted with oil control. Provided the oil shield will fit over an aftermarket valve spring, it does no harm to install the oil shield.

A set of Manley 10750 Street Master stainless-steel intake valves (2.02-inch valve head diameter, 11/32-inch valve stem diameter, 4.911-inch length overall) and Manley 10749 Street Master stainless-steel exhaust valves (1.60-inch valve head diameter, 11/32-inch valve stem diameter, 4.911-inch length overall) were installed. The current retail price for a set of these intake and exhaust valves is $150. The Enginetech S2927 viton positive-seal valve stem seals were installed as well.

Install hardened steel pushrod guide plates, such as the Manley 42355-8 flat guide plates, in order to help stabilize the valvetrain action. These pushrod guide plates are available for $20 a set. All double hump cylinder heads were equipped with pressed-in rocker arm studs; these should be changed to screw-in studs for street performance use. This job can be easily performed by a competent machine shop, and the estimated cost to do so is $100. The ARP 134-7101 high-performance-series screw-in rocker arm studs (170,000 psi, 3/8-inch diameter) were installed; they have a current retail price of $40. The ends of the rocker arm studs must be ground flat in order to permit the installation of the Manley 42107 rocker

The same GM casting number 3890462 double hump cylinder with the Manley 42335-8 hardened guide plates and the ARP 134-7101 screw-in rocker arm studs installed. The valve assemblies in the background are about to be installed as well.

arm nuts. The current retail price for a set of the poly lock rocker arm nuts is $30. The rocker arm studs should be torqued to 50 ft-lb using Loctite.

The rocker arms installed at the factory on the camel hump cylinder heads are stamped steel and have a ratio of 1.5, although this ratio is not accurate. The Competition Cams 1412-16 Magnum roller tip rocker arms (1.52 ratio, 3/8-inch stud diameter) were installed. These rocker arms have an accurate ratio and grooved rocker arm balls are included in the set. The grooved rocker arm balls permit better oil flow and oil retention, thus preventing galling. The current retail price for a set of these rocker arms is $140.

If the original factory cylinder head bolts are in excellent condition, they can be reused on a street performance engine. The best plan, however, is to purchase a new set, such as the ARP 134-3601 high-performance-series cylinder head bolts, (170,000 psi) available at a current retail price of $60. The cylinder head bolts should be torqued to 65 ft-lb using Permatex aviation form-a-gasket.

Chevrolet factory equipped the 1967 Corvette L79 engine with GM 3767493 die-cast aluminum valve covers. Each valve cover has four bolt holes to secure it to the cylinder head, the Corvette script on it, and there are no openings for a breather, PCV valve, or oil filler tube. These valve covers will buff up beautifully if someone like "Tim, the polishing guy" has a go at them.

Intake System

The 1967 Corvette L79 was equipped with the GM 3893954 (casting number 3890490) cast-aluminum single-quad, dual-plane intake manifold with the attached GM 3758369 oil splash shield. There is an automatic choke assembly fitted to the intake manifold on the right side (passenger's side). This is a very good street performance intake manifold and it is becoming extremely difficult to locate. If a "numbers matching" intake manifold is not a concern, then the

Edelbrock 7101 Performer RPM dual-plane aluminum intake manifold, with a power range from 1,500 to 6,500 rpm, is a good substitute. This intake manifold is currently retailing for $130. The Weiand 8016 Stealth dual-plane aluminum intake manifold, with a power range from idle to 6,800 rpm, is another good choice. The current retail price for the Weiand intake manifold is $145.

The factory installed the Holley 0-3810 (GM 3906631) four-barrel carburetor (585 cfm) on all the 1967 Corvette 327-ci engines, and it has an automatic choke. This carburetor is still available from Holley for the current sum of $630—gulp! The chrome air cleaner assembly supplied with the 1967 Corvette L79 engine consists of: base, top, flame arrestor assembly, PCV hose, wing nut, air filter, and air cleaner decal.

There is a tendency for some engine builders to install an after-market fuel pump pushrod in the small-block Chevrolet engines. Many of these fuel pump pushrods are for racing purposes and are manufactured using hardened steel, which will soon wear the pushrod surface of a street camshaft. Stick with the original GM 3704817 fuel pump pushrod. Install the fuel pump pushrod in the engine block and then bolt the GM 3719599 fuel pump plate onto the engine block. Bolt the fuel pump to the fuel pump plate. The GM 6416712 (casting number 6440433) fuel pump is the factory original model installed on the 1967 Corvette L79 engine with the GM 3892693 fuel line. A reproduction "numbers matching" AC-Delco fuel pump is available today for the outrageous sum of $140, and the fuel line is a lowly $20.

The GM 3827369 cast-iron water outlet elbow (thermostat housing) used on the 1967 Corvette L79 engine is a rare bird indeed. The model stands out by itself because it looks as if someone sat on it. It was installed on many of the Corvette 327-ci engines, and the current retail price for a reproduction unit is $30. The 1967 Corvette L79 engine was one of the few 327-ci engines equipped with a water pump bypass hose. If the thermostat ever sticks shut, the cooling system will still function. The water pump bypass connections consist of the GM 3829819 thermal bypass 87-degree connector, the GM 3794094 bypass hose, and the GM 3921915 thermal bypass connector installed in the front of the intake manifold. The Chevrolet bypass hose is totally overpriced; the Goodyear 63394 hose is the same type and costs only a few dollars.

Ignition System

The GM 1111196 distributor was installed on the 1967 Corvette L79 engine and was equipped with points and a tachometer drive. Corvette offered a transistor ignition option for that year as well. In order to bring the engine described here into modern times, the distributor was converted to a breakerless unit using the Mallory 501 Unilite conversion kit. A new distributor cap, rotor, and vacuum control were added as well.

Many of the small-block Corvette 327-ci engines were equipped with stainless-steel ignition shielding in order to reduce radio interference. This ignition shielding looks very nice, but it is expensive to replace ($475 for a reproduction set) and is a real nuisance when it is time to change the spark plugs.

The firing order for all the small-block Chevrolet engines is: 1, 8, 4, 3, 6, 5, 7, and 2. The left (driver's side) bank from the front: 1, 3, 5, and 7 cylinders. The right (passenger's side) bank from the front: 2, 4, 6, and 8 cylinders.

The owner finally relented on his stock look campaign and agreed to purchase a new Powermaster 17102 chrome alternator (80 amps, 14 volts). These are available for the current retail price of $90 and they look terrific on any small-block Chevrolet 327-ci engine.

The GM 3846565 alternator support bracket, which was mounted on the front of the left (driver's side) exhaust manifold, and the GM 3868882 curved brace were used to mount the alternator on the 1967 Corvette L79 engine.

A Summit Racing Equipment G1668 chrome high-torque, 168-tooth starting motor was installed. This starting motor is reputed to have 25 percent more torque than the stock-style starting motors. The snout on the starting motor had to be changed to the GM 1968122 snout, which is used with 153-tooth flywheels. Always use the GM 14097279 starting motor bolts; they have a shoulder that supports the starting motor. It does no harm to install the GM 354353 starting motor brace; it is bolted to the oil pan and supports the end of the starting motor.

Cooling and Exhaust Systems

A Summit Racing Equipment 311015 chrome short-style water pump was installed. The current retail price for this water pump is $120. I may have influenced the owner to agree to the chrome alternator, starting motor, and water pump. The GM casting 3859326 short-style water pump was installed on the 1967 Corvette L79 engine, and rebuilt units with the correct casting number can be purchased for $125.

The GM 3916141 thermal fan clutch, with a 5/8-inch pilot shaft hole, was installed on most 1960 to 1970 small-block Chevrolet engines. The fan clutch is thermostatically controlled. When the engine coolant temperature rises above 180 degrees (Fahrenheit), the fan clutch engages until the temperature again drops below 180 degrees (Fahrenheit). The thermal fan clutch bolts to the front of the fan. Unless it is imperative to have a GM 3916141 thermal fan clutch, the Derale 22012 or the Hayden 2719 thermal fan clutches are available as replacements at the current retail price of $35.

The GM 3770529 fan with five blades and a 17-inch diameter was installed on the 1960 to 1967 small-block Chevrolet engines. The GM 3931002 fan with seven blades and an 18-inch diameter was installed on the 1963 to 1968 Chevrolet 327-ci engines equipped with air conditioning.

The cast-iron ram horn exhaust manifolds installed on the 1967 Corvette L79 engine had a 2-inch outlet and were identified with the Chevrolet casting numbers of GM 3846559 for the left side

The completed GM casting number 3890462 double hump cylinder heads. The GM 3836755 valve stem oil shields are visible at the top of the valve springs. The area around the valves on the combustion chamber walls has been unshrouded to ensure better air/fuel flow, and the cylinder heads have been surfaced.

(driver's side) and GM 372243 for the right side (passenger's side) or both sides. The exhaust manifolds were secured to the cylinder heads using bolts with French locks (curved straps). Reconditioned "numbers matching" exhaust manifolds are available at the current retail price of $350 for the pair. The exhaust manifolds were sand blasted and painted with V.H.T. SP-106 flat silver-grey high-temperature coating. A permanent and far superior finish would be obtained if the exhaust manifolds were metallic-ceramic coated.

If performance is the main concern and "numbers matching" is not, purchase a set of Hedman Hedders 68300 exhaust headers. These exhaust headers will fit all small-block Chevrolet non-emission engines installed in 1963 to 1982 Corvettes, and the headers work with power steering, air conditioning, standard or automatic transmissions, and angle-plug cylinder heads. The headers have 1 5/8-inch-diameter primary tubes and 3-inch-diameter collectors, and they are available for the current retail price of $120. Have them metallic-ceramic coated prior to installing them.

Engine Summary

Note: This engine was completed at the end of September 1996 and installed in a 1967 Corvette convertible. The engine was started, the ignition timing was set, and the engine was allowed to run at 2,000 rpm for 30 minutes in order to break in the camshaft. The owner then drove off grinning, and he has been a happy camper ever since.

Engine block

• 1964 Chevrolet Corvette 327-ci L75 engine block; casting number 3858180; casting date: B1264 (February 12, 1964); stock bore:

The Chevrolet 327-ci engine is now ready for the valve covers and the intake manifold. The Competition Cams 1412-16 Magnum roller tip rocker arms and the GM 6416712 fuel pump are visible.

4.001 inches, and stock stroke: 3.25 inches; two-bolt main bearing caps; 300 horsepower at 5,000 rpm and 360 ft-lb torque at 3,200 rpm; engine block weight (bare): 150 pounds; $100

• Engine block hot tanked; engine block and main bearing caps and bolts Magnafluxed; main bearing caps and bolts shot peened; main bearing caps deburred; all threads retapped; cylinder head bolt holes chamfered; valve lifter bosses deglazed, allowing for 0.002-inch valve lifter clearance; No. 5 main bearing cap oil pump cavity polished; valve lifter gallery ground smooth and painted with Glyptal G-1228A medium-grey gloss enamel; exterior surface of engine block sanded, detailed, and painted with Plasti-Kote 200 Chevrolet orange high-gloss engine enamel; Weatherhead 3152-4 polished-brass water jacket drain plugs (1/4-inch NPT), installed using pipe thread sealant; Pioneer PE100B brass freeze plugs, oil gallery line plugs, and camshaft rear boss plug installed using Permatex aviation form-a-gasket; $455.25

• Engine block bored 0.030-inch oversize and honed and deglazed using torque plate with Sunnen 800 series 400-grit stones, final bore: 4.030 inches; piston-to-bore clearance: 0.004 inch, measured below bottom of wrist pin perpendicular to wrist pin; $125

• Engine block align honed; $200

• Engine block parallel decked to 0.010-inch average below deck; $110

Engine block total: $990.25

Crankshaft

• 1967 GM 3838495 forged steel crankshaft (casting number 4577), internally balanced; main bearing journal diameter: 2.30 inches, and connecting rod journal diameter: 2.00 inches; crankshaft weight: 60 pounds; $125

• Crankshaft shot peened, Magnafluxed, aligned, main bearing journals ground 0.010-inch undersize, connecting rod journals ground 0.010-inch undersize, oil holes chamfered, journals polished, and crankshaft balanced; $255

• Clevite 77 MS-429P-10 main bearings (0.010-inch oversize), installed allowing for 0.002-inch crankshaft clearance and 0.004-inch end play; main bearing cap bolts torqued to 70 ft-lb, using molykote; $65

• Fluidampr 712430 harmonic balancer, 7 1/4-inch o.d., weight: 13.4 pounds, installed with Mr. Gasket 945 Ultra-Seal crankshaft bolt and flat washer using Loctite and torqued to 85 ft-lb; $313

• GM 3858533 double-groove crankshaft pulley installed with stainless-steel bolts, lockwashers, and flat washers using Loctite and torqued to 30 ft-lb; crankshaft pulley painted with Plasti-Kote 203 black high-gloss engine enamel; $32.75

Crankshaft total: $790.75

Connecting Rods and Pistons

• GM 3927145 forged steel, heat-treated I-beam connecting rods, pressed-in wrist pin; connecting rod length: 5.70 inches (center to center); connecting rod weight: 567 grams each; connecting rod ratio: 1.75 (with 3.25-inch stroke crankshaft); $56

• Connecting rods shot peened, Magnafluxed, debeamed, aligned, resized, pin fitted, and balanced; ARP 134-6001 high-performance-series connecting rod bolts, 190,000 psi, 8740 chrome-moly steel, 11/32-inch diameter, installed; $356.67

• Clevite 77 CB-745P-10 connecting rod bearings, 0.010-inch oversize, installed allowing for 0.002-inch connecting rod clearance and 0.010-inch side clearance per pair of connecting rods; connecting rod bolts torqued to 50 ft-lb, using molykote and allowing for 0.006-inch stretch; $38

• TRW L2166NF-30 power-forged aluminum racing pistons, 0.030-inch oversize, 11.0:1 compression ratio, domed top; piston weight: 589 grams each; pressed-in, heat-treated, and casehardened 4340 chrome-moly steel straight-wall wrist pins; wrist pin weight: 141 grams; piston ring grooves: top compression ring groove: 5/64 inch; second compression ring groove: 5/64 inch; oil ring groove: 3/16 inch; Sealed Power (Federal Mogul) E251K-30 moly-coated ductile iron top piston ring set, 0.030-inch oversize, installed within manufacturer's recommended arc; top compression ring gap: 0.018 inch; second compression ring gap: 0.016 inch; oil ring gap: 0.016 inch; piston tops painted with V.H.T. SP-101 white high-temperature coating; intake-valve-to-piston clearance: 0.160 inch, and exhaust-valve-to-piston clearance: 0.180 inch (without gaskets); new displacement: 331.6 ci (5.4 liters); $320

• Complete V-8 engine balance; Fel-Pro KS2600 (current Fel-Pro 2802) complete gasket set installed; $230

Connecting rods and pistons total: $1,000.67

Lubrication System

• Melling M55 standard-volume oil pump with pressure balance grooves; oil pump end clearance: 0.00025 inch; GM 3830080 oil pump pickup tube welded to oil pump body; oil pump cover gasket installed using silicone sealant and bolts torqued to 80 in-lb, using Loctite; Moroso 22070 oil pump driveshaft installed; Manley 42339 oil pump stud installed using Loctite and torqued to 65 ft-lb; $44

• GM 3728502 crankcase ventilator, 5 3/4 inches long, installed; GM 3927136 windage tray installed with GM 3872718 windage tray studs using Loctite and torqued to 25 ft-lb; GM 359942 (1964 Corvette) stamped steel oil pan with internal baffle, installed using stainless-steel bolts, AN flat washers, and lockwashers with Loctite and torqued to 15 ft-lb; oil pan gaskets and rear oil seals installed using silicone sealant; oil pan painted with Plasti-Kote 200 Chevrolet orange high-gloss engine enamel; Mr. Gasket 15 magnetic oil drain plug installed; Trans-Dapt 4957 chrome dip stick and dip stick tube installed; GM 5514219 oil canister assembly installed with GM 5574535 (body) and GM 5573979 (valve) oil filter adapter; AC-Delco PF141 oil filter installed; engine lubricated with 6 quarts Pennzoil HD-30-weight motor oil; $245.57

Lubrication system total: $289.57

Camshaft and Cylinder Heads

• Clevite 77 SH-290S camshaft bearings installed with 0.002-inch camshaft clearance and 0.002-inch end play; No. 1 bearing: SH-290, housing bore diameter: 2.019 to 2.021 inches; No. 2 and No. 5 bearing: SH-288, housing bore diameter: 2.009 to 2.012 inches; No. 3 and No. 4 bearing: SH-287, housing bore diameter: 1.990 to 2.001 inches; camshaft journal diameter: 1.870 inches; $30

• Competition Cams 122102 High Energy hydraulic lifter camshaft with advertised duration: 268 degrees intake and exhaust; duration at 0.050-inch lift: 218 degrees intake and exhaust; lobe separation angle: 110 degrees; net valve lift: 0.454 inch intake and exhaust; valve lash: zero; $95

• Competition Cams 812-16 High Energy hydraulic valve lifters and Competition Cams 7812-16 heat-treated pushrods, 5/16-inch diameter by 7.790-inch length, installed; camshaft degreed; $120

• Cloyes 93100 double-roller timing chain set, heat-treated sprockets, multi-keyway crankshaft sprocket, installed; Manley 42114 camshaft locking plate and bolts installed using Loctite and torqued to 20 ft-lb; Manley 42146 aluminum camshaft button installed; GM 361925 chrome timing gear cover installed with ARP 400-1501 polished stainless-steel bolt kit, 12-point heads, using Loctite and torqued to 15 ft-lb; timing gear cover gasket installed using silicone sealant; GM 3980267 front one-piece oil seal installed; Trans-Dapt 9178 chrome timing gear cover adjustable timing tab installed; $129.53

• GM 3890462 (casting number) double hump closed-chamber cast-iron cylinder heads, 64-cc combustion chamber volume, 160-cc intake runner volume, installed; cylinder heads hot tanked, glass beaded, pressure tested, Magnafluxed, and painted with Plasti-Kote 200 Chevrolet orange high-gloss engine enamel; intake and exhaust ports fully ported and polished and gasket matched; combustion chambers polished and cc'd; K-Line 9832STA phosphor bronze valve guide liners installed; K-Line 1625-1 hardened interlocking ductile iron exhaust valve seat inserts installed; valves unshrouded; cylinder heads surfaced; Serdi-machined multi-angle blueprint valve grind performed; Enginetech S2927 viton positive seal valve stem seals and Competition Cams 501-16 valve stem seals installed; ARP 134-3601 high-performance-series cylinder head bolts, 170,000 psi, installed using Permatex aviation form-a-gasket and torqued to 65 ft-lb; $1,124.53

• Manley 10750 Street Master stainless-steel intake valves, 2.02-inch valve head diameter, 11/32-inch valve stem diameter, 4.911-inch length overall, installed; weight: 109 grams each; Manley 10749 Street Master stainless-steel exhaust valves, 1.60-inch valve head diameter, 11/32-inch valve stem diameter; 4.911-inch length overall, installed; weight: 101 grams each; $143.20

• Competition Cams 981-16 single valve springs with damper, 1.250-inch o.d. and 0.880-inch i.d.; installed height: 110 pounds at 1.70 inches valves closed and 285 pounds at 1.25 inches valves open; coil bind: 1.13 inches; Competition Cams 742-16 valve spring retainers, 11/32-inch stem, and Competition Cams 601-16 stamped steel valve stem locks (7-degree, 11/32-inch stem) installed; GM 3836755 valve stem oil shields installed; $182

• ARP 134-7101 high-performance-series screw-in rocker arm studs (3/8-inch diameter, 170,000 psi) installed using Loctite and torqued to 50 ft-lb; Manley 42355-8 hardened-steel flat pushrod guide plates for 5/16-inch-diameter pushrods, installed; Competition Cams 1412-16 Magnum roller tip rocker arms, 1.52 ratio, installed with Manley 42107 rocker arm nuts, 3/8-inch studs, using anti-seize compound; $230

• 1967 GM 3767493 polished die-cast aluminum Corvette valve covers installed with polished stainless-steel bolts and lockwashers, using Loctite and torqued to 15 ft-lb; valve cover gaskets installed using silicone sealant; $147.77

Camshaft and cylinder heads total: $2,202.03

Intake System

• GM 3893954 (casting number: 3890490) cast-aluminum 1967 Corvette single-quad, dual-plane intake manifold with GM 3758369 oil splash shield attached, installed with ARP 434-2001 polished stainless-steel intake manifold bolts, 12-point heads, using Loctite and torqued to 25 ft-lb; intake manifold gaskets installed using silicone sealant; $310.95

• Holley 0-3810 (GM 390663) four-barrel carburetor, 585 cfm, automatic choke, installed; $630

• GM 3893243 automatic choke assembly, GM 159853 choke cover screw, GM 3876794 dirt seal washer, GM 3917616 choke rod, GM 3864866 thermostat cover, GM 3887148 thermostat, and GM

7007137 choke rod clip installed; Zip Products CZ-751 carburetor return spring installed; $37.15

• GM 3704817 fuel pump pushrod and GM 3719599 fuel pump mounting plate installed with stainless-steel bolts and lock-washers torqued to 20 ft-lb using Loctite; fuel pump mounting plate gasket installed using silicone sealant; GM 6416712 (casting number 6440433) fuel pump installed with polished stainless-steel bolts and lockwashers and torqued to 20 ft-lb using Loctite; fuel pump gasket installed using silicone sealant; GM 3892693 fuel line (fuel pump to carburetor) installed; $175.10

• GM 6423909 chrome air cleaner assembly, AC-Delco AC-35 air cleaner wing nut, GM 3849856 flame arrestor assembly, GM 3902350 PCV hose (rear of engine to air cleaner) 15/16-inch i.d., GM 3849733 vent tube, GM 6422721 crankcase ventilation valve (PCV CV-726C), GM 3877445 hose clamps, GM 3831055 front PCV hose, GM 3888362 chrome oil filler tube, GM 3881854 chrome oil filler tube cap, and Auto Accessories of America 0299 air cleaner decal, "327 Turbo-Fire 350 Horsepower" installed; $335.20

Intake system total: $1,488.40

The finished product ready to be installed—it looks better than any Corvette L79 engine that ever left the factory. That is Max (Luke Balogh's dog) giving his approval and permission to install the engine.

Ignition System

• GM 1111196 tachometer drive distributor converted to breaker-less unit using Mallory 501 Unilite photo-optic infrared LED system; GM 1971244 distributor cap, GM 1852722 rotor, GM 1116236 vacuum advance control, GM 9433153 vacuum advance hose, 5/32-inch i.d., GM 3903332 chrome vacuum advance tube, and Zip Products CZ-542 vacuum advance line clip installed; GM 3770598 distributor clamp installed with stainless-steel bolt and lockwasher using anti-seize compound; $121.50

• GM 1115202 ignition coil, 1.8 ohms, installed; Auto Accessories of America 22024 spark plug wire set installed; Eckler's IS-340 ignition shielding kit installed; NGK XR5 resistor-type 14-millimeter spark plugs installed with 0.040-inch gap; $605.65

• Powermaster 17102 chrome alternator (80 amps, 14 volts) installed with GM 3846565 chrome alternator support bracket and GM 3868882 chrome alternator curved adjusting brace using polished stainless-steel bolts, flat washers, lockwashers, and nylocks; $160

• Summit Racing Equipment G1668 chrome high-torque starting motor and GM 1968122 snout (153-tooth flywheel) installed with GM 14097279 starting motor bolts using anti-seize compound; GM 354353 starting motor brace installed; starting motor brace painted with Plasti-Kote 203 black high-gloss engine enamel; $114.99

Ignition system total: $1,002.14

Cooling and Exhaust Systems

• Summit Racing Equipment 311015 chrome short-style water pump installed with polished stainless-steel bolts and lockwashers using Loctite and torqued to 20 ft-lb; water pump gaskets installed using silicone sealant; GM 3829819 thermal bypass 87-degree connector, GM 3921915 intake manifold bypass hose connector, and GM 3794094 bypass hose installed with stainless-steel line clamps; GM 1513321 water temperature sending unit installed using pipe thread sealant; Chicago Corvette A2006 temperature sending unit wire brackets installed; GM 3890419 chrome single-groove water pump pulley, Hayden 2719 thermal fan clutch, and GM 3770529 fan (five blades, 17-inch diameter) installed with polished stainless-steel bolts and lockwashers using Loctite and torqued to 20 ft-lb; Gates 11A1360 crankshaft/alternator/water pump v-belt (7/16-inch by 53 1/2-inch) installed; $189.63

• GM 3846559 left exhaust manifold and GM 372243 right exhaust manifold sandblasted and painted with V.H.T. SP-106 flat silver-grey high-temperature coating; new Paragon Reproductions PR-693-4K exhaust manifold bolts and French locks installed using Loctite and torqued to 25 ft-lb; exhaust manifold gaskets installed using Permatex ultra-copper high-temperature silicone sealant; Paragon Reproductions PR-728K stainless-steel exhaust manifold outlet studs installed using anti-seize compound; $438.65

Cooling and exhaust systems total: $628.28

Labor

• Labor for checking clearances, gapping piston rings, degree camshaft, valvetrain assembly, detailing, trial engine assembly, final engine assembly, and initial engine start-up; $800

Labor total: $800

Engine Grand Total: $9,192.09 (U.S.)

Note: The estimated output of this engine is 351 horsepower at 6,000 rpm and 358 ft-lb torque at 4,000 rpm (see Appendix A—Dyno Print-Outs).

CHAPTER 11
1970 CORVETTE 350-ci ENGINE (LT-1 CLONE)

I purchased my first Corvette—a 1972 Corvette LT-1 with a small-block 350-ci engine—in the summer of 1974. The engine was rated at 255 horsepower at 5,000 rpm and 280 ft-lb torque at 4,000 rpm. The Corvette LT-1 was only produced for three years, from 1970 to 1972, and the 1970 Corvette LT-1 was equipped with the most powerful Generation I small-block 350-ci engine Chevrolet ever offered. The 1970 Corvette LT-1 was rated at 370 horsepower at 6,000 rpm and 380 ft-lb torque at 4,800 rpm.

The engine that was in the car when I bought it was pretty well trashed. I built a new engine that lasted for about a year until I completely destroyed it one very late evening. I will not go into details as to how this occurred, but I will say one of the forged steel connecting rods was sheared off at the piston skirt, another one was twisted 90 degrees, the camshaft disintegrated, the oil pan had nineteen holes through it, and the radiator had two holes in it—all in all, it was a great night out!

Each engine I built for my LT-1 was better than the previous engine, as I was experimenting with a lot of new equipment and combinations. The final engine I built for that car was a great runner. When the throttle was hammered and the two double pumpers opened up, the car almost flipped over backward. Due to a lot of

business traveling at the time, the car sat for many years in my garage and I finally sold it in 1981.

In 1983, I decided to build a 1923 Ford Model T Roadster Pickup. My obvious choice for an engine was a modified 1970 Corvette LT-1 engine. I was only interested in finding a good used small-block Chevrolet 350-ci engine block with four-bolt main bearing caps and not concerned about correct casting numbers and dates. In a very short period of time, I located and purchased a standard-bore 1973 Corvette L82, four-bolt main bearing cap engine block, and a NOS (new old stock) forged steel crankshaft. I finally completed building my hot rod in 1993. This chapter contains the complete buildup information for that engine.

Components Description
Engine Block

The specifications for the 1970 Corvette LT-1 engine are:
- 350-ci (5.7-liter) displacement
- 4.001-inch stock bore and 3.484-inch stock stroke
- Stock compression ratio: 11.0:1
- 370 horsepower at 6,000 rpm and 380 ft-lb torque at 4,800 rpm

Chevrolet first introduced the Generation I small-block 350-ci engine in the 1967 Camaro. This style of engine block was not changed until 1986 when a one-piece rear oil seal and taller valve lifter bores were introduced. The four-bolt main bearing cap engine

The first engine I built for my 1972 Corvette LT-1 with the original LT-1 valve covers and GM 3991004 single-quad dual-plane intake manifold. The Mallory dual-point distributor and Hooker headers can be seen as well.

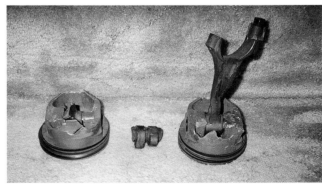

The shrapnel remaining from an awesome explosion of my 1972 Corvette LT-1 engine. The force it took to twist the forged steel connecting rod 90 degrees is simply amazing. Those two lumps in the middle are the remains of the camshaft.

The last engine I built for my LT-1. That is an Edelbrock 2560 (Model STR-10) crossram intake manifold with two Holley 650-cfm double pumpers and marine flame arrestors for hood clearance. This was a wild beast!

The digits "010" and "020" are cast into the front of this Chevrolet 350-ci engine block. The "010" represents 1 percent additional tin content, and the "020" represents 2 percent additional nickel content. This is a four-bolt main bearing cap engine block.

block was first offered in 1969. There must have been literally millions of the small-block Chevrolet 350-ci engine blocks produced from 1967 to 1986; however, there were only approximately 5,000 Corvette LT-1 engines produced from 1970 to 1972.

The small-block Chevrolet 350-ci engine blocks with a casting number of 3970010 are some of the best. You will find the digits "010" and "020" behind the camshaft gear at the front of the engine block. The "010" represents 1 percent additional tin content and the "020" represents 2 percent additional nickel content. The casting number 3970010 engine block was manufactured from 1969 to 1980, and some of the engines have four-bolt main bearing caps while others have two-bolt main bearing caps. You must remove the oil pan in order to determine what type of main bearing caps are installed; there is no way to establish this from outward appearance.

Here is a list of the 1967 to 1986 casting numbers for the cast-iron 350-ci engine blocks (manufactured in the United States) with four-bolt main bearing caps:

376450
460703
3932386
3932388
3956618 (also two-bolt)
3970010 (also two-bolt)
3970014 (also two-bolt)
14010207 (also two-bolt)
14010209
14011064

These are the casting numbers I am aware of; there may well be others. If you have a passion to find an original Corvette LT-1 engine block, look for the following last three letters of the VIN stamped

on the right front (passenger's side) of the engine block deck:

1970: CTR, CTU, and CTV
1971: CGZ, CGY, and CJK
1972: CKY, CKZ, and CRT

Refer to Chapter 1 for information about engine block cleaning, detailing, and painting. Install the Milodon 23150 lifter valley screen kit to keep debris in the valve lifter gallery from ending up in the oil pan and eventually the bearings. The Milodon kit is available for $13.

It might prove difficult, or even impossible, to find a decent small-block Chevrolet 350-ci engine block with four-bolt main bearing caps. Do not despair—you can convert an engine block with two-bolt main bearing caps into a four-bolt main bearing cap engine block by installing the Milodon 11150 splayed four-bolt main bearing cap conversion kit. Only a qualified machine shop should perform this job. The engine block will have to be align bored and honed after it has been converted to four-bolt main bearing caps. The Milodon 11150 conversion kit currently retails for $197.95, and the estimated cost to install it is $200.

The cylinders in the Chevrolet 350-ci engine block can be safely bored to 0.040-inch oversize and usually to 0.060-inch oversize. Have the cylinders sonic tested if the engine block is going to be bored to 0.060-inch oversize in order to be certain there will be enough material left in the cylinder walls after the engine block has been bored.

Have the engine block align honed or align bored if you fit it with new main bearings caps, and then have it parallel decked to ensure all the critical surfaces of the engine block are perfectly true. Refer to Chapter 1.

In order to provide better lubrication for the camshaft gear and

A set of shot peened four-bolt main bearing caps for a Chevrolet 350-ci engine block.

The GM 3941184 (casting number 3941182) forged steel crankshaft is used in the high-performance Corvette LT-1 engines.

timing gear chain, drill a 0.030-inch hole in the center lower face of the front camshaft boss (behind the camshaft gear), especially if you plan to install a gear drive. There are three valve lifter gallery oil line expansion plugs at the front of the engine block behind the camshaft gear. Drill and tap the three holes, and install new stainless-steel 1/4-inch NPT plugs using Permatex aviation form-a-gasket. Drill a 0.030-inch hole in the center plug to assist in bleeding off any air in the oil gallery line.

I followed the advice of a well-respected engine builder many years ago by installing two (one on each side) GM 992956 engine block heaters at the rear of the engine block. In theory, if the engine block is heated prior to the initial start-up, it will take less time for the engine to reach operating temperature. As a result, tuning and break-in are put on the fast track.

Crankshaft

All the pre-1986 Chevrolet 350-ci engines have a 3.484-inch stroke crankshaft, which was manufactured from cast nodular iron or forged steel. The diameter of the main bearing journals is 2.4484 to 2.4493 inches, and the connecting rod journal diameter is 2.0988 to 2.0998 inches. The diameter of the main bearing housing bores is 2.6406 to 2.6415 inches. All the Chevrolet 350-ci crankshafts manufactured from 1986 onward have a special flywheel flange for use with the one-piece rear oil seal and cannot be used with the pre-1986 small-block Chevrolet engines. If you are designing a street performance engine for serious horsepower, fit it with a forged steel crankshaft. Look for the original GM 3941184 forged steel crankshaft, casting number 3941182. This crankshaft was manufactured using 1053 steel, and it was Tuftrided at the factory.

When searching for the GM 3941184 forged steel crankshaft, remember that the main bearing journals cannot be ground more than

0.060-inch undersize and the connecting rod journals cannot be ground more than 0.050-inch undersize. If the crankshaft needs to be ground in excess of those sizes, bearings are not currently available.

All is not lost if you cannot locate an original GM 3941184 forged steel crankshaft. Scat Enterprises (see Appendix B—Resources) now offers forged steel, standard-weight (approximately 54 to 56 pounds) crankshafts for use with different length connecting rods; they are available with stock or longer strokes. For example, the Scat Enterprises 4-350-3750-6000 is manufactured using 4340 forged steel, the journals are nitrided, the oil holes are the straight shot design and chamfered. This particular model is designed for use with 6.00-inch-long connecting rods and has a 3.75-inch stroke, resulting in a displacement of 383 ci (with a 4.030-inch bore). The current retail price is $665 for this Scat Enterprises forged steel crankshaft. All the Scat Enterprises crankshafts and connecting rods are manufactured in the United States.

Purchasing a good used crankshaft and paying to hot tank, shot peen, Magnaflux, align, regrind, chamfer the oil holes, and polish the journals will most likely cost more than a new Scat Enterprises forged steel crankshaft, as described above. The Scat Enterprises crankshaft offers the added benefit of increased displacement for the same price as a stock stroke crankshaft. More cubic inches equates to more horsepower.

The Clevite 77 MS-909P main bearings are available in standard size, 0.001-, 0.002-, 0.010-, 0.020-, 0.030-, and 0.040-inch oversize. The current retail price for a set of these main bearings is $41. The Federal Mogul 4663M main bearings are available in standard size, 0.001-, 0.002-, 0.010-, 0.020-, 0.030-, 0.040-, 0.050-, and 0.060-inch oversize. The current retail price for a set of these main bearings is $42. The Clevite 77 and the Federal Mogul bearings are available at automotive parts outlets. The factory-recommended main bearing clearance is 0.0013 to 0.0025 inch for No. 1, 2, 3, and

The GM 3923282 (currently GM 14031310) common small-block Chevrolet connecting rod for the large-journal crankshafts has been available since 1967. These connecting rods are designed for use with a pressed-in wrist pin and have 3/8-inch-diameter bolts.

A TRW L2304 power-forged aluminum racing piston (0.030-inch oversize). This piston has a compression ratio of 11.0:1 with a combustion chamber volume of 64 cc. The piston was used in the 1970 Corvette LT-1 350-ci engine.

4 main bearings and 0.0017 to 0.0033 inch for No. 5 main bearing, which is also the thrust bearing. The factory-recommended crankshaft end play is 0.002 to 0.006 inch. Torque the inner main bearing cap bolts to 70 ft-lb, and torque the outer main bearing cap bolts to 65 ft-lb using molykote.

Do not use the factory-installed harmonic balancer on a street performance engine. The Fluidampr 712430 harmonic balancer meets SFI specs 18.1, has a 7 1/4-inch o.d., and weighs 13.4 pounds. This harmonic balancer is designed for an internally balanced engine. The current retail price for the Fluidampr 712430 harmonic balancer is $295, and it is available at speed shops. Use a quality crankshaft bolt and washer, such as the ARP 134-2501 (available for $18), to secure the harmonic balancer.

Connecting Rods and Pistons

The best connecting rods offered by Chevrolet for its pre-1986 small-block engines are the GM 3973386 (current GM 14096846), more recently referred to as the "pink rods" because of a dab of pink paint applied at the factory. These I-beam connecting rods were manufactured using 1038 forged steel, 5.695 to 5.705 inches long (center to center), pressed-in wrist pin, 3/8-inch-diameter connecting rod bolts, and they weigh 590 grams each. The GM 3973386 connecting rods were heat treated, shot peened, and Magnafluxed at the factory. Production of these connecting rods commenced in 1970, and they were used in the Corvette LT-1 and Camaro Z-28 engines. The diameter of the crankshaft end (the big end) is 2.2247 to 2.2252 inches. Upgrade the connecting rod bolts with the ARP 134-6003 high-performance-series connecting rod bolts, rated at 190,000 psi. These connecting rod bolts currently retail for $60.

As an alternative, you can use the Scat Enterprises forged 4340 steel, H-beam connecting rods with ARP 8740 steel connecting rods bolts. If you're able to purchase a good used set of the GM 3973386 connecting rods, have them shot peened, aligned, Magnafluxed, resized, pin fitted, and install new connecting rod bolts, but be warned, it may end up costing more than a new set of Scat Enterprises H-beam connecting rods. A set of the Scat Enterprises 2-350-6000-2100 H-beam connecting rods, with a 6.00-inch length (center to center), currently retails for $429.

Dozens of companies sell connecting rods for the small-block Chevrolet engines, and some of the connecting rods are excellent. Some companies, however, sell connecting rods that were manufactured overseas and are of questionable quality; perhaps more precisely, they are junk. I have seen connecting rods from overseas where there was a difference of 0.002 to 0.003 inch in the crankshaft end (the big end) of the connecting rods in a set. Purchase connecting rods from a manufacturer with a long and reputable track record.

The Clevite 77 CB-663P connecting rod bearings are available in standard size, 0.001-, 0.002-, 0.010-, 0.020-, 0.030-, and 0.040-inch oversize. The current retail price for a set of these connecting rod bearings is $31. The Federal Mogul 8-2555CP connecting rod bearings are available in standard size, 0.001-, 0.002-, 0.010-, 0.020-, 0.030-, 0.040-, and 0.050-inch oversize. The current retail price for a set of these connecting rod bearings is $32. The factory-recommended connecting rod bearing clearance is 0.0013 to 0.0035 inch, and the side clearance per pair of connecting rods is 0.008 to 0.014 inch. Torque the connecting rod bolts to 50 ft-lb using molykote and allow for 0.006-inch stretch. Refer to Chapter 3 for a photograph of the Clevite 77 CB-663P-10 connecting rod bearings.

The GM 3942541 forged aluminum pistons with a pressed-in wrist pin, a domed top, and a compression ratio of 11.0:1 with a

The GM 3941184 forged steel crankshaft and GM 3973386 forged steel connecting rods have been installed. Notice the GM 3960312 windage tray studs and the debeamed connecting rods. That is a GM 992956 engine block heater at the rear of the engine block.

The TRW 50065 high-volume oil pump with the TRW 52039 oil pump pickup tube and the GM 3927136 windage tray installed. Some may say I got a little carried away by chroming the Lakewood 15705 block protector!

64-cc combustion chamber, were installed in the 1970 Corvette LT-1 engine, along with the TRW L2304 replacement piston.

I gave much consideration to the compression ratio of this engine. Street performance engines should have a maximum compression ratio of 10.0:1 with high-octane, unleaded gasoline. This being the case, I decided to install a set of Speed-Pro 2244P-030 power-forged aluminum racing pistons (0.030-inch oversize) with a flat top containing four valve notches. These pistons have a pressed-in wrist pin, a compression ratio of 9.72:1 with a 64-cc combustion chamber, and they weigh 640 grams each. When I purchased the pistons in 1983, they cost $300 for the set, including the moly piston rings.

For a street performance small-block Chevrolet engine, install Ross Racing Pistons 99526 forged aluminum pistons with full-floating wrist pins and a compression ratio of 9.5:1 with a 64-cc combustion chamber. They weigh 432 grams each. The stocking pistons, wrist pins, and double Spiro-Lox retainers currently retail for $704.20. The Ross Racing Pistons 99526 pistons are designed for a 4.030-inch bore and 3.75-inch stroke using a 6.00-inch-long (center to center) connecting rod. Ross Racing Pistons can supply its own moly piston ring set with these pistons.

The Fel-Pro KS-2600 complete gasket set was originally installed in the engine described here and it retailed for $40. The Fel-Pro 2802 complete gasket set is available today at a retail price of $90.

Lubrication System

Refer to Chapter 10 for information regarding small-block Chevrolet oil pumps. The Milodon 25010 extended oil pump shaft, with a 1-inch aluminum block extension for the oil pump, was installed in this engine. Rather than using a longer oil pump pickup tube, extend the oil pump deeper into the oil pan to make it easier for the oil pump to push oil than to pull oil. It is questionable how 1 inch can make a difference in oil pump performance. One thing is certain, however—oil pump extensions are seldom used in this day and age in street performance engines.

The Milodon 25010 oil pump extension kit permits the use of the stock GM 3830080 oil pump pickup screen with a Melling M55HV high-volume oil pump. The Milodon 18314 oil pump pickup screen, combined with the Melling M55HV high-volume oil pump, eliminates the need for the Milodon 25010 oil pump extension shaft and spacer. This extension kit is currently available for $30.

The GM 359942 stamped steel oil pan was fitted with an internal oil baffle and has a capacity for 6 quarts of oil (with a cartridge-style oil filter). This oil pan was used on some of the 1963 to 1965 Corvette engines as well as the 1969 to 1972 Camaro Z-28 and Corvette LT-1 engines.

This engine was going to be installed in a hot rod, which should have additional oil capacity. A Milodon 30900 low-profile oil pan with a capacity for 6 quarts of oil was chrome plated and installed. This oil pan has the dip stick located on the left side (driver's side), which is the same side as the stock Chevrolet oil pan. A small-block Chevrolet engine with the Milodon 30900 oil pan will fit perfectly in any 1968 to 1972 Corvette. Refer to Chapter 10 for a description of windage trays and windage tray studs.

The GM 3952301 oil filter adapter was bolted to all the Corvette LT-1 engines along with a 1-quart oil filter, such as the Fram PH-13. I installed a Trans-Dapt 1067 chrome oil filter cover on my engine in order to be compatible with the chrome oil pan. The right-side (passenger's side) Corvette LT-1 valve cover was fitted with the GM 3989348 rubber grommet (3/4-inch o.d. by 3/8-inch i.d.) and

The Milodon 30900 chrome oil pan has been bolted in place. It is almost a shame to flip this baby over.

The engine in the trial assembly stage. The GM 5231585 edge orifice solid lifters and GM 3796243 blue tip 5/16-inch-diameter pushrods can be seen.

the GM 6484525 crankcase ventilation valve (PCV CV-746C). The left-side (driver's side) Corvette LT-1 valve cover was fitted with the GM 3851735 chrome oil filler cap. The GM 3965542 Corvette crossed flags emblem was attached to the right front of the right-side (passenger's side) valve cover.

A threaded oil line hole is in the center front of the engine block between the bottom of the intake manifold and the top of the timing gear cover. This hole is usually plugged with a 1/8-inch NPT plug, but it can be used for an additional oil pressure gauge line.

Camshaft and Cylinder Heads

The Clevite SH-290S camshaft bearings are available at a current retail price of $27 for a set. The Federal Mogul 1235M camshaft bearings are available at a current retail price of $28 for a set. All 1967 to 1977 Chevrolet 350-ci engines use the same camshaft bearings.

The GM 3972178 solid (mechanical) lifter camshaft was the special high-performance model installed in the Corvette LT-1 and Camaro Z-28 engines. It is a good street performance camshaft. The Chevrolet specifications for this camshaft are: advertised duration: 307 degrees intake and 319 degrees exhaust; duration at 0.050-inch lift: 229 degrees intake and 237 degrees exhaust; lobe separation angle: 110 degrees; valve lift (with 1.50 ratio rocker arms): 0.452 inch intake and 0.455 inch exhaust; valve lash (hot): 0.024 inch intake and 0.030 inch exhaust.

The GM 3927140 solid (mechanical) lifter camshaft was the first off-road racing design introduced by Chevrolet in 1969 for its small-block engines. This is a terrific camshaft to use in a street performance engine, and I managed to purchase a NOS camshaft and a set of the GM 5231585 solid lifters from a Chevrolet dealer in a small town in Oregon. The camshaft and lifters cost $200 in 1983. I have encountered at least eight different specifications for the GM 3927140 camshaft and three of the conflicting specifications were

in different Chevrolet manuals. The specifications I have found to be the most accurate are: advertised duration: 316 degrees intake and 323 degrees exhaust; duration at 0.050-inch lift: 243 degrees intake and 254 degrees exhaust; lobe separation angle: 112 degrees; valve lift (with 1.50 ratio rocker arms): 0.475 inch intake and 0.495 inch exhaust; valve lash (hot): 0.024 inch intake and 0.026 inch exhaust. The Crane Cams 968821 Blueprint factory replacement solid lifter camshaft, which is very similar to the GM 3927140 camshaft, is available today for the retail price of $80.

The GM 5231585 solid (mechanical) lifters originally used in the early high-performance Chevrolet 327-ci engines were also known as "edge orifice" lifters. The lifters restrict the overhead oiling to the rocker arms, and there is a procedure that must be performed in order to correct the restriction if stock rocker arms are being installed. There is a wide recess around the middle of the valve lifter body, and there is a lubrication hole in the side of the valve lifter body approximately 1/8 inch (0.125 inch) above the wide recess. Use a high-speed grinder with a small carbide bit to grind a vertical groove in the valve lifter body downward from the lubrication hole to the wide recess. The vertical groove should be approximately 1/16-inch (0.06250-inch) wide and 1/32-inch (0.03125-inch) deep. Do not perform the operation if you plan to install roller rocker arms. The GM 3927140 camshaft and the GM 5231585 solid lifters are a very good combination. Always match the valve lifters with the camshaft by purchasing the camshaft and the valve lifters from the same manufacturer.

The Crower Cams & Equipment 00321 solid lifter camshaft is similar to the GM 3927140 solid lifter camshaft. This camshaft has a power range from 2,400 rpm to 6,400 rpm, and the specifications are: advertised duration: 274 degrees intake and 282 degrees exhaust; duration at 0.050-inch lift: 242 degrees intake and 248 degrees exhaust; lobe separation angle: 114 degrees; valve lift (with 1.50 ratio rocker

This small-block Chevrolet timing gear cover with attached timing tab is designed for use with a 6 3/4-inch-diameter harmonic balancer and has been painted with PPG DGHS black 9000 high-gloss polyurethane. The GM 3980267 one-piece oil seal is installed.

arms): 0.482 inch intake and 0.504 inch exhaust. If this camshaft was installed in the engine described here, the estimated output would be: 470 horsepower at 6,000 rpm and 444 ft-lb torque at 5,000 rpm. See Chapter 10 for information on the coolface solid lifters.

If your boss has just given you an unexpected bonus, rush out and buy a roller camshaft. The Crower Cams & Equipment Company 00425 solid roller camshaft has a power range from 2,500 to 6,500 rpm, and the specifications are: advertised duration: 280 degrees intake and 288 degrees exhaust; duration at 0.050-inch lift: 246 degrees intake and 248 degrees exhaust; lobe separation angle: 112 degrees; valve lift (with 1.50 ratio rocker arms): 0.554 inch intake and 0.567 inch exhaust. If this camshaft was installed in the engine described here, the estimated output would be: 480 horsepower at 6,000 rpm and 464 ft-lb torque at 5,000 rpm. This is a great camshaft, and its current retail price is $330. The Crower Cams & Equipment Company 66200 solid roller lifters are available for an additional retail cost of $385.

The GM 3796243 pushrods are also referred to as "blue tip" pushrods due to the dark blue paint near the guide plate ends. These heavy-duty thick-wall pushrods are 5/16-inch diameter by 7.790-inch length and they have hardened tips for use with pushrod guide plates. The 5/16-inch-diameter pushrods are entirely satisfactory for use in most street performance engines unless the camshaft has a ridiculous net valve lift or the engine will be used for racing. If that is the case, install 3/8-inch-diameter pushrods along with the correct pushrod guide plates. Some aluminum aftermarket cylinder heads require longer-than-stock pushrods. Crower Cams & Equipment Company offers heat-treated pushrods in 5/16-inch and 3/8-inch diameters and a number of different lengths.

If you plan to install a timing chain set, purchase a Cloyes 93100 double-roller model. Refer to Chapter 10 for information about this

A Crane Cams 11871 turbo Fireball angle-plug cast-iron cylinder head (casting number 340292) with 2.02-inch-diameter intake valves and 1.60-inch-diameter exhaust valves.

part. Timing chains are subject to stretching over a period of time, while a dual idler gear drive will not. The Pete Jackson 327-1C quiet dual idler gear drive is a good product for street performance engines. The kit comes complete with a roller camshaft button and a camshaft gear locking plate with bolts. The Edelbrock 7890 Accu-Drive dual idler gear drive is also a good product and comes with all the mounting hardware. The current retail price for a Pete Jackson gear drive is $140, and the current retail price for the Edelbrock Accu-Drive is $160. These parts are available at most speed equipment outlets.

The GM 3991433 timing gear cover was installed on the Corvette LT-1 and Camaro Z-28 engines. This same part number was also used on all the 1969 to 1980 Chevrolet 350-ci engines. It has an attached timing tab that will clear the 8-inch diameter GM 3947712 harmonic balancer used on the Corvette LT-1 engine. The Mr. Gasket 1099 chrome quick-change timing gear cover is a good product. It is a two-piece timing gear cover that permits the camshaft to be removed without removing the oil pan. This item costs about $50.

The GM 3987376 cast-iron cylinder head (casting number 3991492) was the factory replacement model for the early small-block Chevrolet high-performance engines. This cylinder head is also referred to as a "492" head. It came equipped with 2.02-inch head diameter intake valves and 1.60-inch head diameter exhaust valves. The combustion chamber volume was said to be 65 cc. These same 3991492 (casting number) cylinder heads were offered under

The valve lifter gallery and the top of the cylinder heads painted with Glyptal G-1228A medium-grey gloss enamel. The Moroso 2505 lifter gallery oil splash shield and Competition Cams 1412-16 Magnum roller tip rocker arms are visible.

Left-side view of the engine shows the 1968 Cal Custom 40-2300 polished die-cast aluminum ribbed valve cover. The air cleaner tops were cast locally over 30 years ago.

another part number with the smaller head diameter valves installed. The biggest changes to the small-block Chevrolet cast-iron cylinder heads came in 1970 with the introduction of new 14-millimeter tapered spark plug seats, screw-in rocker arm studs with guide plates, and the famous angle-plug cast-iron cylinder heads.

The 1970 GM 3965742 angle-plug cylinder heads have the same 3991492 casting number and the same 65-cc combustion chamber volume as the straight plug cylinder heads. In 1972, GM offered the 336746 (with the same 3991492 casting number) angle-plug cylinder head, an improved version of the 1970 model. In 1973, GM introduced the 3965784 angle-plug cast-iron cylinder head (casting number 340292). This cylinder head was also known as the "turbo" head and was a major improvement over the two earlier angle-plug cylinder head designs.

The Crane Cams 11871 turbo Fireball angle-plug cylinder head was available in the late 1970s and the early 1980s. It was the GM 3965784 cast-iron cylinder head (casting number 340292), and Crane Cams did an excellent job of preparing the cylinder heads. The cylinder heads were fully assembled and ready to bolt on. They had 180-cc intake runner volume, 64-cc exhaust runner volume, 64.5-cc combustion chamber volume, the intake and exhaust ports were fully ported and polished and gasket matched, the combustion chambers were polished and cc'd, 2.02-inch head diameter intake valves and 1.60-inch head diameter exhaust valves were installed with a three-angle valve grind, combustion chambers were unshrouded (laying back), hardened steel screw-in rocker arm studs and guide plates were installed, and valve stem seals were provided. The dual valve springs were manufactured using Swedish Oteva

steel. The cylinder heads' aluminum valve spring retainers should not be installed in a street performance engine. I discovered a NOS set of the Crane Cams 11871 angle-plug cylinder heads at a speed shop in the State of Washington in 1986 and paid $850 for the fully assembled pair.

Purchase a pair of Edelbrock 6071 Performer RPM (non-emission) aluminum angle-plug cylinder heads for the Chevrolet 350-ci engine. The Edelbrock 6071 cylinder heads are fully assembled, and they have 170-cc intake runner volume, 60-cc exhaust runner volume, and 70-cc combustion chamber volume. The cylinder heads have been CNC machined for precise port design and gasket fit, they have 2.02-inch head diameter stainless-steel intake valves, 1.60-inch head diameter stainless-steel exhaust valves installed with a Serdi-machined multi-angle valve grind, bronze valve guides, ductile iron interlocking exhaust valve seat inserts, hardened-steel screw-in rocker arm studs and guide plates, valve springs, valve spring retainers and locks, and valve stem seals. The current retail price for the Edelbrock 6071 cylinder heads is $960. The Edelbrock 6071 cylinder heads require pushrods that are 0.100-inch longer than stock pushrods and the Edelbrock 8550 cylinder head bolt kit.

One of the best sources of stainless-steel valves is Dale Wilch's RPM Catalog (see Appendix B—Resources). The valves are manufactured in Argentina, and the quality is as good as any of the name-brand stainless-steel valves sold at much higher prices. The RPM Catalog 43246 intake valves are 2.02-inch head diameter by 11/32-inch stem diameter, and the RPM Catalog 43245 exhaust valves are 1.60-inch head diameter by 11/32-inch stem diameter. A complete set of these intake and exhaust valves currently costs $64. A few years

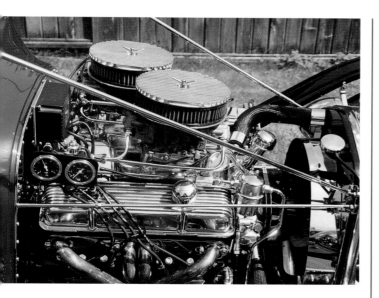

Right-side view of my engine shows the Mickey Thompson 3746427 Power Ram polished-aluminum ram-log intake manifold, the Cal Custom 40-2300 valve cover, and the Sanderson block hugger stainless-steel exhaust header.

ago, I decided to make some changes to my small-block Chevrolet 350-ci engine, including installing a set of RPM Catalog 43246 and 43245 stainless-steel valves. Refer to Chapter 10 for information pertaining to screw-in rocker arm studs, guide plates, roller tip rocker arms, rocker arm nuts, and cylinder head bolts.

If you still have money left after buying a roller camshaft and roller lifters, buy a set of Crower Cams & Equipment Company 73600 stainless-steel, 1.50-ratio roller rocker arms. These are probably the best roller rocker arms available today and the set includes the poly locknuts. The current retail price is $380 for a set.

Do not be too quick to discard the GM 3965541 and 3965542 die-cast aluminum valve covers for the Corvette LT-1 and replace them with some aftermarket billet-look valve covers. The Corvette LT-1 valve covers have dripper tabs on the underside to lubricate the rocker arms, and they also have a proper baffle for the PCV valve. Many aftermarket valve covers do not have these features.

Although I built an engine based on the Corvette LT-1 engine for my hot rod, I did not want it to look like a Corvette LT-1 engine. The first valve covers I installed were the Edelbrock 4649 Signature Series chrome tall valve covers with proper baffles. A few years ago, I decided to give my engine an early 1960s look. I located a pair of the original Cal Custom 40-2300 die-cast ribbed valve covers in Florida for $80. They are great-looking valve covers, although they do not have dripper tabs and are not properly baffled. If you use a PCV valve with one of these valve covers, oil will be sucked through the valve cover and into the carburetor, resulting in a smoke screen that any tank commander would be proud of. To overcome this situation, fit an oil separator between the PCV valve and the carburetor. Install the Edelbrock 4404 valve cover hold-down tabs with any

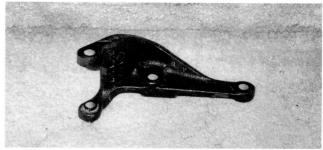

The GM 3951337 alternator mounting bracket used on the Corvette LT-1 engines. The bracket is bolted to the front of the left cylinder head.

valve covers, as they spread the tension from the bolts over a wider area. The retail price for a set is $10.

Intake System

The GM 3972114 (casting number 3972110) single four-barrel high-rise aluminum intake manifold was used on the 1970 Corvette LT-1 and Camaro Z-28 engines. The GM 3991004 (casting number 3959594) single four-barrel high-rise aluminum intake manifold was used on the 1971 and 1972 Corvette LT-1 and Camaro Z-28 engines. The two intake manifolds are excellent street performance dual-plane intake manifolds and are as good, if not better, than any aftermarket brand.

The factory installed the GM 3758369 oil splash shield on the GM 3972114 and GM 3991004 intake manifolds. The Moroso 2505 valve lifter gallery oil splash shield is a good item to install in any Chevrolet 350-ci engine. Check the splash shield after it is installed to ensure there is no interference with any of the valve lifters. The Moroso 2505 oil splash shield will not work with roller lifters.

The Corvette LT-1 engines include a factory-installed Holley 0-6239 model 4150 four-barrel 780-cfm carburetor. Refer to Chapter 10 for information regarding aftermarket single-quad, dual-plane aluminum intake manifolds, and carburetors.

The first intake system I installed on my Chevrolet 350-ci hot rod engine consisted of a Weiand 1984 dual quad tunnel-ram aluminum intake manifold with two Holley 0-4777 double pumper four-barrel, 650-cfm carburetors. The base of the intake manifold was polished, and the top was chromed. It was a very impressive-looking setup for a street performance engine, but it was also a huge mistake. When the car was at a stoplight, the intake manifold used to load up with fuel and I would have to rev the engine up to clear the fuel out in order to leave the stoplight without backfiring or stalling. This intake system is designed for drag racing and is not practical for the street, where the engine is operating under 3,000 rpm.

A few years back, I purchased a very rare 1965 Mickey Thompson 3746427 Power Ram dual four-barrel ram-log aluminum intake manifold from a gentleman in Kentucky. The

My Chevrolet 350-ci engine installed in the 1923 Ford Model T hot rod frame. Everything is chrome except the frame. I originally built the engine with the Weiand 1984 tunnel-ram intake manifold and two Holley 650-cfm double pumper carburetors—big mistake!

power range for this intake manifold is said to be 2,500 to 7,000 rpm, and it is one of the finest-looking intake manifolds I have ever seen. The ends of the crossram intake runners are curved, unlike most crossrams, which are square at the ends of the intake runners. "Tim, the polishing guy" carried out a spectacular buffing job on the intake manifold—it looks like chrome plating. After I installed the Mickey Thompson 3746427 intake manifold, my engine performance improved dramatically. My hot rod is now a real pleasure to drive—the intake manifold does not load up with fuel, there is no hesitation, and the engine even sounds better. I used the same Holley 0-4777 double pumper 650-cfm carburetors.

If I had not installed the Mickey Thompson 3746427 Power Ram intake manifold, I would have installed my 1972 Edelbrock 2850 (model SY-1) smoky ram single quad aluminum intake manifold. I would love to see how my hot rod performs with that intake manifold and the recommended Holley 0-4781 double pumper four-barrel, 850-cfm carburetor. Refer to Chapter 6 for information about fuel pressure regulators, fuel pressure gauges, and fuel lines.

Ignition System

The 1970 Corvette LT-1 was equipped the GM 1111491 distributor, the 1971 Corvette LT-1 was equipped with the GM 1112038 distributor, and the 1972 Corvette LT-1 was equipped with the GM 1112150 distributor. All three distributors operate with points. I prefer the Mallory Unilite or Mallory magnetic breakerless distributors for their compactness, reliability, and efficiency. Refer to Chapter 7 for information on distributors, ignition coils, spark plug wires, alternators, and starting motors. Refer to Chapter 10 for information pertaining to the firing order.

The Corvette LT-1 alternator mounts on the front of the left (driver's side) cylinder head using the GM 3951337 alternator mounting bracket, and the GM 460754 curved brace attaches to the upper left (driver's side) water pump stud. This bracket and brace are designed for use with a short-style water pump. It is a very neat and simple mounting system that should have been used on all the Chevrolet 350-ci engines.

Cooling and Exhaust Systems

Refer to Chapter 8 for the information regarding water pumps.

I installed a pair of Sanderson polished stainless-steel block-hugger exhaust headers on my Chevrolet 350-ci engine. I wanted the exhaust headers inside the frame, unlike most 1923 Ford Model T hot rods that have the exhaust headers outside the frame. The one drawback to stainless steel is that it tends to tarnish, resulting in a blue color. Had metallic-ceramic coating been available as an option when I purchased the block-hugger exhaust headers, I would have had them coated.

Engine Summary

Note: The engine block, crankshaft, and connecting rod prices are the prices I paid for them in 1983. They will cost more today, and they will be much harder to locate.

Engine Block

• 1973 Chevrolet Corvette 350-ci L82 engine block; casting number 39270010; casting date: L192 (December 19, 1972); stock bore: 4.001 inches; stock stroke: 3.484 inches; four-bolt main bearing caps; 250 horsepower at 5,200 rpm and 285 ft-lb torque at 4,000 rpm; engine block weight (bare): 150 pounds; $50

• Engine block hot tanked; engine block and main bearing caps and bolts Magnafluxed; main bearing caps and bolts shot peened; all threads retapped; cylinder head bolt holes chamfered; valve lifter bosses deglazed, allowing for 0.002-inch valve lifter clearance; No. 5 main bearing cap oil pump cavity polished; 0.030-inch hole drilled in bottom center of front camshaft boss and center of middle valve lifter gallery oil line plug; front valve lifter gallery oil line holes drilled and tapped, and 1/4-inch NPT plugs installed using pipe thread sealant; valve lifter gallery ground smooth and painted with Glyptal G-1228A medium-grey gloss enamel; Milodon 23150 lifter valley screen kit installed; exterior surface of engine block ground smooth and painted with Plasti-Kote 203 black high-gloss engine enamel; Weatherhead 3152-4 polished-brass water jacket drain plugs (1/4-inch NPT) installed using pipe thread sealant; GM 992956 engine block heaters, Pioneer PE100 freeze plugs, and rear camshaft boss plug installed using Permatex aviation form-a-gasket; $496.75

• Engine block bored 0.030-inch oversize and honed and deglazed using torque plate and Sunnen 800 series 400-grit stones, final bore: 4.030 inches; piston-to-bore clearance: 0.004 inch, measured below bottom of wrist pin perpendicular to wrist pin; $125

• Engine block align honed; $200

• Engine block parallel decked to 0.010-inch average below deck; $110

Engine block total: $981.75

Crankshaft

• NOS GM 3941184 (casting number 1182) forged 1053 steel crankshaft, journals nitrided, internally balanced; main bearing journal diameter: 2.45 inches, and connecting rod journal diameter: 2.10 inches; crankshaft weight: 65 pounds; $150

• Crankshaft shot peened, Magnafluxed, aligned, oil holes chamfered, journals polished, and crankshaft balanced; $105

• Clevite 77 MS-909P main bearings, standard size, installed allowing for 0.002-inch crankshaft clearance and 0.004-inch end play; GM 3932480 inner main bearing cap bolts and GM 3960312 windage tray studs torqued to 70 ft-lb; GM 3877669 outer main bearing cap bolts torqued to 65 ft-lb using molykote; $105

• Fluidampr 712430 harmonic balancer, 7 1/4-inch o.d., weight: 13.4 pounds, installed with Mr. Gasket 1150 chrome crankshaft bolt and flat washer using Loctite and torqued to 85 ft-lb; $313

• Luke's Custom Machine & Design chrome-plated aluminum single-groove crankshaft pulley, 5 1/2-inch o.d., installed with chrome Grade 8 bolts, lockwashers, and flat washers using Loctite and torqued to 25 ft-lb; $95

Crankshaft total: $768

Connecting Rods and Pistons

• GM 3973386 forged 1053 steel I-beam connecting rods, pressed-in wrist pin; connecting rod length: 5.70 inches (center to center); connecting rod weight: 590 grams each; connecting rod ratio: 1.64

(with 3.484-inch stroke crankshaft); $40

• Connecting rods shot peened, Magnafluxed, debeamed, aligned, resized, pin fitted, and balanced; Maxalloy 9271 connecting rod bolts (190,000 psi, 3/8-inch diameter) installed; $356.67

• Clevite 77 CB-663P connecting rod bearings, standard size, installed allowing for 0.002-inch connecting rod clearance and 0.010-inch side clearance per pair of connecting rods; connecting rod bolts torqued to 50 ft-lb using molykote and allowing for 0.006-inch stretch; $31

• Speed-Pro 2244P-030 power-forged aluminum racing pistons (0.030-inch oversize), 9.72:1 compression ratio, flat top (with four valve reliefs); piston weight: 640 grams each; pressed-in, heat-treated, and casehardened 4340 chrome-moly steel straight-wall wrist pins; wrist pin weight: 141 grams; wrist pin diameter: 0.927 inch; piston ring grooves: top compression ring groove: 1/16 inch; second compression ring groove: 1/16 inch; oil ring groove: 3/16 inch; Speed-Pro R-9771-035 plasma moly-coated ductile iron-top piston ring set with standard tension oil ring (0.035-inch oversize) installed within manufacturer's recommended arc; top compression ring gap: 0.018 inch; second compression ring gap: 0.016 inch; oil ring gap: 0.016 inch; piston tops painted with V.H.T. SP-101 white high-temperature coating; intake-valve-to-piston clearance: 0.140 inch and exhaust-valve-to-piston clearance: 0.160 inch (without gasket); new displacement: 355.5 ci (5.8 liters); $300

• Complete V-8 engine balance; Fel-Pro KS2600 (current Fel-Pro 2802) complete gasket set installed; $230

Connecting rods and pistons total: $957.67

Lubrication System

• TRW 50065 high-volume oil pump with pressure balance grooves; oil pump end clearance: 0.00025 inch; TRW 52039 oil pump pickup tube welded to oil pump body; oil pump cover gasket installed using silicone sealant and bolts torqued to 80 in-lb using Loctite; Milodon 25010 oil pump extension kit with 1-inch extended oil pump shaft, 4130 chrome-moly steel, heat-treated ends, and 1-inch oil pump spacer plate installed; Milodon 17050 oil pump stud kit installed using Loctite and torqued to 65 ft-lb; $57

• GM 3927136 windage tray installed using Loctite on studs and torqued to 25 ft-lb; Milodon 30900 chrome low-profile oil pan installed with Mr. Gasket 6085 Ultra-Seal chrome oil pan bolts using Loctite and torqued to 15 ft-lb; oil pan gaskets and rear oil seals installed using silicone sealant; Trans-Dapt 9783 chrome dip stick and dip stick tube installed; GM 3952301 oil filter adapter installed using Loctite on bolts and torqued to 20 ft-lb; Fram PH-13 oil filter installed with Trans-Dapt 1067 chrome oil filter cover; engine lubricated with 7 quarts Pennzoil HD-30-weight motor oil; Weatherhead 3152-2 polished-brass pipe plug, 1/8-inch NPT; installed in oil pressure hole above timing gear cover; $264.57

Lubrication system total: $321.57

Camshaft and Cylinder Heads

• Clevite 77 SH-290S camshaft bearings installed with 0.002-inch camshaft clearance and 0.002-inch end play; No. 1 bearing: SH-290, housing bore diameter: 2.019 to 2.021 inches; No. 2 and 5 bearing: SH-288, housing bore diameter: 2.009 to 2.012 inches; No. 3 and 4 bearing: SH-287, housing bore diameter: 1.990 to 2.001 inches; camshaft journal diameter: 1.870 inches; $27

• 1969 GM 3927140 first off-road racing design solid (mechanical) lifter camshaft with advertised duration: 316 degrees intake and 323 degrees exhaust; duration at 0.050-inch lift: 243 degrees intake and 254 degrees exhaust; lobe separation angle: 112 degrees; net valve lift: 0.475 inch intake and 0.495 inch exhaust; valve lash (hot): 0.024 inch intake and 0.026 inch exhaust; camshaft degreed; $127

• GM 5231585 edge orifice solid (mechanical) lifters with grooved oil hole and bases micropolished; GM 3796243 blue tip heavy-duty thick wall pushrods (5/16-inch diameter by 7.790-inch length), installed; Moroso 2505 lifter gallery oil splash shield installed; $162

• Cloyes 93100 double-roller timing chain set, heat-treated sprockets, multi-keyway crankshaft sprocket, installed; Manley 42114 camshaft locking plate and bolts installed using Loctite and torqued to 20 ft-lb; Manley 42146 aluminum camshaft button installed; GM 3991433 chrome timing gear cover installed with Trans-Dapt 2950 chrome timing gear cover bolts using Loctite and torqued to 15 ft-lb; timing gear cover gasket installed using silicone sealant; GM 3980267 front one-piece oil seal installed; Trans-Dapt 4960 chrome timing tab installed; $119.53

• NOS Crane Cams 11871 turbo Fireball angle-plug cast-iron cylinder heads, GM 3965784 (casting number 340292); cylinder heads Magnafluxed and surfaced; intake runner volume: 180 cc; exhaust runner volume: 64 cc; combustion chamber volume: 64.5 cc; intake and exhaust ports fully ported and polished and gasket matched; combustion chambers unshrouded (laying back), polished, and cc'd; K-Line 9832STA bronze valve guide liners installed; K-Line 1625-1 hardened interlocking ductile iron exhaust valve seat inserts installed, Serdi-machined multi-angle blueprint valve grind performed; area beneath valve covers painted with Glyptal G-1228A medium-grey gloss enamel; exterior surface of cylinder heads painted with Plasti-Kote 203 black high-gloss engine enamel; cylinder heads installed with Fel-Pro 7733PT-2 perma-torque blue stripe cylinder head gaskets and Mr. Gasket 940 chrome cylinder head bolts using Permatex aviation form-a-gasket and torqued to 65 ft-lb; $921.51

• (Dale Wilch's) RPM Catalog 43246 stainless-steel intake valves (2.02-inch head diameter, 11/32-inch stem diameter, 4.915-inch length overall), swirl polished, hardened tips, and RPM Catalog 43245 stainless-steel exhaust valves (1.60-inch head diameter, 11/32-inch stem diameter, 4.915-inch length overall), swirl polished, hardened tips, installed with Serdi-machined multi-angle blueprint valve grind; GM 3836755 O-ring valve stem seals and

Enginetech S2927 viton positive seal valve stem seals installed; $231

• Crane Cams Oteva steel 99858 inner and 99836 (current Crane Cams 99834) outer valve springs with installed height: 120 pounds at 1.734 inches valves closed and 303 pounds at 1.130 inches valves open; 1.415-inch o.d. and 1.026-inch/0.700-inch i.d.; coil bind: 1.075 inches; Manley 23645 valve spring retainers, heat-treated black oxide finish, 11/32-inch stem diameter; Crane Cams 99097-1 valve stem locks, machined heat-treated steel, 7-degree, 11/32-inch stem diameter, stock height; $116.85

• GM 3973418 heat-treated steel pushrod guide plates (5/16-inch diameter pushrods) installed with GM 3973416 heat-treated steel rocker arm studs (3/8-inch diameter) using Loctite and torqued to 50 ft-lb; Competition Cams 1412-16 Magnum roller tip rocker arms (1.52 ratio) installed with Manley 42107 rocker arm nuts (3/8-inch studs) using anti-seize compound; $230

• 1968 Cal Custom 40-2300 polished die-cast aluminum ribbed valve covers installed with Mr. Gasket 9827 chrome valve cover spreader bars and Mr. Gasket 9824 chrome valve cover lift-off wing bolts; Fel-Pro 1602 valve cover gaskets installed using silicone sealant; GM 3894337 valve cover grommet installed with polished aluminum PCV valve block-off plug; Trans-Dapt 4803 chrome twist-on breather caps installed; $111.18

Camshaft and cylinder heads total: $2,046.07

Intake System

• 1965 Mickey Thompson 3746427 Power Ram polished aluminum dual quad ram-log intake manifold installed with Trans-Dapt 4924 chrome socket head intake manifold bolts and AN flat washers using Loctite and torqued to 25 ft-lb; power range: 2,500 to 7,000 rpm; Fel-Pro 1205 intake manifold gaskets (1.28- by 2.09-inch ports) installed using silicone sealant; intake ports gasket matched and underside of intake manifold painted with V.H.T. SP-101 white high-temperature coating; Papco 1010CB brass expansion plugs (1-inch diameter) installed in intake manifold using Permatex aviation form-a-gasket; Weatherhead 3350-8 polished-brass 45-degree elbow (1/2-inch NPT); Weatherhead 129-8-8 polished-brass water pump bypass fitting (1/2-inch NPT) to 3/4-inch i.d. hose; Weatherhead 3152-6 polished-brass pipe plug (3/8-inch NPT) installed using pipe thread sealant; $502.97

• Holley 0-4777 double pumper four-barrel carburetors, 650 cfm each, installed; choke assemblies removed; (Gary) Lang 9 polished die-cast aluminum ribbed air cleaners (10-inch diameter) installed with K&N E-1050 air filters (9-inch diameter by 2-inch height) and Mr. Gasket 6398 chrome wing-style air cleaner nuts; Edelbrock 8710 polished aluminum carburetor spacers (1 inch high) installed with Trans-Dapt 2046 carburetor studs using anti-seize compound; $707.47

• Holley 12-834 chrome mechanical fuel pump (6 to 8 psi, 110 gph) installed with GM 3719599 chrome fuel pump plate using chrome Grade 8 bolts and lockwashers with Loctite and torqued to

20 ft-lb; fuel pump and fuel pump plate gaskets installed using silicone sealant; Weatherhead 3220-6-4 polished-brass adapter (3/8-inch NPT to 1/4-inch NPT) and Weatherhead 402-6-6 polished-brass 90-degree elbow (3/8-inch tube to 3/8-inch NPT) installed using pipe thread sealant; GM 3704817 fuel pump pushrod (1/2-inch diameter by 5 3/4-inch length) installed; $69.85

• Mr. Gasket 3661 chrome thermostat housing installed with Robert Shaw 330-160 extra performance balanced 160-degree (Fahrenheit) thermostat using chrome bolts and lockwashers with anti-seize compound; Fel-Pro 35062 thermostat housing gasket installed using silicone sealant; Trans-Dapt 4955 chrome oil filler tube installed with Mr. Gasket 2060 chrome oil filler tube breather cap; Enderle 72-103 ball bearing carburetor linkage modified and installed with Mr. Gasket 14 and Edelbrock 8005 chrome universal throttle return spring kits; $184.28

• Holley 162-510 chrome inline fuel filter; Holley 12-803 chrome fuel pressure regulators, adjustable from 4 1/2 to 9 psi; Weatherhead 402-6-6 polished-brass 90-degree elbows (3/8-inch tube to 3/8-inch NPT), Weatherhead 3152-6 polished-brass pipe plugs (3/8-inch NPT), Weatherhead 3325-6-2 polished-brass adapters (3/8-inch NPT to 1/8-inch NPT), installed using pipe thread sealant; Mr. Gasket 1552 chrome dual-inlet fuel lines (9 5/16-inch center to center) installed; Stewart-Warner 82405 mechanical fuel pressure gauge, Stewart-Warner 82411 vacuum gauge, Auto-Meter 3232 gauge mounting bracket, with Weatherhead 3400-6 polished-brass 90-degree elbow (3/8-inch NPT), and Weatherhead 3220-6-2 polished-brass adapter (3/8-inch NPT to 1/8-inch NPT) installed using pipe thread sealant; Mr. Gasket 1557 chrome universal "T" hex fuel block with Weatherhead 3220-6-4 polished-brass adapters (3/8-inch tube to 1/4-inch NPT) and Weatherhead 202-6-6 polished-brass adapters (3/8-inch tube to 3/8-inch NPT) installed using pipe thread sealant; Summit Racing Equipment 220238 polished stainless-steel fuel line (3/8-inch o.d. by 0.028-inch wall by 4-foot length) installed with Weatherhead 100-6 chrome inverted flare nuts (3/8-inch tube) using pipe thread sealant; $274.60

Intake system total: $1,739.17

Ignition System

• Mallory 3748201 Unilite distributor with photo-optic infrared LED system, 356 T-6 aluminum housing, mechanical advance, installed with NOS Cal Custom 6161 chrome distributor clamp; Mallory 29440 Promaster ignition coil and Mallory 29026 HyFire electronic ignition control installed with chrome mounting brackets; $332.80

• Taylor/Vertex 70051 pro universal 8-millimeter high-performance spark plug wires, black 90-degree boots, installed; Mallory 1122956 chrome high-lift spark plug wire looms and

Taylor 42800 black plastic spark plug wire separators kit installed; Accel 276S short spark plugs installed with 0.050-inch gap and torqued to 15 ft-lb; $79.80

• Aries KC-11 chrome internally regulated alternator (63 amps) installed with GM 3951337 chrome alternator mounting bracket and GM 460754 chrome curved alternator adjustment brace using chrome Grade 8 bolts and lockwashers with Loctite; $166.62

• Aries 765-41 chrome high-torque starting motor with GM 1968122 chrome gear housing installed with GM 14097279 chrome starting motor bolts using anti-seize compound; GM 3826928 chrome starting motor brace installed; $131.66

Ignition system total: $710.88

Cooling and Exhaust Systems

• Brassworks 1888P Flowkooler polished aluminum short-style high-performance water pump installed with chrome Grade 8 bolts and lockwashers using Loctite and torqued to 25 ft-lb; water pump gaskets installed using silicone sealant; GM 3921915 water pump bypass hose fitting, GM 3794094 water pump bypass hose, and Weatherhead 3152-8 polished-brass pipe plug (1/2-inch NPT) installed using pipe thread sealant; water pump bypass hose installed with stainless-steel line clamps and covered with Spectre 3001A black nylabraid and Spectre 3208B chrome champclamps; GM 3905995 chrome single-groove water pump pulley, Mr. Gasket 2393 polished aluminum 2-inch fan spacer, Flex-A-Lite 5715 polished stainless-steel flex fan (15-inch diameter) installed with chrome Grade 8 bolts and lockwashers using Loctite and torqued to 25 ft-lb; Motorcraft JB-546L crankshaft/alternator/water pump v-belt installed; $352.13

• Sanderson CC158 block hugger polished stainless-steel exhaust headers (1 5/8-inch primary tubes and 3-inch-diameter collectors) installed with Trans-Dapt 8911 Stage 8 polished stainless-steel locking header bolt kit using Loctite and torqued to 25 ft-lb; Mr. Gasket 5902 Ultra-Seal exhaust manifold gaskets (1 5/8-inch-diameter ports) installed using Permatex ultra-copper high-temperature silicone sealant; $331.95

Cooling and exhaust systems total: $684.08

Labor

• Labor for checking clearances, gapping piston rings, degree camshaft, valvetrain assembly, detailing, trial engine assembly, final engine assembly, and initial engine start-up; $800

Labor total: $800

Engine Grand Total: $9,009.19 (U.S.)

Note: The estimated output of this engine is 472 horsepower at 6,000 rpm and 441 ft-lb torque at 5,000 rpm (see Appendix A—Dyno Print-Outs).

CHAPTER 12
1970 CORVETTE 454-ci ENGINE (LS7 CLONE)

In 1965, Chevrolet introduced its first big-block passenger car engine—the Mark IV 396-ci engine. Chevrolet produced the Mark IV big-block engines until 1990, when it introduced the Mark V big-block engine. The most powerful of all the Mark IV engines was the 1970 Chevrolet LS7 Turbo-Jet 454-ci engine. It was offered as an option for the 1970 Corvette, although there is no evidence to indicate whether or not the factory ever installed one. This engine was rated at 460 horsepower at 5,600 rpm and 490 ft-lb torque at 3,600 rpm. These huge horsepower and torque numbers must have really shaken up the fanatics crusading for fuel economy.

The Chevrolet 454-ci Mark IV engine block (casting number 14015445). The valve lifter gallery has been ground smooth, and the engine block is now ready to be hot tanked.

Jerry Olsen is one of the owners of J & M Autobody & Paint (see Appendix B—Resources), a body shop that has also been restoring Corvettes for over 30 years. Jerry and I have been friends for that period of time and discussed building a Corvette from the ground up together on a number of occasions. In January 1994, I purchased a 1969 Corvette coupe for the sum of $1,350 (U.S.). Before anyone thinks this was the deal of the century, it had no running gear, no front end, the back end was smashed, someone had tried to install flares in the rear quarter panels, and most of the interior was missing.

I assembled the frame, suspension, steering, brakes, engine, transmission, and rear end. Jerry Olsen and his crew completely rebuilt the body (the only original body panels are the two doors), installed all the wiring, and completed the project with a fabulous Pearl Teal paint job. The car was finished in 1995 and won the "best in class" and "best paint" awards in a custom car and hot rod show with over 500 entries. Since then, I have won many "best in class" awards for this beautiful vehicle.

Prior to purchasing the 1969 Corvette, I decided I wanted to build a modified 1970 Corvette LS7 engine. Once again, I was not concerned about correct casting numbers or casting dates. I just wanted a good Chevrolet 454-ci Mark IV engine block with four-bolt main bearing caps, a forged steel crankshaft, and forged steel connecting rods. Bud Child of High Performance Engines had all of these parts from a 1989 Chevrolet light-duty truck that had been driven for only 7,000 miles before it was demolished in an accident. This chapter contains the complete buildup information for that engine.

Components Description
Engine Block
The specifications for the 1970 Corvette LS7 engine are:
- 454-ci (7.4-liter) displacement
- 4.251-inch stock bore and 4.00-inch stock stroke
- Stock compression ratio: 11.25:1
- 460 horsepower at 5,600 rpm and 490 ft-lb torque at 3,600 rpm

Chevrolet introduced its 454-ci engine in 1970, the last big-horsepower year for the American automotive manufacturers. As a result of its late arrival, the Chevrolet 454-ci engine is often overlooked by engine builders as a source of very serious horsepower and perform-

A Chevrolet 454-ci engine with two-bolt main bearing caps—quite satisfactory for most street performance engines.

ance. It is common knowledge that more cubic inches equate to more horsepower and torque. The big-block Chevrolet Mark IV engines are readily available today and the prices are still reasonable.

In this chapter, I will limit my description of the Chevrolet 454-ci engines to the Mark IV model. The Mark IV engine blocks have a standard deck height of 9.80 inches, and the truck engine blocks have a deck height of 10.20 inches. Some of the engine blocks were fitted with four-bolt main bearing caps and others, with the same casting number, were fitted with two-bolt main bearing caps. Remove the oil pan to determine what type of main bearing caps is installed; there is no way to detect this from the outward appearance of an engine block. The designations "High-Per" and "Pass" or "Hiperf" were cast into the engine block behind the timing gear cover, above the oil filter boss, or at the rear of the engine block. Before you start jumping up and down believing you have a rare high-performance engine block, it has been reported that the majority of the Chevrolet 454-ci Mark IV engine blocks had these letters cast in them.

If you intend to use a Chevrolet 454-ci engine block as the basis for a big-horsepower street performance engine, locate an engine block with the four-bolt main bearing caps. My intention was to achieve more horsepower from the engine described here than a Chevrolet LS7 engine, which dictates a four-bolt main bearing cap engine block be used. The same casting numbers were sometimes used on both the 427-ci and 454-ci engines. Here is a list of some of the engine blocks with four-bolt main bearing caps:

361959 (also two-bolt)

3963512 (also two-bolt)

3969854 (also two-bolt)

10068286

14015443

14015445 (also two-bolt)

There are more than likely a few more Chevrolet 454-ci Mark IV engine block casting numbers for engine blocks equipped with four-bolt main bearing caps than I have listed. The GM 14044809 (casting number 3963512) engine block was used for the Chevrolet

454-ci LS6 engine. It was probably the same engine block used for the Chevrolet 454-ci LS7 engine, since it was manufactured in 1970 and 1971.

Refer to Chapter 1 for information regarding the preparation of the engine block. Install a valve lifter gallery screen kit, such as the Moroso 25001, to keep any debris from ending up in the oil pan. The Moroso 25001 kit costs about $13.

Unlike the small-block Chevrolet engines, the big-block Chevrolet 454-ci Mark IV two-bolt main bearing cap engine blocks cannot be converted to four-bolt main bearing cap engine blocks using splayed main bearing caps. There is an oil line inside the engine block on the left side above the oil pan rail. Splayed main bearing cap bolts would penetrate into this oil line. The Milodon 11205 main bearing cap kit with straight bolts is designed for the Chevrolet 454-ci engine block already fitted with four-bolt main bearing caps. The four-bolt main bearing caps fitted at the factory in the Chevrolet 454-ci engine block have sufficient strength to withstand the rigors of even a wild street performance machine.

The cylinders in the Chevrolet 454-ci engine block can safely be bored 0.060-inch oversize, which is about the maximum over-bore recommended for a street performance engine. Refer to Chapter 1 for information regarding cylinder boring, align honing, and parallel decking.

In order to provide better lubrication for the camshaft gear and timing chain gear chain, drill a 0.030-inch hole in the center of the lower face of the front camshaft boss (behind the camshaft gear). Also drill the two top front oil gallery line plugs with a 0.030-inch hole if you plan to install a gear drive.

Crankshaft

All the crankshafts used in the Chevrolet 454-ci engines have a 4.00-inch stroke and are externally balanced. The main bearing journal diameter for the No. 1 journal is 2.7492 inches; the No. 2, 3, and 4 main bearing journals are 2.7498 inches; and the No. 5 main bearing journal is 2.750 inches. The connecting rod journal diameter is 2.1990 to 2.200 inches. The diameter of the main bearing housing bores is 2.9370 to 2.9380 inches. All the Chevrolet 454-ci Mark V crankshafts, manufactured from 1991 onward, have a special flywheel flange for use with the one-piece rear oil seal that cannot be used with the Mark IV engine blocks.

The GM 3963523 (casting number 3520) is one of the best crankshafts for the Chevrolet 454-ci engines. This crankshaft was manufactured using forged 1053 steel, the journals are nitrided, the oil holes are cross-drilled, and it was offered by Chevrolet for use in the 454-ci LS6 and LS7 engines. If you locate a GM 3963523 forged steel crankshaft, the main bearing journals cannot be ground more than 0.040-inch undersize and the connecting rod journals cannot be ground more than 0.050-inch undersize. If the crankshaft needs to be ground in excess of those sizes, bearings are not currently available.

A GM 3963523 (casting number 3520) forged 1053 steel crankshaft that has been shot peened, Magnafluxed, the journals ground 0.010-inch undersize, the oil holes chamfered, the journals polished, and balanced.

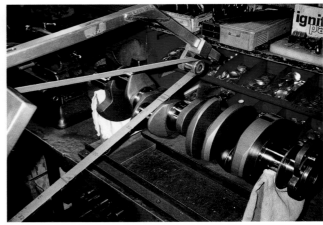

The journals are being polished on this GM 3963523 (casting number 3520) forged steel crankshaft. "Mario," the engine balancing and trapeze artist, is performing this task at High Performance Engines.

If you cannot locate a good used Chevrolet 454-ci crankshaft, Scat Enterprises sells forged steel standard-weight (approximately 69 pounds) crankshafts for use with different length connecting rods and they are available with stock or longer strokes. For example, the Scat Enterprises 4-454-4250-6385 is manufactured using forged 4340 steel, the journals are nitrided, the oil holes are the straight-shot design, and they are chamfered. This model is designed for use with 6.385-inch-long connecting rods and has a 4.25-inch stroke, resulting in a displacement of 496 ci (with a 4.310-inch bore). The current retail price for this crankshaft is $750.

It would likely cost more to purchase a good used crankshaft and pay to hot tank, shot peen, Magnaflux, align, regrind, chamfer the oil holes, and polish the journals than to buy a new Scat Enterprises forged steel crankshaft, as described above. Scat Enterprises forged steel crankshafts also provide increased displacement for the same price as a stock stroke crankshaft. Refer to Chapter 2 for information on crankshaft preparation.

The Clevite 77 MS-829P main bearings are available in standard size, 0.001-, 0.010-, 0.020-, 0.030-, and 0.040-inch oversize. The current retail price for a set of these bearings is $55. The Federal Mogul 4400M main bearings are available in standard size, 0.001-, 0.002-, 0.010-, 0.0020-, 0.030-, and 0.040-inch oversize. The current retail price for a set of these main bearings is $61. The factory-recommended main bearing clearance is 0.0013 to 0.0025 inch, and the No. 5 main bearing is the thrust bearing. The factory-recommended crankshaft end play is 0.006 to 0.010 inch. Torque the inner and outer main bearing caps bolts to 110 ft-lb using molykote.

Do not use the factory-installed harmonic balancer on a street performance engine. The Fluidampr 712105 harmonic balancer meets SFI specs 18.1, has an 8-inch o.d., and weighs 17.3 pounds. This harmonic balancer is designed for an externally balanced engine. The current retail price for the Fluidampr 712105 harmonic balancer is $310. It is available at most high-performance parts outlets. Use a good-quality crankshaft bolt and washer, such as the ARP 235-2501 (available for about $20) to secure the harmonic balancer.

Connecting Rods and Pistons

The GM 3969804 forged 4340 steel I-beam connecting rods, for use with full floating wrist pins, were fitted in the big-block 1969 Chevrolet L88 and ZL-1 engines. They are the strongest connecting rods that Chevrolet ever manufactured for the Mark IV engines, and they are far superior to many aftermarket connecting rods. These connecting rods have the GM 3969864 boron 10B39 steel bolts (7/16 inch by 2.34 inches, 220,000 psi) and GM 3942410 nuts installed. The connecting rods and the bolts were shot peened and Magnafluxed at the factory; the boron steel bolts can be reused many times without the need for replacement. The GM 3969804 connecting rods were also referred to as "dimple rods," due to a small green dot between the ribs near the wrist pin hole. They were torqued to 80 ft-lb, allowing for 0.009-inch stretch. The crankshaft end (the big end) diameter of the GM 3969804 connecting rods is 2.3247 to 2.3252 inches, the length (center to center) is 6.130 to 6.140 inches, and they have an average weight of 790 grams.

The second-best choice for big-block Chevrolet connecting rods are the GM 3963552 forged 4340 steel I-beam connecting rods, for use with pressed-in wrist pins, installed in the 1970 to 1971 big-block Chevrolet LS6 and LS7 engines. These connecting rods have the GM 3981092 knurled shank connecting rod bolt (7/16-inch diameter) installed, and they were torqued to 73 ft-lb, allowing for 0.007-inch stretch. Refer to Chapter 3 for information on the preparation of connecting rods.

The Clevite 77 CB-743P connecting rod bearings are available in standard size, 0.001-, 0.002-, 0.010-, 0.020-, 0.030-, 0.040-, and 0.050-inch oversize. The current retail price for these connecting rod bearings is $50. The Federal Mogul 8-3190CP connecting rod bearings are available in standard size, 0.001-, 0.002-, 0.010-, 0.020-, 0.030-, and 0.040-inch oversize. The current retail price

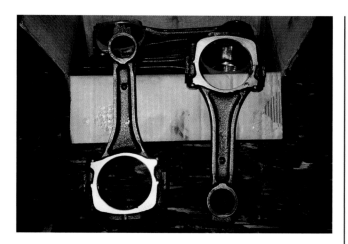

A set of GM 3969804 forged 4340 steel I-beam connecting rods (designed for use with full-floating wrist pins) with the GM 3969864 boron steel 7/16-inch bolts and GM 3942410 nuts installed. These are the best connecting rods that Chevrolet made for the Mark IV engines. Notice the dimple between the ribs.

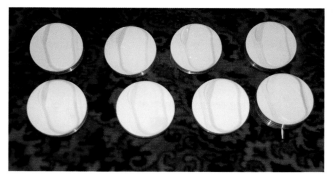

A set of TRW 2399F forged aluminum full-floating racing pistons. They have a compression ratio of 9.0:1 with a combustion chamber volume of 118 cc. The V.H.T. SP-101 white high-temperature coating is great for photographs.

A Melling M77 standard-volume oil pump with a Moroso 24440 oil pump pickup screen.

for these connecting rod bearings is $53. The factory-recommended connecting rod bearing clearance is 0.0014 to 0.003 inch, and the side clearance per pair of connecting rods is 0.015 to 0.021 inch.

The GM 3981075 forged aluminum pistons with pressed-in wrist pins and 12.5:1 compression ratio were offered for the 1970 Chevrolet LS7 engine. These pistons were used with the GM 3963552 connecting rods for use with pressed-in wrist pins, and they were the open chamber design.

I gave much consideration to the compression ratio of this engine. A street performance engine, operating with high-octane, unleaded gasoline, should have a maximum compression ratio of 10.0:1. This being the case, I installed a set of TRW 2399F forged aluminum racing pistons (standard size, open chamber design) with a slightly domed 13.8-cc top. These pistons have a full-floating wrist pin, a compression ratio of 9.0:1 with a 118-cc combustion chamber volume, or a compression ratio of 9.75:1 with a 110-cc combustion chamber volume, and are advertised as being similar to the GM 6262979 pistons used in the 1971 Chevrolet 454-ci LS6 engine. The TRW 2399F forged aluminum pistons are available at a current retail price of $500 for a set, including a moly-coated top piston ring set. The TRW pistons and rings are available through most speed equipment dealers.

I installed the Fel-Pro 2805 complete gasket set in this engine. The current retail price for this gasket set is $110, and the set is available at most automotive parts outlets.

Lubrication System

The 1969 Corvette ZL-1 and 1970 Chevrolet LS7 engines are equipped with the GM 3969870 standard-volume oil pump and

GM 6269895 oil pump pickup screen. This excellent oil pump and oil pump pickup screen combination works well in a street performance big-block Chevrolet 454-ci engine. The oil pump and pickup screen are still available today from your Chevrolet dealers for a current retail price of $90. The GM 10051105 high-volume oil pump is available for a current retail price of $65.

The Melling M77 is the standard-volume replacement oil pump for the big-block Chevrolet 454-ci engines. This oil pump costs a lot less than the factory oil pumps and is available for the current retail price of $25. The Melling M77HV is the high-volume replacement oil pump available at a current retail price of $25.

Install a new oil pump driveshaft in any street performance Chevrolet 454-ci engine. The ARP 135-7901 oil pump driveshaft is manufactured using chrome-moly steel rated at 170,000 psi and its current retail price is $12. The Milodon 17050 oil pump stud kit, manufactured using heat-treated 8740 steel, is available at a current retail price of $6.

Chevrolet used the GM 3977591 oil pan with the GM 3967854 baffle on its LS7 engines. The oil pan has a capacity of 6 quarts of oil. I installed a Milodon 30950 low-profile oil pan with

The Milodon 32260 Diamond Stripper windage tray and the Melling M77 standard-volume oil pump with the GM 6269895 oil pump pickup screen attached. (This is the engine described in this chapter.)

The GM 3967854 flat metal windage tray with a Melling M77HV high-volume oil pump.

the right side (passenger's side) dip stick and a capacity of 6 quarts of oil. This oil pan is an excellent choice for any big-block Chevrolet 454-ci engine using a rear sump oil pan, and it provides sufficient frame and steering clearance in the 1968 to 1972 Corvettes. The current retail price for this oil pan is $160. The Milodon 30960 chrome oil pan retails for $200.

If you install an aftermarket oil pan, purchase the matching oil pump pickup screen (or tube). Use the Milodon 18301 oil pump pickup screen with the Melling M77HV high-volume oil pump and the Milodon 30950 or 30960 oil pan. The current retail price for the Milodon 18301 oil pump pickup screen is $35. Milodon products are available at most speed equipment outlets.

Chevrolet used the GM 3967854 flat metal windage tray in its LS7 engine. This windage tray requires the use of the GM 3902885 windage tray studs (four). The windage tray is available at a current retail price of $12, and the windage tray studs (four) will cost an additional $26. The Milodon 32260 Diamond Stripper windage is an excellent product, especially when used with the Milodon 30950 or 30960 oil pans. The Milodon 32260 windage tray is available at a current retail price of $85.

Chevrolet installed the GM 3952301 oil filter adapter in all its Mark IV big-block 454-ci engines. Use the Fram PH-13 oil filter, or similar type, with this oil filter adapter.

Camshaft and Cylinder Heads

The Clevite 77 SH-616S camshaft bearings are available at a current retail price of $35. The Federal Mogul 1404M camshaft bearings are available at a retail price of $38. The camshaft journal diameter is 1.950 inches. Refer to Chapter 5 for a photograph of the Clevite 77 SH-616S camshaft bearings.

The GM 3959180 solid (mechanical) lifter camshaft was the Chevrolet general competition model installed in the 1969 Corvette ZL-1 and 1970 Chevrolet LS7 engines with a recommended compression ratio of at least 11.25:1. The Chevrolet specifications for this camshaft are: advertised duration: 347 degrees intake and 359 degrees exhaust; duration at 0.050-inch lift: 262 degrees intake and 273 degrees exhaust; lobe separation angle: 110 degrees; valve lift (with 1.70 ratio rocker arms): 0.560 inch intake and 0.600 inch exhaust; valve lash (hot): 0.024 inch intake and 0.026 inch exhaust. This is strictly a drag racing camshaft and should not be considered for the street. It amazes me today when I hear people mention they would love to own and drive a "numbers matching" L88-, ZL-1-, or LS7-powered vehicle on the street. The compression ratios range from 11.25:1 to 12.5:1 and the factory camshafts in those engines were designed to operate from 3,500 rpm upward, which would make these vehicles almost impossible to use as daily drivers. Throw in today's unleaded gasoline and you'd have a nightmare.

In order to operate a Chevrolet 454-ci engine in a street performance vehicle today, you must install a sensible camshaft. The Crower Cams & Equipment Company 01321 294F solid (mechanical) lifter camshaft is an excellent choice. This camshaft has an advertised duration of 294 degrees intake and 300 degrees exhaust; duration at 0.050-inch lift: 244 degrees intake and 246 degrees exhaust; lobe separation angle: 114 degrees; valve lift (with 1.70-ratio rocker arms): 0.517 inch intake and 0.530 inch exhaust; valve lash (hot): 0.022 inch intake and 0.024 inch exhaust. This is the camshaft that was installed in the engine described here. The estimated output will be: 523 horsepower at 5,500 rpm and 534 ft-lb torque at 4,500 rpm. The current retail price for the camshaft is

A GM 6260482 (casting number 6272990) open combustion chamber design cast-iron cylinder head. The intake port runner volume is 325 cc, the exhaust port runner volume is 127 cc, and the combustion chamber volume is 118 cc.

$115. There is a nice torque curve from 2,000 rpm to 4,500 rpm, which shows that the correct camshaft was chosen for street use. I was able to obtain more horsepower and torque from this engine than the horsepower and torque listed for a Chevrolet LS7 engine—exactly the result I wanted.

The Crower Cams & Equipment Company 01475 286R street solid (mechanical) roller camshaft is another good choice for a Chevrolet 454-ci street performance engine. The advertised duration is: 286 degrees intake and 290 degrees exhaust; duration at 0.050-inch lift: 242 degrees intake and 250 degrees exhaust; lobe separation angle: 112 degrees; valve lift (with 1.70-ratio rocker arms): 0.580 inch intake and 0.573 inch exhaust; valve lash (hot): 0.026 inch intake and 0.028 inch exhaust. The estimated output is: 560 horsepower at 6,000 rpm and 570 ft-lb torque at 4,500 rpm. Once again, there is a nice torque curve from 2,000 rpm to 4,500 rpm, indicating this would be a good camshaft for the 454-ci engine. The current retail price for this camshaft is $320.

The GM 5231585 edge orifice solid (mechanical) lifters were used with the Chevrolet solid lifter camshafts in the 1960s and the early 1970s. Refer to Chapter 11 for an explanation of these solid lifters. The Crower Cams & Equipment Company 66900 solid lifters with the 66980 coolface oiling system will be installed in the engine described here; their current retail price is $120. Refer to Chapter 5 for an explanation of the coolface lubrication system.

The GM 3942416 intake pushrods and GM 3942415 exhaust pushrods, when used with pushrod guide plates, are the best pushrods offered by Chevrolet for the 454-ci engine with a solid lifter camshaft. These nonadjustable pushrods were used in the 1969 ZL-1 and L88 engines and are 7/16-inch diameter. The stock length of the Chevrolet pushrods is 8.250-inch intake and 9.250-inch exhaust. It would appear that many of the aftermarket cylinder heads require the use of longer pushrods than the stock length pushrods. The cylinder heads that will be installed on the engine described here require the use of the Crower Cams & Equipment Company 70308-1 nonadjustable RC60 heat-treated pushrods,

0.050 inch longer than stock. These pushrods are 7/16-inch diameter, the intake length is 8.300 inches, and the exhaust length is 9.300 inches. The current retail price for a set of these pushrods is $140. Refer to Chapter 5 for a photograph of the Crower Cams & Equipment Company 70308-1 pushrods.

Instead of the usual timing chain and gear set, we will install a Pete Jackson 427-5C quiet dual idler gear drive in this engine. The dual idler gear drives offer precise camshaft timing, which is definitely necessary when an engine approaches the 500-horsepower mark. The GM 330850 timing gear cover was installed on the 1970 to 1974 Corvette 454-ci engines. The Pete Jackson 427-5C gear drive currently retails for $155.

The GM 6260482 (casting number 6272990) is one of the best cast-iron large rectangular port big-block Chevrolet cylinder heads from the early 1970s. This open combustion chamber design cylinder head was the special high-performance model offered in 1971. It was fitted with 2.19-inch head diameter intake valves and 1.88-inch head diameter exhaust valves. The intake port runner volume was said to be 325 cc, the exhaust port runner volume 127 cc, and the combustion chamber volume 118 cc.

The GM 353047 (casting number 353049) is one of the best cast-iron large oval port big-block Chevrolet cylinder heads from the early 1970s. This semi-open combustion chamber design cylinder head was offered in 1973. It was fitted with 2.06-inch head diameter intake valves and 1.72-inch head diameter exhaust valves. The intake port runner volume was said to be 240 cc, the exhaust port runner volume 119 cc, and the combustion chamber volume 113 cc. The larger 2.19-inch head diameter intake valves and the 1.88-inch head diameter exhaust can be installed for street performance use, provided the combustion chambers are unshrouded (laying back).

The GM 3946072 (casting number 3946074) is the best aluminum large rectangular port big-block Chevrolet cylinder head from the late 1960s. This open combustion chamber design cylinder head was installed on the 1969 ZL-1 and L88 engines, and it was fitted with 2.19-inch head diameter intake valves and 1.88-inch head diameter exhaust valves. The intake port runner volume was said to be 325 cc, the exhaust port runner volume 122 cc, and the combustion chamber volume 115 cc.

Since the introduction of the big-block Chevrolet cylinder heads in 1965, all have had screw-in rocker arm studs and guide plates. In 1968, the temperature-sending unit was installed in a boss in the left (driver's side) cylinder head. In 1969, Chevrolet introduced the open combustion chamber design cylinder heads. In 1970, Chevrolet changed to the 5/8-inch hex head spark plugs with a tapered seat. In 1973, Chevrolet introduced hardened exhaust valve seat inserts for use with unleaded gasoline.

Purchase used cylinder heads with caution—many cylinder heads have been improperly assembled and may have poor intake and exhaust port work or they may have been damaged beyond

A World Products 3003B (bare) Merlin cast-iron cylinder head that has been assembled with 2.19-inch head diameter stainless-steel intake valves and 1.88-inch head diameter stainless-steel exhaust valves.

The cylinder heads are complete with 2.19-inch head diameter stainless-steel intake valves, 1.88-inch head diameter stainless-steel exhaust valves, valves springs, valve spring retainers, valve stem locks, valve stem seals, hardened interlocking ductile iron exhaust valve seat inserts, bronze valve guides, CNC-shaped intake and exhaust ports, matched gaskets, 7/16-inch diameter heat-treated rocker arm studs, and hardened steel guide plates. The Edelbrock 6045 cylinder heads are currently available at a retail price of $1,719 for a fully assembled pair.

In my desire to outperform the Chevrolet LS7 engine, I made the classic mistake of installing a set of World Products 3003B (bare) Merlin large rectangular port cast-iron cylinder heads on the engine described here. These open chamber design cylinder heads were some of the earliest cylinder heads that World Products introduced, and they have an intake port runner volume of 320 cc, an exhaust port runner volume of 110 cc, and a combustion chamber volume of 122 cc. In retrospect, I should have purchased a set of the World Products 3004B (bare) large oval port cast-iron cylinder heads. Those cylinder heads have an intake port runner volume of 269 cc and a combustion chamber volume of 119 cc. The World Products 3003B (bare) Merlin cylinder heads have too much intake port runner volume for street performance use with a Chevrolet 454-ci engine. The engine described here did not have the throttle response under 3,000 rpm that it should have. If the engine had a displacement over 490-ci, the Merlin large rectangular port cylinder heads would have been ideal.

The early World Products 3003B (bare) cylinder heads required a lot of porting and polishing work, as well as gasket matching. The current World Products 030030 (bare) cast-iron large rectangular port cylinder heads are CNC machined and require little, if any, preparation work. The current retail price for a set of World Products Merlin cast-iron cylinder heads is $960 for the bare rectangular port or oval port castings. The World Products Merlin cast-iron cylinder heads require the use of the World Products 7301 or GM

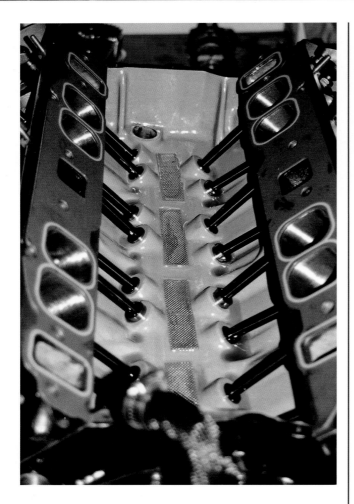

A set of big-block Chevrolet (casting number 336781) cast-iron oval port cylinder heads with a semi-open combustion chamber design. The intake port runner volume is 225 cc, the exhaust port runner volume is 114 cc, and the combustion chamber volume is 113 cc. Those are Iskenderian Racing Cams 203-96 seamless chrome-moly steel 7/16-inch-diameter pushrods.

repair. Used cylinder heads must be cleaned, Magnafluxed, pressure tested, ported and polished and gasket matched, the combustion chambers cc'd, hardened interlocking ductile iron exhaust valve seat inserts installed, and bronze valve guide liners installed. The cost of all these procedures, plus the initial purchase price of the cylinder heads, will add up very quickly. It is far more economical to purchase a new set of cylinder heads that have been CNC machined to precise tolerances.

The Edelbrock 6045 Performer RPM (non-emission) aluminum oval port cylinder heads with semi-open combustion chamber design are some of the best cylinder heads for street performance big-block Chevrolet 454-ci engines. These cylinder heads have a 290-cc intake port runner volume, 110-cc exhaust port runner volume, and a combustion chamber volume of 110 cc.

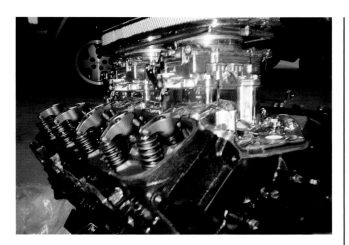

The Competition Cams 1411-16 Magnum roller tip rocker arms installed on the World Products 3003B (bare) Merlin cast-iron cylinder heads.

3977170 eight-cylinder head bolts. These are 1 inch longer than stock, and they currently retail at $20 for the eight pieces.

The Manley 11528 Race Master stainless-steel intake valves (2.19-inch head diameter by 3/8-inch stem diameter) and the Manley 11527 Race Master stainless-steel exhaust valves (1.88-inch head diameter by 3/8-inch stem diameter) were installed in the World Products 3003B (bare) cylinder heads with a Serdi-machined multi-angle blueprint valve grind. Enginetech S2890 viton positive seal valve stem seals were installed. The Manley intake and exhaust valves have a current retail price of $175 for the 16 valves.

The Crower Cams & Equipment Company 68340 tungsalloy dual valve springs with damper have an installed height of: 128 pounds at 1.875 inches valves closed and 335 pounds at 1.350 inches valves open; these valve springs were installed. The Crower Cams & Equipment Company 87063 chrome-moly steel 7-degree valve spring retainers and the Crower Cams & Equipment Company 86102 stamped steel 7-degree valve stem locks (3/8-inch stem diameter) were also installed. The Crower Cams & Equipment Company valve springs, valve spring retainers, and valve stem locks have a current retail price of $160.

There were some 1973 to 1981 big-block Chevrolet cast-iron cylinder heads that had exhaust valve rotators installed. If you choose to use dual valve springs, you will have to install valve spring seat spacers, or exhaust valve rotator eliminators, such as the Hastings 4779-8 model.

A new set of Manley 42149 hardened-steel raised guide plates was installed with a set of ARP 135-7101 high-performance-series rocker arm studs (7/16-inch diameter). The current retail price of the Manley guide plates and the ARP rocker arm studs is $90. A new set of Competition Cams 1411-16 Magnum roller tip rocker arms (1.72 ratio) was installed, and the current retail price for the set is $146. Refer to Chapter 5 for a photograph of the Manley 42149 guide plates.

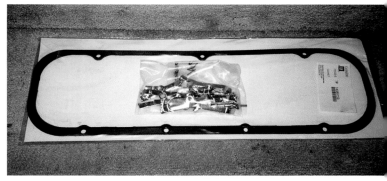

A GM 14085759 valve cover gasket and Moroso 68516 chrome valve cover hold-down tabs.

New GM 3877668 and GM 3877669 cylinder head bolts were installed. The long bolts are torqued to 75 ft-lb, and the short bolts are torqued to 65 ft-lb using Permatex aviation form-a-gasket. The ARP 135-3603 professional series (170,000 psi) cylinder head bolts are designed for use with the World Products Merlin cast-iron cylinder heads and are available at a current retail price of $90.

The GM 14085759 valve cover gaskets are some of the best valve cover gaskets to use on a big-block Chevrolet 454-ci engine. The gaskets are manufactured using neoprene rubber with a steel core and can be reused numerous times. They are available from Chevrolet dealers for the current retail price of $35 for two. A new set of Zip Products VC-207 chrome Corvette valve covers, with dripper rails and power brake slant, was installed with Moroso 68516 chrome valve cover hold-down tabs. The valve covers have a current retail price of $130, and the valve cover hold-down tabs cost about $20 for a set of 14. Refer to Chapter 5 for photographs of the Zip Products VC-207 chrome valve covers.

Intake System

Chevrolet offered a number of high-performance cast-aluminum intake manifolds for the Mark IV big-block engines. The GM 3933163 (casting number 3933163) dual-plane high-rise, single four-barrel intake manifold (intended for use with large rectangular ports) was installed on the 1965 to 1969 Chevrolet special high-performance engines. The GM 977609 (casting number 3963569) dual-plane low-rise, single four-barrel intake manifold (intended for use with large rectangular ports) was installed on the LS6 engine. The GM 3957994 (casting number 3947801) dual-plane low-rise, single four-barrel intake manifold (intended for use with large oval ports) was installed on the 1968 to 1969 Corvette engines.

It is very difficult in this day and age to find an original big-block Chevrolet intake manifold from the 1960s and 1970s in decent condition. Unless you need a specific intake manifold for a "numbers matching" vehicle, you will be better off with one of the

A Weiand 7544 single-plane aluminum intake manifold for a big-block Chevrolet engine with large oval port cylinder heads. The power range is from 1,500 to 7,000 rpm. "Tim, the polishing guy" has been at this gem!

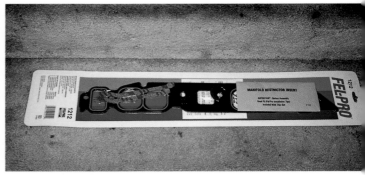

A Fel-Pro 1212 intake manifold gasket set for use with large oval port cylinder heads.

many aftermarket aluminum intake manifolds available that will suit just about any type of application.

The GM 12555320 intake manifold oil splash shield is an excellent item to install in any big-block Chevrolet engine. The part fits beneath the intake manifold, over the valve lifter gallery, and is available at a current retail price of $15. Refer to Chapter 4 for a photograph of this item.

When I started to build this engine, I decided that I wanted something different for the intake system in my 1969 Corvette. I settled on an Offenhauser 5594 low-profile large rectangular port aluminum, dual-quad intake manifold with two Edelbrock 1405 performer series 600-cfm carburetors. Even though I had a high-rise L88 hood and a low-rise intake manifold, I was still faced with a clearance problem between the top of the air cleaner and the underside of the hood. Luke's Custom Machine & Design milled a section approximately 6 inches long by 1 inch high from the top of the air cleaner, thus permitting a minimum of hood clearance.

The Chevrolet 454-ci engine requires a mechanical fuel pump capable of providing a sufficient volume of fuel. The Holley 12-454 performance fuel pump, (6 to 8 psi, 110 gph) with its chrome-like appearance, is a good choice. The lower part of this fuel pump can rotate, permitting the fuel inlet and outlet fittings to be placed in the best position. The current retail price for the Holley 12-454 fuel pump is $70. The GM 3704817 fuel pump pushrod (1/2-inch diameter by 5 3/4-inch length) was installed in all the Chevrolet V-8 engines from 1955 to 1980.

Ignition System

A Mallory 3864501 Unilite distributor with the mechanical tachometer drive will be installed in the engine described here. Refer to Chapter 7 for information on distributors, ignition coils, spark plug wires, alternators, and starting motors.

The firing order for all the Mark IV big-block Chevrolet engines is: 1, 8, 4, 3, 6, 5, 7, and 2. The left (driver's side) bank from the

front: 1, 3, 5, and 7 cylinders. The right (passenger's side) bank from the front: 2, 4, 6, and 8 cylinders.

A number of brackets and braces are required to install the alternator and power steering pump in the 1968 to 1972 Corvettes equipped with a big-block Chevrolet engine. These are: the GM 3878236 alternator bracket, the GM 3946000 alternator/power steering pump brace, the GM 3986109 alternator upper support bracket, and the GM 3878240 alternator lower support bracket. The air conditioning compressor is mounted using the GM 3894364 rear mounting bracket, the GM 3894362 front mounting bracket, and the GM 3887167 front support bracket.

Cooling and Exhaust Systems

Install the water pump bypass hose on a big-block Chevrolet engine. Depending on the location of the water pump bypass hose fitting in the intake manifold, it might not be possible to install the stock Chevrolet fittings. Weatherhead produces brass fittings of all types to overcome this problem.

A set of Hedman Hedders 68090 metallic-ceramic-coated exhaust headers were installed on this engine. Refer to Chapter 8 to view a photograph of these exhaust headers.

Engine Summary

Note: This is the first engine I installed in my 1969 Corvette coupe. Even though I should have installed large oval port cylinder heads on this engine, it performed very well, especially with the camshaft designed for street performance use. I accomplished my original goal of achieving more horsepower and torque than the 1970 Corvette LS7 engine.

Engine Block

• 1989 Chevrolet 454-ci L19 engine block; casting number 14015445; casting date: E249 (May 24, 1989); stock bore: 4.251 inches; stock stroke: 4.00 inches; four-bolt main bearing caps; 9.80-

The Offenhauser 5594 dual-quad intake manifold. The forward section of the air cleaner had to be milled for hood clearance.

All the brackets and braces required to mount the alternator, power steering pump, and air conditioning compressor in a 1968 to 1972 Corvette equipped with a big-block Chevrolet engine.

inch deck height; light-duty truck, 230 horsepower; engine block weight (bare): 195 pounds; $285

• Engine block hot tanked; engine block and main bearing caps and bolts Magnafluxed; main bearing caps and bolts shot peened; all threads retapped; cylinder head bolt holes chamfered; valve lifter bosses deglazed, allowing for 0.002-inch valve lifter clearance; No. 5 main bearing cap oil pump cavity polished; 0.0625-inch hole drilled in bottom center of face of front camshaft boss, and 0.041-inch hole drilled in top front oil gallery line plugs for additional oiling; valve lifter gallery and front of engine block ground smooth and painted with Glyptal G-1228A medium-grey gloss enamel; Moroso 25001 oil gallery screen kit installed; exterior surface of engine block sanded, detailed, and painted with Plasti-Kote 203 black high-gloss engine enamel; Dorman 565-034 brass freeze plugs, rear camshaft boss plug, and stainless-steel oil gallery line plugs installed using Permatex aviation form-a-gasket; Weatherhead 3152-4 polished-brass water jacket drain plugs (1/4-inch NPT) installed using pipe thread sealant; $471.75

• Engine block cylinders honed and deglazed using torque plate and Sunnen 800 series 400-grit stones, final bore: 4.251 inches; piston-to-bore clearance: 0.004 inch measured below bottom of wrist pin perpendicular to wrist pin; $65

• Engine block align honed; $200

• Engine block parallel decked to 0.010-inch average below deck; $110

Engine block total: $1,131.75

Crankshaft

• GM 3963523 (casting number 3520) forged 1053 steel, journals nitrided, externally balanced; main bearing journal diameter: 2.750 inches; connecting rod journal diameter: 2.20 inches; crankshaft weight: 70 pounds; $525

• Crankshaft shot peened, Magnafluxed, aligned; main bearing journals ground 0.020-inch undersize, connecting rod journals ground 0.010-inch undersize; oil holes chamfered, journals polished, and crankshaft balanced; Moroso 41100 roller pilot bearing installed using anti-seize compound; $235

• Clevite 77 MS-829P-20 main bearings (0.020-inch oversize) installed allowing for 0.002-inch crankshaft clearance and 0.007-inch end play; GM 3909834 inner main bearing cap bolts, GM 3902885 windage tray studs, and 3859927 outer main bearing cap bolts torqued to 110 ft-lb using molykote; $87

• Fluidampr 712105 harmonic balancer (8-inch o.d., weight: 17.3 pounds) installed with Mr. Gasket 946 chrome crankshaft bolt and flat washer using Loctite and torqued to 85 ft-lb; $330

• GM 3921923 chrome double-groove crankshaft pulley (6 3/4-inch o.d.) installed with polished stainless-steel bolts, lockwashers, and flat washers using Loctite and torqued to 30 ft-lb; $75

Crankshaft total: $1,252

Connecting Rods and Pistons

• GM 3969804 (green dot) forged 4340 steel I-beam connecting rods, full-floating wrist pins (6.135-inch stock length) with GM 3969864 boron 10B39 steel connecting rod bolts (7/16-inch diameter by 2 3/4-inch length, 220,000 psi), and GM 3942410 connecting rod bolt nuts installed; connecting rod weight: 790 grams each; connecting rod ratio: 1.53 (with 4.00-inch stroke crankshaft); $525

• Connecting rods shot peened, Magnafluxed, debeamed, aligned, resized, pin fitted allowing for 0.002-inch wrist pin clearance, and balanced; $300

• Clevite 77 CB-743P-10 connecting rod bearings (0.010-inch oversize) installed allowing for 0.002-inch connecting rod clearance and 0.017-inch side clearance per pair of connecting rods; connecting rod bolts torqued to 80 ft-lb using molykote and allowing for 0.009-inch stretch; $50

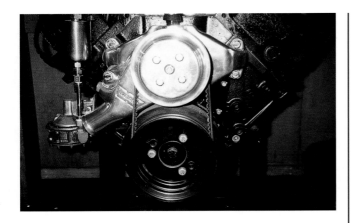

A Weiand 8212 short-style polished-aluminum water pump mounted on a big-block Chevrolet 454-ci engine with a GM 3921923 double v-belt crankshaft pulley. A Holley 12-454 mechanical fuel pump is visible as well.

• TRW 2399F power-forged standard-size aluminum racing pistons, 9.00:1 compression ratio, 13.8-cc slight domed top, open combustion chamber design; piston weight: 658 grams each; full-floating heat-treated and casehardened 4340 chrome-moly straight-wall wrist pins installed allowing for 0.002-inch connecting rod clearance; wrist pin weight: 152 grams; Tru-Arc wrist pin retainers installed; piston ring grooves: top compression ring: 5/64 inch; second compression ring: 5/64 inch; oil ring: 3/16 inch; Sealed Power (Federal Mogul) R9590-5 plasma-moly-coated top piston ring set installed within manufacturer's recommended arc; top compression ring gap: 0.020 inch; second compression ring gap: 0.018 inch; oil ring gap: 0.018 inch; piston tops painted with V.H.T. SP-101 white high-temperature coating; intake-valve-to-piston clearance: 0.175 inch; exhaust-valve-to-piston clearance (without gasket): 0.190 inch; $500

• Complete V-8 engine balance; Fel-Pro 2805 complete gasket set installed; $300

Connecting rods and pistons total: $1,675

Lubrication System

• Melling M77 standard-volume oil pump with pressure balance grooves and GM 6269895 oil pump pickup screen tack welded in place; oil pump cover end clearance: 0.00025 inch; oil pump cover gasket installed using silicone sealant and bolts torqued to 80 in-lb using Loctite; Melling 12577 oil pump driveshaft (6 1/2 inches long) with heat-treated ends installed; Manley 42339 oil pump stud kit installed using Loctite and torqued to 65 ft-lb; $78

• Milodon 32260 Diamond Stripper windage tray installed with nuts torqued to 25 ft-lb using Loctite; Milodon 30950 chrome low-profile oil pan (7-quart capacity) installed with ARP 435-1802 polished stainless-steel bolts (six-point head, 170,000 psi) using Loctite and torqued to 15 ft-lb; oil pan gaskets and rear oil seals installed using silicone sealant; Trans-Dapt 4958 chrome dip stick

and dip stick tube installed; GM 3952301 oil filter adapter installed using Loctite on bolts and torqued to 20 ft-lb; Fram PH-13 oil filter installed with Trans-Dapt 1067 chrome oil filter cover; engine lubricated with 7 quarts Pennzoil HD-30-weight motor oil; $373.67

Lubrication system total: $451.67

Camshaft and Cylinder Heads

• Clevite 77 SH-616S camshaft bearings installed with 0.002-inch camshaft clearance and 0.002-inch camshaft end play; No. 1 bearing: SH-615, housing bore: 2.1395 to 2.1405 inches; No. 2 and 5 bearing: SH-616, housing bore: 2.1295 to 2.1305 inches; No. 3 and 4 bearing: SH-617, housing bore: 2.1195 to 2.1205 inches; camshaft journal diameter: 1.950 inches; $35

• Crower Cams & Equipment Company 01321 294F solid (mechanical) lifter camshaft with advertised duration: 294 degrees intake and 300 degrees exhaust; duration at 0.050-inch lift: 244 degrees intake and 246 degrees exhaust; lobe separation angle: 114 degrees; net valve lift (with 1.72 ratio rocker arms): 0.501 inch intake and 0.513 inch exhaust; valve lash (hot): 0.022 inch intake and 0.024 inch exhaust; camshaft degreed; $115

• Crower Cams & Equipment Company 66900 precision-ground radius face solid lifters (0.842-inch diameter), stock pushrod seat height with new 66980 coolface 0.024-inch oil metering hole; Crower Cams & Equipment Company 70308-1 nonadjustable pushrods (7/16-inch diameter), 4130 seamless chrome-moly steel, ends heat-treated to surface hardness RC60, 0.050 inch longer than stock; intake pushrod length: 8.30 inches, and exhaust pushrod length: 9.30 inches; GM 12555320 intake manifold oil splash shield painted with Glyptal G-1228A medium-grey gloss enamel and installed; $270

• Pete Jackson 427-5C quiet dual idler gear drive with roller camshaft button installed with camshaft bolts torqued to 20 ft-lb using Loctite; GM 330850 chrome timing gear cover installed with ARP 400-1501 polished stainless-steel bolt kit (12-point heads) using Loctite and torqued to 15 ft-lb; Trans-Dapt 4961 chrome timing gear cover tab installed; GM 10191640 timing gear cover oil seal installed; $195

• World Products 3003B (bare) Merlin large rectangular port, open combustion chamber, high-density cast-iron cylinder heads; cylinder heads surfaced; intake port runner volume: 320 cc; exhaust port runner volume: 110 cc; combustion chamber volume: 118 cc; intake and exhaust ports fully ported, polished, and gasket matched; combustion chambers polished and cc'd; hardened interlocking ductile iron exhaust valve seat inserts installed; K-Line KL1842STA bronze bullet universal-length (3/8-inch diameter) bronze valve guide liners installed; Serdi-machined multi-angle blueprint valve grind performed; exterior surface of cylinder heads painted with Plasti-Kote 203 black high-gloss engine enamel; cylinder heads installed with Fel-Pro 8180PT-1 permatorque blue stripe cylinder head gaskets; GM 3877668 (long) and GM

3877669 (short) cylinder head bolts and World Products 7301 (eight) cylinder head bolts (1 inch longer than stock) installed using Permatex aviation form-a-gasket with the long bolts torqued to 75 ft-lb and the short bolts torqued to 65 ft-lb; $1,755

• Manley 11528 Race Master stainless-steel intake valves (2.19-inch head diameter, 3/8-inch stem diameter, 4.951-inch length overall), hardened tips swirl polished; weight: 135 grams each; Manley 11527 Race Master stainless steel exhaust valves (1.88-inch head diameter, 3/8-inch stem diameter, 4.951-inch length), hardened tips swirl polished; weight: 131 grams each; Enginetech S2890 viton positive seal valve stem seals installed; $191.20

• Crower Cams & Equipment Company 68340 tungsalloy dual valve springs with damper; installed height: 128 pounds at 1.875 inches valves closed and 335 pounds at 1.350 inches valves open; 1.505 inches o.d. and 1.125 inches/0.760 inch i.d.; coil bind: 1.100 inches; Crower Cams & Equipment Company 87063 chrome-moly steel 7-degree valve spring retainers (3/8-inch stem diameter) and 86102 stamped heat-treated steel 7-degree valve stem locks (3/8-inch stem diameter) stock height, installed; $154.13

• Manley 42149 hardened-steel raised pushrod guide plates, for 7/16-inch pushrods, installed with ARP 135-7101 high-performance-series 8740 chrome-moly steel rocker arm studs (7/16-inch diameter, 170,000 psi) using Loctite and torqued to 50 ft-lb; Competition Cams 1411-16 Magnum roller tip rocker arms (1.72 ratio) with grooved rocker arm balls, installed with Manley 42112 heat-treated chrome-moly steel sure-lock rocker arm nuts (7/16-inch studs) using anti-seize compound; $232.32

• Zip Products VC-207 chrome Corvette valve covers, with dripper rails and power brake slant, installed with GM 14085759 valve cover gaskets using silicone sealant; Moroso 68516 chrome valve cover hold-down tabs installed with polished stainless-steel bolts and lockwashers using Loctite and torqued to 15 ft-lb; Trans-Dapt 4878 rubber grommet installed with Trans-Dapt 4870 chrome push-in breather; Trans-Dapt 4998 rubber grommet installed with a Motorcraft EV-49-B PCV valve; Gates 3225 PCV valve line (5/16-inch i.d. by 1 foot long) installed with Spectre 3001A black nylabraid and Spectre 3208B chrome champclamps; Zip Products IS-226A and IS-226C spark plug wire supports/dividers installed; Chicago Corvette Supply B2363 right-hand valve cover decal "Tonawanda #1 Team" installed; Dr. Rebuild 1758122 chrome oil filler cap installed; $264.32

Camshaft and cylinder heads total: $3,211.97

Intake System

• Offenhauser 5594 equa-flow, 360-degree, low-profile polished aluminum dual-quad intake manifold with large rectangular ports, gasket matched; port size: 1 5/8 inches by 2 5/16 inches; power range: 1,500 to 6,000 rpm; underside of intake manifold painted with V.H.T. SP-101 white high-temperature coating; Fel-

The water pump bypass fittings and the temperature-sending unit used on a big-block Chevrolet engine.

Pro 1275 intake manifold gaskets (port size: 1.82 inches by 2.54 inches) installed using silicone sealant; Trans-Dapt 9266 chrome intake manifold bolts and AN flat washers installed using Loctite and torqued to 25 ft-lb; $450.32

• Edelbrock 1405 performer series 600-cfm carburetors, square flange, manual choke, installed with Trans-Dapt 2046 carburetor stud kits using anti-seize compound; Edelbrock 8090 inverted flare nut fittings installed; $413.30

• Speedway Motors 925-11903 Cobra Style polished cast-aluminum air cleaner installed with K&N E-1960 air filter (21 inches long by 10 inches wide by 1.80 inches high); $289.95

• Trans-Dapt 9229 chrome O-ring thermostat housing with Robert Shaw 330-160 extra performance balanced 160-degree (Fahrenheit) thermostat installed with chrome bolts and lockwashers using silicone sealant and torqued to 20 ft-lb; stainless-steel 1/2-inch NPT plug installed using pipe thread sealant; Stewart-Warner 284-E mechanical fuel-pressure gauge and Stewart-Warner 284-AH vacuum gauge installed with Stewart-Warner 814143-F chrome mounting bracket; Moroso 64926 chrome throttle cable return spring and bracket installed; $123.70

• Holley 12-454 chrome performance mechanical fuel pump (6 to 8 psi, 110 gph) installed with polished stainless-steel bolts and lockwashers using Loctite and torqued to 20 ft-lb; fuel pump gasket installed using silicone sealant; Weatherhead 3200-6-4 polished-brass adapter (3/8-inch NPT to 1/4-inch NPT) and Weatherhead 402-6-6 polished-brass 90-degree elbow (3/8-inch tube to 3/8-inch NPT) installed using pipe thread sealant; GM 3704817 fuel pump pushrod (1/2-inch diameter by 5 3/4-inch length) installed; Holley 162-530 chrome inline fuel filter (discontinued) installed with Weatherhead 100-6 polished-brass inverted flare nuts (3/8-inch tube), and Bundyflex B612 chrome fuel lines (3/8-inch tube by 2-foot length) using pipe thread sealant; $127.68

Intake system total: $1,404.95

Ignition System

• Mallory 3864501 Unilite distributor, with photo-optic infrared LED system, mechanical tachometer drive, 356 T-6 billet

This great-looking engine was installed in my 1969 Corvette coupe frame. I spent many long days building the engine up to this condition.

My Chevrolet 454-ci engine installed in the 1969 Corvette coupe frame. The frame is painted with Endura EX-2C black 160 high-gloss polyurethane, and all the bolts, fuel lines, and brake lines are stainless steel. That is a Muncie M-20 four-speed manual transmission behind the engine.

aluminum housing, mechanical advance, installed with GM 14007385 chrome distributor clamp and polished stainless-steel bolt and lockwasher using anti-seize compound; Mallory 29440 Promaster ignition coil and Mallory 29026 HyFire electronic ignition control installed; $463.85

• Taylor/Vertex 70053 Pro Series black 8-millimeter high-performance spark plug wires, 135-degree boots, Spiro-Pro Kelvar resistor core, installed; Taylor 42800 black plastic spark plug wire separator kit installed; NGK UR4 v-power resistor-type spark plugs installed with 0.050-inch gap; $75.57

• Aries KC-11 chrome internally regulated alternator (63 amps) installed with GM 3878236 chrome alternator bracket, GM 3946000 chrome alternator/power steering pump brace, GM 3986109 chrome alternator upper support bracket, and GM 3878240 chrome alternator lower support bracket using new polished stainless-steel bolts, lockwashers, flat washers, and nylocks; Gates 11A0800 crankshaft/water pump pulley v-belt (7/16-inch by 31 1/2-inch length) installed; Gates 11A1370 crankshaft/power steering pump/alternator pulley v-belt (7/16-inch by 54-inch length) installed; $347.28

• TCI Automotive 351100 high-torque racing starter, draws 25 amps and produces 2.5 horsepower of cranking output, installed with new bolts using anti-seize compound; $200.95

Ignition total: $1,087.65

Cooling and Exhaust Systems

• Edelbrock 8852 Victor Series polished 356 T-6 aluminum water pump (3/4-inch pilot shaft) installed with polished stainless-steel bolts and lockwashers using Loctite and torqued to 25 ft-lb; water pump gaskets installed using silicone sealant; GM 3992071BE chrome water pump pulley (5 1/2-inch diameter, triple groove) installed with polished stainless-steel bolts and lockwashers using Loctite and torqued to 25 ft-lb; Turbo-Flex 24200 polished-aluminum fan spacer (2 inches thick) and Hayden 3717 polished

stainless-steel heavy-duty 17-inch-diameter fan installed; GM 3829819 chrome thermal bypass connector (water pump fitting), Weatherhead 1430 polished-brass hose connector (1/2-inch NPT to 3/4-inch i.d. hose; intake manifold fitting), and GM 1485552 water pump bypass hose installed with stainless-steel line clamps; hose covered with Spectre 3001A black nylabraid and Spectre 3208B chrome champclamps; $473.85

• GM 5910741 rebuilt chrome air conditioning compressor installed with GM 3894364 chrome rear compressor mounting bracket, GM 3894362 chrome front compressor mounting bracket, and GM 3887167 chrome front compressor support bracket using polished stainless-steel bolts and lockwashers with Loctite; Gates 11A1195 air conditioning compressor/water pump pulley v-belt (7/16 inch by 47 inches long) installed; $610

• Hedman Hedders 68090 metallic-ceramic-coated exhaust headers installed with Fel-Pro 1412 exhaust manifold gaskets, 2.13-inch-diameter exhaust ports, using Permatex ultra copper high-temperature silicone sealant; Trans-Dapt 8912 Stage 8 polished stainless-steel self-locking exhaust header bolts installed using Loctite and torqued to 25 ft-lb; $466.14

Cooling and exhaust systems total: $1,549.99

Labor

• Labor for checking clearances, gapping piston rings, degree camshaft, valvetrain assembly, detailing, trial engine assembly, final engine assembly, and initial engine start-up; $800

Labor total: $800

Engine Grand Total: $12,564.98 (U.S.)

Note: The estimated output of this engine is 521 horsepower at 5,500 rpm and 533 ft-lb torque at 4,500 rpm (see Appendix A—Dyno Print-Outs).

CHAPTER 13
CHEVROLET
492-ci ENGINE

Five years after I completed my 1969 Corvette coupe, I decided it was time to do something about the engine, although it ran beautifully. The fact I had installed large rectangular port cylinder heads instead of the large oval port cylinder heads continued to bother me. I had two options. I could build a set of large oval port cylinder heads and install them, or I could build a new engine and keep the large rectangular port cylinder heads. I decided on the second option.

In one respect, it is easier to remove a big-block Chevrolet engine from a 1969 Corvette than it is to change the cylinder heads. There is not a lot of room in the engine compartment of my Corvette due to the power brake booster on one side and the air conditioning/heater housing on the other side. Besides, it was time for a seasonal upgrade. A larger displacement engine was the order of the day, and this chapter will explain the complete buildup of that engine.

Components Description
Engine Block

Once I had decided to proceed with the building of a new engine, I located a 1990 Chevrolet 454-ci engine block with four-bolt main bearing caps that was originally installed in a light-duty

The Chevrolet 492-ci engine block. All the machine work has been carried out and the engine block is O-ringed. The valve lifter gallery has been painted with Glyptal G-1228A medium-grey gloss enamel, and a Moroso 25001 oil gallery screen kit has been installed using epoxy.

truck. The purchase price was $400, subject to Magnafluxing and inspection. The previous owner told me that the engine block had just been freshly bored 0.030-inch oversize and align honed. I sent the engine block to High Performance Engines, where they discovered the cylinder boring and align honing work was less than professional. The engine block had to be rebored to 0.040-inch oversize in order to clean up the cylinders and had to be align honed (again). Other than these minor problems, the engine block was in excellent shape.

I had the engine block bored to 0.040-inch oversize in order to have enough material left in the cylinder walls to bore it 0.060-inch oversize if the need ever arose. Refer to Chapter 1 for all the information regarding engine block preparation.

In the event this engine block would someday be equipped with a blower, I also had the engine block O-ringed. There is no harm in doing this for an unblown engine, and the process guarantees a super head gasket seal.

Crankshaft

I decided prior to commencing the buildup of this engine that it would have a large displacement. The Summit Racing Equipment SES-3-91-05-C385 Proline forged 4340 aircraft-quality steel, non-twisted crankshaft was one of the best deals around at the time and retailed for $1,095. Unfortunately, this crankshaft is no longer available. The heat-treated and stress-relieved crankshaft has a 4.250-inch stroke for use with 6.385-inch-long connecting rods and is internally balanced, journal surfaces nitrided to 60 Rockwell C hardness, computer-designed counterweight positioning, rounded airplane-wing counterweight leading edges, 0.125-inch radius on journals, oil holes cross-drilled and chamfered, gun drilled No. 1 and 4 connecting rod pins, journals polished, and the crankshaft weight is 78 pounds, prior to balancing. The crankshaft is slightly on the heavy side; however, it was installed in a street performance engine and not a drag race engine, where lower crankshaft weight is critical. The crankshaft weight was reduced to 70 pounds after balancing by removing some excess weight from the crankshaft counterweights. This is the same weight as a stock crankshaft used in a Mark IV Chevrolet 454-ci engine.

The Lunati (Holley) BP421IN Racer Series forged non-twisted crankshaft is manufactured using 4340 aircraft-quality

The Summit Racing Equipment SES-3-91-05-C385 Proline forged non-twisted crankshaft with Clevite 77 MS-829H chamfered main bearings and Clevite 77 CB-743H chamfered connecting rod bearings.

The Ross Racing Pistons forged aluminum racing pistons that will be installed in the Chevrolet 492-ci engine. The piston tops have been painted with V.H.T. SP-101 white high-temperature coating.

steel and is similar to the Summit Racing Equipment Proline crankshaft previously mentioned. The Racer Series crankshafts have 0.140-inch radii on all the journals, the journals undergo a plasma gas nitrite heat treatment, the counterweights have a contoured wing design, and the oiling system is similar to the one used by Chevrolet. The Lunati BP421IN crankshaft is available for a current retail price of $1,299.

Because there is a 0.125-inch radius on the journals, you must use special chamfered bearings to build your own version of this engine. The Clevite 77 MS-829H main bearings are available in standard size, 0.001-, 0.010-, and 0.020-inch oversize. The current retail price for these main bearings is $119. The Federal Mogul 141M main bearings are available in standard size, 0.001-, 0.009-, 0.010-, 0.019-, 0.020-, 0.021-, and 0.030-inch oversize. The current retail price for these main bearings is $108.

The Summit Racing Equipment SES-3-91-05-C385 crankshaft is internally balanced and requires an internally balanced harmonic balancer. The Fluidampr 712440 harmonic balancer is designed for use with an internally balanced engine. It meets SFI specs 18.1, has a 7 1/4-inch o.d., and weighs 14.2 pounds. The current retail price for this harmonic balancer is $310, and it is available at most speed equipment dealers.

Connecting Rods and Pistons

The aftermarket is the only source for connecting rods that are longer (center to center) than stock connecting rods. If you install a stroker crankshaft in this engine, upgrade the connecting rods as well to ensure the strongest possible bottom end in the street performance engine.

The Manley forged 4340 steel H-beam connecting rods are some of the best connecting rods for street performance engines. The connecting rods are designed for use with full-floating wrist

pins. The connecting rods have been fully machined, stress relieved, shot peened, and Magnafluxed. The wrist pin bores (the small end) and crankshaft bores (the big end) are all within 0.0002-inch tolerance. The wrist pin bushings are a bronze alloy. The Manley H-beam connecting rods are designed for use with the standard Chevrolet 2.200-inch-diameter connecting rod journal, and they are available with center-to-center lengths of 6.135, 6.385, and 6.535 inches. The connecting rod bolts are ARP 42361 cap screw bolts (8740 steel, 12-point, 190,000 psi, 7/16-inch diameter). I used Manley Performance Parts 14062-8 forged 4340 steel H-beam connecting rods in this engine. They have a length of 6.385 inches (center to center) and weigh 813 grams each. The current retail price for a set of these connecting rods is $699.

Manley recommends that you soak the connecting rod bolts for these connecting rods in 30-weight motor oil and torque them to 80 ft-lb, allowing for 0.0052- to 0.0056-inch stretch. Manley also recommends a wrist pin clearance in the connecting rods of 0.0008 to 0.015 inch.

The Clevite 77 CB-743H chamfered connecting rod bearings are available in standard size, 0.001-, 0.010-, and 0.020-inch oversize. The current retail price for these connecting rod bearings is $121. The Federal Mogul 8-7200CH chamfered connecting rod bearings are available in standard size, 0.001-, 0.009-, 0.010-, 0.020-, 0.021-, and 0.030-inch oversize. The current retail price for these connecting rod bearings is $113.

If you need to have an engine bored to 0.040-inch oversize, you will need to order custom pistons. Forged aluminum pistons for the big-block Chevrolet 454-ci engine are usually available in standard size, 0.030-inch oversize, and 0.060-inch oversize. The 0.040-inch oversize is an oddball size. Purchase a set of Ross Racing Pistons forged aluminum racing pistons (0.040-inch oversize, stipulating a 10.0:1 compression ratio) with full-floating

The bottom end is complete and ready for the oil pan installation. The Melling M77HV high-volume oil pump with the Milodon 18301 oil pump screen, the Milodon 32260 Diamond Stripper windage tray, and the Manley 14062-8 H-beam connecting rods are all in plain sight.

The Crower Cams & Equipment Company 01476 street solid roller camshaft.

wrist pins, designed for use with a 4.250-inch stroke crankshaft and 6.385-inch-long (center to center) connecting rods. These pistons have a 0.185-inch-high dome designed for use with open combustion chambers, and they weigh 583 grams each. The current retail price for a set of these pistons is $750, including straight-wall wrist pins. Because the oil ring intersects the wrist pin hole in the piston, Ross Racing Pistons provides oil ring support rails and double Spiro-Lox retainers with the pistons.

Purchase a set of Sealed Power (Federal Mogul) E-233K-40 moly top ring piston rings. These piston rings are designed for a top compression ring groove width of 5/64 inch, a second compression ring groove width of 5/64 inch, and an oil ring groove width of 3/16 inch. The current retail price for a set of these moly top ring piston rings is $55.

Lubrication System

Drill a 0.0625-inch hole in the bottom center of the face of the front camshaft boss and drill 0.041-inch holes in the two top oil gallery line plugs to provide additional oiling for the dual idler camshaft gear drive.

Due to the large displacement of this engine, I installed a Melling M77HV high-volume oil pump with pressure-balance grooves and tack welded a Milodon 18301 CNC-machined billet oil pump screen to the oil pump. This oil pump pickup is compatible with the Milodon 30950 low-profile oil pan. Refer to Chapter 12 for information about oil pans, oil pump driveshafts and stud kits, and windage trays.

I decided to paint the oil pan for this engine with Endura EX-2C black 160 high-gloss polyurethane, rather than chrome plating it like the oil pan on the first engine described in Chapter 12. It is almost impossible to keep a chrome oil pan polished in a 1969 Corvette that is driven on the street. If you have a chrome oil pan and do not keep it polished, it will soon break out with tiny rust spots. As much as it hurts, there are times when you must take a practical approach to building an engine.

Camshaft and Cylinder Heads

Refer to Chapter 12 for information regarding camshaft bearings.

The Chevrolet 492-ci engine requires a camshaft capable of delivering the necessary performance that is also suitable for street use. For those reasons, I chose the Crower Cams & Equipment Company 01476 290R street solid (mechanical) roller lifter camshaft. This camshaft has an advertised duration of 290 degrees intake and 296 degrees exhaust; duration at 0.050-inch lift: 252 degrees intake and 254 degrees exhaust; lobe separation angle: 112 degrees; valve lift: 0.585 inch intake and 0.578 inch exhaust; valve lash (hot): 0.026 inch intake and 0.028 inch exhaust. The current retail price for this camshaft is $245.

Crower Cams & Equipment recommends the use of the GM 992869 engine oil supplement (EOS) for the break-in period of its camshafts. Pour a can of this product in the valve lifter gallery, over the camshaft lifters, prior to installing the intake manifold.

Use the Crower Cams & Equipment Company 66201 solid roller lifters with the camshaft mentioned previously. These roller lifters are made of CNC-machine milled chrome-moly steel with heat-treated expanded edge orifice metering system, crowned bearings and crowned outer race, Torrington oversize control contoured tapered needle bearings, Torque-Lock fasteners, stock pushrod seat height, and 0.842-inch o.d. The current retail price for the Crower Cams & Equipment Company 66201 solid roller

The World Products 3003B (bare) cast-iron cylinder heads ready for assembly. The K-Line 9832STA bronze valve guide liners and Serdi-machined valve seat insert work are visible.

The Manley 42149 hardened-steel raised guide plates and ARP 134-7101 high-performance-series 7/16-inch rocker arm studs have been installed. The area around these items has been painted with Glyptal G-1228A medium-grey gloss enamel.

lifters is $285. You can find a photograph of these solid roller lifters in Chapter 5.

Reuse the Crower Cams & Equipment Company 70308-1 nonadjustable pushrods. These pushrods are manufactured using 4130 seamless chrome-moly steel (7/16-inch diameter and 0.050 inch longer than stock), and the ends are heat-treated to surface hardness RC60. There is a photograph of these pushrods in Chapter 5.

Purchase an Edelbrock 7891 Accu-Drive dual idler gear drive with SAE (Society of Automotive Engineers) 8620 steel gears, currently available for the retail price of $200. Do not reuse the GM 330850 chrome timing gear cover because it is almost impossible to polish once the water pump is installed. For a more practical approach, paint the timing gear cover with polyurethane paint.

As previously mentioned, I used the cylinder heads from the Chevrolet 454-ci engine described in Chapter 12 on this engine. The World Products Merlin large rectangular port cast-iron cylinder heads were in excellent shape due to the low number of miles they had been used. As a result of the limited use, I did not have to have them Magnafluxed again or resurfaced. The larger displacement of this engine required the installation of larger intake and exhaust valves. Have the cylinder heads disassembled, hot tanked, and painted. Have the combustion chambers unshrouded (laying back) to accommodate the 2.25-inch head diameter intake valves and 1.90-inch head diameter exhaust valves. Install new bronze valve guide liners for the use of 11/32-inch stem diameter valves. Once again, have a Serdi-machined multi-angle blueprint valve grind performed.

Install Manley 11874 Race Master stainless-steel intake valves

(2.25-inch head diameter by 11/32-inch stem diameter) and Manley 11883 Race Master stainless-steel exhaust valves (1.90-inch head diameter by 11/32-inch stem diameter) along with the Serdi-machined multi-angle blueprint valve grind. Install Enginetech S2927 viton positive seal valve stem seals. The current retail price for the Manley stainless-steel valves, described above, is $240.

Install Crower Cams & Equipment Company 68389 dual silicone valve springs with damper and an installed height of: 125 pounds at 1.90 inches valves closed and 360 pounds at 1.30 inches valves open. Also install Crower Cams & Equipment Company 87060 heat-treated chrome-moly steel 10-degree valve spring retainers and Crower Cams & Equipment Company 86110-1 jumbo split-lock 10-degree valve stem locks (11/32-inch stem diameter, 0.050 inch longer than stock). These items have a current retail price of $175. There is a photograph of the Crower Cams & Equipment Company 68389 valve springs in Chapter 5.

I retained the Manley 42149 guide plates and the ARP 135-7101 rocker arm studs. Cut the Manley guide plates vertically in half, and then align and weld them back together in order to correctly center the pushrods (a common problem with many aftermarket cylinder heads). Check the alignment of the pushrods with the rocker arms and the clearance of the pushrods in the guide plates. If you neglect this procedure, pushrod failure is almost guaranteed.

Install a set of the Crower Cams & Equipment Company 73605 rollarized rocker arms (17-4PH stainless-steel, 1025 heat-treated, Torrington oversized needle bearings, 52100 ball race steel tip roller, 1.70 ratio). These superb roller rocker arms come with the Crower Cams & Equipment Company 86050 sure-lock heat-treated chrome-moly steel rocker arm stud nuts (7/16-inch stud diameter). The current retail price for these stainless steel roller rocker arms is $375.

I retained the GM 3877668 and 3877669 cylinder head bolts and the eight World Products 7301 extra-length cylinder head bolts.

I wanted to retain the chrome Corvette valve covers for this engine since the left side (driver's side) valve cover clears the power brake booster and the right side (passenger's side) valve cover is clear of the air conditioning/heater housing in my 1969 Corvette. However, these stock valve covers will not clear the Crower Cams & Equipment Company 73605 roller rocker arms. I had Luke's Custom Machine & Design fabricate a set of 1/2-inch-thick aluminum valve cover spacers. The valve covers are now clear of everything, and unless you look closely, it does not appear as if there are valve cover spacers installed.

Intake System

Building a new engine also means installing a new intake system. I sold the complete intake system for the Chevrolet 454-ci engine described in Chapter 12 for the same price I had originally paid for it. I decided to install a single four-barrel high-rise intake manifold; however, there was the problem of hood clearance in my 1969 Corvette. I spent a considerable amount of time at my local speed equipment shop (thank you, Bud Bennett) measuring the height of different dual-plane and single-plane intake manifolds.

I finally decided to purchase a Weiand (Holley) 7513 X-celerator single-plane cast-aluminum four-barrel carburetor intake manifold. This intake manifold is a 360-degree design for large rectangular port cylinder heads; its port size is 1 9/16 inches by 2 5/16 inches. Many engine builders recommend only a dual-plane intake manifold for street performance use, although the Weiand 7513 single-plane intake manifold is said to have a power range from 1,800 to 7,300 rpm.

Polished-aluminum intake manifolds look terrific just after they are buffed, but they are extremely difficult to keep shiny in some vehicles. To keep it shiny, spray the intake manifold with Eastwood Company 10200Z diamond-clear gloss finish. As soon as the intake manifold is buffed, clean it thoroughly with wax-and-grease remover, and then spray it with the Eastwood Company diamond-clear finish. The finish is impervious to gasoline and it really works. As usual, I had "Tim, the polishing guy" buff my new Weiand intake manifold.

You can usually take the Holley and Edelbrock four-barrel carburetors manufactured today right out of the box and install them on a street performance engine. You may need to make some minor jet changes. A carburetor for a large displacement engine is a different matter, and you should rely on the services of a respected carburetor company to determine the best carburetor to install. Jet Performance Products (see Appendix B—Resources), formerly Mike Jones Carburetion, has been in business for 35

The Crower Cams & Equipment 68389 valve springs, 87060 valve spring retainers, and 86110-1 valve stem locks with the Manley 11874 intake valves and 11883 exhaust valves laid out at High Performance Engines by "T-Bone," the wizard of all cylinder heads, prior to the installation in the World Products Merlin cylinder head.

years and specializes in all types of fuel systems. I ordered one of its Holley 0-4781 stage 2 850-cfm double pumper carburetors with chrome fuel bowls and linkage and black powder-coated center section and base. The Jet Performance Products stage 2 carburetors have all the gasket surfaces checked for straightness, the boosters are aligned in the venturi, the throttle bores are aligned for proper sealing, the fuel metering circuits are blue-printed, the secondary power valve is blocked off, the air horn is milled, there are four corner idle circuits, an anti-backfire check valve kit is installed, there are clear view sight plugs for adjusting the float level, and the carburetor is flow bench tested. This fantastic-looking carburetor now flows at 990 cfm, and the performance is superb. The current retail price is $850.

Refer to Chapter 12 for information regarding fuel pressure regulators and fuel pressure gauges.

As I have previously mentioned, the air-cleaner-to-hood clearance is an issue with my 1969 Corvette. After carefully measuring everything about 50 times, I was convinced that the Mr. Gasket 6477 Rodware chrome heavy-breather louvered air cleaner (14-inch o.d. by 2 1/2-inch height) was the only decent-looking air cleaner that would fit on my Weiand intake manifold and Holley carburetor. This air cleaner looks similar to the 1958 to 1960 Corvette chrome air cleaner with the louvers around the side of the top section. There is a photograph of the Mr. Gasket 6477 air cleaner in Chapter 5, and the current retail price is $46.

Install a new K&N E-2865 air filter to replace the restrictive paper filter element supplied with most air cleaners. This air filter

The GM 12555320 intake manifold oil splash shield has been painted with Glyptal G-1228A medium-grey gloss enamel and installed. This is a good photograph of the Crower Cams & Equipment 73605 stainless-steel roller rocker arms prior to installing the valve covers.

is 13-inch o.d. by 2.312-inch height and it currently sells for $47. To check the clearance, install the engine with the air cleaner in place and bolt the hood back in position. I placed some putty on the top front of the air cleaner and carefully closed the hood. When I reopened the hood, I discovered I had 1/2-inch (0.500-inch) clearance between the top of the air cleaner and the underside of the hood, and that is plenty!

Ignition System

I retained the Mallory 3864501 Unilite distributor, Mallory 29440 Promaster ignition coil, and the Mallory 29026 HyFire ignition control, as well as the Aries KC-11 chrome alternator and all the chrome alternator brackets.

The Crower Cams & Equipment Company 01476 solid roller camshaft is manufactured from 8620 cast steel billet and requires an aluminum/bronze distributor gear. I purchased a Mallory 29426 aluminum/bronze distributor gear (0.491-inch o.d. shaft) at its current retail price of $50.

Cooling and Exhaust Systems

I retained all the items listed for the cooling and exhaust systems in Chapter 12.

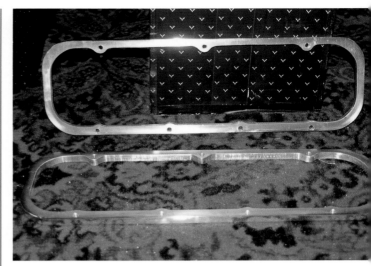

A set of 1/2-inch-thick aluminum valve cover spacers for a Chevrolet 454-ci engine fabricated by Luke's Custom Machine & Design.

Engine Summary

Note: This is the second engine I installed in my 1969 Corvette coupe. This engine runs beautifully on the street and the throttle response is extremely impressive. In all likelihood I will not upgrade it again . . . maybe.

Engine Block

• 1990 Chevrolet 454-ci L19 engine block; casting number 10068286; casting date: C070 (March 7, 1990); stock bore: 4.251 inches; stock stroke: 4.00 inches; four-bolt main bearing caps; 9.80-inch deck height; light-duty truck, 230 horsepower; engine block weight (bare): 195 pounds; $200

• Engine block hot tanked; engine block and main bearing caps and bolts Magnafluxed; main bearing caps and bolts shot peened; all threads retapped; cylinder head bolt holes chamfered; valve lifter bosses deglazed allowing for 0.002-inch valve lifter clearance; and No. 5 main bearing cap oil pump cavity polished; 0.0625-inch hole drilled in bottom center of face of front camshaft boss and 0.041-inch hole drilled in top front oil gallery line plugs for additional oiling; valve lifter gallery and front of engine block ground smooth and painted with Glyptal G-1228A medium-grey gloss enamel; Moroso 25001 oil gallery screen kit installed; exterior surface of engine block sanded and detailed and painted with Plasti-Kote 203 black high-gloss engine enamel; Federal Mogul 3818009 brass freeze plugs and rear camshaft boss plug and new stainless-steel oil gallery line plugs installed using Permatex aviation form-a-gasket; Weatherhead 3152-4 polished-brass water jacket drain plugs (1/4-inch NPT) installed using pipe thread sealant; $471.75

• Engine block bored 0.040-inch oversize and cylinders honed and deglazed using torque plate with Sunnen 800 series 400-grit stones; final bore: 4.290 inches; piston-to-bore clearance: 0.004 inch, measured below bottom of wrist pin perpendicular to wrist pin; $125

- Engine block align honed; $200
- Engine block parallel decked to 0.010-inch average below deck; $110
- Engine block O-ringed using 0.035-inch-diameter stainless-steel wire; $100

Engine block total: $1,206.75

Crankshaft

- Summit Racing Equipment SES-3-91-05-C385 Proline forged 4340 aircraft-quality non-twisted steel crankshaft; crankshaft Magnafluxed; shot peened; internally balanced; journals surface nitrided to 60 Rockwell C hardness; core heat treated and stress relieved; gun drilled No. 1 and 4 connecting rod pins; computer-designed counterweight positioning; rounded airplane-wing counterweight leading edges; journals radiused 0.125 inch and polished; and oil holes cross-drilled and chamfered; crankshaft stroke: 4.250 inches for use with 6.385-inch-long (center to center) connecting rods; crankshaft weight (after balancing): 70 pounds; $1,095
- Clevite 77 MS-829H chamfered main bearings, standard size, installed allowing for 0.002-inch crankshaft clearance and 0.006-inch end play; ARP 235-5701 main bearing cap stud kit (for windage trays; 8740 chrome-moly steel, 190,000 psi) threads rolled to MIL-S-8879 specifications, black oxide finish, hardened washers and nuts, installed; inner and outer main bearing cap studs torqued to 110 ft-lb using molykote; $215.95
- Fluidampr 712440 harmonic balancer (7 1/4-inch o.d., weight: 14.2 pounds) installed with ARP 235-2501 harmonic balancer bolt and washer (190,000 psi) using Loctite and torqued to 85 ft-lb; Moroso 41100 roller pilot bearing installed using anti-seize compound; $356
- GM 3921923 double-groove crankshaft pulley (6 3/4-inch o.d.) installed with polished stainless-steel bolts, lockwashers, and flat washers using Loctite and torqued to 30 ft-lb; crankshaft pulley painted with Endura EX-2C black 160 high-gloss polyurethane; $75

Crankshaft total: $1,741.95

Connecting Rods and Pistons

- Manley 14062-8 forged 4340 steel H-beam connecting rods, 6.385-inch length (center to center); fully machined and stress relieved; shot peened; Magnafluxed; bronze alloy wrist pin bushings; wrist pin bores and crankshaft journal bores honed to +/- 0.0002-inch tolerance; wrist pin end (the small end) diameter: 0.9911 inch; ARP 42361 connecting rod cap screw bolts (8740 steel, 7/16-inch diameter, 12-point, 190,000 psi) installed; connecting rod weight: 880 grams each; connecting rod ratio: 1.50 (with 4.25-inch stroke crankshaft); $699

- Clevite 77 CB-743H chamfered connecting rod bearings, standard size, installed allowing for 0.002-inch connecting rod clearance and 0.016-inch side clearance per pair of connecting rods; connecting rod bolts torqued to 80 ft-lb using 30-weight motor oil and allowing for 0.0063- to 0.0067-inch stretch; $121
- Ross Racing Pistons forged 2618 T-61 aluminum racing pistons (0.040-inch oversize, 10.0:1 compression ratio, 0.185-inch slight domed top), intake and exhaust valve reliefs, open combustion chamber design; piston weight: 583 grams each; Ross Racing Pistons 990-01-29 full-floating heat-treated and casehardened 4340 chrome-moly steel straight-wall wrist pins installed allowing for 0.0015-inch connecting rod clearance; wrist pin length: 2.930 inches; wrist pin diameter: 0.990 inch; wrist pin weight: 149 grams each; Ross Racing Pistons 4004-E double Spiro-Lox wrist pin retainers installed; piston ring grooves: top compression ring width: 5/64 inch; second compression ring width: 5/64 inch; oil ring width: 3/16 inch; Sealed Power (Federal Mogul) E-233K-40 plasma-moly-coated top piston ring set installed within manufacturer's recommended arc; top compression ring gap: 0.020 inch; second compression ring gap: 0.018 inch; oil ring gap: 0.018 inch; Ross Racing Pistons ORS-425 oil ring support rails installed with 0.010-inch clearance; piston tops painted with V.H.T. SP-101 white high-temperature coating; intake-valve-to-piston clearance: 0.170 inch, and exhaust-valve-to-piston-clearance: 0.160 inch (without gasket); new displacement: 491.5 ci (8.1 liters); $805
- Complete V-8 engine balance; $190

Connecting rods and pistons total: $1,815

Lubrication System

- Melling M77HV high-volume oil pump with pressure-balance grooves and Milodon 18301 CNC-machined billet oil pump screen tack welded to oil pump; oil pump cover end clearance: 0.00025 inch; oil pump cover gasket installed using silicone sealant and bolts torqued to 80 in-lb using Loctite; Milodon 23060 oil pump driveshaft, 4130 chrome-moly steel, heat-treated ends, installed; ARP 230-7003 oil pump stud kit installed using Loctite and torqued to 65 ft-lb; $78
- Milodon 32260 Diamond Stripper windage tray installed with nuts torqued to 25 ft-lb using Loctite; Milodon 30950 low-profile oil pan (7-quart capacity) installed with ARP 435-1901 polished stainless-steel oil pan stud kit (170,000 psi) using Loctite and torqued to 15 ft-lb; Fel-Pro 1804 oil pan gaskets and McCord BS210 viton material rear main bearing seals installed using silicone sealant; Trans-Dapt 4958 chrome dip stick and dip stick tube installed; GM 3952301 oil filter adapter installed using Loctite on bolts and torqued to 20 ft-lb; Fram PH-13 oil filter installed with Trans-Dapt 1067 chrome oil filter cover; engine lubricated with 7 quarts Pennzoil HD-30-weight motor oil; oil pan painted with Endura EX-2C black 160 high-gloss polyurethane; $407.57

Lubrication system total: $485.57

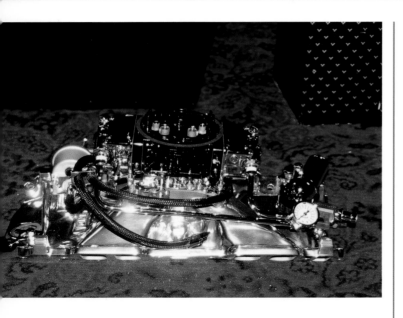

The Weiand 7513 X-celerator intake manifold with the Jet Performance Products stage 2 Holley 0-4781 double pumper 850-cfm carburetor installed.

Camshaft and Cylinder Heads

• Clevite 77 SH-616S camshaft bearings installed with 0.002-inch camshaft clearance and 0.002-inch camshaft end play; No. 1 bearing: SH-615, housing bore: 2.1395 to 2.1405 inches; No. 2 and 5 bearing: SH-616, housing bore: 2.1295 to 2.1305 inches; No. 3 and 4 bearing: SH-617, housing bore: 2.1195 to 2.1205 inches; camshaft journal diameter: 1.950 inches; $35

• Crower Cams & Equipment Company 01476 290R street solid (mechanical) roller lifter 8620 cast steel billet camshaft with advertised duration: 290 degrees intake and 296 degrees exhaust; duration at 0.050-inch lift: 252 degrees intake and 254 degrees exhaust; lobe separation angle: 112 degrees; net valve lift (with 1.70 ratio rocker arms): 0.559 inch intake and 0.550 inch exhaust; valve lash (hot): 0.026 inch intake and 0.028 inch exhaust; camshaft degreed; $245

• Crower Cams & Equipment Company 66201 solid roller lifters with Torque-Lock fasteners, CNC-machine-milled chrome-moly heat-treated steel (0.842-inch o.d., stock pushrod seat height); Crower Cams & Equipment Company 70308-1 nonadjustable pushrods (7/16-inch diameter, 4130 seamless chrome-moly steel, ends heat-treated to surface hardness RC60, 0.050 inch longer than stock); intake pushrod length: 8.30 inches, and exhaust pushrod length: 9.30 inches; GM 12555320 intake manifold oil splash shield painted with Glyptal G-1228A medium-grey gloss enamel and installed; $440

• Edelbrock 7891 Accu-Drive dual idler gear drive, SAE (Society of Automotive Engineers) 8620 steel gears, with roller camshaft button, installed with camshaft bolts torqued to 20 ft-

lb using Loctite; GM 330850 timing gear cover installed with ARP 400-1401 polished stainless-steel timing gear cover stud kit (170,000 psi) using Loctite and torqued to 15 ft-lb; GM 10114142 timing gear cover gasket installed using silicone sealant; GM 10191640 timing gear cover oil seal installed; timing gear cover painted with Endura EX-2C black 160 high-gloss polyurethane; $245

• World Products 3003B (bare) Merlin large rectangular port, open combustion chamber, high-density cast-iron cylinder heads; cylinder heads surfaced; intake runner volume: 320 cc; exhaust runner volume: 110 cc; combustion chamber volume: 118 cc; intake and exhaust ports fully ported and polished and gasket matched; combustion chambers polished and cc'd; hardened interlocking ductile iron exhaust valve seat inserts installed; K-Line 9832STA bronze bullet universal-length (11/32-inch diameter) valve guide liners installed; and valves unshrouded (laying back); Serdi-machined multi-angle blueprint valve grind performed; area beneath valve covers painted with Glyptal G-1228A medium-grey gloss enamel; exterior surface of cylinder heads painted with Plasti-Kote 203 black high-gloss engine enamel; cylinder heads installed with Fel-Pro 8180PT-2 perma-torque blue stripe cylinder head gaskets; GM 3877668 (long) and new GM 3877669 (short) cylinder head bolts and World Products 7301 cylinder head bolts (eight), 1 inch longer than stock, installed using Permatex aviation form-a-gasket with the long bolts torqued to 75 ft-lb and the short bolts torqued to 65 ft-lb; cylinder head weight (bare): 75 pounds each; $1,755

• Manley 11874 Race Master stainless-steel intake valves (2.25-inch head diameter, 11/32-inch stem diameter, 5.244-inch length overall, hardened tips, swirl polished); weight: 140 grams each; Manley 11883 Race Master stainless-steel exhaust valves (1.90-inch head diameter, 11/32-inch stem diameter, 5.422-inch length overall, hardened tips, swirl polished); weight: 123 grams each; Enginetech S2927 viton positive seal valve stem seals installed; $256

• Crower Cams & Equipment Company 68389 dual silicone valve springs with damper; installed height: 125 pounds at 1.90 inches valves closed and 360 pounds at 1.30 inches valves open; 1.510-inch o.d. and 1.118-inch/0.750-inch i.d.; coil bind: 1.130 inches; color: lime green/purple; Crower Cams & Equipment 87060 heat-treated chrome-moly steel 10-degree valve spring retainers (11/32-inch stem diameter) and 86110-1 jumbo split-lock 10-degree valve stem locks, heat-treated chrome-moly steel (11/32-inch stem diameter, 0.050 inch longer than stock) installed; $175

• Manley 42149 hardened-steel raised pushrod guide plates (for 7/16-inch pushrods) installed with ARP 135-7101 high-performance-series 8740 chrome-moly steel rocker arm studs (7/16-inch diameter, 170,000 psi) using Loctite and torqued to 50 ft-lb; Crower Cams & Equipment Company 73605 stainless

17-4PH steel roller rocker arms (1025 heat-treated, 1.70 ratio) installed with Crower Cams & Equipment Company 86050 sure-lock rocker arm stud nuts (heat-treated chrome-moly steel, 7/16-inch stud diameter) using anti-seize compound; $465

• Zip Products VC-207 chrome Corvette valve covers, with dripper rails and power brake slant, installed with Luke's Custom Machine & Design polished-aluminum valve cover spacers (1/2-inch thickness) and GM 14085759 valve cover gaskets using silicone sealant; Moroso 68516 chrome valve cover hold-down tabs installed with Mr. Gasket 6304 Rodware chrome tall acorn nuts and stainless-steel studs, AN flat washers and lockwashers using Loctite and torqued to 15 ft-lb; Trans-Dapt 4878 rubber grommet installed with Trans-Dapt 4870 chrome push-in breather; Trans-Dapt 4998 rubber grommet installed with Motorcraft EV-49-B PCV valve; Gates 3225 PCV valve line (5/16-inch i.d. by 1-foot length) installed with Spectre 3001A black nylabraid and Spectre 3208B chrome champclamps; Zip Products IS-226A and IS-226C spark plug wire supports/dividers installed; Chicago Corvette Supply B2363 right-hand valve cover decal "Tonawanda #1 Team" installed; Dr. Rebuild 1758122 chrome oil filler cap installed; $591.60

Camshaft and cylinder heads total: $4,207.60

Intake System

• Weiand 7513 X-celerator polished-aluminum, 360-degree design, high-rise single-quad intake manifold with large rectangular ports, gasket matched; port size: 1 9/16 inches by 2 5/16 inches; power range: 1,800 to 7,300 rpm; underside of intake manifold painted with V.H.T. SP-101 white high-temperature coating; Fel-Pro 1275 intake manifold gaskets, port size: 1.82 inches by 2.54 inches, installed using silicone sealant; ARP 435-2001 polished stainless-steel intake manifold bolts (six-point head, 170,000 psi) installed using Loctite and torqued to 25 ft-lb; $335

• Jet Performance Products stage 2 Holley 0-4781, chrome and black powder-coated, 990-cfm double pumper carburetor installed with ARP 400-2401 polished stainless-steel carburetor stud kit using anti-seize compound; $861

• Mr. Gasket 6477 Rodware chrome heavy-breather louvered air cleaner (14-inch o.d. by 2 1/2-inch height) installed with K&N E-2865 air filter (13-inch o.d. by 2.31-inch height); $93

• Trans-Dapt 9229 chrome O-ring thermostat housing with Robert Shaw 330-160 extra performance balanced 160-degree (Fahrenheit) thermostat installed with chrome bolts and lockwashers using silicone sealant and torqued to 20 ft-lb; stainless-steel 1/2-inch NPT plug installed using pipe thread sealant; Auto-Meter 4484 Pro Comp Ultra-Lite vacuum gauge (0 to 30 in.hg.) installed with Holley 12-803 chrome fuel pressure regulator bracket using polished stainless-steel bolts and lockwashers

The Chevrolet 492-ci engine ready to be installed in my 1969 Corvette coupe. A lot of thought and detailing went into building this engine.

with anti-seize compound; Trans-Dapt 2291 chrome carburetor return spring and bracket installed; $75.85

• Holley 12-454 chrome performance mechanical fuel pump (6 to 8 psi, 110 gph) installed with ARP 430-1602 polished stainless-steel bolts (six-point head, 170,000 psi) using Loctite and torqued to 20 ft-lb; fuel pump gasket installed using silicone sealant; Weatherhead 3200-6-4 polished-brass adapter (3/8-inch NPT to 1/4-inch NPT) and Weatherhead 402-6-6 polished-brass 90-degree elbow (3/8-inch tube to 3/8-inch NPT) installed using pipe thread sealant; GM 3704817 fuel pump pushrod (1/2-inch diameter by 5 3/4-inch length) installed; Holley 162-530 chrome inline fuel filter (discontinued) installed with Weatherhead 100-6 polished-brass inverted flare nuts (3/8-inch tube) and Summit Racing Equipment 220238 polished stainless-steel fuel line (3/8-inch tube by 0.028-inch wall by 2-foot length) using pipe thread sealant; $127.68

• Holley 12-803 chrome fuel pressure regulator, adjustable from 4 1/2 to 9 psi, installed with Weatherhead 402-6-6 polished-brass 90-degree elbow (3/8-inch tube to 3/8-inch NPT, inlet line), Weatherhead 3152-6 polished-brass pipe plug (3/8-inch NPT, outlet line), and Weatherhead 3325-6-2 polished-brass adapter (1/8-inch NPT to 3/8-inch NPT, outlet line) using pipe thread sealant; Summit Racing Equipment G3122 chrome fuel pressure gauge (0 to 15 psi) installed with Trans-Dapt 2197 chrome dual inlet fuel line (9 5/16-inch center to center) using pipe thread sealant; $63.89

Intake system total: $1,556.42

Ignition System

• Mallory 3864501 Unilite distributor with photo-optic LED system, mechanical tachometer drive, 356 T-6 billet aluminum

A great photograph of the Chevrolet 492-ci engine installed in my 1969 Corvette prior to putting the hood back on. There is no room left in the engine compartment for additional parts after one of these brutes has been bolted in.

housing, mechanical advance, installed with GM 14007385 chrome distributor clamp and polished stainless-steel bolt and lockwashers using anti-seize compound; Mallory 29440 Promaster ignition coil and Mallory 29026 HyFire electronic ignition control installed; Mallory 29426 aluminum/bronze distributor gear (0.491-inch shaft) installed; $513.85

• Taylor/Vertex 70053 Pro Series black 8-millimeter high-performance spark plug wires (135-degree boots, Spiro-Pro Kelvar resistor core) installed; Taylor 42800 black plastic spark plug wire separator kit installed; NGK UR4 v-power resistor type spark plugs installed with 0.050-inch gap; $75.57

• Aries KC-11 chrome internally regulated alternator (63 amps) installed with GM 3878236 chrome alternator bracket, GM 3946000 chrome alternator/power steering pump brace, GM 3986109 chrome alternator upper support bracket, and GM 3878240 chrome alternator lower support bracket using polished stainless-steel bolts, lockwashers, flat washers, and nylocks; Gates 11A0800 crankshaft/water pump v-belt (7/16-inch by 31 1/2-inch length) installed; Gates 11A1370 crankshaft/power steering pump/alternator v-belt (7/16-inch by 54-inch length) installed; $347.28

• TCI Automotive 351100 high-torque racing starter (draws 25 amps and produces 2.5 horsepower of cranking output)

installed with new bolts using anti-seize compound; $200.95

Ignition system total: $1,137.65

Cooling and Exhaust Systems

• Edelbrock 8852 Victor Series polished 356 T-6 aluminum water pump (3/4-inch pilot shaft) installed with polished stainless-steel bolts and lockwashers using Loctite and torqued to 25 ft-lb; water pump gaskets installed using silicone sealant; GM 3992071BE chrome water pump pulley (5 1/2-inch diameter, triple groove) installed with polished stainless-steel bolts and lockwashers using Loctite and torqued to 25 ft-lb; Turbo-Flex 24200 polished-aluminum fan spacer (2-inch thickness) and Hayden 3717 polished stainless-steel heavy-duty 17-inch-diameter fan installed; GM 3829819 chrome thermal bypass connector (water pump fitting), Weatherhead 1430 polished-brass hose connector (1/2-inch NPT to 3/4-inch i.d. hose, intake manifold fitting), and GM 1485552 water pump bypass hose installed with stainless-steel line clamps; hose covered with Spectre 3001A black nylabraid and Spectre 3208B chrome champclamps; $473.85

• GM 5910741 rebuilt chrome air conditioning compressor installed with GM 3894364 chrome rear compressor mounting bracket, GM 3894362 chrome front compressor mounting bracket, and GM 3887167 chrome front compressor support bracket using new polished stainless-steel bolts and lockwashers with Loctite; Gates 11A1195 air conditioning compressor/water pump pulley v-belt (7/16-inch by 47-inch length) installed; $610

• Hedman Hedders 68090 metallic-ceramic-coated exhaust headers installed with Fel-Pro 1412 exhaust manifold gaskets (2.13-inch diameter exhaust ports) using Permatex ultra copper high-temperature silicone sealant; Trans-Dapt 8912 Stage 8 polished stainless-steel self-locking exhaust header bolts installed using Loctite and torqued to 25 ft-lb; $466.14

Cooling and exhaust systems total: $1,549.99

Labor

• Labor for checking clearances, gapping piston rings, degree camshaft, valvetrain assembly, detailing, trial engine assembly, final engine assembly, and initial engine start-up; $800

Labor total: $800

Engine Grand Total: $14,500.93 (U.S.)

Note: The estimated output of this engine is 647 horsepower at 6,000 rpm and 635 ft-lb torque at 4,500 rpm (see Appendix A—Dyno Print-Outs).

CHAPTER 14
BLOWN KEITH BLACK 541-ci ENGINE

A year after I completed building my 1969 Corvette coupe, Jerry Olsen of J & M Autobody & Paint suggested we build a second Corvette. A mutual friend of ours had a 1972 Corvette coupe for sale. I purchased the car for $1,800 (U.S.).

This vehicle had no running gear, there was no front end, the back end had been hit, an attempt had been made to install rear fender flares, and the interior was in shambles. (At least I am consistent when I buy Corvettes!)

I assembled the frame, suspension, steering, brakes, engine, transmission, and rear end. Jerry Olsen, with his partner, Larry Woida, and the rest of his crew, rebuilt the body (the only original body panels are the two doors), installed all the wiring, and completed the project with a spectacular Claret Red Pearlcoat

The Keith Black Racing Engines model KB500 aluminum Chevrolet engine block after "Tim, the polishing guy" attacked it. Notice the size of the cross-webs in the valve lifter gallery and the four-bolt main bearing caps.

paint job. In 1998, it won the "best in class" and the "outstanding engine" award at a custom car and hot rod show with over 500 entries. I entered both of my Corvettes in the show, and my 1969 Corvette Coupe won "second in class." It is a sad day when a person competes against his own cars for trophies!

In 1986, I saw a completely polished aluminum Chevrolet engine block with polished-aluminum cylinder heads in an edition of *Hot Rod* magazine. I knew right then and there that one day I would have to own a completely polished aluminum and chrome engine. I wanted a really wild engine for the 1972 Corvette coupe, so I purchased a Keith Black Racing Engines aluminum Mark IV Chevrolet engine block, which reminded me of the 1969 Corvette ZL-1 aluminum engine option. Only two were ever installed in Corvettes. This chapter contains the complete buildup information for that engine.

Components Description
Engine Block

Keith Black Racing Engines dates back to the mid-1950s, renowned today for the quality aluminum Hemi drag race engine blocks, aluminum cylinder heads, and other components it designs and produces. In the mid-1980s, Keith Black Racing Engines started manufacturing Chevrolet aluminum engine blocks. I decided from the start of this project that I wanted the best product available—naturally, that is a Keith Black Racing Engines aluminum engine block.

This engine block is manufactured using 356 T-6 virgin aluminum; it is fully machined and will accept all Mark IV Chevrolet engine parts; the cylinder sleeves are removable; four-bolt billet steel main bearing caps are supplied; the camshaft bearings are installed; there are anodized aluminum screw-in freeze plugs; the dowels for the cylinder heads and the timing gear cover are installed; a variety of cylinder head stud kits is provided; the purchaser has a choice of whether to install Chevrolet, Brodix, Dart, or Pontiac cylinder heads; the engine block is available in standard 9.80-inch deck height or a +0.400-inch tall deck version; the cylinder bores are available in 4.250 inches or 4.500 inches; and the engine block is clearanced for a 4.25-inch stroke crankshaft, although the engine block will accept up to a 4.750-inch stroke crankshaft with forged steel connecting rods.

A set of Manley 14062-8 forged 4340 steel H-beam connecting rods (6.385-inch length, center to center).

The Keith Black Racing Engines model KB500 engine block is meticulously manufactured and is one of the rare aftermarket engine blocks that will accept all the internal and external parts without having to custom fit everything. This, in itself, is a huge labor-cost saver. The Block Inspection Report sheet (a checklist of all the measurements in the engine block, including each and every bolt hole) comes with the engine block. This is truly professional and typical of Keith Black Racing Engines.

The Keith Black Racing Engines 52000 (model KB500) engine block I ordered was the standard 9.80-inch deck height with 4.50-inch cylinder bores. I also requested the engine block be O-ringed. The current retail price for one of these engine blocks is $4,500. I purchased the Keith Black Racing Engines 71905 windage tray stud kit for the sum of $35.

Naturally, the engine block had to be polished. When I told "Tim, the polishing guy," he thought he had died and gone to heaven—I have never seen him so happy.

After the engine block was buffed, it was thoroughly cleaned with wax-and-grease remover, all the internal openings were masked off, and the engine block was sprayed with Eastwood Company 10200Z diamond-clear gloss finish. It would be virtually impossible to keep every nook and cranny of the engine block polished once it's installed in the 1972 Corvette, and I used the Eastwood Company coating to protect the aluminum from the elements.

Crankshaft

I installed a Summit Racing Equipment SES-3-91-05-C385 Pro-line forged 4340 aircraft-quality, non-twisted crankshaft in the engine described here. Refer to Chapter 13 for information about this crankshaft, crankshaft bearings, and the harmonic balancer.

Connecting Rods and Pistons

I also installed a set of Manley 14062-8 forged 4340 steel H-beam connecting rods in this engine. Refer to Chapter 13 for information regarding these connecting rods and connecting rod bearings.

Because this engine block has a 4.50-inch bore with a 4.250-inch stroke and I planned to install a blower, I ordered a custom set of Ross Racing Pistons blower pistons. These pistons are

The Ross Racing Pistons blower pistons for a Keith Black Racing Engines (model KB500) aluminum engine block with a 4.50-inch bore. As usual, the piston tops have been painted with V.H.T. SP-101 white high-temperature coating.

manufactured using 2618 T-61 aluminum and have a slight dished top for use with open combustion chamber cylinder heads. The wrist pins are the super-duty full-floating type with double Spiro-Lox retainers. Ross Racing Pistons includes oil ring support rails with the pistons. The current retail price for the blower pistons with the super-duty wrist pins is $830.

The Childs & Albert ductile dura-moly zero-gap second ring piston ring set contains the best types of piston rings available today. The zero-gap piston ring has an overlapping step gap design, which almost eliminates end gap blowby. These piston rings are advertised as having a 0 to 1 percent leak-down reading in a fresh engine, and they are ideal for a blown engine. The Childs & Albert dura-moly piston rings used in this engine are designed for a top compression ring groove width of 1/16 inch, a second compression ring groove width of 1/6 inch, and an oil ring groove width of 3/16 inch. The recommended end gap is 0.0045 inch by the bore size, for a blown street engine using gasoline. I installed a set of Childs & Albert RS-43ZX4.505 ZGS piston rings in the engine; the set's current retail price is $230.

Lubrication System

I installed a Melling M77HV high-volume oil pump with a Milodon 18301 oil pump pickup screen in this engine. Refer to Chapter 12 for information pertaining to oil pans, oil pump driveshafts and stud kits, and windage trays.

In Chapter 13, I suggest painting the oil pan with polyurethane. Because this engine block is completely polished, however, I had to make an exception. I had the Milodon 30950 low-profile oil pan chrome plated, and it is now completely compatible with the engine block.

Camshaft and Cylinder Heads

Refer to Chapter 12 for information regarding camshaft bearings.

I requested the assistance of Jerry MacLaughlin at Crower Cams & Equipment Company in choosing the correct camshaft for this engine. Although it is a monster-cubic-inch engine with a blower, I wanted to be able to drive my Corvette on the street without having to fight it in rush hour traffic or at stop signs. Jerry recommended the Crower Cams & Equipment Company 01404 236HR245 street hydraulic roller lifter camshaft. This camshaft has an advertised duration of: 292 degrees intake and 303 degrees exhaust; duration at 0.050-inch lift: 236 degrees intake and 245 degrees exhaust; lobe separation angle: 110 degrees; valve lift: 0.586 inch intake and 0.612 inch exhaust; valve lash (hot): zero. The current retail price for this camshaft is $245.

Use Crower Cams & Equipment Company 66321 hydraulic roller lifters with the camshaft mentioned above. These roller lifters are made of CNC-machine-milled chrome-moly heat-treated steel with crowned bearings and crowned outer race, Torrington oversize control-contoured tapered needle bearings,

The Keith Black Racing Engines (model KB500) polished-aluminum engine block with the Summit Racing Equipment SES-3-91-05-C385 Proline forged non-twisted steel crankshaft and Manley 14062-8 forged steel H-beam connecting rods.

Torque-Lock fasteners, stock pushrod seat height, and 0.842-inch o.d. The current retail price for a set of the Crower Cams & Equipment Company 66320 hydraulic roller lifters is $400.

Purchase the Crower Cams & Equipment Company 70302 nonadjustable pushrods. These pushrods are manufactured using 4130 seamless chrome-moly steel (3/8-inch diameter, stock length for use with the 66321 hydraulic roller lifters), and the ends are heat treated to surface hardness RC60. The current retail price for a set of these pushrods is $140.

Install a Pete Jackson 427-5C quiet dual idler gear drive with a GM 330850 chrome timing gear cover.

At the time I started to assemble the parts for this engine, Edelbrock had just released its new aluminum big-block Chevrolet (non-emission) cylinder heads. Due to the demand for these cylinder heads, I had to wait about two months to receive my order, but it was well worth the wait. The Edelbrock 6054 (bare) Performer RPM 356 T-6 aluminum large rectangular port open combustion chamber cylinder heads are superb products. The intake port runner volume is 315 cc, the exhaust port runner volume is 110 cc, and the combustion chamber volume is 118 cc. Install phosphor bronze valve guides, hardened interlocking ductile iron exhaust valve seat inserts, and cylinder heads that have

been CNC machine ported and gasket matched. The performance range is said to be 1,500 to 7,000 rpm, and the current retail price for a set of these cylinder heads (bare) is $1,300.

I presented the cylinder heads to "Tim, the polishing guy" for his buffing delight, after which they were thoroughly cleaned with wax-and-grease remover and sprayed with Eastwood Company 10200Z diamond-clear gloss finish. Then, I delivered the cylinder heads to "T-Bone," the wizard of all cylinder heads at High Performance Engines, who performed his usual magic and also machined receiver groove O-rings (0.039 inch wide) in the cylinder heads. I purchased the Keith Black Racing Engines 61021 copper cylinder head gaskets for a retail price of $80.

Install Manley 11874 Race Master stainless-steel intake valves (2.25-inch head diameter by 11/32-inch stem diameter) and Manley 11881 Race Master stainless-steel exhaust valves (1.88-inch head diameter by 11/32-inch stem diameter) with a Serdi-machined multi-angle blueprint valve grind. Have the cylinder head combustion chambers unshrouded (laying back), and install Enginetech S2927 viton positive seal valve stem seals.

Install Crower Cams & Equipment 68932 heat-treated chrome-moly steel valve spring seat cups (which retail for $45) and Crower Cams & Equipment Company 68340 tungsalloy dual valve springs with damper and an installed height of: 128 pounds at 1.875 inches valves closed and 335 pounds at 1.350 inches valves open. Install Crower Cams & Equipment Company 87064 heat-treated chrome-moly steel 10-degree valve spring retainers, the 86110-1 jumbo split-lock 10-degree valve stem locks (11/32-inch stem diameter, 0.050 inch longer than stock), and the 86121S heat-treated chrome-moly steel lash caps (0.060-inch depth, 11/32-inch valve stems). The current retail price for lash caps is $30.

Install a set of the Manley 42164 hardened-steel raised guide plates and the Crower Cams & Equipment Company 88402L rocker arm studs. Fortunately, the guide plates aligned perfectly on this engine and do not need to be cut to install on the Edelbrock 6054 aluminum cylinder heads.

Install a set of the Crower Cams & Equipment Company 73605 roller rocker arms (1.70 ratio). Refer to Chapter 13 for information regarding these roller rocker arms.

Install the Keith Black Racing Engines 52200CD cylinder head stud kit, included with the engine block. The Keith Black Racing Engines model KB500 aluminum engine block is equipped with blind bolt holes that are not open to the water passages. Install the cylinder head studs in the engine block using anti-seize compound. Always coat any bolts installed in aluminum with anti-seize compound, not Loctite.

Install a set of Corvette chrome valve covers and Luke's Custom Machine & Design 1/2-inch-thick aluminum valve cover spacers. Refer to Chapter 13 for information regarding the valve covers and the valve cover spacers.

Intake System

Gene Mooneyham, the owner and founder of Mooneyham Blowers, is credited with developing the tented floor in big-block Chevrolet blower intake manifolds. This innovation ensures that the forward cylinders are not deprived of the fuel/air mixture when the engine is under hard acceleration.

I installed a Blower Drive Service 8026 polished-aluminum street blower intake manifold on this engine. This intake manifold is designed for the GMC 6-71 blower, although it will accept blowers up to 14-71. This intake manifold has a tented floor, large rectangular intake ports, a pop-off valve (backfire valve), intake manifold gaskets, and a 1401 polished-aluminum thermostat housing and gasket with a 180-degree (Fahrenheit) thermostat. Polishing the intake manifold is optional for $150. The current retail price for the Blower Drive Service 8026 polished-aluminum intake manifold is $575. Edelbrock recommends Fel-Pro 1211 intake manifold gaskets with its 6054 aluminum large rectangular port cylinder heads. Have the intake manifold ports gasket matched.

The Blower Drive Service 8026 blower intake manifold does not have any heat riser passages, which is quite beneficial as there is a substantial amount of heat introduced into the intake manifold when the blower is under boost.

The pressure balance grooves that have been ground into the top cover and the sides and bottom of the main body of a Melling M77HV high-volume oil pump.

I ordered two Jet Performance Products stage 2 Holley 0-4781 double pumper 850-cfm carburetors. The carburetors flow 990 cfm each and have chrome fuel bowls and linkage and black powder-coated center sections and bases. Refer to Chapter 13 for information about these carburetors. Refer to Chapter 12 for information about fuel pressure regulators and fuel pressure gauges.

In order to install the carburetors on the blower, you'll need to install a Weiand (Holley) 7163 polished-aluminum 1-inch-high carburetor adapter. The Holley carburetors require a pair of Trans-Dapt 2084 polished-aluminum 1-inch-high spacers to permit the Holley carburetor linkage to clear the Weiand 7163 adapter. Install ARP 200-2402 polished stainless-steel carburetor stud kits. The current retail price for the carburetor adapter, carburetor spacers, and the carburetor stud kits is $135.

Install the Weiand (Holley) 7166 side-mount carburetor linkage kit. This is a premium-quality linkage kit with ball bearing shaft supports and heim joints. The current retail price for the Weiand 7166 linkage kit is $130.

I have always liked the appearance of the Hilborn-style fuel injector scoops on engines, although I do not like the new models of this scoop paired with carburetors where the air filter element(s) can be seen from the front of the scoop when looking inside. I decided to purchase a Mr. Gasket 5233 Rodware polished-aluminum Hilborn-style scoop. This scoop has a steel mesh in the front preventing any debris from ending up inside the scoop, and the air filters are hidden from view. The current retail price is $215. I installed two K&N E-3260 air filters to replace the restrictive paper air filters provided with the scoop. The current retail price for the two K&N E-3260 air filters is $47.

I purchased a NOS GM 5138725 blower/supercharger (model 6-71), casting date: 3-9-70 (March 9, 1970), from Luke Balogh. He originally bought two NOS 6-71 blowers at the Portland,

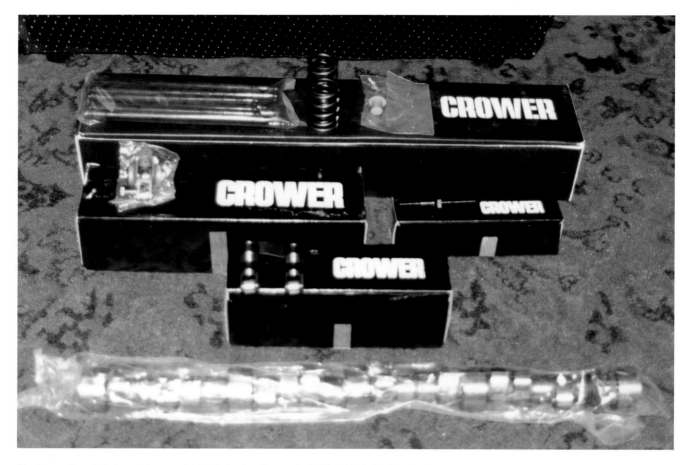

The Crower Cams & Equipment Company 01404 hydraulic roller camshaft with 66321 hydraulic roller lifters, 73605 roller rocker arms, 88402L rocker arm studs, 70302 pushrods, 68340 dual valve springs, and 86086 phenolic camshaft thrust plug.

Oregon, swap meet approximately 20 years ago. The GM 5114442 later model die-cast front cover and GM 5122363 later model die-cast front and rear bearing plates came equipped with the blower case. "Tim, the polishing guy" sanded the blower case area between the vertical ribs so that all these areas are the same depth. This is a tremendous amount of work because this area of the blower case is such a rough casting. The finished result was a beautifully buffed blower case. Refer to Chapter 6 for the blower information.

Install a Luke's Custom Machine & Design LS2000 sculptured blower snout with the LS2200 shaft and LS4100 gear coupler. Luke's Custom Machine & Design used to individually fabricate the sculptured blower snout, snout shaft, and gear coupler on a lathe as each order was placed. Demand for this product soon proved there are not enough hours in a day to produce the number of snouts required to fill the orders. The sculptured snout, snout shaft, and gear coupler are now manufactured by CNC machining. Refer to Chapter 6 for information about blower snouts.

I wanted to use the stock mounting brackets to keep the alternator and power steering pump in the stock position in my 1972 Corvette. Luke's Custom Machine & Design fabri-cated a polished-aluminum 1/2-inch-thick plate that bolts to the front of the water pump using 2 1/8-inch-long spacers. This plate is the idler pulley mounting bracket and it fits perfectly, allowing all the stock mounting brackets to be utilized. The aluminum idler pulley produced by Luke's Custom Machine & Design is another work of art—it has 10 beveled holes drilled in its face. Refer to Chapter 6 for a photograph of an aluminum idler pulley bracket.

The Blower Drive Service 6931 blower pulley is manufactured using 6061 T-6 aluminum (it is 31 teeth by 3.50 inches wide) and is designed for use with a 13.9-millimeter blower belt. This pulley will serve as the crankshaft drive pulley. The Blower Drive Service 6925 blower pulley is also manufactured using 6061 T-6 aluminum (it is 25 teeth by 3.50 inches wide) and is designed for use with a 13.9-millimeter blower belt. This pulley will serve as the blower drive pulley. This combination of pulleys will result in a blower drive ratio of 24 percent overdrive and approximately 11.5 pounds of boost. This is really on the borderline for the maximum boost appropriate in a street performance engine. Of course, everything about this engine is borderline insane. The Blower Drive Service 6931 and

A great photograph of the Keith Black Racing Engines (model KB500) aluminum engine block with the Pete Jackson 427-5C quiet dual idler gear drive installed. Check out the size of those four-bolt billet steel main bearing caps—brute strength!

6925 blower belt pulleys are hard anodized, but I prefer them polished. "Tim, the polishing guy" had a real task sanding off the tough-as-nails hard anodizing before he could buff the pulleys. The current retail price for these two blower pulleys is $200.

Luke's Custom Machine & Design fabricated an aluminum 2-inch-thick crankshaft blower pulley spacer that fits inside the GM 3921923 double-groove crankshaft pulley. This permits the crankshaft blower pulley to be mounted in front of the crankshaft v-belt pulley.

Install a Blower Drive Service 1543-75 Kelvar-lined polyurethane blower belt. This blower belt is 13.9 millimeters by 60.75 inches (length) by 3 inches (width). The 13.9-millimeter blower belt is really intended for Top Fuel drag race use, but it looks very impressive on a street performance engine. The current retail price for the Blower Drive Service 1543-75 blower belt is $200. Refer to Chapter 6 for information regarding blower pulleys and blower belts.

Refer to Chapter 12 for information regarding fuel pressure regulators and fuel pressure gauges.

Ignition System

Install a Mallory 3864501 Unilite distributor, a Mallory 29440 Promaster ignition coil, and a Mallory 697 HyFire IV ignition control.

Refer to Chapter 7 for more information on these products, information about spark plug wires, and information about alternators.

In keeping with the polished-and-chrome theme throughout this engine, install a Proform 66259 chrome high-torque mini-starter. The current retail price for this item is $200.

Cooling and Exhaust Systems

Refer to Chapter 12 for information regarding cooling and exhaust systems. There is a photograph of a set of Hedman Hedders 68090 metallic-ceramic-coated exhaust headers in Chapter 8.

Engine Summary

Note: My original goal was achieved with the building of a completely polished and chrome engine. This is a truly spectacular engine, and it runs beautifully. Perhaps this engine should be referred to as a super ZL-1 clone.

Engine Block

• Keith Black Racing Engines 52000 (model KB500) polished 356 T-6 virgin aluminum engine block with 4.50-inch bore; O-ringed using 0.039-inch-diameter stainless-steel wire; 9.80-inch standard deck height;

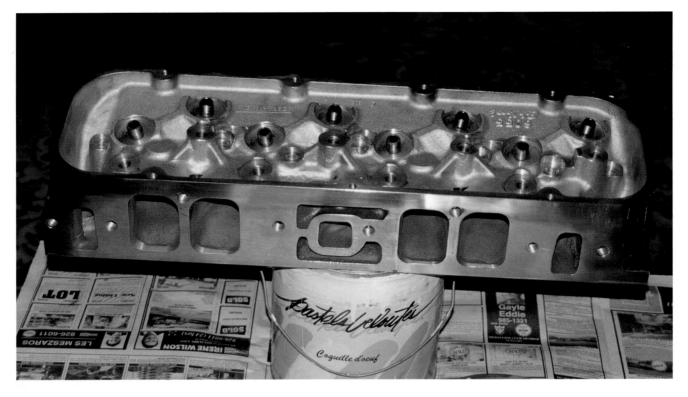

An Edelbrock 6054 (bare) Performer RPM aluminum cylinder head after I sprayed it with Eastwood Company 10200Z diamond-clear gloss finish. The large rectangular intake ports and the bronze valve guides are visible.

No. 5 main bearing cap oil pump cavity polished; cylinder head bolt holes chamfered; billet steel four-bolt main bearing caps installed; 0.0625-inch hole drilled in bottom center of face of front camshaft boss and 0.041-inch hole drilled in top front oil gallery line plugs for additional oiling; Keith Black Racing Engines blue anodized screw-in engine block freeze plugs; stainless steel oil gallery line plugs; Weatherhead 3152-4 polished-brass water jacket drain plugs (1/4-inch NPT); rear blue anodized screw-in camshaft boss plug installed using Permatex aviation form-a-gasket; engine block weight: 165 pounds; engine block coated with Eastwood Company 10200Z diamond-clear gloss finish; $4,500

• Engine block cylinders honed and deglazed using torque plate and Sunnen 800 series 400-grit stones; final bore: 4.50 inches; piston-to-bore clearance: 0.008 inch, measured below bottom of wrist pin perpendicular to wrist pin; $55

Engine block total: $4,555

Crankshaft

• Summit Racing Equipment SES-3-91-05-C385 Proline forged 4340 aircraft-quality non-twisted steel crankshaft; crankshaft Magnafluxed, shot peened, internally balanced; journals surface nitrided to 60 Rockwell C hardness; core heat treated and stress relieved; gun drilled No. 1 and 4 connecting rod pins; computer-designed counterweight positioning; rounded airplane-wing counterweight leading edges; journals radiused 0.125 inch and

The Edelbrock 6054 aluminum cylinder heads have been installed. With one Crower Cams & Equipment Company 73605 roller rocker arm in position, we can check the pushrod length and clearance with the valve spring retainer. The Edelbrock 8852 aluminum water pump and the Fluidampr 712440 harmonic balancer are visible.

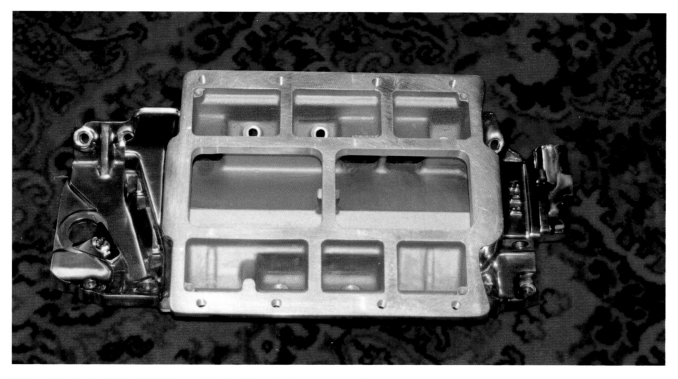

A Blower Drive Service 8026 polished-aluminum big-block Chevrolet blower intake manifold. This intake manifold has a tented floor and a Blower Drive Service 1401 polished-aluminum thermostat housing.

polished; oil holes cross-drilled and chamfered; crankshaft stroke: 4.250 inches for use with 6.385-inch-long (center to center) connecting rods; crankshaft weight (after balancing): 70 pounds; $1,095

• Clevite 77 MS-829H chamfered main bearings, standard size, installed allowing for 0.002-inch crankshaft clearance and 0.006-inch end play; Keith Black Racing Engines 71905 windage tray stud kit installed; inner and outer main bearing cap studs torqued to 100 ft-lb using molykote; $119

• Fluidampr 712440 harmonic balancer (7 1/4-inch o.d., weight: 14.2 pounds) installed with ARP 235-2501 harmonic balancer bolt and washer (190,000 psi) using Loctite and torqued to 85 ft-lb; $330

• GM 3921923 chrome double-groove crankshaft pulley (6 3/4-inch o.d.) and Luke's Custom Machine & Design aluminum crankshaft blower pulley spacer (2-inch thickness) installed with stainless-steel bolts, lockwashers, and flat washers using Loctite and torqued to 30 ft-lb; $155

Crankshaft total: $1,699

Connecting Rods and Pistons

• Manley 14062-8 forged 4340 steel H-beam connecting rods, 6.385-inch length (center to center); fully machined and stress relieved, shot peened, Magnafluxed; bronze alloy wrist pin bushings; wrist pin and crankshaft journal bores honed to +/- 0.0002-inch tolerance; wrist pin end (the small end) diameter: 0.9911 inch; ARP 42361 connecting rod cap screw bolts (8740 steel, 7/16-inch diameter, 12-point, 190,000 psi); connecting rod weight: 880 grams each; connecting rod ratio: 1.50 (with 4.25-inch stroke crankshaft); $699

• Clevite 77 CB-743H chamfered connecting rod bearings, standard size, installed allowing for 0.002-inch crankshaft clearance and 0.016-inch side clearance per pair of connecting rods; connecting rod bolts torqued to 80 ft-lb using 30-weight motor oil and allowing for 0.0063- to 0.0067-inch stretch; $121

• Ross Racing Pistons forged 2618 T-61 aluminum blower pistons, 4.50-inch bore, 8.0:1 compression ratio, slight dished top, intake and exhaust valve reliefs, open combustion chamber design; piston weight: 585 grams each; Ross Racing Pistons 990-04-29 super-duty full-floating heat-treated and casehardened billet 4340 chrome-moly steel taper-wall wrist pins installed allowing for 0.0015-inch connecting rod clearance; wrist pin length: 2.930 inches; wrist pin diameter: 0.990 inches; wrist pin weight: 153 grams each; Ross Racing Pistons 4004-E double Spiro-Lox wrist pin retainers installed; piston ring grooves: top compression ring width: 1/16 inch; second compression ring width: 1/16 inch; oil ring width: 3/16 inch; Childs & Albert RS43ZX505 ZGS dura-moly zero-gap second ring piston ring set installed within manufacturer's recommended arc; top compression

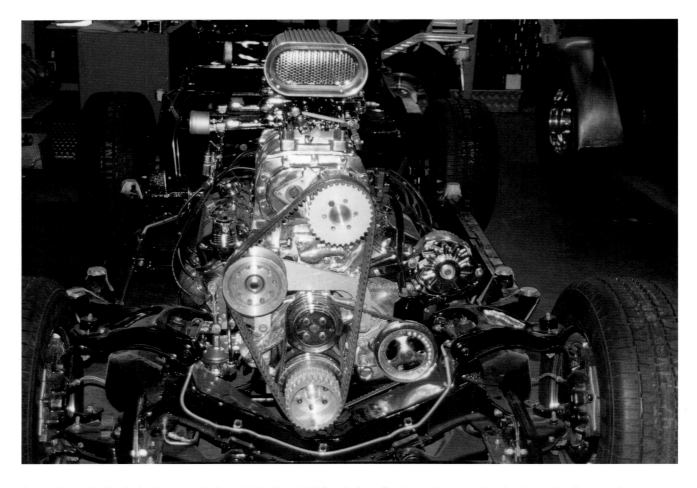

A great photograph of the front of the engine after it was installed in my 1972 Corvette frame. The stock water pump pulley, alternator, crankshaft pulley, and power steering pump were all mounted in the factory position. The crankshaft and blower drive pulleys were the same diameter, although just for the initial start-up of the engine.

ring gap: 0.020 inch; second compression ring gap: 0.018 inch; oil ring gap: 0.018 inch; Ross Racing Pistons ORS-425 oil ring support rails installed with 0.010-inch clearance; piston tops painted with V.H.T. SP-101 white high-temperature coating; intake-valve-to-piston clearance: 0.190 inch, and exhaust-valve-to-piston clearance: 0.160 inch (without gasket); new displacement: 540.7 ci (8.9 liters); $1,060

- Complete V-8 engine balance; $190

Connecting rods and pistons total: $2,070

Lubrication System

- Melling M77HV high-volume oil pump with pressure-balance grooves and Milodon 18301 CNC-machined billet oil pump screen tack welded to oil pump; oil pump cover end clearance: 0.00025 inch; oil pump cover gasket installed using silicone sealant and bolts torqued to 80 in-lb using Loctite; Melling 12577 oil pump driveshaft, 4130 chrome-moly steel, heat-treated ends; Manley 42339 oil pump stud kit installed using anti-seize compound and torqued to 65 ft-lb; $78

- Milodon 32260 Diamond Stripper windage tray installed with nuts torqued to 25 ft-lb using Loctite; Milodon 30950 chrome low-profile oil pan (7-quart capacity) installed with ARP 435-1901 polished stainless-steel oil pan stud kit (170,000 psi) using anti-seize compound and torqued to 15 ft-lb; Fel-Pro 1804 oil pan gaskets and McCord BS210 viton material rear main bearing seals installed using silicone sealant; Trans-Dapt 4958 chrome dip stick and dip stick tube installed; GM 3952301 oil filter adapter installed using anti-seize compound on bolts and torqued to 20 ft-lb; Fram PH-13 oil filter installed with Trans-Dapt 1067 chrome oil filter cover; engine lubricated with 7 quarts Pennzoil HD-30-weight motor oil; $407.57

Lubrication system total: $485.57

Camshaft and Cylinder Heads

- Clevite 77 SH-616S camshaft bearings installed with 0.002-inch camshaft clearance and 0.002-inch end play; No. 1 bearing: SH-615, housing bore: 2.1395 to 2.1405 inches; No. 2 and 5 bearing: SH-616, housing bore: 2.1295 to 2.1305 inches; No. 3

A right side (passenger's side) photograph of the finished product. I spent many nights detailing this engine and the final result is an awesome-looking engine.

and 4 bearing: SH-617, housing bore: 2.1195 to 2.1205 inches; camshaft journal diameter: 1.950 inches; $35

• Crower Cams & Equipment Company 01404 236HR245 street hydraulic roller lifter 8620 cast steel billet camshaft with advertised duration: 292 degrees intake and 303 degrees exhaust; duration at 0.050-inch lift: 236 degrees intake and 245 degrees exhaust; lobe separation angle: 110 degrees; valve lift (with 1.70 ratio rocker arms): 0.586 inch intake and 0.612 inch exhaust; valve lash (hot): zero; camshaft degreed; $245

• Crower Cams & Equipment Company 66231 hydraulic roller lifters with Torque-Lock fasteners, CNC-machine-milled chrome-moly heat-treated steel, stock pushrod seat height, 0.842-inch o.d.; Crower Cams & Equipment 70302 nonadjustable pushrods (3/8-inch diameter, 4130 seamless chrome-moly steel), ends heat treated to surface hardness RC60; intake pushrod length: 7.620 inches, and exhaust pushrod length: 8.620 inches; $540

• Pete Jackson 427-5C quiet dual idler gear drive with camshaft thrust roller button installed with camshaft bolts torqued to 20 ft-lb using Loctite; GM 330850 chrome timing gear cover installed with ARP 400-1401 polished stainless-steel timing gear cover stud kit (170,000 psi) using anti-seize compound and torqued to 15 ft-lb; GM 10114142 timing gear cover gasket installed using silicone sealant; GM 10191640 timing gear cover oil seal installed; $195

• Edelbrock 6054 (bare) Performer RPM polished 356 T-6 aluminum large rectangular port open combustion chamber cylinder heads; intake port runner volume: 315 cc; exhaust port runner volume: 110 cc; combustion chamber volume: 118 cc; intake and exhaust ports fully ported and polished and gasket matched; combustion chambers unshrouded (laying back), polished and cc'd; hardened interlocking ductile iron exhaust valve seat inserts installed; phosphor bronze valve guides installed; cylinder heads receiver groove O-ringed; Serdi-machined multi-angle blueprint valve grind performed; performance range: 1,500 to 7,000 rpm; cylinder heads coated with Eastwood Company 10200Z diamond-clear gloss finish; Keith Black Racing Engines 61021 copper cylinder head gaskets installed using Permatex copper spray-a-gasket; Keith Black Racing Engines 52200CD cylinder head stud kit installed using anti-seize compound with long studs torqued to 65 ft-lb and short studs torqued to 55 ft-lb; $1,565

• Manley 11874 Race Master stainless-steel intake valves (2.25-inch head diameter, 11/32-inch stem diameter; 5.244-inch length overall), hardened tips, swirl polished; weight: 140 grams each; Manley 11881 Race Master stainless-steel exhaust valves (1.88-inch head diameter; 11/32-inch stem diameter; 5.422-inch length overall), hardened tips, swirl polished; weight: 122 grams each; Enginetech S2927 viton positive seal valve stem seals installed; $256

• Crower Cams & Equipment Company 68932 heat-treated chrome-moly steel valve spring seat cups installed with Crower Cams & Equipment Company 68340 tungsalloy dual valve springs with damper; installed height: 137 pounds at 1.850 inches valves open and 383 pounds at 1.250 inches valves closed; 1.505-inch o.d. and 1.125-inch/0.760-inch i.d.; coil bind: 1.10 inches; Crower Cams & Equipment Company 87064 heat-treated chrome-moly steel 10-degree valve spring retainers (11/32-inch stem diameter), new 86110-1 jumbo split-lock 10-degree valve stem locks (heat-treated chrome-moly steel, 11/32-inch stem diameter, 0.050 inch longer than stock), and 86121S heat-treated chrome-moly steel lash caps (0.060-inch depth, 11/32-inch stem diameter) installed; $250

• Manley 42164 hardened-steel raised pushrod guide plates for 3/8-inch-diameter pushrods installed with Edelbrock 88402L heat-treated chrome-moly steel rocker arm studs (7/16-inch diameter) using anti-seize compound and torqued to 45 ft-lb; Crower Cams & Equipment Company 73605 stainless 17-4PH steel roller rocker arms (1025 heat-treated, 1.70 ratio) installed with Crower Cams & Equipment Company 86050 sure-lock rocker arm nuts (heat-treated chrome-moly steel, 7/16-inch stud diameter) using anti-seize compound; $465

• Zip Products VC-207 chrome Corvette valve covers with dripper rails and power brake slant installed with Luke's Custom Machine & Design polished-aluminum valve cover spacers (1/2-inch thickness) and GM 14085759 valve cover gaskets using silicone sealant; Moroso 68516 chrome valve cover hold-down tabs installed with Mr. Gasket 6304 Rodware chrome tall acorn nuts and stainless-steel studs, AN flat washers, and lockwashers using anti-seize compound and torqued to 15 ft-lb; Trans-Dapt 4878 rubber grommet installed with Trans-Dapt 4870 chrome push-in breather; Trans-Dapt 4998 rubber grommet installed with Motorcraft EV-49-B PCV valve; Gates 3225 PCV valve line (5/16-inch i.d. by 2-foot length) installed with Spectre 3001A black nylabraid and Spectre 3208B chrome champclamps; Zip Products IS-226A and IS-226C spark plug wire supports/dividers installed; Chicago Corvette Supply B2363 right-hand valve cover decal "Tonawanda #1 Team" installed; Corvette Central 263216 ZL-1 data plate installed on left-hand valve cover; Dr. Rebuild 1758122

chrome oil filler cap installed; $604.45

Camshaft and cylinder heads total: $4,155.45

Intake System

• Blower Drive Service 8026 polished-aluminum blower intake manifold with large rectangular ports, gasket matched; port size: 1 9/16 inches by 2 5/16 inches; intake manifold coated with Eastwood Company 10200Z diamond-clear gloss finish and underside painted with V.H.T. SP-101 white high-temperature coating; Fel-Pro 1211 intake manifold gaskets, port size: 1.82 inches by 2.54 inches, installed using silicone sealant; ARP 435-2001 polished stainless-steel intake manifold bolts (six-point head, 170,000 psi) installed using anti-seize compound and torqued to 25 ft-lb; $615.57

• NOS GM 5138725 polished-aluminum large bore die-cast supercharger (blower) case (model 6-71), casting date: 3-9-70 (March 9, 1970); GM 5122363 polished die-cast front and rear bearing plates and GM 5114442 polished die-cast front cover; Blower Drive Service 671SL1 bearing seals, 5205HD front bearings, and 62052RS rear bearings installed; Blower Drive Service 671-GK complete gasket set installed using Permatex aviation form-a-gasket; Luke's Custom Machine & Design aluminum bearing support rings and polished-aluminum rear bearing caps installed with polished stainless-steel bolts and lockwashers using anti-seize compound; rotors double-pinned and clearanced; Blower Drive Service 555 pressure relief valve and 556 oil sight gauge installed; stainless-steel oil filler and oil drain plugs (3/8-inch NPT) installed using pipe thread sealant; blower assembled with polished stainless-steel socket head bolts, lockwashers, and AN flat washers using Permatex aviation form-a-gasket; Armstrong N-8090 blower-to-intake-manifold gasket installed using anti-seize compound; Mooneyham 10884 anodized aluminum blower stud kit installed using anti-seize compound; $1,368.95

• Luke's Custom Machine & Design LS2000 polished sculptured blower snout with LS2200 snout shaft, and LS4100 gear coupler installed with polished stainless-steel socket head bolts and lockwashers using Permatex aviation form-a-gasket; $505

• Blower Drive Service 6931 polished 6061 T-6 aluminum crankshaft blower pulley (13.9 millimeters by 31 teeth by 3.5 inches wide) and 6925 polished 6061 T-6 aluminum blower snout pulley (13.9 millimeters by 25 teeth by 3.5 inches wide) installed with polished stainless-steel socket head bolts, lockwashers, and AN flat washers using anti-seize compound; Blower Drive Service 1543-75 Kelvar lined polyurethane blower belt (13.9 millimeters by 60.75 inches long by 3 inches wide) installed; blower drive ratio: 24.0 percent overdrive; blower boost: 11.5 pounds (estimated); $410

• Luke's Custom Machine & Design polished-aluminum idler pulley bracket (1/2-inch thickness) installed with chrome steel water pump spacers (2 1/8-inch length) and polished stainless-steel bolts, lockwashers, and AN flat washers using anti-seize compound and torqued to 25 ft-lb; Luke's Custom Machine & Design polished-aluminum idler pulley installed with 4140 chrome-moly steel stand-off using anti-seize compound; $604.88

• Weiand 7163 polished-aluminum 2x4-barrel carburetor adapter (1 inch high) installed with Weiand 7080 carburetor adapter to blower gasket using polished stainless-steel bolts and lockwashers with anti-seize compound; Trans-Dapt 2084 polished-aluminum carburetor spacers (1 inch high) installed; $135

• Jet Performance Products stage 2 Holley 0-4781, chrome and black powder-coated, 990-cfm double pumper carburetors installed with ARP 400-2402 polished stainless-steel carburetor stud kits using anti-seize compound; $1,722

• Mr. Gasket 5233 Rodware polished-aluminum Hilborn-style scoop installed with K&N E-3260 air filters (6.375-inch o.d. by 2.50-inch height); $262

• Weiand 7166 polished dual side-mount ball bearing carburetor linkage installed using anti-seize compound; $130

• Blower Drive Service 1401 polished-aluminum thermostat housing installed with Robert Shaw 330-160 extra performance balanced 160-degree (Fahrenheit) thermostat; Fel-Pro 35062 thermostat housing gasket installed using silicone sealant with polished stainless-steel bolts and lockwashers torqued to 20 ft-lb using anti-seize compound; Auto-Meter 4401 Pro Comp Ultra-Lite vacuum/boost gauge (0 to 30 inches vacuum/0 to 20 psi boost) installed with Holley 12-803 chrome fuel pressure gauge brackets using polished stainless-steel bolts and lockwashers with anti-seize compound; Trans-Dapt 2291 chrome carburetor return springs and brackets installed; $75.85

• Holley 12-454 chrome mechanical performance fuel pump (6 to 8 psi, 110 gph) installed with ARP 430-1602 polished stainless-steel bolts (six-point head, 170,000 psi) using anti-seize compound and torqued to 20 ft-lb; fuel pump gasket installed using silicone sealant; Weatherhead 3200-6-4 polished-brass adapter (3/8-inch NPT to 1/4-inch NPT) and Weatherhead 402-6-6 polished-brass 90-degree elbow (3/8-inch tube to 3/8-inch NPT) installed using pipe thread sealant; GM 3704817 fuel pump pushrod (1/2-inch diameter by 5 3/4-inch length) installed; Holley 162-530 chrome inline fuel filter (discontinued) installed with Weatherhead 100-6 polished-brass inverted flare nuts (3/8-inch tube) and Summit Racing Equipment 220238 polished stainless-steel fuel line (3/8-inch tube by 0.028-inch wall by 2-foot length) using pipe thread sealant; $127.68

• Holley 12-803 fuel pressure regulators, adjustable from 4 1/2 to 9 psi, installed with Weatherhead 402-6-6 polished-brass 90-degree elbows (3/8-inch tube to 3/8-inch NPT, inlet and outlet lines), and Weatherhead 3325-6-2 polished-brass adapter (1/8-inch NPT to 3/8-inch NPT, outlet line), using pipe thread sealant; Auto-Meter 4411 Pro Comp Ultra-Lite fuel pressure gauge (0 to 15 psi) installed; Summit Racing Equipment 220238 polished stainless-

steel fuel lines (3/8-inch tube by 0.028-inch wall by 5-foot length) installed with Weatherhead 100-6 polished-brass inverted flare nuts (3/8-inch tube) using pipe thread sealant; $167.73

Intake system total: $6,124.66

Ignition System

• Mallory 3864501 Unilite distributor with photo-optic LED system, mechanical tachometer drive, 356 T-6 aluminum housing, mechanical advance, installed with GM 14007385 chrome distributor clamp and polished stainless-steel bolt and lockwasher using anti-seize compound; Mallory 29440 Promaster ignition coil and Mallory 697 HyFire IVA electronic ignition control installed; Mallory 29426 aluminum/bronze distributor drive gear (0.491-inch-diameter shaft) installed; $557.85

• Taylor/Vertex 70053 Pro Series black 8-millimeter high-performance spark plug wires, 135-degree boots, Spiro-Pro Kelvar resistor core, installed; Taylor 42800 black plastic spark plug wire separator kit installed; Champion RC12YC copper plus resistor type spark plugs installed with 0.050-inch gap using anti-seize compound and torqued to 10 ft-lb; $75.57

• Aries KC-11 chrome internally regulated alternator (63 amps) installed with GM 3878236 chrome alternator bracket, GM 3946000 chrome alternator/power steering pump brace, GM 3986109 chrome alternator upper support bracket, and GM 3878240 chrome alternator lower support bracket using polished stainless-steel bolts, lockwashers, flat washers, and nylocks; Gates 11A0785 crankshaft/water pump v-belt (7/16-inch by 31-inch length) installed; Gates 11A0785 alternator belt (7/16-inch by 31-inch length) installed; $347.28

• Proform 66259 chrome high-torque mini-starter, draws 25 amps and produces 2 horsepower of cranking output, installed with new bolts using anti-seize compound; $200

Ignition total: $1,180.70

Cooling and Exhaust Systems

• Edelbrock 8852 Victor Series polished 356 T-6 aluminum water pump (3/4-inch pilot shaft) installed with polished stainless-steel bolts and lockwashers using anti-seize compound and torqued to 25 ft-lb; water pump gaskets installed using silicone sealant; Luke's Custom Machine & Design polished-aluminum water pump pulley (5 1/2-inch diameter, double groove) installed with polished stainless-steel bolts and lockwashers using Loctite and torqued to 25 ft-lb; GM 3829819 chrome thermal bypass connector (water pump fitting), Weatherhead 1430 polished-brass hose connector (1/2-inch NPT to 3/4-inch i.d. hose, intake manifold fitting), and GM 1485552 water pump bypass hose installed with stainless-steel line clamps; hose covered with Spectre 3001A black nylabraid and Spectre 3208B chrome champclamps; $451.95

• Hedman Hedders 68090 metallic-ceramic-coated exhaust headers installed with Fel-Pro 1411 exhaust manifold gaskets

The left side of the blown Keith Black 541-ci polished and chrome engine in my 1972 Corvette coupe.

(1.94-inch-diameter exhaust ports) using Permatex ultra copper high-temperature silicone sealant; Trans-Dapt 8912 Stage 8 polished stainless-steel self-locking exhaust header bolts installed using anti-seize compound and torqued to 25 ft-lb; $466.14

Cooling and exhaust systems total: $918.09

Labor

• Labor for checking clearances, gapping piston rings, degree camshaft, valvetrain assembly, blower setup, detailing, trial engine assembly, final engine assembly, and initial engine start-up; $1,200

Labor total: $1,200

Engine Grand Total: $22,388.47 (U.S.)

Note: The estimated output of this engine is 753 horsepower at 5,500 rpm and 801 ft-lb torque at 4,000 rpm (see Appendix A—Dyno Print-Outs).

CHAPTER 15
1956 CHRYSLER 354-ci HEMI ENGINE

This chapter describes one of the true hot rod legends, the Chrysler hemispherical combustion chamber engine. The Chrysler Hemi saga began in 1951 with the introduction of the Chrysler 331-ci Hemi engine. In 1956, Chrysler introduced the 354-ci Hemi engine, and in 1957, the Chrysler 392-ci Hemi engine made its debut. The 1959 Dodge Truck was the last vehicle to have one of the early Hemi engines installed.

The first Hemi engine described in this book is a naturally aspirated 1956 Chrysler FirePower 354-ci model that was originally installed in a Canadian Chrysler New Yorker. This mild street performance engine was built at Luke's Custom Machine & Design and completed at the end of October 2003. The owner intends to install it in his daily driven 1931 Ford Model A five-window coupe.

Components Description
Engine Block

The specifications for the 1956 Chrysler FirePower 354-ci Hemi engine are:

The 1956 and 1957 Passenger Car Parts List, published by Chrysler Corporation of Canada Limited. These manuals for the parts division were issued in Windsor, Ontario (Canada). The 1956 version is WM 4328, and the 1957 version is WM 4364. It is almost impossible to locate a copy of this type of parts catalog today. This photograph was taken at Wilkinson's Automobilia.

- 354-ci (5.8-liter) displacement
- 3.9375 inches stock bore and 3.625 inches stock stroke
- Stock compression ratio: 9.0:1
- 280 horsepower at 4,600 rpm and 380 ft-lb torque at 2,800 rpm

Over the years, I have come across identification lists for the early Chrysler Hemi engines that explain the year and the application of an engine based on the serial number and casting codes and dates. The lists generally include which vehicles the engines were installed in as well. The serial numbers for the Canadian-manufactured Chrysler Hemi engine blocks, however, are not as well documented, although many early Chrysler Hemi engine blocks were produced in Canada. One of the most authentic places to research information is in the *Passenger Car Parts List* published by Chrysler Corporation for its parts division during every year the early Hemi engines were produced. These parts catalogs are extremely scarce today, although they occasionally turn up on eBay (www.ebay.com) or are advertised for sale in Hemmings Motor News (www.hemmings.com). Wilkinson's Automobilia (see Appendix B—Resources) is an excellent source for this type of publication.

I have encountered early Chrysler Hemi engine blocks over the years that have serial numbers not listed in any of the common publications. Unless you are building a "numbers matching" vehicle, you should not be concerned about the serial number. The most important thing to remember is that you have an early Hemi engine block. It is not my intention to write a casting number or serial number book, although I will list the original source for each Chrysler Hemi engine I describe in this book along with any other relevant information I have obtained for that particular engine block. I will also limit my description of components strictly to the 1956-and-later Chrysler Hemi engines. Many of the parts used with the DeSoto, Dodge, Dodge Truck, industrial, and marine engines are not interchangeable with the Chrysler engines; therefore, I do not intend to list them.

The Chrysler 354-ci Hemi engine block is a good casting and its factory machining is of the highest quality. This engine block was produced for the Chrysler passenger cars in 1956 only and for the Dodge Trucks from 1956 to 1959. The prefixes for the 1956 Chrysler FirePower engine blocks are NE56 and C72 (Canada), the prefix for the 1956 Chrysler 300B engine block is 3NE56, and

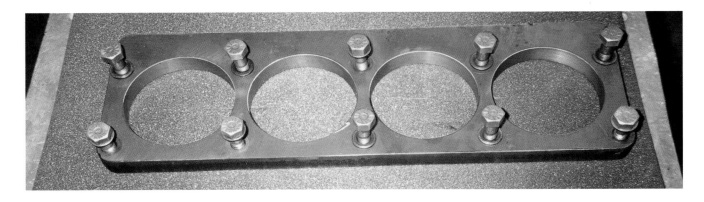

Luke's Custom Machine & Design fabricated this torque plate for the early Chrysler Hemi engines. Use a torque plate whenever a cylinder block is undergoing boring or cylinder honing and deglazing.

the prefix for the 1956 Chrysler Imperial engine block is CE56. There are more than 30 prefixes for the 1956 to 1959 Dodge Truck engine blocks. The 1954 Chrysler 331-ci Hemi engine block was the first Chrysler Hemi engine block that did not have the integral bell housing. This is a real plus because modern transmissions can be adapted fairly easily to the 1954-and-later Chrysler Hemi engine blocks. You can locate a Chrysler 354-ci Hemi engine block today without a great deal of effort, which is quite interesting considering the limited number of engine blocks that were manufactured. The current price for one of these engine blocks in very good condition is estimated to be $400.

Limit the bore of the Chrysler 354-ci Hemi engine block to 0.030-inch oversize in order to leave as much material in the cylinder walls as possible to prevent overheating, especially in a street performance engine. If this is not possible, you can safely have the Chrysler 354-ci Hemi engine block bored 0.0625-inch oversize to a cylinder bore size of 4.00 inches. Refer to Chapter 1 for information pertaining to engine block preparation and machining procedures. The engine block described in this chapter will be bored 0.030-inch oversize.

The Chrysler 354-ci Hemi engine block was manufactured with two-bolt main bearing caps. These main bearing caps are of sufficient strength for most street performance engines, even blown engines, provided the boost does not exceed 6 pounds. There is a photograph of a set of these main bearing caps and bolts in Chapter 1. The ARP 140-5001 high-performance-series main bearing cap bolts (170,000 psi) are available at a current retail price of $40. If you decide to install four-bolt main bearing caps, the Milodon 11320 splayed four-bolt main bearing caps are currently available at most speed equipment dealers for the retail price of $300. Have the engine block align bored and honed after installing four-bolt main bearings caps. The diameter of the main bearing housing bores is 2.6565 to 2.6570 inches. The Chrysler 1408853 rear main bearing cap dowel (or sleeve) is fitted in the engine block on the left side (driver's side) and aligns the rear main bearing cap. The distance from the crankshaft centerline to the deck is 10.390 inches. This engine block did not require align honing but did require parallel decking.

Dorman 568-010 quick-seal copper freeze plugs are available for the Chrysler 354-ci Hemi engine block. Install this type of freeze plug by turning the brass acorn nut that in turn locks a copper expansion plug into the freeze plug opening. Also use Permatex aviation form-a-gasket when installing these freeze plugs. The Dorman 568-010 quick-seal freeze plugs are available at automotive parts outlets for the current retail price of $40. There is a photograph of these freeze plugs in Chapter 1.

The freeze plug sets for most OHV (overhead valve) V-8 engines include the rear camshaft boss plug—not so for the Dorman 568-010 quick-seal freeze plugs. Luke's Custom Machine & Design fabricates a solid brass rear camshaft boss plug to make up for this shortfall. The 1.760-inch-diameter brass plug is available for $15. At the rear of the engine block, on the left side (driver's side) of the Chrysler 354-ci Hemi engine block, there is an oil gallery line that is closed off with a 1/2-inch NPT plug. Inside this oil gallery line you must install a 3/8-inch NPT plug. If you forget to install this plug, there will be no oil pressure. At the front of the engine block, there are two oil gallery line holes that are blocked off when the camshaft retainer plate is installed. Drill and tap the two holes and install new stainless-steel 1/4-inch NPT plugs. Install all the oil gallery line plugs and the rear camshaft boss plug using Permatex aviation form-a-gasket.

Crankshaft

The Chrysler 331-ci and 354-ci Hemi crankshafts are quality items that were manufactured using forged steel, heattreated, Magnafluxed, and shot peened at the factory. The 354-ci crankshaft has slightly different counterweight balancing due to heavier pistons; however, the two models are interchangeable. The stock stroke is

The Luke's Custom Machine & Design solid brass 1.760-inch-diameter rear camshaft boss plug for the early Chrysler Hemi engine blocks.

3.625 inches, the main bearing journals are 2.4995- to 2.5005-inch diameter, and the connecting rod journals are 2.249- to 2.250-inch diameter. After almost 50 years, it is still possible to find a decent Chrysler 331-ci or 354-ci Hemi crankshaft. The current price for one of these crankshafts is estimated to be $250. Caution: If you need to grind the main bearing journals or the connecting rod journals more than 0.040-inch undersize, bearings are not currently available. The only solution to this problem is to have the journals built up. Refer to Chapter 2 for information about this subject. There is a photograph in Chapter 2 of the crankshaft that will be installed in the engine described in this chapter.

The 1951 to 1955 Chrysler 331-ci Hemi crankshaft casting numbers are:
    1323335
    1335001
    1409421
    1419421
The Chrysler 354-ci Hemi crankshaft casting numbers are:
    1409421
    1419421
    1523335
    1617184
    1619647
    1635690

These are the casting numbers I am aware of; there may well be others. Refer to Chapter 2 for information on crankshaft preparation.

The Federal Mogul 916M main bearings are available in standard size and 0.010-inch oversize. The current retail price for a set of these main bearings is $290. The Clevite 77 main bearings are not currently available. The King Engine Bearings main bearings are available in standard size, 0.010-, 0.020-, 0.030-, and 0.040-inch oversize. The current retail price for a set of these main bearings is $110. The King Engine Bearings are available from Hot Heads Research & Racing (23110) and PAW HEM-MOM354. The factory-recommended main bearing clearance was 0.0005 to 0.0015 inches, and the recommended crankshaft

end play was 0.002 to 0.007 inches. The No. 3 main bearing is the thrust bearing. The main bearing cap bolts are torqued to 85 ft-lb using molykote, starting with No. 3 main bearing cap.

The Chrysler 1735045 harmonic balancer is no longer available, but do not install a used harmonic balancer on a street performance engine. The Mopar Performance (Chrysler Corporation) P4452816 harmonic balancer for the small-block Chrysler 340-ci engines bolts onto the 1956 Chrysler 1634860 crankshaft directly and is designed for an internally balanced engine. The outside diameter is 7 1/4 inches. This harmonic balancer will, however, require a wider Woodruff keyway and will have to be degreed—a simple procedure for a competent machine shop. The current retail price for the Mopar Performance P4452816 harmonic balancer is $140, and it is available at Chrysler dealers. The Fluidampr 716395 harmonic balancer is made for the Chrysler 354-ci Hemi engine. This premium-quality harmonic balancer is designed for an internally balanced engine; the outside diameter is 7 1/4 inches, and the weight is 13.7 pounds. The Fluidampr 716395 harmonic balancer is available from speed shops for the current retail price of $300. Install the Chrysler 1618686 oil slinger on the crankshaft snout in front of the crankshaft gear. Glass bead and paint the oil slinger with Glyptal G-1228A medium-grey gloss enamel.

The Mopar Performance P4452816 and the Fluidampr 712420 harmonic balancers have six bolt holes each for mounting the Chrysler 1732941 double v-belt crankshaft pulley. If you plan to install an aftermarket aluminum timing gear cover and a Chevrolet short-style water pump, you cannot use the Chrysler 1732941 double v-belt 5 3/4-inch-diameter crankshaft pulley as it will protrude out too far from the front of the engine for the v-belts to line up. Install a Super Sunny 8841 polished-aluminum single v-belt 6 1/2-inch-diameter crankshaft pulley. Have a 3/8-inch-thick aluminum spacer fabricated to fit between the crankshaft pulley and the harmonic balancer in order to achieve correct v-belt alignment. The current retail price for the Super Sunny 8841 aluminum crankshaft pulley is $25.

Connecting Rods and Pistons
The drop-forged steel I-beam connecting rods used in the Chrysler 331-ci and the Chrysler 354-ci Hemi engines are excellent connecting rods, entirely suitable for most street performance engines. These connecting rods are designed for use with full-floating wrist pins, they are 6.625 inches long (center to center), and they weigh 714 grams each. The casting numbers for the early Chrysler 331-ci and the 354-ci Hemi connecting rods are 1324222 and 1821345. The diameter of the crankshaft end (the big end) is 2.3750 to 2.3755 inches, and the thickness of the crankshaft end (the big end) is 1.00 inch. Refer to Chapter 3 for information regarding connecting rod preparation.

Upgrade the connecting rod bolts with ARP 145-6002 high-performance-series connecting rod bolts (3/8-inch diameter, 8740

A 1956 Chrysler 1634860 (casting number 1619647) forged steel crankshaft. This crankshaft has been shot peened, aligned, Magnafluxed, the main and connecting rod journals have been ground 0.020-inch undersize, the oil holes chamfered, and the journals polished.

A set of Federal Mogul 916M10 main bearings (0.010-inch oversize) for the Chrysler 354-ci Hemi engine.

chrome-moly steel, 190,000 psi). If your engine is going to produce some very serious horsepower, install the ARP 245-6402 pro-series wave-loc connecting rod bolts (3/8-inch diameter, ARP2000 material, 220,000 psi). The current retail price for the ARP 145-6002 connecting rod bolts is $40, and the current retail price for the ARP 245-6402 connecting rod bolts is $85. These connecting rod bolts are designed for the big-block Chrysler 383-ci and 440-ci engines. The ARP 145-6002 connecting rod bolts are torqued to 45 ft-lb using molykote, allowing for 0.006-inch stretch.

The Federal Mogul 1800-CP connecting rod bearings are available in standard size, 0.010-inch oversize, and 0.020-inch oversize. The current retail price for a set of these connecting rod bearings is $195. The Clevite 77 connecting rod bearings are not currently available. The King Engine Bearings are available in standard size, 0.010-, 0.020-, 0.030-, and 0.040-inch oversize. The current retail price for a set of these connecting rod bearings is $95. The King Engine Bearings are available from Hot Heads Research & Racing (23120) and PAW (HEM-MOR354). The factory-recommended connecting rod bearing clearance is 0.0005 to 0.0015 inches, and the recommended side clearance per pair of connecting rods is 0.006 to 0.014 inches.

The Federal Mogul 1804V full-floating wrist pin bushing is a good product to use in the Chrysler 331-ci and the 354-ci Hemi connecting rods. The current retail price for a set of these wrist pin bushings is $35. Federal Mogul products are available at automotive parts dealers.

As previously mentioned, this engine is a mild street performance motor. This being the case, the owner purchased a set of Egge Parts House L1089-8.030 cast-aluminum slipper-skirt pistons (0.030-inch oversize). These pistons have a compression ratio of 9.0:1. The full-floating wrist pins are heat treated and casehardened and Tru-Arc

wrist pin retainers are supplied with them. The Grant Piston Rings 3158 cast-iron piston ring set has a top compression ring width of 3/32 inch, a second compression ring width of 3/32 inch, and an oil ring width of 5/32 inch. Always follow the piston ring manufacturer's recommendation for the piston ring gap. The current retail price for a set of these pistons with wrist pins and cast-iron piston rings is $300. Egge Parts House (see Appendix B—Resources) is one of the best sources for early Chrysler Hemi parts. The factory-recommended cast-aluminum piston clearance is 0.0005 to 0.0015 inches.

Most cast-aluminum pistons for the early Chrysler Hemi engines have an arrow or an "F" marked on the top or the side to indicate which direction should face the front of the engine block. The pistons will be turned differently on each side of the engine block. Pay strict attention to this detail as it is critical for the valve-to-piston clearance. As a general rule, the larger notch in the piston top is located at the top of the engine block nearest the valve lifter gallery because the intake valve usually has the larger diameter of the two valves. Always follow the piston manufacturer's instructions when installing the pistons.

The Fel-Pro FS7908PT-4 is the correct gasket set to use with the early Chrysler 354-ci Hemi engine. The current retail price for this complete gasket set is $135.

Lubrication System

The 1956 Chrysler 1630248 oil pump was an excellent oil pump for the Chrysler 354-ci Hemi engine and was used with the Chrysler 1324213 oil pump pickup screen. This oil pump is no

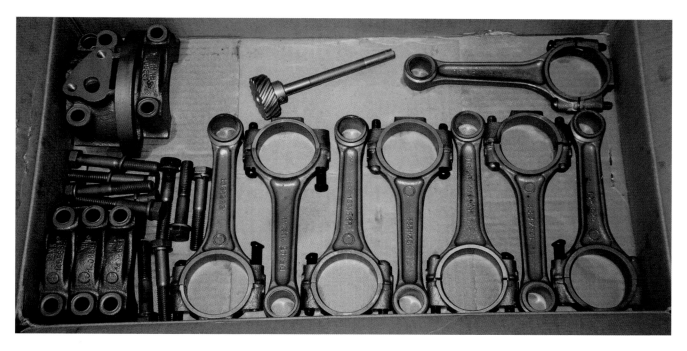

A set of Chrysler 354-ci Hemi I-beam connecting rods (casting number 1324222), a set of the main bearing caps and bolts, and the oil pump intermediate shaft and gear. The connecting rods have been shot peened and aligned and are now ready for the machine shop. The main bearing caps have been shot peened.

longer available from Chrysler Corporation. The most common oil pump installed today in the Chrysler 354-ci Hemi engine is the Chrysler 4286590 high-volume oil pump, currently used in the small-block Chrysler 340-ci engines. An adapter is required to bolt it to the rear main bearing cap in the early Chrysler Hemi engines. The owner of this engine managed to locate a NOS 1956 Chrysler 1630248 oil pump and 1324213 oil pump pickup screen. They will be used with a 1956 Chrysler 1553766 rear sump oil pan. The Chrysler 354-ci and 392-ci Hemi oil pans are interchangeable.

The Milodon 20155 high-volume oil pump is provided with an attached pickup screen and is designed for use with the early Chrysler Hemi rear sump oil pans. The Milodon 20150 high-volume oil pump with the Milodon 18342 oil pump pickup screen is designed for use with the Milodon 30932 low-profile rear sump oil pan. The Milodon oil pumps, with the pickup screens, currently retail for $200. The Milodon 30932 oil pan is available at a current retail price of $195 on an exchange basis only. If you want one of those Milodon oil pans, you will have to beat the bushes and locate a stock early Chrysler Hemi oil pan in fairly decent shape. Install the oil pan with 20 pieces: 5/16 NC by 1-inch-long stainless-steel hex head bolts, lockwashers, and AN flat washers.

The PAW HEM-5300 cast-aluminum, rear sump oil pan is a nice addition to any street performance early Chrysler Hemi engine, and is designed for use with the Milodon 21055 high-volume oil pump and oil pump pickup screen assembly. The current retail price for this oil pan is $300, or $400 for the HEM-5300P polished version.

The Chrysler 354-ci Hemi engine had an oil pressure relief valve fitted underneath the rear main bearing cap in the right side (passenger's side) of the engine block. During periods of low rpm, such as when the engine was cold, the oil pressure relief valve would open, permitting unfiltered oil to enter the oiling system—not acceptable for a street performance engine. Remove the Chrysler 1535905 oil pressure relief valve body and install a PAW HEM-5340 oil diverter valve, available for the current retail price of $20.

Use the PAW HEM-5340 oil diverter valve in conjunction with a spin-on oil filter mounting bracket such as the Hot Heads Research & Racing 20101 vertical position model. These two items will create a true full-flow oil system. The Hot Heads Research & Racing 20101 aluminum oil filter mounting bracket bolts to the stock mounting pad located on the right side (passenger's side) of the Chrysler 354-ci Hemi engine block and accepts a typical spin-on oil filter such as the Fram PH-8A. The current retail price for this oil filter adapter is $55.

The Chrysler 354-ci Hemi engine was equipped with an intermediate driveshaft for the oil pump. The Chrysler 1323369 oil pump intermediate driveshaft (6.030-inch length) with the Chrysler 601268 gear was located between the oil pump and the distributor. The oil pump intermediate driveshaft was lowered from the top of the valve lifter gallery through the Chrysler 1324281 intermediate driveshaft bushing to connect with the oil pump. The gear is at the top of the oil pump intermediate driveshaft in the valve lifter gallery. The Hot Heads Research &

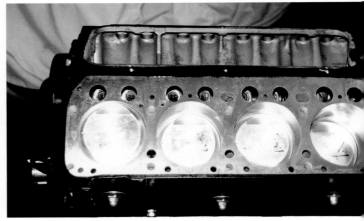

Egge Parts House L1089-8.030 cast-aluminum pistons (0.030-inch oversize) have been installed in this Chrysler 354-ci Hemi engine block.

A set of PAW HEM-MOR354 (King Engine Bearings) main bearings (0.010-inch oversize) for the Chrysler 354-ci Hemi engine.

Racing 21945 oil pump intermediate driveshaft (6.030-inch length) is designed for use with the 1956 Chrysler 1642392 distributor used in the 354-ci Hemi engine. The Hot Heads Research & Racing 21947 oil pump intermediate driveshaft (6.360-inch length) is designed for use with a small-block Chrysler 360-ci distributor. The current retail price for each of these intermediate driveshafts is $30. The Hot Heads Research & Racing 21950 intermediate driveshaft bushing is available for $4.

The dip stick and dip stick tube are often missing from early Chrysler Hemi engines. The Hot Heads Research & Racing 21955 chrome angled dip stick and tube are available for $18. The Hot Heads Research & Racing 21956 chrome straight dip stick and tube are available for $13.

Camshaft and Cylinder Heads

The Federal Mogul 1149M camshaft bearings are available at the current retail price of $60 for a set. The Clevite 77 SH-313S camshaft bearings are available at the current retail price of $55 for a set. The Chrysler 354-ci Hemi camshaft journal diameter is 2.00 inches.

Chrysler hydraulic lifter and solid lifter camshafts are not suitable candidates for a street performance engine. Hot Heads Research & Racing is one of the few outlets today that sells a street performance solid (mechanical) lifter camshaft for the Chrysler 354-ci Hemi engine. The company offers three different designs. Luke's Custom Machine & Design had a few 1956 Chrysler 1632425 solid (mechanical) lifter camshafts custom-ground years ago by a legendary local camshaft grinding company, Shadbolt Cams. One of these camshafts was discovered buried at the back

of a shelf and will be used in this engine. The specifications for this camshaft are: advertised duration: 290 degrees intake and exhaust; duration at 0.050-inch lift: 230 degrees intake and exhaust; lobe separation angle: 110 degrees; net valve lift (with 1.50 ratio rocker arms): 0.458 inch intake and 0.457 inch exhaust; and valve lash (hot): 0.020 inch intake and 0.021 inch exhaust. This is a very good camshaft for a naturally aspirated early Chrysler 354-ci Hemi engine. The torque curve is almost straight from 2,000 to 4,500 rpm.

The 1955 to 1958 Chrysler 300-series engines were the only early Chrysler Hemi engines installed in passenger cars that the factory equipped with a solid lifter camshaft, nonadjustable pushrods, and adjustable rocker arms. The factory equipped all the other early Chrysler Hemi engines installed in passenger cars with hydraulic lifter camshafts, nonadjustable pushrods, and nonadjustable rocker arms. Hot Heads Research & Racing offers three types of hydraulic lifter camshafts for the Chrysler 354-ci Hemi engine. PAW offers five hydraulic lifter camshafts for normally aspirated engines and three hydraulic lifter blower grind camshafts. The Hot Heads Research & Racing and the PAW camshafts retail for $225 outright, with no core exchange.

Prior to 1955, the Chrysler Hemi camshafts had a long threaded snout for installing the camshaft timing gear and a large fuel pump eccentric. In 1955, Chrysler introduced a short snout for installing the camshaft gear and a small fuel pump eccentric. The pre-1955 camshafts and the 1955-and-later camshafts are interchangeable, provided the timing chain set and fuel pump eccentric that are matched with each model of camshaft are changed with the camshaft. This only applies to the Chrysler 331-ci and 354-ci Hemi engines.

The Chrysler 1634267 thrust plate was attached to the front of the engine block with four bolts and secured the camshaft in position. This plate, by definition, controls the end thrust of the camshaft. The Chrysler 1618717 camshaft sprocket spacer is a metal beveled ring that fits over the snout of the camshaft and provides the clearance between the camshaft sprocket and the front of the engine block. The bottom two bolts secure the Chrysler 1328644 oil trough to the camshaft thrust plate. The oil trough is a practical item that lubricates the camshaft timing chain. The Chrysler 1632426 camshaft eccentric is used with a mechanical fuel pump. The items just described were installed in the 1955-and-later Chrysler Hemi engines. Refer to Chapter 5 for a photograph of the camshaft thrust plate and the oil trough.

Most aluminum aftermarket timing gear covers do not have a mechanical fuel pump boss; therefore, you will need to use an electric fuel pump. Remove the Chrysler 1632426 camshaft eccentric. The Hot Heads Research & Racing 20200 camshaft bolt and washer kit replaces the factory camshaft eccentric and is available for $13. The PAW HEM-5270 camshaft retainer plate kit (consisting of the camshaft thrust plate and bolts, the camshaft bolt and washer kit, and the camshaft sprocket spacer) is available for the current retail price of $50.

There are only a few sources of aftermarket solid (mechanical) lifters for the Chrysler 354-ci Hemi engine. Automotive parts outlets sell the Sealed Power AT-2084 Johnson solid lifters for about $60 a set. The PAW HEM-937 solid lifters are available for a current retail price of $50 for a set. There is a photograph of a set of solid lifters in Chapter 5. A reputable camshaft grinding company can resurface a set of the 1956 Chrysler 1635737 solid lifters if they are in very good condition, although it may cost more than a new set. The solid lifters used in the big-block Chrysler 383-ci and 440-ci engines will fit the Chrysler 354-ci Hemi engine block and do have the correct pushrod seat height. Crower Cams & Equipment Company 66932 precision-ground radius face solid lifters are available for the current retail price of $70 for a set. The 1956 Chrysler 1555176 hydraulic lifters are no longer listed. PAW HEM-812 heavy-duty hydraulic lifters are available at the current retail price of $65 for a set.

You will need to install an aftermarket camshaft in a Chrysler 354-ci Hemi engine that is being built as a street performance engine. Replace the factory pushrods with longer aftermarket pushrods. Use adjustable pushrods with nonadjustable rocker arms and nonadjustable pushrods with adjustable rocker arms. Smith Brothers Pushrods (see Appendix B—Resources) is one of the finest sources for custom-length pushrods and its prices are reasonable. As a matter of interest, the Chrysler 1486906 nonadjustable intake valve pushrods (5/16-inch diameter by 9.610-inch length) and the Chrysler 1486907 nonadjustable exhaust valve pushrods (5/16-inch diameter by 10.958-inch length) were used with the 1956 Chrysler hydraulic lifter camshaft. The Chrysler 1538121 nonadjustable intake valve pushrods (5/16-inch diameter by 9.752-inch length) and the Chrysler 1538122

The Milodon 20155 high-volume oil pump with attached oil pump pickup screen and the PAW HEM-5300 aluminum oil pan.

nonadjustable exhaust valve pushrods (5/16-inch length by 11.207-inch length) were used with the 1956 Chrysler solid lifter camshaft.

A number of economy timing chain sets are available for the Chrysler 354-ci Hemi engine. The Cloyes 93103 true roller timing chain set with a heat-treated, multi-keyway crankshaft sprocket for advancing or retarding the camshaft timing is a quality model. The current retail price for the Cloyes 93103 true roller timing chain set is $95. The timing chain sets used in the small-block Chrysler 340-ci and 360-ci engines will fit a Chrysler 354-ci Hemi engine. New on the market, the JP Performance 5895 billet steel double-roller timing chain set with a multi-keyway crankshaft sprocket is also an excellent model. This premium-quality timing chain set for the Chrysler 354-ci engine is manufactured in Australia, and its current retail price is a very low $60.

The Chrysler 1639273 stamped steel timing gear cover is not compatible with a Chevrolet short-style water pump. There is a photograph of one of these timing gear covers in Chapter 5. The Hot Heads Research & Racing 20215 aluminum timing gear cover is designed for the 1955 to 1958 Chrysler 331-ci, 354-ci, and the 392-ci Hemi engines. This excellent product is equipped with an adjustable timing pointer, utilizes the stock early Chrysler Hemi one-piece oil seal, and is complete with stainless-steel socket head bolts. Have someone like "Tim, the polishing guy" tackle this piece of aluminum. The current retail price for the Hot Heads Research & Racing 20215 aluminum timing gear cover is $140.

We will install the Chrysler 1738375 stamped steel one-piece valley cover (for a 1957 Chrysler 300C Hemi engine) on this engine. This valley cover has an attached breather tube with a dent in it about halfway up the tube. The dent was introduced at the factory to clear the 2x4-barrel carburetor setup. Most of the early Chrysler Hemi valley covers consisted of two pieces: a lower unit and an upper unit. Install the valley cover with eight pieces: 5/16-inch NC by 3/4-inch-long stainless-steel hex head bolts, lockwashers, and AN flat washers.

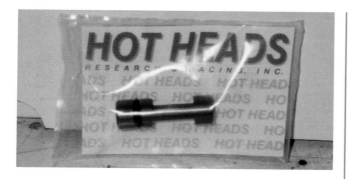

The Hot Heads Research & Racing 20120 oil diverter valve for use in the early Chrysler Hemi engines.

The Chrysler 1323369 shorter (6.030-inch length) oil pump intermediate driveshaft on the left is designed for a Chrysler 354-ci Hemi engine. The Chrysler 1732826 longer (6.345-inch length) oil pump intermediate driveshaft on the right is designed for a Chrysler 392-ci Hemi engine.

The Chrysler hemispherical combustion chamber cylinder heads are probably the most efficient cylinder heads ever installed on an engine manufactured in the United States. The intake and exhaust ports in these cast-iron cylinder heads are short in length, gently curved, and symmetrical. The intake and exhaust valves are at the optimum angle for combustion chamber efficiency. Very little can be done to these cylinder heads to improve them aside from surfacing, gasket matching, and cc'ing the combustion chambers. Any porting and polishing work involves some minor cleanup in the runners; the ports are actually quite smooth due to the high quality of the casting.

The 1955 Chrysler 331-ci Hemi cylinder heads are almost identical to the 1956 Chrysler 354-ci Hemi cylinder heads. Both models have water passage openings at each end of the cylinder head; the water passages are blocked off with removable plates.

The Hot Heads Research & Racing 20101 polished-aluminum oil filter adapter. The Dorman 568-010 quick-seal freeze plugs are visible.

The 1955 Chrysler 331-ci Hemi cylinder head casting number is 1556157, and the 1956 Chrysler 354-ci Hemi cylinder head casting number is 1619823. These are the casting numbers I am aware of; there may well be others. The estimated cost for a pair of 1955 or 1956 Chrysler Hemi cylinder heads without the rocker arms or valve assemblies (bare) is $300.

Have the early Chrysler Hemi cylinder heads hot tanked to remove the usual grime that builds up after many years of service or lying in someone's garage for a lengthy period of time. Have the cylinder heads pressure tested to ensure there are no hidden cracks. After this is done, carry out the porting and polishing and the gasket matching. Use a high-speed grinder with sanding discs and detail the exterior surface of the cylinder head. Then, send the cylinder heads out to be Redi-Stripped to ensure the water passages are completely clean. As soon as the cylinder heads return from being Redi-Stripped, mask off the outside, place plastic covers over the valve guides, and paint the surface beneath the valve covers with Glyptal G-1228A medium-grey gloss enamel. This paint will prevent rust from forming if there ever is moisture present on the cylinder heads and it will also aid with the oil return. Mask off the top and bottom sides of the cylinder heads and the intake and exhaust ports, and then paint the cylinder heads with the same color as the engine block. Retap the intake and exhaust manifold bolt holes and the spark plug holes. The cylinder heads are now ready for the machine shop.

The valve guides in the 1955 and 1956 Chrysler Hemi cylinder heads are cast iron. They are removable to permit easy replacement of damaged or worn valve guides. Have a competent machine shop handle any valve guide removal and replacement to avoid serious damage to the cylinder heads. The Hot Heads Research & Racing 40030 (intake) and 40040 (exhaust) cast-iron valve guides for 3/8-inch stem diameter valves are available at a current retail price of $96 for the complete intake and exhaust set.

The Chrysler 331-ci and 354-ci Hemi cylinder heads are equipped with valve seat inserts. The intake valve dimensions are: 1.9375-inch head diameter by 3/8-inch stem diameter by 5.03125-inch length overall. The exhaust valve dimensions are: 1.75-inch head diameter by 3/8-inch stem diameter by 5.03125-inch length overall. The engine described in this chapter is a mild street performance engine; therefore, stock dimension valves will be installed. The owner was able to purchase a NOS set of Federal Mogul V-2190 SAE (Society of Automotive Engineers) 1041 steel replacement intake valves (1.9375-inch head diameter by 3/8-inch stem diameter by 5.049-inch length overall). Additionally, the owner purchased a NOS set of 1956 Chrysler 1634744 exhaust valves (1.75-inch head diameter by 3/8-inch stem diameter by 5.0375-inch length overall). A Serdi-machined multi-angle blueprint valve grind will be performed on the cylinder heads. Egge Parts House supplies replacement valves for early Chrysler Hemi engines for about $10 each.

A number of engine building shops install valve stem seals only on the intake valves in the early Chrysler Hemi cylinder heads. They do not believe it is necessary to install valve stem seals on the exhaust valves due to the angle of the exhaust valves. It does no harm to install valve stem seals on the exhaust valves. The Enginetech S2890 viton positive seal valve stem seals will be installed on the intake and exhaust valves in the engine described here.

Many machine shops advocate the installation of hardened exhaust valve seat inserts for use with today's unleaded gasoline. Luke Balogh, the owner of Luke's Custom Machine & Design, drove his own Ford van, equipped with a mid-engine 1957 Chrysler 392-ci Hemi, for almost 300,000 miles using unleaded gasoline before the engine finally packed it in. Luke's Hemi engine died because of a spun connecting rod bearing and not because of non-hardened exhaust valve seat inserts. Unless the intake or exhaust valve seat inserts in the Chrysler Hemi cylinder head are badly pitted or cracked, leave them alone. Most street performance vehicles equipped with an early Chrysler Hemi engine will be used for limited driving at the best of times.

The 1956 Chrysler 354-ci Hemi cylinder heads were equipped with single valve springs that are only suitable for use with a stock camshaft. Because this is a mild street performance engine, install a new set of Federal Mogul VS-510 single valve springs with an installed height of: 80 pounds at 1.70 inches valves closed and 200 pounds at 1.250 inches valves open; 1.40-inch o.d. and 1.00-inch i.d.; coil bind: 1.15 inches. Install 1956 Chrysler 1619636 heat-treated valve spring retainers and 1956 Chrysler 1614666 valve stem locks for use with the four-groove Chrysler valves. The

A set of Clevite 77 SH-313S camshaft bearings for the Chrysler 354-ci engines.

Federal Mogul VS-510 single valve springs are available at the current retail price of $50.

The rocker arm assemblies installed on all the early Chrysler Hemi 331-ci, 354-ci, and 392-ci passenger car engines are the same with the exception of the Chrysler 300-series, which has adjustable rocker arms. The rocker arm ratio is 1.50. Disassemble and clean the early Chrysler Hemi rocker arm assemblies, and glass bead the rocker arms, springs, and stands. Paint the rocker arms and stands with Glyptal G-1228A medium-grey gloss enamel (providing the shaft holes are plugged) after they have been glass beaded to assist with oil return and prevent rust from forming if there is moisture present. Remove the 5/8-inch-diameter rocker arm shaft end plugs from each end of the shaft and thoroughly clean the shafts. There are eight oiling holes in each shaft that must be clear. The oiling holes in the rocker arms themselves must be clear as well. Polish the shafts on a lathe with 600-grit wet sandpaper. The rocker arm pallets (tips) that contact the valves might have to be refaced. If refacing is necessary, have a premium-quality machine shop perform the work to avoid the complete destruction of the rocker arms. If using adjustable rocker arms, coat the adjusting screws with anti-seize compound when reassembling them. Have the rocker arm shafts hard chromed when building a high-horsepower street performance engine. The recommended shaft clearance for the rocker arms is 0.0015 to 0.002 inch. The estimated cost for a used pair of early Chrysler Hemi rocker arm assemblies in good condition is $300.

The following is a complete list of all the rocker arm assembly parts (for one cylinder head) for a 1956 Chrysler 354-ci Hemi engine using nonadjustable rocker arms:

The Shadbolt Cams street-grind solid (mechanical) lifter camshaft and a new set of Sealed Power (Federal Mogul) AT-2084 Johnson solid lifters for the Chrysler 354-ci Hemi engine.

On the left: the 1956 Chrysler 1486906 intake pushrod and 1486907 exhaust pushrod are used with the Chrysler hydraulic lifter. On the right: the 1956 Chrysler 1538121 intake pushrod and 1538122 exhaust pushrod are used with the Chrysler solid lifter.

- One each: 1327449, casting number 1323355, left end bracket (stand)
- One each: 1327450, casting number 1323356, left inner bracket (stand)
- Two each: 1327451, casting number 1323357, center and right inner bracket (stand)
- One each: 1327452, casting number 1323358, right end bracket (stand)
- Four each: 1323353, casting number 1323353, nonadjustable intake rocker arms
- Four each: 1323354, casting number 1323354, nonadjustable exhaust rocker arms

- One each: 1324481 intake rocker arm shaft, 7/8-inch diameter
- One each: 1324482 exhaust rocker arm shaft, 7/8-inch diameter
- Eight each: 1324449 rocker arm locating springs
- Two each: 142520 tapered pins (for end bracket)
- Two each: 103380 cotter pins (for end bracket)
- Four each: 1324268 end plugs, 5/8-inch o.d. (Papco 260-126 expansion plugs)

If adjustable rocker arms are used, these are:
- Four each: 1535011, casting number 1535011, adjustable intake rocker arms
- Four each: 1535012, casting number 1535012, adjustable exhaust rocker arms
- Four each: 1535013 rocker arm adjusting screws
- Four each: 1535014 rocker arm adjusting screw jam nuts

PAW offers completely rebuilt early Chrysler Hemi nonadjustable rocker assemblies with hard-chromed rocker arm shafts, bronze rocker arm bushings, refaced rocker arms pallets (tips), and milled tops of the rocker arm stands. The current retail price for each rebuilt rocker arm assembly is $175, on an exchange basis only.

The Chrysler 1324452 long cylinder head bolts (10) and the Chrysler 1323310 short cylinder head bolts (10) can be reused, provided they are in good condition and not badly pitted or rusted. These quality cylinder head bolts are suitable for a street performance engine.

The Chrysler 1323310 FirePower stamped steel valve covers are a nice addition to any early Chrysler Hemi engine when they have been chrome plated, although they will only clear nonadjustable rocker arm assemblies. Install the valve covers using 1 1/2-inch-long engine studs that are 5/16-inch NC on the end installed in the cylinder head and 5/16-inch NF on the valve cover end. Use Permatex aviation form-a-gasket when installing the valve cover studs in the cylinder heads. Purchase 12 pieces: 5/16-inch NF stainless-steel acorn nuts, lockwashers, and AN flat washers. Buff the acorn nuts and apply anti-seize compound to the top of the studs when installing the acorn nuts.

Intake System

The only high-performance intake manifold offered for the early Chrysler Hemi engines was the 2x4-barrel carburetor dual-plane cast-iron intake manifold. This intake setup was only available on the 1955 to 1958 Chrysler 300-series engines. The Chrysler 1675930 (casting number 1634285) dual four-barrel intake manifold was installed on the 1956 Chrysler 300B engine and is not the greatest of designs. The Weiand (Holley) 7263 cast-aluminum dual-quad, dual-plane high-rise intake manifold is still available at a current retail price of $230. The advertised power range is: 2,000 to 6,800 rpm.

A Hot Heads Research & Racing 50020 polished cast-aluminum single quad, dual-plane high-rise intake manifold will be installed on this engine. This well-designed intake manifold retails for $275 for the unpolished version. Its advertised power range is idle to 5,500 rpm. The stainless-steel socket head intake manifold bolts are supplied with the intake manifold.

An Edelbrock 1405 Performer (non-emission) 600-cfm carburetor with manual choke will be installed on this engine. The current retail price for this carburetor is $200. Purchase an ARP 400-2401 polished stainless-steel carburetor stud kit to match the polished intake manifold. The current retail price for the ARP 400-2401 carburetor stud kit is $11. Install the carburetor studs in the intake manifold using anti-seize compound. Refer to Chapter 6 for information regarding fuel pressure regulators and fuel pressure gauges. Install a Mr. Gasket 6477 Rodware chrome air cleaner (14-inch o.d. by 2 1/2-inch height).

The 1957 Chrysler 1738375 valley cover for the Chrysler 300C engine has a hole in the top rear section where a rubber grommet and PCV valve can be installed. Fresh air will now be pulled through the breather cap at the front of the valley cover, and the engine will be vented through the PCV valve to the carburetor.

Ignition System

Install an electronic ignition in your street performance early Chrysler Hemi engine. Refer to Chapter 7 for information about distributors. The Proform 66991 electronic distributor with vacuum advance and a control unit will fit the 1956 Chrysler 354-ci Hemi engine if you install the Hot Heads Research & Racing 21947 oil pump intermediate driveshaft. There is an explanation of oil pump intermediate driveshafts earlier in this chapter. The Proform 66991 distributor for the small-block Chrysler 360-ci engine currently retails for $175. Use the Chrysler 1326835 distributor clamp to secure the distributor in position. Many aftermarket steel distributor clamps are poorly manufactured and will bend when they are tightened. Refer to Chapter 7 for information about ignition coils.

One of the new JP Performance 5985 billet steel double-roller timing chain sets manufactured in Australia.

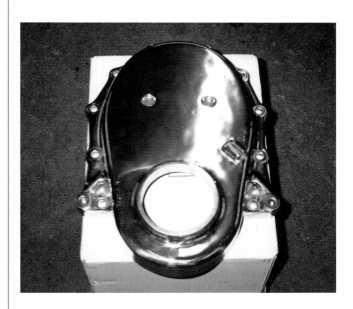

A Hot Heads Research & Racing 20215 polished-aluminum timing gear cover for the early Chrysler Hemi engine.

The firing order for the 1956 Chrysler 354-ci Hemi engine is: 1, 8, 4, 3, 6, 5, 7, and 2 cylinders. The left side (driver's side) bank from the front is: 1, 3, 5, and 7. The right side (passenger's side) bank from the front is: 2, 4, 6, and 8.

Install Mopar Performance (Chrysler Corporation) 4120808 Hemi spark plug tube and insulator kits with Taylor/Vertex 35071 Spiro-Pro black 8-millimeter spark plug wire. Cut the spark plug wire to length for each cylinder. Slide the spark plug tube seals

A 1955 Chrysler 331-ci Hemi cast-iron cylinder head (casting number 1556157) that has been cut apart in order to show the port and valve layout. The runners are gently curved and quite smooth, direct from the factory. The valves are at the optimum angle for combustion chamber efficiency.

A pair of 1955 Chrysler 331-ci Hemi cylinder heads (casting number 1556157) that have been Redi-Stripped, ported and polished, and the area beneath the valve covers has been painted with Glyptal G-1228A medium-grey gloss enamel. These cylinder heads are ready for the machine shop.

(contained in the Fel-Pro FS7908PT-4 complete gasket set) onto the Chrysler 1737379 aluminum spark plug tubes. Gap the spark plugs (for this engine it is 0.050 inch) and slide them into the spark plug tubes. Gently slide the spark plug tubes through the valve covers and into the cylinder heads. Torque the spark plugs to 25 ft-lb (for cast-iron cylinder heads). Place Luke's Custom Machine & Design beveled aluminum spark plug tube washers on the ends of the spark plug tubes (beveled side up), and peen the end of the spark plug tube over the spark plug tube washer. Apply dielectric grease to one end of the spark plug wire, slide the Hemi boot onto the spark plug wire, slide the plastic insulator onto the spark plug wire, slide the rubber spark plug boot onto the spark plug wire, and then crimp the spark plug connector onto the end of the spark plug wire. Slide the rubber spark plug boot down until the end is over the spark plug connector, slide the plastic insulator onto the rubber spark plug boot, connect the spark plug wire to the spark plug, and then slide the Hemi boot down the spark plug wire onto the valve cover so it slips into place around the beveled spark plug tube washer. Connect the other end of each spark plug wire to the distributor. Refer to Chapter 7 for a photograph of the Mopar Performance 4120808 spark plug tube and insulator kit. Refer to Chapter 7 for information pertaining to alternators.

The NGK BP6ES resistor-type 18-millimeter spark plugs are quality spark plugs for early Chrysler Hemi street performance engines. The Splitfire 6E spark plugs are considered premium-quality 18-millimeter spark plugs and they are more expensive. Gap the spark plugs to 0.050 inch when using an electronic ignition with a control box.

The Mopar Performance (Chrysler Corporation) P5249644 lightweight starting motor is available from Chrysler dealers for the current retail price of $135. This starting motor is frequently used with transmission adapters. The Powermaster 19530 chrome XS Torque starting motor is available for the 1951 to 1956 Chrysler Hemi engines using a 146-tooth flywheel. The current retail price for this starting motor is $290.

Cooling and Exhaust Systems

Install Hot Heads Research & Racing 20701 aluminum water pump adapters in order to mount the Weiand 8212 action-plus aluminum big-block Chevrolet short-style water pump. Use the Hot Heads Research & Racing 20215 aluminum timing gear cover with this combination. Install the Hot Heads Research & Racing 21301 aluminum water crossover manifold with offset water outlet by connecting it to the water outlet openings at the front of each cylinder head. The current retail price for the Hot Heads Research & Racing 20701 water pump adapters is $33, the Weiand 8212 water pump is $110, and the Hot Heads Research & Racing 21301 crossover manifold is $190. These items are not polished. Stainless-steel socket head bolts are supplied with the water pump adapters

On the left is the 1956 Chrysler 1634790 intake valve guide with the beveled top. On the right is the 1956 Chrysler 1486911 exhaust valve guide.

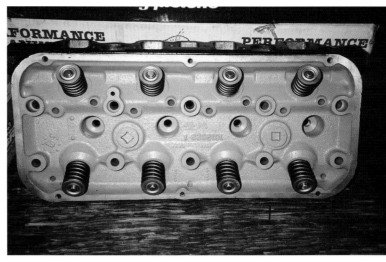

One of the 1956 Chrysler 1671141 (casting number 1619823) Hemi cylinder heads that will be used on the engine. Those are Federal Mogul VS-510 single valve springs and 1956 Chrysler 1619636 valve spring retainers with 1956 Chrysler 1614666 valve stem locks.

and crossover manifold. Use a Mr. Gasket 2660 chrome water outlet elbow (1955 to 1964 Chevrolet) with the crossover manifold. The current retail price for this water outlet elbow is $10.

The Chrysler 1732885 triple-groove (5 3/4-inch diameter) water pump pulley cannot be used with the Chevrolet short-style water pump because the pulley protrudes too far forward of the engine for the v-belt to properly align with the crankshaft pulley. Install a Trans-Dapt 9478 polished-aluminum single-groove water pump pulley (6-inch diameter). Purchase four 5/16-inch NF by 3/4-inch-long stainless-steel socket head countersunk bolts for securing the water pump pulley to the water pump. Buff the heads of the bolts to match the polished water pump and water pump pulley. The current retail price for the Trans-Dapt 9478 water pump pulley is $45.

Attach the exhaust manifolds to the cylinder heads using 2-inch-long engine studs. The part of the stud that is installed in the cylinder head is 3/8-inch NC, and the part of the stud where the exhaust manifold is attached is 3/8-inch NF. Install the studs in the cylinder heads using Permatex aviation form-a-gasket. There are a limited number of exhaust headers available for the early Chrysler Hemi engines. The PAW HEM-5500 block hugger headers with starter tubes are available at the current retail price of $300, or $400 for the HEM-5501 metallic-ceramic-coated version. The Hot Heads Research & Racing 60020 full-length headers are available at the current retail price of $400, or $637 for the metallic-ceramic-coated version. The Hot Heads Research & Racing 60010 block hugger headers retail for $300, or $449 for the metallic-ceramic-coated version. If you need to build custom exhaust headers, the Hot Heads Research & Racing 60005 steel exhaust header flange kit (3/8-inch thickness) is available at the current retail price of $60.

Engine Summary

Note: Exhaust headers are not listed in this engine summary because a custom set will have to be fabricated.

Engine Block

• 1956 Canadian Chrysler New Yorker 354-ci engine block; serial number prefix: C72; casting number 1619829; casting date: J275 (October 27, 1955); stock bore: 3.9375 inches; stock stroke: 3.625 inches; two-bolt main bearing caps; 9.0:1 compression ratio; 280 horsepower at 4,600 rpm and 380 ft-lb torque at 2,800 rpm; engine block weight (bare): 186 pounds; $400

• Engine block hot tanked; engine block and main bearing caps and bolts Magnafluxed; main bearing caps and bolts shot peened; all threads retapped; cylinder head bolt holes chamfered; valve lifter bosses deglazed allowing for 0.002-inch valve lifter clearance; engine block Redi-Stripped; Dorman 568-010 quick-seal copper freeze plugs (1 5/8-inch diameter), Luke's Custom Machine & Design brass rear camshaft boss plug (1.76-inch diameter), stainless-steel oil gallery line plugs, and Weatherhead 3152-4 polished-brass water jacket drain plugs (1/4-inch NPT) installed using Permatex aviation form-a-gasket; exterior surface of engine block sanded, detailed, and painted with Plasti-Kote 203 black high-gloss engine enamel; $448.33

• Engine block bored 0.030-inch oversize and honed and deglazed using torque plate and Sunnen 600 series 280-grit stones, final bore: 3.9675 inches; piston-to-bore clearance: 0.002 inch, measured below bottom of wrist pin perpendicular to wrist pin; $125

• Engine block parallel decked to 0.010-inch average below deck; $110

Engine block total: $1,083.33

The underside of this 1957 Chrysler 1738375 one-piece valley cover has been painted with Glyptal G-1228A medium-grey gloss enamel.

Crankshaft

• 1956 Chrysler 1634860 forged steel crankshaft, casting number 1619647; crankshaft heat treated, shot peened, and Magnafluxed; main bearing journal diameter: 2.50 inches, and connecting rod journal diameter: 2.25 inches; crankshaft weight: 63 pounds; $250

• Crankshaft aligned, main bearing journals ground 0.020-inch undersize, connecting rod journals ground 0.020-inch undersize, oil holes chamfered, journals polished, and crankshaft balanced; $225

• PAW (King Engine Bearings) HEM-MOM354 main bearings (0.020-inch oversize) installed allowing for 0.002-inch crankshaft clearance and 0.005-inch end play; main bearing cap bolts installed using molykote and torqued to 85 ft-lb; $110

• Mopar Performance P4452816 harmonic balancer (7 1/4-inch o.d.) installed with Chrysler 152191 Woodruff key and Chrysler 1731525 crankshaft bolt and 1324265 washer using Loctite and torqued to 85 ft-lb; harmonic balancer painted with Plasti-Kote 203 black high-gloss engine enamel; Luke's Custom Machine & Design aluminum crankshaft pulley spacer (3/8-inch thickness) installed; Super Sunny 8841 polished-aluminum crankshaft pulley (single v-belt, 6 1/2-inch diameter) installed with polished stainless-steel bolts, lockwashers, and flat washers using Loctite and torqued to 20 ft-lb; Chrysler 1618686 oil slinger painted with Glyptal G-1228A medium-grey gloss enamel; $235

Crankshaft total: $820

Connecting Rods and Pistons

• Chrysler 1323338, casting number 1324222, forged steel I-beam connecting rods, full-floating wrist pins (6.625-inch length,

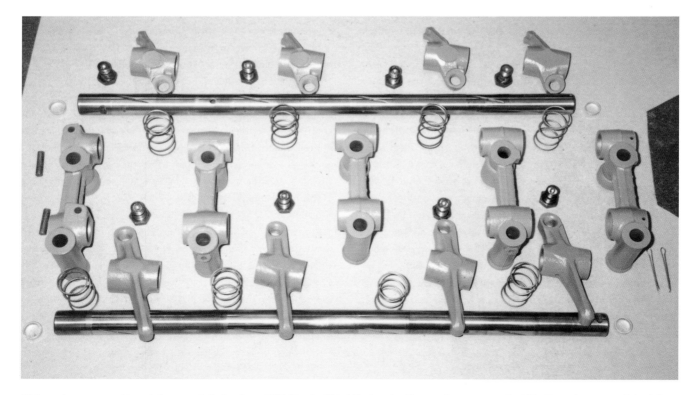

All the rocker arm assembly parts for one cylinder head on a 1956 Chrysler 354-ci Hemi engine. These rocker arms are adjustable. The rocker arms and stands have been cleaned, glass beaded, and painted with Glyptal G-1228A medium-grey gloss enamel. The rocker arm shafts have been polished.

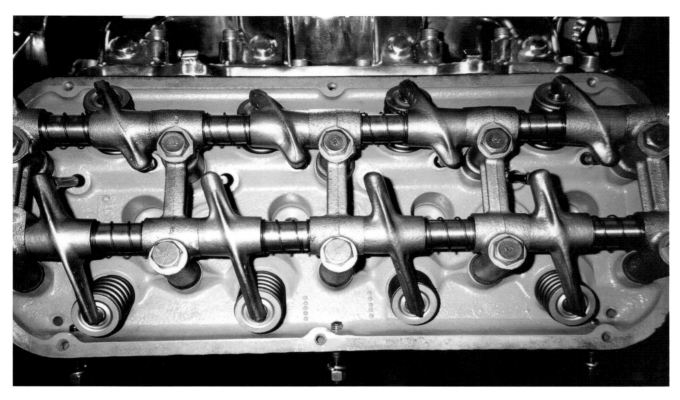

One of the 1956 Chrysler 354-ci Hemi cylinder heads installed on the engine and a rocker arm assembly I rebuilt for Luke's Custom Machine & Design.

center to center); connecting rod weight: 714 grams each; connecting rod ratio: 1.83 (with 3.625-inch stroke); $120

• Connecting rods shot peened, aligned, Magnafluxed, resized, balanced, and Federal Mogul 1804V wrist pin bushings installed allowing for 0.002-inch wrist pin clearance; ARP 145-6002 high-performance-series connecting rod bolts (3/8-inch diameter, 8740 chrome-moly steel, 190,000 psi) installed; $390

• Federal Mogul 1800-CP20 connecting rod bearings (0.020-inch oversize) installed allowing for 0.002-inch connecting rod clearance and 0.010-inch side clearance per pair of connecting rods; connecting rod bolts torqued to 45 ft-lb using molykote and allowing for 0.006-inch stretch; $195

• Egge Parts House L1089-8.030 cast-aluminum slipper-skirt pistons (0.030-inch oversize) with 9.0:1 compression ratio; heat treated and casehardened 4340 chrome-moly steel straight-wall wrist pins installed with Tru-Arc wrist pin retainers; piston grooves: top compression ring groove width: 3/32 inch; second compression ring groove width: 3/32 inch; oil ring groove width: 5/32 inch; Grant Piston Rings 3158 cast-iron piston ring set (0.030-inch oversize) installed within manufacturer's recommended arc; top compression ring gap: 0.016 inch; second compression ring gap: 0.016 inch; oil ring gap: 0.016 inch; intake-valve-to-piston clearance: 0.235 inch, and exhaust-valve-to-piston clearance: 0.235 inch (with gasket); new displacement: 359.6 ci (5.9 liters); $300

• Complete V-8 engine balance; Fel-Pro FS7908PT-4 complete gasket set installed; $325

Connecting rods and pistons total: $1,330

Lubrication System

• NOS 1956 Chrysler 1630248 oil pump and Chrysler 1324213 oil pump pickup screen installed; 1956 Chrysler 1408853 rear main bearing cap dowel installed; Hot Heads Research & Racing 21947 oil pump intermediate driveshaft (6.360-inch length) installed with Chrysler 601268 oil pump intermediate driveshaft gear and Hot Heads Research & Racing 21950 oil pump intermediate driveshaft bushing; PAW HEM-5340 oil diverter valve installed; $154.85

• 1956 Chrysler 1553766 stamped steel rear sump oil pan (5-quart capacity) installed with stainless-steel bolts, lockwashers, and AN flat washers using Loctite and torqued to 15 ft-lb; oil pan gaskets and seals installed using silicone sealant; Hot Heads Research & Racing 20101 polished-aluminum vertical oil filter adapter installed with stainless-steel socket head bolts using Loctite and torqued to 20 ft-lb; oil filter adapter gasket installed using silicone sealant; Fram PH-8A oil filter installed; engine lubricated with 6 quarts Pennzoil HD-30-weight motor oil; oil pan painted with Plasti-Kote 203 black high-gloss engine enamel; Hot Heads Research & Racing 21955 chrome angled dip stick and dip stick tube installed; $238.11

A pair of 1956 Chrysler 1323310 FirePower stamped steel valve covers that have been chrome plated.

A Hot Heads Research & Racing 50020 polished-aluminum single-quad, dual-plane high-rise intake manifold for the early Chrysler Hemi engines.

Lubrication system total: $392.96

Camshaft and Cylinder Heads

• Clevite 77 SH-313S camshaft bearings installed with 0.002-inch camshaft clearance and 0.002-inch end play; No. 1 bearing: SH-313, housing bore: 2.1295 to 2.1305 inches; No. 2, 3, and 4 bearing: SH-314, housing bore: 2.1295 to 2.1305 inches; No. 5 bearing: SH-315, housing bore: 1.5670 to 1.5680 inches; camshaft journal diameter: 2.00 inches; $55

• 1956 Chrysler 1632425 solid (mechanical) lifter camshaft reground by Shadbolt Cams, street grind with advertised duration: 290 degrees intake and exhaust; duration at 0.050-inch lift: 230 degrees intake and exhaust; lobe separation angle: 110 degrees; net valve lift (with 1.50 ratio rocker arms): 0.458 inch intake and 0.457 inch exhaust; valve lash (hot): 0.020 inch intake and 0.021 inch exhaust; camshaft degreed; $200

• Chrysler 1634267 camshaft thrust plate installed with Grade 8 bolts and lockwashers using Loctite and torqued to 25 ft-lb; Chrysler 1618717 camshaft sprocket spacer, Chrysler 106751 Woodruff key, and Chrysler 1328644 oil trough installed; Hot Heads Research & Racing 20200 camshaft bolt and washer kit installed; $60

• Sealed Power (Federal Mogul) AT-2084 Johnson hardenable iron alloy solid (mechanical) lifters (0.903-inch diameter, stock pushrod seat height) installed; Smith Brothers adjustable pushrods (4130 seamless chrome-moly steel, 5/16-inch diameter by 0.049-inch wall) installed; intake valve pushrod length: 9.750 inches, and exhaust valve pushrod length: 11.225 inches; $215

The Edelbrock 1405 Performer 600-cfm carburetor is installed on a Hot Heads Research & Racing 50020 polished-aluminum single-quad high-rise intake manifold. This is a practical setup for an early Chrysler Hemi street performance engine.

• Dynagear 78103 precision double-roller timing chain set, multi-keyway crankshaft sprocket, installed; Hot Heads Research & Racing 20215 polishing cast-aluminum timing gear cover with adjustable timing pointer installed with stainless-steel socket head bolts and AN flat washers and torqued to 15 ft-lb using Loctite; timing gear cover gasket installed using silicone sealant; $240

• 1957 Chrysler 1738375 (model 300C) one-piece valley

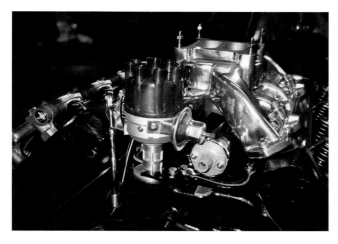

A Proform 66991 electronic distributor designed for the small-block Chrysler 360-ci engine. In order for this distributor to function, a Hot Heads Research & Racing 21947 oil pump intermediate driveshaft has been installed.

Luke's Custom Machine & Design beveled aluminum spark plug tube washers are seen on the ends of the spark plug tubes. These spark plug tube washers are designed to work with the Hemi spark plug boots contained in the Mopar Performance 4120808 kits.

cover installed with polished stainless-steel bolts, lockwashers, and AN flat washers using Loctite and torqued to 15 ft-lb; valley cover gasket installed using silicone sealant; valley cover painted with Plasti-Kote 203 black high-gloss engine enamel; underside of valley cover painted with Glyptal G-1228A medium-grey gloss enamel; Motormite 242344 PCV valve grommet and Motomaster 17-9288-4 PCV valve installed; Mr. Gasket 2060 chrome oil filler/crankcase breather cap installed; $130.26

• 1956 Chrysler 1671141 (casting numbers 1619823-1) cast-iron hemispherical combustion chamber cylinder heads; cylinder head weight: 66 pounds each; $300

• Cylinder heads hot tanked and Redi-Stripped; intake and exhaust ports fully ported and polished and gasket matched; combustion chambers polished and cc'd; surfaced; NOS 1956 Chrysler 1634790 intake valve guides and 1486911 exhaust valve guides (3/8-inch stem diameter) installed; Serdi-machined multi-angle blueprint valve grind performed; area beneath valve covers painted with Glyptal G-1228A medium-grey gloss enamel; exterior surface of cylinder heads sanded, detailed, and painted with Plasti-Kote 203 black high-gloss engine enamel; $748.22

• NOS Federal Mogul V-2190 SAE (Society of Automotive Engineers) 1041 steel intake valves (1.9375-inch head diameter by 3/8-inch stem diameter by 5.049-inch length overall) installed; NOS 1956 Chrysler 1634744 exhaust valves (1.75-inch head diameter by 3/8-inch stem diameter by 5.0375-inch length overall) installed; Serdi-machined multi-angle blueprint valve grind performed; Enginetech S2890 viton positive seal valve stem seals installed; $176

• Sealed Power (Federal Mogul) VS-510 single valve springs with installed height: 80 pounds at 1.70 inches valves closed and 200 pounds at 1.250 inches valves open; 1.40-inch o.d. and 1.00-inch i.d.; coil bind: 1.150 inches; 1956 Chrysler 1619636

A Hot Heads Research & Racing 21301 water crossover manifold and 20701 aluminum water pump adapters with a Mr. Gasket 2660 chrome water outlet elbow.

heat-treated steel valve spring retainers (3/8-inch stem diameter) and 1956 Chrysler 1614666 valve stem locks (3/8-inch stem diameter for four-groove valves) installed; $105

• 1956 Chrysler nonadjustable rocker arm assemblies rebuilt by Luke's Custom Machine & Design (rocker arm ratio: 1.50); rocker arm assemblies and cylinder heads installed with Chrysler 1324452 long cylinder head bolts and Chrysler 1323310 short cylinder head bolts using anti-seize compound and torqued to 85 ft-lb; $600

• 1956 Chrysler 1323310 chrome FirePower valve covers installed with Papco 264-016 engine studs (5/16-inch by 1 3/4-inch length, reduced to 1 1/2-inch length), polished stainless-steel

A pair of Hot Heads Research & Racing 60010 block hugger exhaust headers for the early Chrysler Hemi engines. The flanges are 3/8 inch thick.

A good front view of the 1956 Chrysler 354-ci Hemi engine.

acorn nuts, lockwashers, and AN flat washers using anti-seize compound and torqued to 15 ft-lb; valve cover gaskets installed using silicone sealant; $460

Camshaft and cylinder heads total: $3,289.48

Intake System

• Hot Heads Research & Racing 50020 polished cast-aluminum single-quad, dual-plane high-rise intake manifold installed with stainless-steel socket head bolts and AN flat washers using Loctite and torqued to 25 ft-lb; intake manifold gaskets installed using silicone sealant; ARP 400-2401 polished stainless-steel carburetor stud kit installed using anti-seize compound; $436

• Edelbrock 1405 Performer (non-emission) silver finish, 600-cfm, four-barrel carburetor, manual choke, installed; Mr. Gasket 6477 Rodware chrome heavy-breather louvered air cleaner (14-inch o.d. by 2 1/2 inches high) installed with K&N E-2865 air filter (13-inch o.d. by 2.312 inches high); $293

• Holley 12-803 chrome fuel pressure regulator, adjustable from 4 1/2 to 9 psi, installed with Weatherhead 402-6-6 polished-brass 90-degree elbow (3/8-inch tube to 3/8-inch NPT, outlet line); Weatherhead 1069-6 polished-brass 90-degree male elbow (3/8-inch i.d. hose to 1/8-inch NPT) and Weatherhead 3220-6-2 polished-brass adapter (1/8-inch NPT to 3/8-inch NPT, inlet line); Weatherhead 3220-6-2 polished-brass adapter (1/8-inch NPT to 3/8-inch NPT) and Holley 26-500 fuel pressure gauge (0 to 15 psi, 1 1/2-inch diameter face) installed using pipe thread sealant; Summit Racing Equipment 220238 polished stainless-steel fuel line (3/8-inch tube by 0.028-inch wall by 1-foot length) installed with Weatherhead 100-6 polished-brass inverted flare nuts (3/8-inch tube) using pipe thread sealant; $75.95

Intake system total: $804.95

Ignition System

• Proform 66991 electronic distributor and control unit installed with Chrysler 1326835 distributor clamp and polished stainless-steel bolt and lockwasher using anti-seize compound; MSD 8200 Blaster 2 chrome ignition coil (45,000 volts) installed with Mr. Gasket 9777 chrome ignition coil bracket; distributor clamp painted with Plasti-Kote 203 black high-gloss engine enamel; $219

• Chrysler 1737379 aluminum spark plug tubes installed with Luke's Custom Machine & Design beveled spark plug tube washers; NGK BP6ES resistor-type 18-millimeter spark plugs installed with 0.050-inch gap and torqued to 25 ft-lb; Taylor/Vertex 35071 Pro Series black 8-millimeter high-performance spark plug wire, Spiro-Pro Kelvar resistor core, installed with Mopar Performance (Chrysler Corporation) 4120808 Hemi spark plug tube and insulator kit (Standard ST113 spark plug terminals, Standard TN9 distributor cap nipples, Standard ST26 distributor cap terminals) and Spectre 4245 chrome/plastic spark plug wire separators; $191.28

The left side of the completed 1956 Chrysler 354-ci Hemi engine. This engine puts out enough horsepower to keep any 1931 Ford happy.

• Proform 66445 chrome GM alternator (internally regulated, 65 amps) installed with Luke's Custom Machine & Design polished-aluminum mounting bracket and steel brace using polished stainless-steels bolts, lockwashers, and AN flat washers; alternator brace painted with Plasti-Kote 203 black high-gloss engine enamel; $205.62

• Mopar Performance (Chrysler Corporation) P5249644 lightweight starting motor installed; Gates 11A1285 XL crankshaft/water pump/alternator v-belt (7/16-inch by 50 1/2-inch length) installed; $155.67

Ignition system total: $771.57

Cooling System

• Hot Heads Research & Racing 20701 polished-aluminum water pump adapters installed with stainless-steel socket head bolts using Loctite and torqued to 25 ft-lb; water pump adapter gaskets installed using silicone sealant; Weiand 8212 action-plus polished-aluminum big-block Chevrolet short-style water pump installed with polished stainless-steel bolts and lock washers using anti-seize compound and torqued to 25 ft-lb; water pump gaskets installed using silicone sealant; Trans-Dapt 9478 polished T-6 aluminum single-groove (6-inch diameter) water pump pulley installed with polished

stainless-steel socket head countersunk bolts using Loctite and torqued to 25 ft-lb; $328

• Hot Heads Research & Racing 21301 aluminum water passage crossover manifold installed with polished stainless-steel bolts and lockwashers using Loctite and torqued to 25 ft-lb; water passage crossover manifold gaskets installed using silicone sealant; Robert Shaw 330-160 extra performance balanced 160-degree (Fahrenheit) thermostat installed; Mr. Gasket 2660 chrome O-ring thermostat housing installed with polished stainless-steel bolts and lockwashers using anti-seize compound and torqued to 20 ft-lb; $240

Cooling system total: $568

Labor

• Labor for checking clearances, gapping piston rings, degree camshaft, valvetrain assembly, detailing, trial engine assembly, final engine assembly, and initial engine start-up; $800

Labor total: $800

Engine Grand Total: $9,860.29 (U.S.)

Note: The estimated output of this engine is 405 horsepower at 5,500 rpm and 427 ft-lb torque at 4,000 rpm (see Appendix A—Dyno Print-Outs).

CHAPTER 16
BLOWN 1958 DODGE TRUCK 354-ci HEMI ENGINE

This second chapter about the early Chrysler Hemi engines pertains to a blown 354-ci engine. The engine block that is the basis for this project originated from a 1958 Dodge Truck, which is the only Dodge part that will be used in the building of this engine.

The supercharger boost was kept on the mild side in order to prevent the owner going bankrupt from buying stronger aftermarket parts for his engine. Luke's Custom Machine & Design completed this engine at the end of November 2003. The owner is going to install it in his daily-driven 1932 Ford Model B five-window coupe.

Components Description
Engine Block
The specifications for the 1958 Dodge Truck 354-ci Hemi engine are:
- 354-ci (5.9-liter) displacement
- 3.9375-inch stock bore and 3.625-inch stock stroke
- Stock compression ratio: 9.1:1
- 218 horsepower at 3,900 rpm and 319 ft-lb torque at 2,400 rpm

The front of the 1958 Dodge Truck engine block is similar to the front of the 1951 to 1954 Chrysler 331-ci Hemi engine blocks. The 1958 Dodge Truck 354-ci Hemi engine and the 1951 to 1954 Chrysler 331-ci Hemi engines did not have a water passage crossover manifold connecting the front of each cylinder head. The cast-iron water pump/timing gear cover connects the water passages on each side of the engine block. Other than this difference, the 1958 Dodge Truck 354-ci Hemi engine block is the same as the 1956 Chrysler 354-ci engine block.

The engine block described in this chapter did not have any serial numbers. Why there were none is anyone's guess. We determined that this mystery engine block came from a 1956 to 1958 Dodge Truck, based on the type of water passages at the front of the engine block and the water pump/timing gear cover. The casting date of 5-21-8 (May 21, 1958) served as the final evidence in determining that this is a 1958 Dodge Truck 354-ci engine block.

Refer to Chapter 1 for information regarding engine block preparation and machining. Refer to Chapter 15 for information

about the 1956 Chrysler 354-ci Hemi engine block. Strengthen the bottom end by installing an ARP 145-5404 main bearing cap stud kit (190,000 psi), currently available for the retail price of $60.

Crankshaft
There is a radius-like groove at the sides of all the journals of the early Chrysler Hemi crankshafts. The steel material in this area has been rolled to provide strength to the ends of the journal.

We installed a 1956 Chrysler 1634860 (casting number 1619647) crankshaft in the 1958 Dodge Truck 354-ci Hemi engine block. There is a photograph of this crankshaft in Chapter 15. Refer to Chapter 2 for information regarding crankshaft preparation and machining. Refer to Chapter 15 for information about Chrysler 354-ci Hemi crankshafts and bearings.

Because this is a blown engine, we did not use a harmonic balancer. Luke's Custom Machine & Design fabricated an aluminum crankshaft pulley (6 1/2-inch diameter) bolted to the hub section from a 1956 to 1958 Chrysler Hemi harmonic

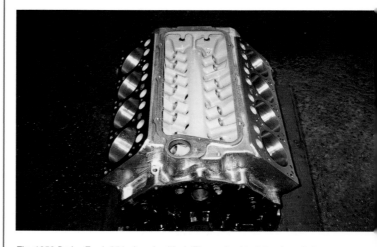

The 1958 Dodge Truck 354-ci engine block. The engine block has been hot tanked, sanded and detailed, and the valve lifter gallery has been painted with Glyptal G-1228A medium-grey gloss enamel. The engine block just arrived back from the machine shop.

The tip of the pen indicates where the radius of this Chrysler 354-ci Hemi crankshaft journal has been rolled in order to provide strength to the ends of the journal.

A set of Chrysler 354-ci Hemi connecting rods (casting number 1324222) that have been shot peened, aligned, debeamed, Magnafluxed, resized, rebushed and pin fitted, balanced, and ARP 145-6002 connecting rod bolts installed.

balancer. The timing adjustment degrees are notched in the outer edge of the crankshaft pulley. The blower belt pulley bolts to the front of the crankshaft pulley.

Connecting Rods and Pistons

Install a set of Chrysler 1323338 (casting number 1324222) forged steel I-beam connecting rods in the Dodge Truck engine. These connecting rods are the same as those described in Chapter 15, except they have been debeamed. The engine's boost is limited to approximately 5 pounds. This being the case, you will not need boxed connecting rods or aftermarket connecting rods. Refer to Chapter 3 for information regarding connecting rod preparation and bearings.

Now that all the machining procedures have been carried out, there should be no discussion about what this Chrysler 354-ci Hemi connecting rod (casting number 1324222) weighs.

If your Chrysler 354-ci Hemi engine is going to produce serious horsepower (i.e., with a blower capable of producing boost over 10 pounds), use the Pontiac 455-ci connecting rods manufactured in the United States by Scat Enterprises. The Scat Enterprises 2-455-6625-2249 forged 4340 steel H-beam connecting rods with ARP 8740 steel connecting rod bolts are the same 6.625-inch length (center to center). The crankshaft end (the big end) diameter is 2.3750 inches—the same as the Chrysler 354-ci Hemi connecting rods, casting numbers 1324222 and 1821345. The crankshaft end (the big end) of the Chrysler 354-ci Hemi connecting rods is 1.00 inch thick, and the crankshaft end (the big end) of the Scat Enterprises 2-455-6625-2249 connecting rods is 0.990 inch thick. This difference of 0.010 inch for each connecting rod will have little effect on a blown street performance engine. This additional side clearance for the connecting rods will permit the oil on the bearings to escape at a faster rate. Have Scat Enterprises provide a set of connecting rods with the 1.00-inch thickness at the crankshaft end (the big end).

If you use pistons with the Chrysler wrist pin diameter of 0.9841 to 0.9843 inch, replace the wrist pin bushing in the Scat Enterprises connecting rods (which is for a 0.980-inch-diameter wrist pin) with the Federal Mogul 1804V wrist pin bushing. If you order custom pistons with a 0.980-inch-diameter wrist pin, the wrist pin end (the small end) in the Scat Enterprises H-beam connecting rods will not need to be machined. The Scat Enterprises 2-455-6625-2249 H-beam connecting rods are available at a current retail price of $549 for a set—less than the cost to purchase a set of Chrysler 354-ci Hemi connecting rods and shot

A set of TRW L2061-030 forged aluminum pistons (0.030-inch oversize) for a Chrysler 354-ci Hemi engine. The wrist pins are the straight-wall design.

A set of Ross Racing Pistons blower pistons (0.0625-inch oversize, 8.0:1 compression ratio) for a Chrysler 354-ci Hemi engine.

peen, debeam, box, align, Magnaflux, resize, rebush, and install new connecting rod bolts. The Scat Enterprises H-beam connecting rods are much stronger and will withstand the horsepower of just about any street performance engine, blown or not.

Scat Enterprises H-beam connecting rod bearings are a lot less expensive for the Pontiac 455-ci engine than they are for the Chrysler 354-ci Hemi engine. The Clevite 77 CB-758P connecting rod bearings are available in standard size, 0.001-, 0.010-, 0.020-, 0.030-, and 0.040-inch oversize. The current retail price for a set of these connecting rod bearings is $50. The Federal Mogul 1555CPA connecting rod bearings are available in standard size, 0.001-, 0.010-, 0.020-, 0.030-, and 0.040-inch oversize. The current retail price for a set of these connecting rod bearings is $55. These connecting rod bearings are for the Pontiac 455-ci engine.

As previously mentioned, the boost will be limited in the Dodge Truck engine. As a result, it is permissible to install forged aluminum pistons rather than true blower pistons. The owner of this engine had a set of TRW L2061-030 power-forged aluminum slipper-skirt pistons (0.030-inch oversize) and a new set of Hastings 636 moly top ring piston rings. The pistons are a flat top design, and the compression ratio will be 8.0:1. He purchased the pistons, wrist pins, and piston rings for $440. Refer to Chapter 15 for information regarding pistons and gasket sets.

Lubrication System

Install a Hot Heads Research & Racing 21905 high-volume oil pump for the small-block Chrysler 340-ci engine in the Dodge Truck engine. This oil pump has a rear sump pickup screen. The current retail price for the oil pump and oil pump pickup screen is $160. Refer to Chapter 15 for information on oil pumps, oil pump intermediate driveshafts, and the oil diverter valve.

The owner of the Dodge Truck engine was concerned about ground clearance with the oil pan. In order to guarantee adequate ground clearance, Luke's Custom Machine & Design sectioned 1 1/2 inches from an early Chrysler Hemi truck oil pan with a full-length sump and welded a baffle to the inside of the oil pan for oil control.

Camshaft and Cylinder Heads

It appears that none of the major camshaft manufacturers in the United States have an off-the-shelf solid (mechanical) lifter blower camshaft for a Chrysler 354-ci Hemi engine. Luke's Custom Machine & Design sent a 1956 Chrysler solid lifter camshaft to Crower Cams & Equipment Company to be reground into a suitable street performance blower camshaft for the Dodge Truck engine. This camshaft now has an advertised duration of: 284 degrees intake and exhaust; duration at 0.050-inch lift: 224 degrees intake and exhaust; lobe separation angle: 112 degrees; net valve lift (with 1.50 rocker ratio): 0.452 inch intake and 0.450 inch exhaust; valve lash (hot): 0.016 inch intake and 0.018 inch exhaust. The current retail price for Crower Cams & Equipment Company to regrind a Chrysler 354-ci Hemi camshaft is $100.

Install a set of Competition Cams 821-16 High Energy solid (mechanical) lifters for the big-block Chrysler 383-ci and 440-ci

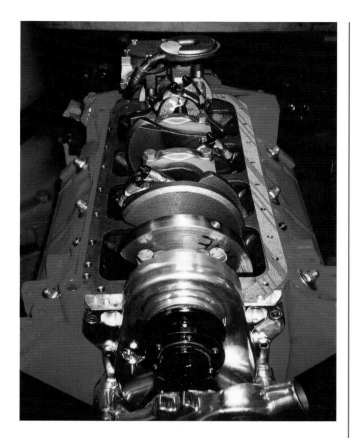

The Hot Heads Research & Racing 21905 oil pump with the rear sump oil pump pickup screen attached. The hub on the front of the crankshaft is from a 1956 to 1958 Chrysler harmonic balancer.

The Chrysler 354-ci solid lifter camshaft that was reground by Crower Cams & Equipment Company for the Dodge Truck Hemi engine.

A set of Competition Cams 821-16 High Energy solid lifters for the big-block Chrysler 383-ci and 440-ci engines. The lifters will be installed in the Dodge Truck engine.

engines in the Dodge Truck engine. The current retail price for these solid (mechanical) lifters is $70.

Because the engine will have a blower, install heat-treated pushrods. In this case, we installed a set of Smith Brothers heat-treated 4130 seamless chrome-moly steel nonadjustable pushrods (5/16-inch diameter) in the Dodge Truck engine. The intake valve pushrod length is 9.750 inches, and the exhaust pushrod length is 11.225 inches. The current retail price for a set of these pushrods is $225. There is a photograph of a set of Smith Brothers pushrods in Chapter 5.

Install a Cloyes 92103 true roller timing chain set in the Dodge Truck engine. Because the Dodge Truck engine block has two additional water passage openings at the lower front, we must use a different timing gear cover. The Hot Heads Research & Racing 20211 aluminum timing gear cover is designed for the 1951 to 1954 Chrysler 331-ci Hemi engine block with a small-block Chevrolet short-style water pump. However, this timing gear cover will fit the 1956 to 1959 Dodge Truck 354-ci engine blocks without modification. The current retail price for the unpolished version of the Hot Heads Research & Racing 20211 aluminum timing gear

cover is $210. There is a photograph of a Howard's finned aluminum timing gear cover for these engines in Chapter 5.

In order to provide an additional touch of class to an early Chrysler Hemi engine, Luke's Custom Machine & Design fabricates a polished-aluminum valley cover. This valley cover is not finned, unlike most aftermarket aluminum valley covers, so that it is easier to keep clean. It is almost impossible to clean a finned valley cover underneath a blower intake manifold on an early Chrysler Hemi engine. The current retail price for one of the fully polished aluminum valley covers from Luke's Custom Machine & Design is $85. Luke's Custom Machine & Design installs a breather tube at the rear of the valley cover and a PCV valve at the front of the valley cover. You may need to install an oil separator between the PCV valve and the carburetor when using any

A Cloyes 92103 true roller timing chain set for a Chrysler 354-ci Hemi engine.

Luke's Custom Machine & Design fabricated this polished-aluminum valley cover for the early Chrysler Hemi engines.

A Luke's Custom Machine & Design polished finned-aluminum oil separator installed on the blown 1958 Dodge Truck Hemi engine.

valley cover other than a stock early Chrysler Hemi valley cover. The early Chrysler Hemi valley covers were two-piece units, which also acted as baffles. Aftermarket valley covers do not have a baffle and permit oil to be drawn through the PCV valve into the carburetor, particularly with blown engines. Luke's Custom Machine & Design produces a good-looking polished finned aluminum oil separator.

Install a pair of 1956 Chrysler 1671141 cast-iron hemispherical combustion chamber cylinder heads (casting number 1619823) on the Dodge Truck engine. Refer to Chapter 15 for information about this type of cylinder head and an explanation of the work carried out to prepare the cylinder heads for the machine shop.

Install the oil seals for the aluminum spark plug tubes. Luke's Custom Machine & Design cuts a groove at the top of the spark plug tube holes in the cylinder heads with a milling machine. Install a Federal Mogul 240736 oil seal in the groove to provide an oil-tight seal for the aluminum spark tube when it is installed, eliminating any seepage of oil into the spark plug tube. The current retail price for eight Federal Mogul 240736 oil seals is $40. The Milodon 27050 spark plug tube seals are available for the current retail price of $80 for a set of eight. No machine work is required for the installation of these oil seals; they are of a press-fit design and have internal O-rings for sealing the aluminum spark plug tubes.

Install a set of Hot Heads Research & Racing 40044 bronze intake valve guides (11/32-inch valve stem diameter) and 40046 bronze exhaust valve guides (11/32-inch valve stem diameter) in the cylinder heads. There is a photograph of these valve guides in

Chapter 5. Install the Hot Heads Research & Racing 40016 stainless-steel intake valves (2.125-inch head diameter by 11/32-inch stem diameter by 5.230-inch length overall) and the 40026 stainless-steel exhaust valves (1.945-inch head diameter by 11/32-inch stem diameter by 5.230-inch length overall) with a Serdi-machined multi-angle blueprint valve grind. Install Enginetech S2927 viton positive seal valve stem seals as well. The current retail price for a set of the Hot Heads Research & Racing stainless-steel intake and exhaust valves is $230 and $124 for a set of bronze intake and exhaust valve guides.

The Chrysler 354-ci Hemi cylinder heads have valve seat inserts. The diameter of the exhaust valve seat inserts is too small to install exhaust valves with a head diameter of 1.945 inches and intake valves with a head diameter of 2.125 inches. Reduce the diameter of the head of the exhaust valve to 1.88 inches in order to use the stock exhaust valve seat inserts. You may also install the

The valves in the background are Hot Heads Research & Racing 40016 stainless-steel 2.125-inch head diameter intake valves, and the valves in the foreground are the 40026 stainless-steel 1.945-inch head diameter exhaust valves.

The 1956 Chrysler Hemi cylinder head (casting number 1619823) and the adjustable rocker arm assembly installed. They have been painted with Glyptal G-1228A medium-grey gloss enamel. The Manley Performance Parts 22400-16 and 22428-16 dual valve springs with the 23645-16 valve spring retainers are highlighted. The groove at the top of the spark plug tube hole for the aluminum spark plug tube oil seal is visible.

Hot Heads Research & Racing 40011 stainless-steel intake valves (2.0625-inch head diameter by 11/32-inch stem diameter by 5.225-inch length) and the 40012 stainless-steel exhaust valves (1.800-inch head diameter by 11/32-inch stem diameter by 5.225-inch length) in the Chrysler 354-ci Hemi cylinder heads. The current retail price for a set of the Hot Heads Research & Racing 40011 intake valves and the 40012 exhaust valves is $282.

Single valves springs are not suitable for an early Chrysler Hemi engine equipped with a blower. Install a set of Manley Performance Parts 22400-16 and 22428-16 Street Master dual valve springs. These valve springs are manufactured using chrome silicon, and they have an installed height of: 120 pounds at 1.820 inches valves closed and 310 pounds at 1.250 inches valves open; 1.437-inch o.d. and 0.720-inch i.d.; coil bind: 1.100 inches. Install new Manley Performance Parts 23645-16 Street Master valve spring retainers manufactured using 4140 chrome-moly steel (11/32-inch valve stem diameter) with Crane Cams 99097-1 machined 4140 heat-treated chrome-moly steel valve stem locks (7-degree, 11/32-inch stem diameter, standard height). The current retail price for the Manley dual valve springs with the valve spring retainers and the Crane Cams valve stem locks is $200.

Install a pair of 1956 Chrysler Hemi adjustable rocker arm assemblies in the Dodge Truck engine. Refer to Chapter 15 for information on these rocker arm assemblies. The rocker arm stands and the rocker arms were glass beaded and painted with Glyptal G-1228A medium-grey gloss enamel.

Although it is not absolutely necessary to use cylinder head studs for a blown street performance engine utilizing a mild amount of boost, it is recommended. One of the best cylinder head

The Milodon 80215 premium cylinder head stud kit for the early Chrysler Hemi engines.

stud kits available today for the early Chrysler Hemi engine is the Milodon 80215 premium cylinder head stud kit. This cylinder head stud kit is manufactured using 8740 chrome-moly steel and is rated at 180,000 psi. The washers and nuts are parallel ground and manufactured using 4130 hardened steel. The current retail price for a Milodon 80215 cylinder head stud kit is $130.

The Weiand WC671 blower intake manifold installed on the Dodge Truck engine. The two pop-off valves (backfire valves) are located on the floor of the intake manifold.

A Hot Heads Research & Racing 50050 cast-aluminum high-rise blower intake manifold for the early Chrysler Hemi engines.

Install a pair of O'Brien Truckers polished cast finned aluminum valve covers with finned spark plug wire covers on the Dodge Truck engine. You may need to grind a small amount of material from the bottom of the inside of each valve cover to provide adequate clearance for the exhaust valve springs. These polished valve covers are available from Hot Heads Research & Racing 21550 for the current retail price of $390.

In order to provide sufficient crankcase ventilation, install a Mooneyes USA MP1800 polished right-angle valve cover breather (3-inch width) at the front of each valve cover. The current retail price for one of these items is $36. There is a photograph of the Mooneyes USA MP1800 valve cover breathers in Chapter 5.

A note of caution when using the 1956 Chrysler 1323310 FirePower valve covers with cylinder head studs: the top of the studs (particularly the bottom row of longer studs) may have to be trimmed in order to clear the valve covers.

Intake System

Install a vintage Weiand WC671 polished-aluminum blower intake manifold on the Dodge Truck Hemi engine. This particular intake manifold has two pop-off valves (backfire valves) in the floor of the intake manifold. The Weiand (Holley) 7138 blower intake manifold is the current model available for the GMC 6-71 blower at a retail cost of $300 for the unpolished version or $400 polished. This semi high-rise intake manifold has the pop-off valve (backfire valve) plate located at the front. The Hot Heads Research & Racing 50040 cast-aluminum blower intake manifold is available at the current retail price of $400 for the unpolished street version. The pop-off valve (backfire valve) is fitted at the front of this high-rise intake manifold.

The owner of the Dodge Truck Hemi engine decided to provide two four-barrel carburetors to give his engine a more nostalgic look. Install two Edelbrock 1405 Performer 600-cfm four-barrel carburetors with a manual choke. This is a lot of carburetion for a 359-ci engine, and two Edelbrock 1404 Performer 500-cfm carburetors would have been a slight improvement. The best scenario for this engine would be to install a single Holley 0-4777 double pumper 650-cfm four-barrel carburetor. The Edelbrock 1405 carburetors are available at the current retail price of $200 each. Refer to Chapter 6 for information regarding fuel pressure regulators and fuel pressure gauges.

A Blower Drive Service 24B6 polished-aluminum carburetor adapter will be installed on the GMC 6-71 blower. This carburetor adapter kit is complete with a blower inlet safety screen (to prevent unwanted critters from ending up in the blower), heat resistant carburetor base gaskets, and the required bolts. The current retail price for this carburetor adapter kit is $130.

The owner provided an O'Brien Truckers finned cast-aluminum air cleaner in order for the dual four-barrel carburetors to match the valve covers. The K&N E-2360 air filters fit this air cleaner assembly. The current retail price for this air cleaner and the K&N air filters is $200.

Luke's Custom Machine & Design assembled the blower for the Dodge Truck Hemi engine. This GMC 6-71 blower has the early GM 5150219 sand-cast front and rear bearing plates and the early GM 5150233 sand-cast front cover. "Tim, the polishing guy" did a spectacular job buffing the entire blower assembly. Refer to Chapter 6 for information about the GMC 6-71 blower.

Install a Luke's Custom Machine & Design LS3000 polished 6061 T-6 aluminum medium blower snout with the LS3300 blower snout shaft and LS4100 gear coupler on the GMC 6-71

The GMC 6-71 blower is mounted on the Dodge Truck Hemi engine, and the O'Brien Truckers polished finned valve covers have been bolted in position. The Mooneyes USA MP1800 polished valve cover breathers can be seen as well.

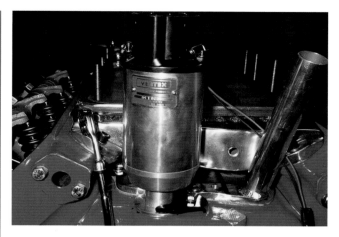

The Taylor/Vertex 541803 distributor with breakerless triggering and an internal HEI coil and control module—truly a self-contained unit. The block-off plates at the ends of the cylinder heads have been tapped for a temperature-sending unit and a heater hose connection.

A set of the Chrysler 1737379 aluminum spark plug tubes that have been glass beaded.

blower. Refer to Chapter 6 for more information about blower snouts. Luke's Custom Machine & Design fabricated the aluminum idler pulley and idler pulley bracket.

Install a Blower Drive Service 6300 aluminum crankshaft blower pulley (1/2-inch pitch [Gilmer] by 30-tooth) and a 6336 aluminum blower snout pulley (1/2-inch pitch [Gilmer] by 36-tooth). Also install a Jason 540H-300 blower belt (1/2-inch pitch [Gilmer] by 54-inch length by 3-inch width). The current retail price for the aluminum blower pulleys and the blower belt is $275. This combination results in an underdrive of 20 percent and an estimated boost of 5.0 pounds.

Ignition System

Install a Taylor/Vertex 541803 self-contained, 356 T-6 aluminum housing, electronic distributor. This centrifugal (mechanical) advance distributor has an internal HEI coil, breakerless triggering, and control module. The Taylor/Vertex 541803 distributor has an appearance similar to a Vertex magneto, and its current retail price is $600. The Taylor/Vertex 541803 distributor has an extended distributor shaft that permits the use of the 1956 Chrysler 1323369 oil pump intermediate driveshaft (6.030-inch length). This is truly a self-contained distributor.

The MSD 8391 distributor for the early Chrysler 331-ci and 354-ci Hemi engines is a vacuum advance distributor referred to as a "ready-to-run" for its built-in inductive ignition module. The MSD 8543 Pro-Billet model is another excellent distributor for the early Chrysler 331-ci and 354-ci Hemi engines. This full centrifugal (mechanical) advance distributor must be used with an MSD ignition control box. Use the Chrysler 1323369 oil

pump intermediate driveshaft (6.030-inch length) with either of these distributors; the current retail price for each is $370.

Do not use the Mopar Performance (Chrysler Corporation) 4120808 Hemi spark plug tube and insulator kits on this engine. Cover the spark plug wires with the O'Brien Truckers finned aluminum spark plug wire covers. Refer to Chapter 15 for information about spark plug tubes, spark plug wires, and starting motors.

Install a Powermaster 17509 chrome Chrysler alternator, rated at 75 amps, on the Dodge Truck Hemi engine using a stainless-steel bracket and brace fabricated by Luke's Custom Machine & Design. The current retail price for the Powermaster 17509 chrome alternator is $120.

Cooling System

The Hot Heads Research & Racing 20211 aluminum timing gear cover has two water pump adapters cast into it. The water pump

The Hot Heads Research & Racing 20211 polished-aluminum timing gear cover, the Weiand 8208 polished-aluminum small-block Chevrolet short-style water pump, the PAW 5775 polished crossover manifold, and the Trans-Dapt 9415 chrome thermostat housing.

The left side of the Dodge Truck Hemi engine after everything has been installed.

adapters are on each side near the top, and that timing gear cover is designed for a small-block Chevrolet short-style water pump. Install a Weiand (Holley) 8208 aluminum water pump on the Dodge Truck Hemi engine. Also install a Trans-Dapt 9478 single-groove aluminum water pump pulley on the water pump. The current retail price for the Weiand 8208 water pump is $95 and the Trans-Dapt 9478 pulley is $45, both unpolished.

Because we installed a Weiand WC671 low-profile blower intake manifold, the Hot Heads Research & Racing 21301 aluminum water passage crossover manifold cannot be installed. The intake manifold is too low to clear that particular crossover manifold. Instead, install a PAW 5775 aluminum water passage crossover manifold with an offset water outlet. Use a Trans-Dapt 9415 chrome water outlet elbow (for Ford 429-ci to 460-ci engines) with this crossover manifold. The current retail price for the PAW 5775 crossover manifold is $180 for the unpolished version, and the Trans-Dapt 9415 water outlet elbow is $13.

Engine Summary

Note: Exhaust headers are not listed in this engine summary because a custom set will have to be fabricated.

Engine Block

• 1958 Dodge Truck 354-ci engine block; casting number 1619829; casting date: 5-21-8 (May 21, 1958); stock bore: 3.9375 inches; stock stroke: 3.625 inches; two-bolt main bearing caps; 9.1:1 compression ratio; 218 horsepower at 3,900 rpm and 319 ft-lb torque at 2,400 rpm; engine block weight (bare): 186 pounds; $600

• Engine block hot tanked; engine block and main bearing caps and bolts Magnafluxed; main bearing caps and bolts shot peened; all threads retapped; cylinder head bolt holes chamfered; valve lifter bosses deglazed allowing for 0.002-inch valve lifter clearance; engine block Redi-Stripped; Dorman 568-010 quick-seal copper freeze plugs (1 5/8-inch diameter), Luke's Custom Machine & Design brass rear camshaft boss plug (1.76-inch diameter), stainless-steel oil gallery line plugs, Weatherhead 3152-4 polished-brass water jacket drain plugs (1/4-inch NPT) installed using Permatex aviation form-a-gasket; valve lifter gallery ground smooth and painted with Glyptal G-1228A medium-grey gloss enamel; exterior surface of engine block sanded and detailed and painted with PPG 74000 red high-gloss polyurethane; $520.54

• Engine block bored 0.030-inch oversize and honed and deglazed using torque plate and Sunnen 800 series 400-grit stones, final bore: 3.9675 inches; piston-to-bore clearance: 0.006 inch, measured below bottom of wrist pin perpendicular to wrist pin; $125

Engine block total: $1,245.54

Crankshaft

• 1956 Chrysler 1634860 forged steel crankshaft, casting number 1619647; crankshaft heat treated, shot peened, and Magnafluxed; main bearing journal diameter: 2.50 inches, and connecting rod journal diameter: 2.25 inches; crankshaft weight: 63 pounds; $250

• Crankshaft aligned, main bearing journals ground 0.010-inch undersize, connecting rod journals ground 0.010-inch undersize, oil holes chamfered, journals polished, and crankshaft balanced; $225

• PAW (King Engine Bearings) HEM-MOM354 main bearings (0.010-inch oversize) installed allowing for 0.002-inch crankshaft clearance and 0.006-inch end play; main bearing cap bolts installed using molykote and torqued to 85 ft-lb; $110

• Luke's Custom Machine & Design polished aluminum crankshaft pulley (6 1/2-inch o.d.) installed with Chrysler 152191 Woodruff key and Chrysler 1731525 crankshaft bolt and 1324264 washer using Loctite and torqued to 85 ft-lb; Chrysler 1618686 oil slinger painted with Glyptal G-1228A medium-grey gloss enamel; $275

Crankshaft total: $860

Connecting Rods and Pistons

• Chrysler 1323338, casting number 1324222, forged steel I-beam connecting rods, full-floating wrist pins (6.625-inch length, center to center), connecting rod weight: 710 grams each; connecting rod ratio: 1.83 (with 3.625-inch stroke); $120

• Connecting rods shot peened, debeamed, aligned, Magnafluxed, resized, balanced, and Federal Mogul 1804V wrist pin bushings installed allowing for 0.002-inch wrist pin clearance; ARP 145-6002 high-performance-series connecting rod bolts (3/8-inch diameter, 8740 chrome-moly steel, 190,000 psi, installed); $496.67

• PAW (King Engine Bearings) HEM-MOR354 connecting rod bearings (0.010-inch oversize) installed allowing for 0.002-inch connecting rod clearance and 0.009-inch side clearance per pair of connecting rods; connecting rod bolts torqued to 45 ft-lb using molykote and allowing for 0.006-inch stretch; $95

• TRW L2061-030 power-forged aluminum slipper-skirt racing pistons (0.030-inch oversize) with 8.0:1 compression ratio; piston weight: 682 grams each; heat-treated and casehardened 4340 chrome-moly steel straight-wall wrist pins installed with Tru-Arc wrist pin retainers; wrist pin weight: 167 grams; piston grooves: top compression ring groove width: 3/32 inch; second compression ring groove width: 3/32 inch; oil ring groove width: 5/32 inch; Hastings 636 moly top ring piston ring set (0.030-inch oversize) installed within manufacturer's recommended arc; top compression ring gap: 0.020 inch; second compression ring gap: 0.024 inch; oil ring gap: 0.018 inch; intake-valve-to-piston clearance: 0.140 inch, and exhaust-valve-to-piston clearance: 0.240 inch (with gasket); new displacement: 359.6 ci (5.9 liters); $440

• Complete V-8 engine balance; Fel-Pro FS7908PT-4 complete gasket set installed; $325

Connecting rods and pistons total: $1,476.67

Lubrication System

• Hot Heads Research & Racing 21905 high-volume oil pump (for small-block Chrysler 340-ci engine) with attached rear sump pickup screen installed; 1956 Chrysler 1408853 rear main bearing cap dowel installed; 1956 Chrysler 1323369 oil pump intermediate driveshaft (6.030-inch length) installed with Chrysler 601268 oil pump intermediate driveshaft gear and Chrysler 1324281 oil pump intermediate driveshaft bushing; PAW HEM-5350 oil diverter valve installed; $214

• 1958 Dodge Truck stamped steel oil pan with full-length sump, sectioned 1 1/2 inches by Luke's Custom Machine & Design; capacity: 7 quarts oil; oil pan installed with stainless-steel hex head bolts, lockwashers, and AN flat washers using Loctite and torqued to 15 ft-lb; oil pan gaskets and seals installed using silicone sealant; Hot Heads Research & Racing 20101 polished-aluminum vertical oil filter adapter installed with stainless-steel socket head bolts using Loctite and torqued to 20 ft-lb; oil filter adapter gasket installed using silicone sealant; Fram PH-8A oil filter installed and engine lubricated with 7 quarts Pennzoil HD-30-weight motor oil; oil pan painted with PPG DGHS 9000 black high-gloss polyurethane; Hot Heads Research & Racing 21955 chrome angled dip stick and dip stick tube installed; $518.11

Lubrication system total: $732.11

Camshaft and Cylinder Heads

• Clevite 77 SH-313S camshaft bearings installed with 0.002-inch camshaft clearance and 0.002-inch end play; No. 1 bearing: SH-313, housing bore: 2.1295 to 2.1305 inches; No. 2, 3, and 4 bearing: SH-314, housing bore: 2.1295 to 2.1305 inches; No. 5 bearing: SH-315, housing bore: 1.5670 to 1.5680 inches; camshaft journal diameter: 2.00 inches; $55

• 1956 Chrysler 1632425 solid (mechanical) lifter camshaft reground by Crower Cams & Equipment Company, blower grind with advertised duration: 284 degrees intake and exhaust; duration at 0.050-inch lift: 224 degrees intake and exhaust; lobe separation angle: 112 degrees; net valve lift (with 1.50 ratio rocker arms): 0.452 inch intake and 0.450 inch exhaust; valve lash (hot): 0.016 inch intake and 0.018 inch exhaust; camshaft degreed; $200

• Chrysler 1634267 camshaft thrust plate installed with Grade 8 bolts and lockwashers using Loctite and torqued to 25 ft-lb; Chrysler 1618717 camshaft sprocket spacer, Chrysler 106751 Woodruff key, and Chrysler 1328644 oil trough installed; Hot Heads Research & Racing 20200 camshaft bolt and washer kit installed; $60

• Competition Cams 821-16 High Energy solid (mechanical) lifters (for big-block Chrysler 383-ci and 440-ci engines; 0.903-inch diameter by 1.803-inch height) installed; Smith Brothers heat-treated 4130 seamless chrome-moly steel nonadjustable pushrods (5/16-inch diameter by 0.083-inch wall) installed; intake valve pushrod length: 9.750 inches, and exhaust valve pushrod length: 11.225 inches; $295

• Cloyes 92103 true roller timing chain set with heat-treated sprockets and multi-keyway crankshaft sprocket installed; Hot Heads Research & Racing 20211 polished-aluminum timing gear cover with adjustable timing pointer, installed with stainless-steel socket head bolts and AN flat washers using Loctite and torqued to 15 ft-lb; timing gear cover gasket installed using silicone sealant; $340

• Luke's Custom Machine & Design polished-aluminum valley cover installed with polished stainless-steel bolts, lockwashers, and AN flat washers using Loctite and torqued to 15 ft-lb; valley cover gasket installed using silicone sealant; Weatherhead 3400-2 polished-brass 90-degree elbow (1/8-inch NPT) installed with Motomaster 17-9259-4 PCV valve using pipe thread sealant; Mr. Gasket 2060 chrome oil filler/crankcase breather cap installed; $165

• 1956 Chrysler 1671141 (casting number 1619823-1) cast-iron hemispherical combustion chamber cylinder heads; cylinder head weight: 66 pounds each; $300

• Cylinder heads hot tanked and Redi-Stripped; intake and exhaust ports fully ported and polished and gasket matched; combustion chambers polished and cc'd, surfaced; Hot Heads Research & Racing 40044 bronze intake valve guides and 40046 bronze exhaust valve guides (11/32-inch stem diameter) installed; Federal Mogul 240736 spark plug tube oil seals installed; Serdi-machined multi-angle blueprint valve grind performed; area beneath valve covers painted with Glyptal G-1228A medium-grey gloss enamel; exterior surface of cylinder heads sanded and detailed and painted with PPG 74000 red high-gloss polyurethane; $936.22

• Hot Heads Research & Racing 40016 stainless-steel intake valves (2.125-inch head diameter by 11/32-inch stem diameter by 5.23-inch length overall) undercut stems at head, hardened tips, swirl polished, installed; weight: 141 grams each; Hot Heads Research & Racing 40026 stainless-steel exhaust valves (1.945-inch head diameter by 11/32-inch stem diameter by 5.23-inch length overall) undercut stems at head, hardened tips, swirl polished, installed; weight: 112 grams each; Serdi-machined multi-angle blueprint valve grind performed; Enginetech S2927 viton positive seal valve stem seals installed; $246

• Manley Performance Parts 22400-16 and 22428-16 Street Master dual valve springs with installed height: 120 pounds at 1.820 inches valves closed and 310 pounds at 1.250 inches valves open; 1.437-inch o.d. and 0.720-inch i.d.; coil bind: 1.100 inches; Manley Performance Parts 23645-16 Street Master valve spring retainers (4140 chrome-moly steel, 11/32-inch stem diameter, 7-degree, 1.440-inch/1.050-inch o.d. and 0.700-inch i.d.) installed with Crane Cams 99097-1 valve stem locks (machined 4140 heat-treated chrome-moly steel, 11/32-inch stem diameter, 7-degree, standard height, black oxide finish); $200

• 1956 Chrysler 300 adjustable rocker arm assemblies rebuilt by Luke's Custom Machine & Design; rocker arm ratio: 1.50; rocker arm stands and rocker arms painted with Glyptal G-1228A medium-grey gloss enamel; rocker arm assemblies and cylinder heads installed with Milodon 80215 premium cylinder head stud kit (aircraft-quality 8740 chrome-moly steel, 180,000 psi, 4130 hardened-steel parallel ground washers and nuts) using anti-seize compound and torqued to 85 ft-lb; $750

• O'Brien Truckers polished cast finned aluminum valve covers with matching polished cast finned aluminum spark plug wire covers installed with Papco 264-016 engine studs (5/16-inch by 1 3/4-inch length), polished stainless-steel acorn nuts, lockwashers, and AN flat washers using anti-seize compound and torqued to 15 ft-lb; valve cover gaskets installed using silicone sealant; Mooneyes USA MP1800 polished-aluminum right-angle valve cover breathers (3-inch width) installed with stainless-steel bolts and lockwashers using Loctite; $522.47

Camshaft and cylinder heads total: $4,069.69

Intake System

• Weiand WC671 polished-aluminum blower intake manifold installed with polished stainless-steel socket head bolts and AN flat washers using Loctite and torqued to 25 ft-lb; intake manifold gaskets installed using silicone sealant; $240

• GM 5155866 polished-aluminum large bore sand-cast supercharger (blower) case (model 6-71); GM 5150219 polished sand-cast front and rear bearing plates and GM 5150233 polished sand-cast front cover; Blower Drive Service 671SL bearing seals, 5205HD front bearings, and 62052RS rear bearings installed; Blower Drive Service 671-GK complete gasket set installed using Permatex aviation form-a-gasket; Luke's Custom Machine & Design aluminum bearing support rings and polished-aluminum rear bearing cover installed with polished stainless-steel bolts and lockwashers using anti-seize compound; rotors double-pinned and clearanced; Blower Drive Service 555 pressure relief valve and 556 oil sight gauge installed; stainless-steel oil filler and oil drain plugs (3/8-inch NPT) installed using pipe thread sealant; blower assembled with polished stainless-steel socket head bolts, lockwashers, and AN flat washers using Permatex aviation form-a-gasket; Armstrong N-8090 blower to intake manifold gasket installed using anti-seize compound; Mooneyham 10884 anodized aluminum blower stud kit installed with polished stainless-steel acorn nuts and AN flat washers using anti-seize compound; $1,368.95

• Luke's Custom Machine & Design LS3000 polished 6061 T-6 aluminum medium blower snout with LS3300 blower snout shaft, and LS4100 gear coupler installed with polished stainless-steel socket head bolts and lockwashers using Permatex aviation form-a-gasket; $385

• Blower Drive Service 6300 polished T-6 aluminum crankshaft blower pulley (1/2-inch pitch [Gilmer] by 30-tooth by 3.5 inches wide) and 6336 polished T-6 aluminum blower snout pulley (1/2-inch pitch [Gilmer] by 36-tooth by 3.5 inches wide) installed with polished stainless-steel socket head bolts, lockwashers, and AN flat washers using anti-seize compound; Jason 540H-300 blower belt (1/2-inch pitch [Gilmer] by 54-inch length by 3-inch width) installed; blower drive ratio: 20 percent underdrive; blower boost: 5.0 pounds (estimated); $275

• Luke's Custom Machine & Design polished-aluminum idler

pulley bracket (1/2-inch thickness) installed with polished-aluminum idler pulley and 4140 chrome-moly steel stand-off; $404.88

• Blower Drive Service 24B6 polished-aluminum 2x4-barrel carburetor adapter (1 inch high) with blower inlet safety screen, installed with polished stainless-steel socket head bolts and AN flat washers using anti-seize compound; carburetor adapter gasket installed using Permatex aviation form-a-gasket; $130

• Edelbrock 1405 Performer silver finish 600-cfm four-barrel carburetors with manual choke installed with ARP 400-2401 polished stainless-steel carburetor stud kits using anti-seize compound; $421.90

• O'Brien Truckers polished cast finned aluminum universal oval air cleaner cover (15-inch length by 7 1/2-inch width by 2 3/4 inches high) installed; K&N E-2360 air filters (6.375-inch diameter by 2.50-inch height) installed; $200

• Holley 12-803 chrome fuel pressure regulators, adjustable from 4 1/2 to 9 psi, installed with Weatherhead 402-6-6 polished-brass 90-degree elbows (3/8-inch tube to 3/8-inch NPT, outlet line), Weatherhead 1069-6 polished-brass 90-degree male elbow (3/8-inch i.d. hose to 1/4-inch NPT), Weatherhead 3220-6-4 polished-brass adapter (1/4-inch NPT to 3/8-inch NPT, inlet line), Weatherhead 3220-6-2 polished-brass adapter (1/8-inch NPT to 3/8-inch NPT), and Holley 26-500 fuel pressure gauge (0 to 15 psi, 1 1/2-inch-diameter face) installed using pipe thread sealant; Summit Racing Equipment 220238 polished stainless-steel fuel line (3/8-inch tube by 0.028-inch wall by 2-foot length) installed with Weatherhead 100-6 polished-brass inverted flare nuts (3/8-inch tube) using pipe thread sealant; $120.59

Intake system total: $3,546.32

Ignition System

• Taylor/Vertex 541803 self-contained, 356 T-6 aluminum housing, electronic distributor, full centrifugal (mechanical) advance, with internal HEI coil, breakerless triggering, and control module; distributor installed with Chrysler 1326835 distributor clamp and polished stainless-steel bolt and lockwasher using anti-seize compound; distributor clamp painted with Plasti-Kote 203 black high-gloss engine enamel; $610

• Chrysler 1737379 aluminum spark plug tubes installed; NGK BP6ES resistor-type 18-millimeter spark plugs installed with 0.050-inch gap and torqued to 25 ft-lb; Taylor/Vertex 35071 Pro Series black 8-millimeter high-performance spark plug wire Spiro-Pro Kelvar resistor core installed with Standard ST113 spark plug terminals; $100

• Powermaster 17509 chrome Chrysler alternator, externally regulated, 75 amps, installed with Luke's Custom Machine & Design polished stainless-steel adjusting brace and mounting bracket using polished stainless-steel bolts, lockwashers, and flat washers; $225.62

It must be Halloween; look at this scary crew! Luke Balogh is on the right in his Hugh Hefner dark blue smoking jacket, and I am on the left. The best part of this photograph is the front of the blown Dodge Truck Hemi engine.

• Mopar Performance (Chrysler Corporation) P5249644 lightweight starting motor installed; Gates 11A1550 XL crankshaft/water pump/alternator v-belt (7/16-inch by 61-inch length) installed; $155.67

Ignition system total: $1,091.29

Cooling System

• Weiand 8208 action-plus polished-aluminum small-block Chevrolet short-style water pump installed with polished stainless-steel bolts and lockwashers using Loctite and torqued to 25 ft-lb; water pump gaskets installed using silicone sealant; Trans Dapt 9478 polished T-6 aluminum single-groove (6-inch diameter) water pump pulley installed with polished stainless-steel socket head countersunk bolts using Loctite and torqued to 25 ft-lb; $97.45

• PAW 5775 polished-aluminum water passage crossover manifold installed with polished stainless-steel bolts and lockwashers using Loctite and torqued to 25 ft-lb; water passage crossover manifold gaskets installed using silicone sealant; Robert Shaw 330-160 extra performance balanced 160-degree (Fahrenheit) thermostat installed; Trans-Dapt 9415 chrome O-ring thermostat housing installed with polished stainless-steel bolts and lockwashers using anti-seize compound and torqued to 20 ft-lb; $243

Cooling system total: $340.45

Labor

• Labor for checking clearances, gapping piston rings, degree camshaft, valvetrain assembly, blower setup, detailing, trial engine assembly, final engine assembly, and initial engine start-up; $1,200

Labor total: $1,200

Engine Grand Total: $14,562.07 (U.S.)

CHAPTER 17
1957 CHRYSLER 392-ci HEMI ENGINE

This chapter contains the next installment of the early Chrysler Hemi engines—the Chrysler 392-ci hemispherical combustion chamber engine. The Chrysler 392-ci Hemi engine was produced in 1957 and 1958 only, for the Chrysler passenger cars. These engine blocks are becoming more difficult to locate because only a limited number were manufactured. Many Chrysler 392-ci Hemi engine blocks ended their careers at drag strips throughout the United States in the late 1950s and 1960s by literally blowing apart. Even these fantastic engines have their limits!

The engine described in this chapter is a naturally aspirated 1957 Chrysler FirePower 392-ci model. The owner is going to install this mild street performance engine in his daily-driven 1950 Ford two-door coupe. Luke's Custom Machine & Design completed the engine at the end of September 2003.

Components Description
Engine Block

The specifications for the 1957 Chrysler FirePower 392-ci Hemi engine are:

- 392-ci (6.4-liter) displacement
- 4.00-inch stock bore and 3.906-inch stock stroke
- Stock compression ratio: 9.25:1
- 325 horsepower at 4,600 rpm and 430 ft-lb torque at 2,800 rpm

The Chrysler 392-ci Hemi engine block is another high-quality product with expert factory machining. The prefixes for the 1956 Chrysler FirePower engine block are NE57 and CF57 (Canada), the prefix for the 1957 Chrysler 300C engine block is 3NE57, and the prefix for the 1957 Chrysler Imperial engine block is CE57. The prefix for the 1958 Chrysler FirePower engine block is 58N, the prefix for the 1958 Chrysler 300D engine block is 58N3, and the prefix for the 1958 Chrysler Imperial engine block is 58C. The estimated price today for a Chrysler 392-ci Hemi engine block is $500.

The Chrysler 392-ci engine block can be safely bored 0.060-inch oversize; however, it is usually best to limit the bore to 0.030-inch oversize if possible. This will prevent overheating, especially in a street performance engine. Refer to Chapter 1 for information about engine block preparation and machining procedures. This engine block will be bored 0.040-inch oversize.

The Chrysler 392-ci Hemi engine block was manufactured with two-bolt main bearing caps. These main bearing caps are of sufficient strength for most street performance engines, even blown engines, provided the boost does not exceed 6 pounds. The ARP 140-5001 high-performance-series main bearing cap bolts (170,000 psi) are available at a current retail price of $40. The ARP 140-5401 main bearing cap stud kit (190,000 psi) is available for $53. If you choose to install four-bolt main bearing caps, the Milodon 11350 splayed four-bolt main bearing caps are currently available for the retail price of $300. Have the engine block align bored and honed after installing the four-bolt main bearing caps. The diameter of the main bearing housing bores is 2.880 to 2.8805 inches. The Chrysler 1408853 rear main bearing cap dowel (or sleeve) is fitted in the engine block on the left side (driver's side)

The 1957 *Passenger Car Parts List, published by Chrysler Corporation of Canada Limited. This edition for the parts division is WM 4402 and was issued in Windsor, Ontario (Canada) in February 1958—another rare publication.*

The No. 1 through No. 4 main bearing caps have been reinforced in this Chrysler 392-ci Hemi engine by the addition of main bearing cap support bridges.

and aligns the rear main bearing cap. The distance from the crank-shaft centerline to the deck is 10.870 inches. This particular engine block did not require align honing but did require parallel decking. Refer to Chapter 15 for information regarding freeze plugs, oil gallery line plugs, and the rear camshaft boss plug.

You may also use main bearing cap support bridges (fabricated with 1045 steel) to strengthen the bottom end of a Chrysler 392-ci Hemi engine block. The dimensions are: 4 5/8 inches long by 1 inch wide by 1 inch high. The main bearing cap support bridges are used for all the main bearing caps except the rear main bearing cap, which is strong enough due to its width. Use aircraft-quality main bearing cap bolts of at least 180,000 psi with the main bearing cap support bridges. The engine block may have to be align honed even though main bearing caps were not installed, due to the different clamping force introduced by the main bearing cap support bridges.

Crankshaft

The Chrysler 392-ci Hemi crankshafts are a top-quality item manufactured using forged steel and then heat treated, Magnafluxed, and shot peened at the factory. The stock stroke is 3.906 inches, the main bearing journals are 2.687 to 2.688 inches in diameter, and the connecting rod journals are 2.374 to 2.375 inches in diameter. These crankshafts are becoming difficult to find; as a result, the current price for one of these crankshafts in decent condition is estimated to be $350. Caution: If the main bearing journals or the connecting rod journals need to be ground more than 0.040-inch undersize, bearings are not currently available. The only solution to this problem is to have the crank-shaft journals built up (refer to Chapter 2).

A 1957 Chrysler 1737919 forged steel crankshaft (casting number 1673755) for a 392-ci engine. The crankshaft has been shot peened, aligned, Magnafluxed, ground, oil holes chamfered, journals polished, and balanced.

The 1957 Chrysler 1737919 crankshaft is designed for the FirePower and Imperial models, and the 1957 Chrysler 1821264 crankshaft is designed for the Chrysler 300 model. The 1958 Chrysler 1827800 crankshaft is designed for the FirePower and Imperial models, and the 1958 Chrysler 1851459 crankshaft is designed for the Chrysler 300 model. There is a common, though incorrect, belief that there is only one Chrysler 392-ci Hemi crankshaft casting number (1673755).

The Federal Mogul 4009M main bearings are available in standard size and 0.010-inch oversize. The current retail price for a set of these main bearings is $215. The Clevite 77 MS-426M main bearings are available in standard size only. The current retail price for a set of these main bearings is $195. The King Engine Bearings main bearings are available in standard size, 0.010-, 0.020-, 0.030-, and 0.040-inch oversize. The current retail price for a set of these main bearings is $110. The King Engine Bearings

The Federal Mogul 4009M10 main bearings (0.010-inch oversize) are being measured with a dial indicator to determine the crankshaft clearance.

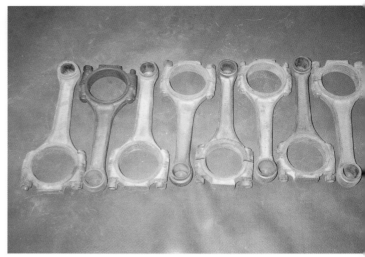

These dirty little rascals are a set of 1957 Chrysler 1673756 (casting number 1673758) forged steel connecting rods. They might not look like much at the moment, but they will be brought back to life, starting with a good shot peening.

A big-block Chrysler 440-ci connecting rod (casting number 2951908) being weighed on a Toledo Digital Scale prior to balancing.

are available from Hot Heads Research & Racing 23130 and PAW HEM-MOM392. The factory-recommended main bearing clearance is 0.0005 to 0.0015 inch, and the recommended crankshaft end play is 0.002 to 0.007 inch. The No. 3 main bearing is the thrust bearing. The main bearing cap bolts are torqued to 85 ft-lb using molykote, starting with No. 3 main bearing cap.

The owner of the engine managed to locate and purchase a NOS Chrysler 1735045 harmonic balancer with the hub and the 1957 Chrysler 1732941 dual v-belt crankshaft pulley. The crankshaft pulley is 5 3/4 inches in diameter. Refer to Chapter 15 for information pertaining to harmonic balancers, the oil slinger, and a crankshaft pulley.

Connecting Rods and Pistons

The drop forged I-beam connecting rods used in the Chrysler 392-ci engine are excellent connecting rods suitable for most street performance engines. These connecting rods are designed for use with full-floating wrist pins, they are 6.956 inches in length (center to center), and they weigh 782 grams each. The casting number for the Chrysler 392-ci Hemi connecting rods is 1673758. The diameter of the crankshaft end (the big end) is 2.500 to 2.5005 inches, and the thickness of the crankshaft end (the big end) is 1.00 inch. Refer to Chapter 3 for information regarding connecting rod preparation.

The Federal Mogul 2235SB connecting rod bearings are available in standard size and 0.010-inch oversize. The current retail price for a set of these connecting rod bearings is $190. The Clevite 77 CB-1213M connecting rod bearings are available in standard size and 0.010-inch oversize. The current retail price for a set of these connecting rod bearings is $175. The King Engine Bearings connecting rod bearings are available in standard size, 0.010-, 0.020-, 0.030-, and 0.040-inch oversize. The current retail price for a set of these connecting rod bearings is $90. The King Engine Bearings are available from PAW HEM-MOR392 or Hot Heads Research & Racing 23140. Refer to Chapter 15 for information about wrist pin bushings.

A number of engine building shops use the big-block Chrysler 440-ci connecting rods as a stronger replacement for the Chrysler 392-ci Hemi connecting rods. The big-block Chrysler 440-ci

The new old stock (NOS) 1957 Chrysler 1752267 cast-aluminum pistons (0.040-inch oversize), the Chrysler 1673756 (casting number 1673758) connecting rods, and the Federal Mogul 2235SB-10 connecting rod bearings (0.010-inch oversize), ready to be installed in the engine.

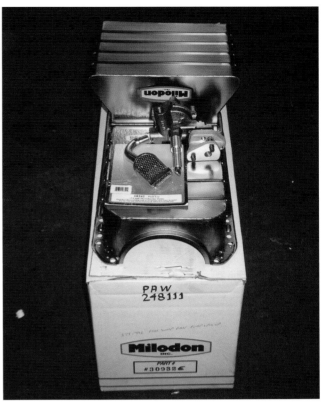

A Milodon 30932 low-profile early Chrysler Hemi oil pan, a Milodon 20150 high-volume oil pump, and a Milodon 18342 oil pump pickup screen.

connecting rods are 6.760 inches in length (center to center), which is 0.196 inches shorter than the Chrysler 392-ci Hemi connecting rods. This shorter length (center to center) places the wrist pin lower down in the piston and limits the amount of material at the bottom of the wrist pin boss in the piston. The 1.094-inch wrist pin diameter used with the big-block Chrysler 440-ci connecting rods is larger than the 0.9841- to 0.9843-inch wrist pin diameter used with the Chrysler 392-ci Hemi connecting rods. Using custom pistons with the big-block Chrysler 440-ci connecting rods, the size of the wrist pin diameter can be reduced to 0.990 inch with the Ross Racing Pistons B1094 bronze wrist pin bushing. The big-block Chrysler 440-ci connecting rods are designed for use with a 2.374-inch-diameter connecting rod journal, and the thickness of the crankshaft end (the big end) is 1.020 inches. The Chrysler 392-ci Hemi connecting rods are designed for use with the same size connecting rod journal diameter but the thickness at the crankshaft end is 1.00 inch, which is 0.020 inch narrower than the big-block Chrysler 440-ci connecting rods. The big block Chrysler 440-ci connecting rods will require the removal of 0.020 inch of material

(0.010 inch from each side) from the sides of the crankshaft end (the big end). The Chrysler 392-ci Hemi connecting rods weigh 782 grams each, and the big-block Chrysler 440-ci connecting rods weigh 922 grams each. To compensate the crankshaft for all this additional weight, add heavy metal (Mallory metal) to the crankshaft counterweights. This is typical of all custom engine building when there is an attempt to interchange engine parts—when one problem is solved, two new problems are created!

If stronger connecting rods are required for a specific Chrysler 392-ci Hemi engine, purchase a set of the Hot Heads Research & Racing 21720 forged steel H-beam connecting rods. These connecting rods are 6.965 inches in length (center to center), they use the big-block Chevrolet 0.990-inch-diameter wrist pin, and they are designed for use with the big-block Chrysler 440-ci connecting rod bearings, which are less expensive than the Chrysler 392-ci Hemi connecting rod bearings. Use custom pistons with the Hot Heads Research & Racing H-beam connecting rods. The current retail price for a set of the Hot Heads Research & Racing 21720 connecting rods is $998. Refer

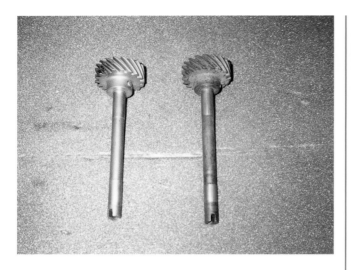

The Chrysler 1323369 shorter (6.030-inch length) oil pump intermediate driveshaft on the left is designed for a Chrysler 354-ci Hemi engine. The Chrysler 1732826 longer (6.345-inch length) oil pump intermediate driveshaft on the right is designed for the Chrysler 392-ci Hemi engine. The Chrysler 601268 gear is on both the shafts.

The camshaft bearings for this Chrysler 392-ci Hemi engine are being installed using a camshaft bearing installation tool. Camshaft bearings must be installed with this type of tool in order to prevent damage to them and to the camshaft bearing housing bores.

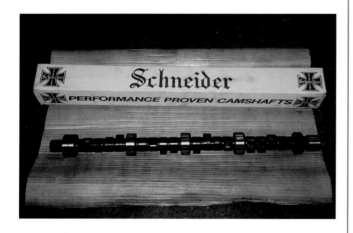

A Schneider Racing Cams 270-H hydraulic lifter camshaft for a Chrysler 392-ci Hemi engine.

to Chapter 15 for information regarding connecting rod bolts.

The owner located a set of NOS 1957 Chrysler 1752267 cast-aluminum pistons with wrist pins and purchased them for $150. The pistons are 0.040-inch oversize (9.25:1 compression ratio) and they weigh 697 grams each. The piston ring groove width is 5/64-inch top and second compression ring grooves, and a 3/16-inch oil ring groove. These pistons are satisfactory for use in a mild street performance engine such as the one described here. Install a Sealed Power E-251K-40 moly-coated ductile iron top piston ring set (0.040-inch oversize). The current retail price for these

piston rings is $43. Refer to Chapter 15 for information about piston installation. The factory-recommended cast-aluminum piston clearance is 0.0005 to 0.0015 inch.

Use the Fel-Pro FS7908PT-4 gasket set with the Chrysler 392-ci Hemi engine. The current retail price for this complete gasket set is $135.

Lubrication System

The 1957 Chrysler 1671902 oil pump was an excellent oil pump for the Chrysler 392-ci Hemi engine and was used with the Chrysler 1737988 oil pump pickup screen. This oil pump is no longer available from Chrysler Corporation. Install a NOS oil pump and an oil pump pickup screen with a 1957 Chrysler 1671887 rear sump oil pan. Refer to Chapter 15 for information about new oil pumps and oil pump pickup screens, the oil diverter valve, and oil filter adapters.

The owner of the engine decided he wanted the engine block, oil pan, and cylinder heads painted with Plasti-Kote T-26 slicker yellow high-gloss engine enamel. Yellow seems to blend in nicely with black and chrome; however, it is just about the worst color to use on an engine. In order to cover a base coat of grey or black, two to three times more paint is required than with any other color.

We equipped the Chrysler 392-ci Hemi engine with an intermediate driveshaft for the oil pump. The Chrysler 1732826 intermediate driveshaft (6.345-inch length) with the Chrysler 601268 gear was located between the oil pump and the distributor. We lowered the oil pump intermediate driveshaft from the top of the valve lifter gallery through the Chrysler 1324281 intermediate

On the left: the 1957 Chrysler 1674608 intake pushrod and 1674609 exhaust pushrod are used with the Chrysler hydraulic lifter. On the right: the 1957 Chrysler 1731558 intake pushrod and the 1731559 exhaust pushrod are used with the Chrysler solid lifter.

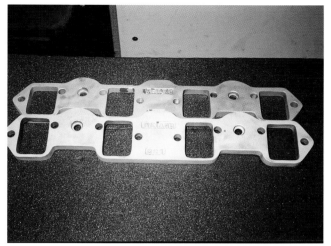

A vintage pair of Weiand 8203 (model CS1) aluminum intake manifold spacers used to install Chrysler 331-ci or 354-ci Hemi cylinder heads on a Chrysler 392-ci engine block.

driveshaft bushing to connect with the oil pump. The gear is at the top of the intermediate driveshaft in the valve lifter gallery. The Hot Heads Research & Racing 21937 oil pump intermediate driveshaft (6.345-inch length) is designed for use with a 1957 Chrysler 1689325 distributor used in the 392-ci Hemi engine. The Hot Heads Research & Racing 21935 oil pump intermediate driveshaft (6.675-inch length) is designed for use with a small-block Chrysler 360-ci distributor. The current retail price for either of these oil pump intermediate driveshafts is $30. The Hot Heads Research & Racing 21950 oil pump intermediate driveshaft bushing is available for $4. Refer to Chapter 15 for information about the dip stick and dip stick tube.

Camshaft and Cylinder Heads

The camshaft bearings used in the Chrysler 354-ci Hemi engine are the same camshaft bearings used in the Chrysler 392-ci Hemi engine. Refer to Chapter 15 for information about these camshaft bearings.

The Chrysler 354-ci Hemi camshafts are not interchangeable with the Chrysler 392-ci Hemi camshafts. The 1957 Chrysler 1735980 hydraulic lifter camshaft and the 1957 Chrysler 1731569 solid (mechanical) lifter camshafts are not suitable candidates for a street performance engine. Schneider Racing Cams (see Appendix B—Resources) is an excellent source of hydraulic lifter, solid (mechanical) lifter, and roller lifter camshafts for the Chrysler 392-ci Hemi engine. The Schneider 270-H hydraulic lifter camshaft will be installed in the engine. The advertised duration is: 270 degrees intake and exhaust; duration at

0.050-inch lift: 214 degrees intake and exhaust; lobe separation angle: 112 degrees; net valve lift (with 1.50 ratio rocker arms): 0.443 inch intake and exhaust; valve lash (hot): zero. The current retail price for this camshaft is $225 outright, with no core exchange. Refer to Chapter 15 for information regarding the camshaft thrust plate and oil trough.

The 1957 to 1958 Chrysler 300-series engines were the only Chrysler 392-ci Hemi engines equipped with a solid lifter camshaft, nonadjustable pushrods, and adjustable rocker arms. The factory equipped all the other Chrysler 392-ci Hemi engines with hydraulic lifter camshafts, nonadjustable pushrods, and nonadjustable rocker arms. The 1957 Chrysler 1673721 solid (mechanical) lifters and the 1957 Chrysler 1555176 hydraulic lifters are no longer available from Chrysler Corporation. Refer to Chapter 15 for information about camshaft lifters.

Install an aftermarket camshaft in a Chrysler 392-ci Hemi engine that is being built as a street performance engine. The aftermarket camshaft will require longer aftermarket pushrods to replace the factory pushrods, since the camshaft will be ground. Adjustable pushrods are required when using nonadjustable rocker arms, and nonadjustable pushrods are required when using adjustable rocker arms. Smith Brothers Pushrods is a fine source for custom-length pushrods and there is a photograph of a set of these pushrods in Chapter 5. As a matter of interest, the Chrysler 1674608 nonadjustable intake valve pushrods (5/16-inch diameter by 10.106-inch length) and the Chrysler 1674609 nonadjustable exhaust valve pushrods (5/16-inch diameter by 11.106-inch length) were used with the 1957 Chrysler 1555176

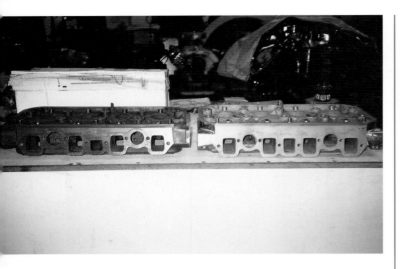

On the left: a Chrysler 354-ci Hemi cylinder head (casting number 1619826) shows the bottom of the intake port castings are 0.530 inch above the tabletop surface. On the right: a Chrysler 392-ci Hemi cylinder head (casting number 1731528) shows the bottom of the intake port castings are flush with the tabletop surface.

A Chrysler 392-ci Hemi cylinder head (casting number 1735282) with the stock dimension 2.00-inch head diameter intake valves and 1.9375-inch head diameter exhaust valves. The valves have been installed with a Serdi-machined multi-angle blueprint valve grind.

hydraulic lifter camshaft. The Chrysler 1731558 nonadjustable intake valve pushrods (5/16-inch diameter by 10.207-inch length) and the Chrysler 1731559 nonadjustable exhaust valve pushrods (5/16-inch diameter by 11.702-inch length) were used with the 1957 Chrysler 1673721 solid (mechanical) lifter camshaft.

Refer to Chapter 15 for information pertaining to timing chain sets. We used a chrome-plated 1957 Chrysler 1730518 stamped steel timing gear cover with the engine and installed a stock-style mechanical fuel pump. As a result, we retained the Chrysler 1632426 camshaft eccentric. The Hot Heads Research & Racing 20215 cast-aluminum timing gear cover with adjustable timing pointer and the PAW HEM-5710 cast-aluminum timing gear cover are available for the Chrysler 392-ci Hemi engine. The Hot Heads Research & Racing model is available at the current retail price of $140, and the PAW model is available at the current retail price of $160. (Prices are for the unpolished version.) We installed a chrome-plated Chrysler 1738375 one-piece stamped steel valley cover for a Chrysler 300C Hemi engine on the engine. Refer to Chapter 15 for information on this valley cover.

The Chrysler 392-ci hemispherical combustion chamber cast-iron cylinder heads are similar to, but not the same as, the Chrysler 354-ci Hemi cylinder heads. The Chrysler 392-ci Hemi cylinder heads did not have valve seat inserts. When viewed from the side, the bottom of the intake port castings of the Chrysler 354-ci Hemi cylinder heads are about 1/2 inch above the engine block deck surface. When viewed from the side, the bottom of the intake port

castings of the Chrysler 392-ci Hemi cylinder heads are flush with the engine block deck surface. The 1955 Chrysler 331-ci and the 1956 Chrysler 354-ci Hemi cylinder heads will bolt onto a Chrysler 392-ci Hemi engine block without any modifications other than the use of 1/2-inch-thick (0.625 inch, including gaskets) intake manifold spacers. The Hot Heads Research & Racing 20209 machined aluminum 1/2-inch-thick intake manifold spacers are available at the current retail price of $95.

The 1957 Chrysler 1737809 cylinder heads are designed for the FirePower and Imperial models, and the 1957 Chrysler 1737807 cylinder heads are designed for the Chrysler 300 model. The 1958 Chrysler 1737809 cylinder heads are designed for the FirePower and Imperial models, and the 1958 Chrysler 1828122 cylinder heads are designed for the Chrysler 300 model. This is slightly mysterious as the only known casting numbers for the Chrysler 392-ci Hemi cylinder heads are 1735282 and 1731528. These are the casting numbers I am aware of; there may well be others. The estimated cost for a pair of 1957 or 1958 Chrysler 392-ci Hemi cylinder heads without the rocker arm or valve assemblies (bare) is $300. Refer to Chapter 15 for information on cylinder head preparation.

Install a set of NOS Chrysler 1634790 cast-iron intake valve guides and Chrysler 1486911 exhaust valve guides (for 3/8-inch valve stem diameter) in the cylinder heads. There is a photograph of these valve guides in Chapter 15.

The Chrysler 392-ci Hemi cylinder heads were equipped with 2.00-inch head diameter by 3/8-inch stem diameter by 5.03125-

A pair of nonadjustable rocker arm assemblies for a Chrysler 392-ci Hemi engine. I also rebuilt this set for Luke's Custom Machine & Design.

A good photograph of an unpolished Mooneyes USA MP656 cast-aluminum early Chrysler Hemi valve cover. These valve covers are complete with spark plug tubes and seals.

inch length overall intake valves and 1.9375-inch head diameter by 3/8-inch stem diameter by 5.03125-inch length overall exhaust valves. The engine is a mild street performance engine; therefore, we installed NOS sets of stock dimension valves. Have a Serdi-machined multi-angle blueprint valve grind performed on the cylinder heads, and install Enginetech S2890 viton positive seal valve stem seals on the intake and exhaust valves. Refer to Chapter 15 for information about hardened valve seat inserts.

Install a set of Federal Mogul VS-510 single valve springs with 1956 Chrysler 1619636 valve spring retainers and 1956 Chrysler 1614666 valve stem locks. Refer to Chapter 15 for information about these items.

The Chrysler 1738375 FirePower valve covers, used on the 300-series engines with adjustable rocker arms, had four bumps stamped horizontally in the center area for exhaust rocker arm clearance. The Chrysler 1323310 FirePower valve covers can be installed with adjustable rocker arms, provided valve cover spacers and extended spark plug tubes are used. These items are available from Titan Speed Engineering (see Appendix B—Resources) for the current retail price of $250. Titan Speed Engineering also manufactures premium-quality billet aluminum rocker arm assemblies for the early Chrysler Hemi engines. Refer to Chapter 15 for information regarding the rocker arm assemblies and cylinder head bolts.

Intake System

The only high-performance intake manifold offered for the Chrysler 392-ci Hemi engine was the 2x4-barrel carburetor, dual-plane cast-iron intake manifold, designed for the Chrysler 300-series engines. The Chrysler 1733477 (casting number 1731560) dual-quad cast-iron intake manifold was installed on the 1957 Chrysler 300C and the 1958 Chrysler 300D Hemi engine. Refer to Chapter 15 for information about intake manifolds. We installed a 1957 Chrysler 1731707 (casting number 1731703-2) cast-iron single-quad, dual-plane intake manifold on this engine. As a point of interest, many of the early Chrysler Hemi cylinder heads and intake manifolds have "CPDD" cast into them. Translated, this means they could be used for the Chrysler, Plymouth, DeSoto, and Dodge engines.

We installed a Carter AFB 9755 (non-emission) 750-cfm carburetor with manual choke on the engine. The current retail price for this carburetor is $205. We also installed an ARP 400-2401 polished stainless-steel carburetor stud kit. To top things off, install a Mr. Gasket 6477 Rodware chrome heavy-breather louvered air cleaner with a K&N E-2865 air filter. Refer to Chapter 15 for information about PCV valves.

Retain the stock timing gear cover to permit the installation of a mechanical fuel pump. Install an AC-Delco 711-4452 mechanical fuel pump capable of producing 6 psi and supplying 80 gph of fuel. The current retail price for this fuel pump is $48.

Ignition System

The MSD 8389 distributor for the early Chrysler 392-ci Hemi

How's this for Hemi city? This photograph, taken at Luke's Custom Machine & Design, shows three Chrysler 392-ci Hemi engines in the final stages of assembly. These engines would look great in anyone's living room!

The Carter AFB 9755 carburetor and Mr. Gasket 6477 Rodware chrome louvered air cleaner.

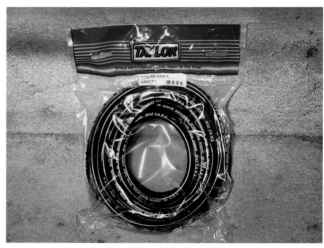

A Mopar Performance 3690430 electronic distributor, designed for a small-block Chrysler 360-ci engine, installed in the Chrysler 392-ci Hemi engine.

A 30-foot roll of Taylor 35071 Spiro-Pro black 8-millimeter resistor-type spark plug wire, good for street performance engines.

engine is a vacuum advance distributor referred to as "ready-to-run" for its built-in inductive ignition module. The MSD 8544 Pro-Billet model is another excellent distributor for the early Chrysler 392-ci Hemi engine. This full centrifugal (mechanical) advance distributor must be used with an MSD ignition control box. Use the Chrysler 1732826 oil pump intermediate driveshaft (6.345 inches in length) with either of these distributors; the current retail price for each is $370.

Install a Mopar Performance (Chrysler Corporation) 3690430 electronic distributor (for the small-block Chrysler 360-ci engine) in this engine. Install the Mopar Performance (Chrysler Corporation) 4007968 upgraded high-performance control unit with the distributor. The current retail price for the distributor and control unit is $200. Install a Hot Heads Research & Racing 21935 oil pump intermediate driveshaft (6.675 inches in length) in order to use this distributor. Refer to Chapter 7 for information regarding ignition coils. Refer to Chapter 15 for information about the distributor clamp, firing order, spark plug tubes, spark

The Proform 66445 chrome GM alternator mounted using Luke's Custom Machine & Design stainless-steel alternator bracket and brace.

The 1957 Chrysler 1671896 water crossover manifold and the 1957 Chrysler 1732885 triple-groove water pump pulley installed.

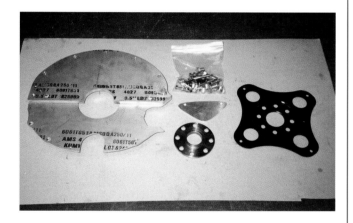

The Luke's Custom Machine & Design complete adapter kit mounts a Chrysler Torqueflite automatic transmission to an early Chrysler Hemi engine.

The spacer plate has been installed as well as the crankshaft flange adapter plate.

plug wires, and spark plugs.

Install a Proform 66445 chrome GM alternator (63 amps) with a Luke's Custom Machine & Design stainless-steel alternator bracket and brace. The current retail price for this alternator is $96.

The Powermaster 19531 chrome XS Torque starting motor is available for the 1957 to 1958 Chrysler 392-ci Hemi engines using a 176-tooth flywheel. The current retail price for this starting motor is $290.

Cooling and Exhaust Systems

Because we kept the stock stamped steel timing gear cover, we retained the 1957 Chrysler 1671895 cast-iron water pump housing as well. Luke's Custom Machine & Design fabricates a stainless-steel adapter plate that permits the installation of a Chrysler P4529102 lightweight aluminum water pump (for a big-block Chrysler 440-ci engine) in the 1957 Chrysler Hemi water pump housing. Install the 1957 Chrysler 1671896 cast-iron cylinder head water passage crossover manifold and the 1957 Chrysler 1730918 cast-iron water outlet elbow.

Using the big-block Chrysler 440-ci water pump requires the installation of a 1/4-inch-thick spacer plate between the 1957 Chrysler 1732885 water pump pulley and the water pump flange in order for the water pump v-belt to be correctly aligned. Install a 1/4-inch-thick spacer plate between the crankshaft pulley and the harmonic balancer as well. The 1957 Chrysler 1732885 water pump triple-groove pulley is 7 1/2 inches in diameter.

Sanderson Headers (see Appendix B—Resources) offers its DD3 block hugger headers for the 331-ci, 354-ci, and the 392-ci

This Chrysler Torqueflite three-speed automatic transmission has been installed using the Luke's Custom Machine & Design complete adapter kit.

early Chrysler Hemi engines installed in 1932 and newer vehicles. The current retail price for the plain steel model is $285, or $435 with metallic-ceramic coating. The Sanderson Headers DR392 roadster headers are designed for use in a Ford Model T with headers outside of the frame. These metallic-ceramic-coated headers are complete with turnouts and mufflers, and the current retail price is $809 for the pair.

Although I have not previously covered the installation of transmissions in this book, it is appropriate to mention one of the most popular transmissions currently being adapted to the early Chrysler Hemi engines—the 1962 to 1988 Chrysler Torqueflite three-speed automatic transmission. Luke's Custom Machine & Design fabricates a complete adapter kit for this transmission and the current retail price is $350.

The early Chrysler Hemi crankshaft flange bolt holes are not threaded. If you plan to install anything other than the stock torque converter, the eight bolt holes must be tapped with a 1/2-inch NF tap. The studs were attached to the stock torque converter.

Engine Summary

Note: Exhaust headers are not listed in this engine summary because a custom set will have to be fabricated.

Engine Block

• 1957 Canadian Chrysler New Yorker 392-ci engine block; serial number prefix: CF57; casting number 1673729; casting date: 4-23-7 (April 23, 1957); stock bore: 4.00 inches; stock stroke: 3.906 inches; two-bolt main bearing caps; 9.25:1 compression ratio; 325 horsepower at 4,600 rpm and 430 ft-lb torque at 2,800 rpm; engine block weight (bare): 209 pounds; $500

• Engine block hot tanked; engine block and main bearing caps and bolts Magnafluxed; main bearing caps and bolts shot peened; all threads retapped; cylinder head bolt holes chamfered; valve lifter bosses deglazed allowing for 0.002-inch valve lifter clearance; and engine block Redi-Stripped; Dorman 568-010 quick-seal copper freeze plugs (1 5/8-inch diameter), Luke's Custom Machine & Design brass rear camshaft boss plug (1.76-inch diameter), stainless-steel oil gallery line plugs, Weatherhead 3152-4 polished-brass water jacket drain plugs (1/4-inch NPT) installed using Permatex aviation form-a-gasket; exterior surface of engine block sanded, detailed, and painted with Plasti-Kote T-26 slicker yellow high-gloss engine enamel; $448.33

• Engine block bored 0.040-inch oversize and honed and deglazed using torque plate and Sunnen 800 series 400-grit stones, final bore: 4.040 inches; piston-to-bore clearance: 0.002 inch, measured below bottom of wrist pin perpendicular to wrist pin; $125

• Engine block parallel decked to 0.010-inch average below deck; $110

Engine block total: $1,183.33

Crankshaft

• 1957 Chrysler 1737919 forged steel crankshaft, casting number 1673755; crankshaft heat treated, shot peened, and Magnafluxed; main bearing journal diameter: 2.687 inches, and connecting rod journal diameter: 2.375 inches; crankshaft weight: 70 pounds; $350

• Crankshaft aligned, main bearing journals ground 0.010-inch undersize, connecting rod journals ground 0.010-inch undersize, oil holes chamfered, journals polished, and crankshaft balanced; $225

• Federal Mogul 4009M-10 main bearings (0.010-inch oversize) installed allowing for 0.002-inch crankshaft clearance and 0.004-inch end play; main bearing cap bolts installed using molykote and torqued to 85 ft-lb; $215

• NOS Chrysler 1735045 harmonic balancer with hub (7 1/4-inch o.d.) installed with Chrysler 152191 Woodruff key and Chrysler 1731525 crankshaft bolt and 1324265 washer using Loctite and torqued to 85 ft-lb; harmonic balancer and crankshaft pulley painted with Plasti-Kote 203 black high-gloss engine enamel; Luke's Custom Machine & Design aluminum crankshaft pulley spacer (1/4-inch thickness) installed; 1957 Chrysler 1732941 double v-belt crankshaft pulley (5 3/4-inch diameter) installed with stainless-steel bolts, lockwashers, and flat washers using Loctite and torqued to 20 ft-lb; Chrysler 1618686 oil slinger painted with Glyptal G-1228A medium-grey gloss enamel; $235

Crankshaft total: $1,025

Connecting Rods and Pistons

• 1957 Chrysler 1673756 forged steel I-beam connecting rods (casting number 1673758), full-floating wrist pins (6.956-inch length, center to center), connecting rod weight: 782 grams each; connecting rod ratio: 1.78 (with 3.906-inch stroke); $120

• Connecting rods shot peened, aligned, Magnafluxed, resized, balanced, and Federal Mogul 1804V wrist pin bushings installed allowing for 0.002-inch wrist pin clearance; ARP 145-6002 high-performance-series connecting rod bolts (3/8-inch diameter, 8740 chrome-moly steel, 190,000 psi) installed; $390

• Federal Mogul 2235SB-10 connecting rod bearings (0.010-inch oversize) installed allowing for 0.002-inch connecting rod clearance and 0.010-inch side clearance per pair of connecting rods; connecting rod bolts torqued to 45 ft-lb using molykote and allowing for 0.006-inch stretch; $190

• NOS 1957 Chrysler 1752267 cast-aluminum slipper-skirt pistons (0.040-inch oversize, with 9.25:1 compression ratio); piston weight: 697 grams each; heat-treated and case-hardened 4340 chrome-moly steel straight-wall wrist pins installed with Tru-Arc wrist pin retainers; wrist pin length: 3.145 inches; wrist pin diameter: 0.9843 inch; wrist pin weight: 173 grams each; piston grooves: top compression ring groove width: 5/64 inch; second compression ring groove width: 5/64 inch; oil ring groove width: 3/16 inch; Sealed Power (Federal Mogul) E-251K-40 moly-coated ductile iron top ring piston ring set (0.040-inch oversize) installed within manufacturer's recommended arc; top compression ring gap: 0.016 inch; second compression ring gap: 0.016 inch; oil ring gap: 0.016 inch; intake-valve-to-piston clearance: 0.185 inch and exhaust-valve-to-piston clearance: 0.180 inch (without gasket); new displacement: 400.6 ci (6.6 liters); $193

• Complete V-8 engine balance; Fel-Pro FS7908PT-4 complete gasket set installed; $325

Connecting rods and pistons total: $1,218

Lubrication System

• NOS 1957 Chrysler 1671902 oil pump and Chrysler 1737988 oil pump pickup screen installed; 1957 Chrysler 1408853 rear main bearing cap dowel installed; Hot Heads Research & Racing 21935 oil pump intermediate driveshaft (6.675-inch length) installed with Chrysler 601268 oil pump intermediate driveshaft gear and Chrysler 1324281 oil pump intermediate driveshaft bushing; PAW HEM-5340 oil diverter valve installed; $154.85

• 1957 Chrysler 1671887 stamped steel rear sump oil pan (5-quart capacity) installed with stainless-steel hex head bolts, lockwashers, and AN flat washers using Loctite and torqued to 15 ft-lb; oil pan gaskets and seals installed using silicone sealant; Hot Heads Research & Racing 20101 polished-aluminum vertical oil filter adapter installed with stainless-steel socket head bolts using Loctite and torqued to 20 ft-lb; oil filter adapter gasket installed using silicone sealant; Fram PH-8A oil filter installed; engine lubricated with 6 quarts Pennzoil HD-30-weight motor oil; oil pan painted with Plasti-Kote T-26 slicker yellow high-gloss engine enamel; Hot Heads Research & Racing 21955 chrome angled dip stick and dip stick tube installed; $238.11

Lubrication system total: $392.96

Camshaft and Cylinder Heads

• Clevite 77 SH-313S camshaft bearings installed with 0.002-inch camshaft clearance and 0.002-inch end play; No. 1 bearing: SH-313, housing bore: 2.1295 to 2.1305 inches; No. 2, 3, and 4 bearing: SH-314, housing bore: 2.1295 to 2.1305 inches; No. 5 bearing: SH-315, housing bore: 1.5670 to 1.5680 inches; camshaft journal diameter: 2.00 inches; $55

• Schneider Racing Cams 270-H hydraulic lifter camshaft with advertised duration: 270 degrees intake and exhaust; duration at 0.050-inch lift: 214 degrees intake and exhaust; lobe separation angle: 112 degrees; net valve lift (with 1.50 ratio rocker arms): 0.443 inch intake and exhaust; valve lash (hot): zero; camshaft degreed; $225

• Chrysler 1634267 camshaft thrust plate installed with Grade 8 bolts and lockwashers using Loctite and torqued to 25 ft-lb; Chrysler 1618717 camshaft sprocket spacer, Chrysler 106751 Woodruff key, Chrysler 1328644 oil trough, and Chrysler 1632426 camshaft eccentric installed; $60

• PAW (Super Stock Industries) HEM-812 heavy-duty hydraulic lifters (0.903-inch diameter, stock pushrod seat height) installed; Smith Brothers Pushrods adjustable pushrods (4130 seamless chrome-moly steel, 3/8-inch diameter by 0.49-inch wall) installed; intake valve pushrod length: 9.75 inches, and exhaust valve pushrod length: 11.225 inches; $215

• Dynagear 78103 precision double-roller timing chain set, multi-keyway crankshaft sprocket, installed; 1957 Chrysler 1730518 chrome timing gear cover installed with polished stainless-steel bolts and lockwashers using Loctite and torqued to 15 ft-lb; timing gear cover gasket installed using silicone sealant; $100

• 1957 Chrysler 1738375 (model 300C) chrome one-piece valley cover installed with polished stainless-steel bolts, lockwashers, and AN flat washers using Loctite and torqued to 15 ft-lb; valley cover gasket installed using silicone sealant; Mr. Gasket 2060 chrome crankcase breather/oil filler cap installed; Motormite 242344 PCV valve grommet and Motomaster 17-9288-4 PCV valve installed; $133.21

• 1957 Chrysler 1737809 (casting number 1735282-1) cast-iron hemispherical combustion chamber cylinder heads; cylinder head weight: 67 pounds each; $300

• Cylinder heads hot tanked and Redi-Stripped; intake and

exhaust ports fully ported and polished and gasket matched; combustion chambers polished and cc'd; surfaced; NOS 1957 Chrysler 1634790 intake valve guides and 1486911 exhaust valve guides (3/8-inch stem diameter) installed; Serdi-machined multi-angle blueprint valve grind performed; exterior surface of cylinder heads sanded, detailed, and painted with Plasti-Kote T-26 slicker yellow high-gloss engine enamel; $675.97

• NOS 1957 Chrysler 1731546 intake valves (2.00-inch head diameter by 3/8-inch stem diameter by 5.03125-inch length overall) installed; NOS 1957 Chrysler 1634744 exhaust valves (1.9375-inch head diameter by 3/8-inch stem diameter by 5.03125-inch length overall) installed; Serdi-machined multi-angle blueprint valve grind performed; Enginetech S2890 viton positive seal valve stem seals installed; $176

• Sealed Power (Federal Mogul) VS-510 single valve springs with installed height: 80 pounds at 1.70 inches valves closed and 200 pounds at 1.250 inches valves open; 1.40-inch o.d. and 1.00-inch i.d.; coil bind: 1.150 inches; 1956 Chrysler heat-treated steel valve spring retainers, 3/8-inch stem diameter, and 1956 Chrysler 1614666 valve stem locks (3/8-inch stem diameter for four-groove valves) installed; $105

• 1957 Chrysler nonadjustable rocker arm assemblies rebuilt by Luke's Custom Machine & Design; rocker arm ratio: 1.50; rocker arm assemblies and cylinder heads installed with Chrysler 1324452 long cylinder head bolts and Chrysler 1323310 short cylinder head bolts using anti-seize compound and torqued to 85 ft-lb; $600

• 1957 Chrysler 1323310 chrome FirePower valve covers installed with Papco 264-016 engine studs (5/16-inch by 1 3/4-inch length, reduced to 1 1/2-inch length), polished stainless-steel acorn nuts, lockwashers, and AN flat washers using anti-seize compound and torqued to 15 ft-lb; valve cover gaskets installed using silicone sealant; $460

Camshaft and cylinder heads total: $3,105.18

Intake System

• 1957 Chrysler 1731707 (casting number 1731703-2) cast-iron single-quad, dual-plane high-rise intake manifold installed with polished stainless steel bolts and AN flat washers using Loctite and torqued to 25 ft-lb; intake manifold gaskets installed using silicone sealant; ARP 400-2401 polished stainless-steel carburetor stud kit installed using anti-seize compound; intake manifold painted with Plasti-Kote T-26 slicker yellow high-gloss engine enamel; $114.28

• Carter AFB 9755 (non-emission) silver finish 750-cfm four-barrel carburetor (manual choke) installed; Mr. Gasket 6477 Rodware chrome heavy-breather louvered air cleaner (14-inch o.d. by 2 1/2 inches high) installed with K&N E-2865 air filter (13-inch o.d. by 2.312 inches high); $298

• AC-Delco 711-4452 mechanical fuel pump (6 psi, 80 gph)

installed with polished stainless-steel bolts and lockwashers using Loctite and torqued to 20 ft-lb; fuel pump gasket installed using silicone sealant; $48

Intake system total: $460.28

Ignition System

• Mopar Performance 3690430 electronic distributor (for small-block Chrysler 360-ci engine) and 4007968 upgraded high-performance control unit installed with Chrysler 1326835 distributor clamp and polished stainless-steel bolt and lockwasher using anti-seize compound; MSD 8200 Blaster 2 chrome ignition coil (45,000 volts) installed with Mr. Gasket 9777 chrome ignition coil bracket; distributor clamp painted with Plasti-Kote 203 black high-gloss engine enamel; $244

• Chrysler 1737379 aluminum spark plug tubes installed with Luke's Custom Machine & Design beveled spark plug tube washers; NGK BP6ES resistor-type 18-millimeter spark plugs installed with 0.050-inch gap and torqued to 25 ft-lb; Taylor/Vertex 35071 Pro Series black 8-millimeter high-performance spark plug wire, Spiro-Pro Kelvar resistor core, installed with Mopar Performance (Chrysler Corporation) 4120808 Hemi spark plug tube and insulator kits, Standard ST113 spark plug terminals, Standard TN9 distributor cap nipples, Standard ST26 distributor cap terminals, and Spectre 4245 chrome/plastic spark plug wire separators; $191.28

• Proform 66445 chrome GM alternator (internally regulated, 65 amps) installed with Luke's Custom Machine & Design stainless-steel adjusting brace and bracket using polished stainless-steel bolts, lockwashers, and flat washers; $205.62

• Mopar Performance (Chrysler Corporation) P5249644 lightweight starting motor installed; Gates 11A1080 crankshaft/water pump/alternator v-belt (7/16 inches by 42 1/2-inch length) installed; $155.67

Ignition system total: $796.57

Cooling System

• 1957 Chrysler 1671895 cast-iron water pump housing installed with polished stainless-steel bolts and lockwashers using Loctite and torqued to 25 ft-lb; water pump housing gasket installed using silicone sealant; water pump housing painted with Plasti-Kote T-26 slicker yellow high-gloss engine enamel; Mopar Performance (Chrysler Corporation) P4529102 polished lightweight aluminum water pump (for big-block Chrysler 440-ci engine) installed with Luke's Custom Machine & Design polished stainless-steel water pump adapter plate using polished stainless-steel bolts and lockwashers with Loctite and torqued to 25 ft-lb; water pump gasket installed using silicone sealant; 1957 Chrysler 1732885 triple-groove water pump pulley (7 1/2-inch diameter) installed with polished stainless-steel bolts, lockwashers, and flat washers

A good front view of the completed 1957 Chrysler 392-ci Hemi engine. This engine should instill some new life into the owner's 1950 Ford two-door coupe.

using Loctite and torqued to 25 ft-lb; water pump pulley painted with Plasti-Kote 203 black high-gloss engine enamel; Goodyear 63394 water pump bypass hose (3/4-inch i.d.) installed with stainless-steel line clamps; $290

• 1957 Chrysler 1671896 cast-iron water passage crossover manifold installed with polished stainless-steel bolts and lockwashers using Loctite and torqued to 25 ft-lb; water passage crossover manifold gaskets installed using silicone sealant; Robert Shaw 330-160 extra performance balanced 160-degree (Fahrenheit) thermostat installed; 1957 Chrysler 1730918 cast-iron thermostat housing installed with polished stainless-steel bolts and lockwashers using Loctite and torqued to 20 ft-lb; thermostat housing gasket installed using silicone sealant. Water passage crossover manifold and thermostat housing painted with Plasti-Kote T-26 slicker yellow high-gloss engine enamel; $100

Cooling system total: $390

Labor

• Labor for checking clearances, gapping piston rings, degree camshaft, valvetrain assembly, detailing, trial engine assembly, final engine assembly, and initial engine start-up; $800

Labor total: $800

Engine Grand Total: $9,371.32 (U.S.)

Note: The estimated output of this engine is 426 horsepower at 5,500 rpm and 454 ft-lb torque at 4,000 rpm (see Appendix A—Dyno Print-Outs).

CHAPTER 18
BLOWN 1957 CHRYSLER 392-ci HEMI ENGINE

This final chapter about the early Chrysler Hemi engines describes the monster of them all: the blown Chrysler 392-ci Hemi engine. This engine was the terror of the American drag strips during the late 1950s and early 1960s. The engine block that is the basis for this engine originated from a 1957 Chrysler Imperial.

The supercharger boost for this engine will be slightly over 15 pounds, which is definitely not for the faint of heart! The owner spared no expense to ensure the best of parts were used in the assembly of this engine, built and completed by Luke's Custom Machine & Design at the end of October 2001. The engine was initially fired up with a single four-barrel carburetor for ease of tuning. After the owner took delivery of his completed engine, he installed a Blower Drive Service electronic fuel injection system for a blown engine. Unfortunately, the new intake system is not shown in this book. The owner intends to install his engine in a daily-driven 1934 Dodge Pickup Truck.

Components Description
Engine Block

The specifications for the 1957 Chrysler Imperial 392-ci engine are:
- 392-ci (6.4-liter) displacement
- 4.00-inch stock bore and 3.906-inch stock stroke
- Stock compression ratio: 9.25:1
- 325 horsepower at 4,600 rpm and 430 ft-lb torque at 2,800 rpm

Install a set of Milodon 11350 splayed four-bolt main bearing caps to strengthen the bottom end of this 1957 Chrysler 392-ci engine block. Luke's Custom Machine & Design fabricated main bearing cap support bridges using 1045 steel, and the support bridges were installed with aircraft-quality main bearing cap bolts (180,000 psi). The dimensions of the main bearing cap support bridges are: 4 5/8-inch length by 1-inch width by 3/4-inch height. Because the outer main bearing cap bolts penetrate the water jacket, install them with Permatex aviation form-a-gasket. Refer to Chapter 1 for information about engine block preparation and machining procedures. This engine block was align bored and honed, parallel decked, and O-ringed.

The owner of the engine wanted to make a statement with his engine, so he decided the color should be RM 79674 purple plum high-gloss polyurethane. Refer to Chapter 15 for information

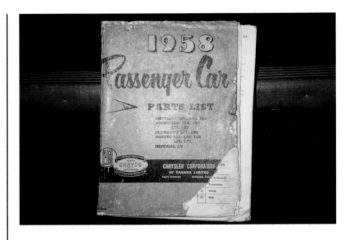

The L Series 1958 Passenger Car Parts List, *published by Chrysler Corporation of Canada Limited. This edition for the parts division is WM 4396 and it was issued in Windsor, Ontario (Canada) in December 1957. These manuals are quite scarce.*

The installation of the Milodon 11350 splayed main bearing caps and the main bearing cap support bridges fabricated by Luke's Custom Machine & Design. Yes, that is a GMC 4-71 blower on the Ford flathead V-8 in the background.

How is this for a wild color? This is a good photograph of the engine block O-rings. The valve lifter gallery has been painted with Glyptal G-1228A medium-grey gloss enamel, which certainly stands out with the RM 79674 purple plum polyurethane.

All the crankshaft journals of this Chrysler 392-ci Hemi crankshaft have been built up using the metal spray method. The surface is quite porous, which is not impressive.

Just to the left of the rear crankshaft journal is the Hot Heads Research & Racing 20120 oil diverter valve (purple ring). To the right of the rear crankshaft journal is the Chrysler 1408853 rear main bearing cap dowel. The Federal Mogul 4009M main bearings and the neoprene rubber rear oil seals are installed.

regarding freeze plugs, the rear camshaft boss plug, and the oil gallery line plugs.

Crankshaft

We installed a 1957 Chrysler 1737919 (casting number 1673755) forged steel crankshaft in the engine. The crankshaft had standard-size main bearing journals and connecting rod journals, which only needed to be polished. Refer to Chapter 2 for information about crankshaft preparation, and refer to Chapter 17 for main bearing data. Install a Luke's Custom Machine & Design aluminum dual-groove degreed crankshaft pulley in place of a harmonic balancer.

Connecting Rods and Pistons

In keeping with the owners "spare no expense" mentality, we installed Cunningham connecting rods. They are the ultimate

A good close-up photograph of the Ross Racing Pistons forged 2618 T-61 aluminum blower pistons for a Chrysler 392-ci Hemi engine.

Lots of Hot Heads Research & Racing goodies are pictured here: a 21804 full sump racing oil pan, 21910 high-volume oil pump and pickup screen, 21955 chrome dip stick and tube, 29010 aluminum distributor clamp, 20701 aluminum water pump adapters, and a set of Dorman 568-010 copper freeze plugs.

The clearance between the oil pump pickup screen and the bottom of the oil pan is being checked. This clearance should be between 3/4 and 1 inch.

connecting rods, and there is a photograph of a set in Chapter 3. These connecting rods are manufactured using custom cross-grain flow pure 4340 chrome-moly steel and they are an "H-I" beam design. The connecting rods are shot peened, fully machined and stress relieved, and Magnafluxed, with bronze alloy wrist pin bushings. The wrist pin end bores (the small end) and the crankshaft end bores (the big end) are sized and finish honed to +/- 0.0002-inch tolerance. The Cunningham AISI H-11 tool steel 12-point connecting rod cap screw bolts (7/16-inch diameter) are rated at an amazing 296,000 psi. The connecting rods are 6.950-inch length (center to center), and they weigh 806 grams each. The manufacturer's recommended torque for the Cunningham connecting rods with 7/16-inch-diameter cap screw bolts is 80 ft-lb, using 80W90 gear lubricant. The current retail price for a custom set of these Cunningham "H-I" beam connecting rods is $1,300. Refer to Chapter 17 for information about connecting rod bearings.

The owner purchased a set of Ross Racing Pistons forged 2618 T-61 aluminum blower pistons with an 8.0:1 compression ratio. These are custom pistons, designed for use with the Cunningham "H-I" beam connecting rods. We installed a Hastings 5508 Power Flex plasma-moly-coated top piston ring set. The top compression ring width is 5/32 inch, the second compression ring width is 5/32 inch, and the oil ring width is 3/16 inch. Refer to Chapter 7 for information about the gasket set.

Lubrication System

Install a Hot Heads Research & Racing 21910 high-volume oil pump (for the small-block Chrysler 340-ci engine) with a rear

A Crower Cams & Equipment Company Imperial 8620 steel billet solid roller camshaft with groove-lock anodized aluminum solid (mechanical) roller lifters. The two buttons on the lifters are visible. This racing camshaft with a 108-degree lobe separation angle was common in the early 1960s.

sump oil pump pickup screen. Tack weld the oil pump pickup screen to the oil pump to prevent it from coming loose. The current retail price for this oil pump with oil pump pickup screen is $160. Install a Chrysler 1732826 oil pump intermediate driveshaft (6.345-inch length) as well.

Install a Hot Heads Research & Racing 21804 full sump racing oil pan with two trapdoors, a louvered windage tray, and an attached crankshaft scraper. This oil pan is manufactured in Australia by KC Racing and is an excellent product. The current retail price for this oil pan is $375. Refer to Chapter 15 for information regarding the oil diverter valve, oil filter adapters, and the dip stick and dip stick tube.

Camshaft and Cylinder Heads

Refer to Chapter 15 for information about camshaft bearings.

Engle Racing Cams is an excellent source of solid (mechanical) lifter, hydraulic lifter, and solid (mechanical) roller lifter camshafts for the Chrysler 392-ci Hemi engine. We selected an Engle Racing Cams RK-48 solid (mechanical) lifter roller camshaft for the engine described in this chapter. The advertised duration is 291 degrees intake and exhaust; duration at 0.050-inch lift: 253 degrees intake and exhaust; lobe separation angle: 112 degrees; net valve lift (with 1.50 ratio rocker arms): 0.591 inch intake and 0.589 inch exhaust; valve lash (hot): 0.018 inch intake and 0.020 inch exhaust. This camshaft is intended for racing rather than street performance, and its current retail price is $500. Refer to Chapter 15 for information about the camshaft retainer plate and oil trough.

The owner purchased a set of the Engle Racing Cams 658 solid (mechanical) roller lifters with the camshaft. These lifters are lightweight, heat treated, stock 0.903-inch diameter and pushrod seat height, and they use the patented bar-slot blade to join two lifters together. The current retail price for a set of these roller lifters is $660.

We installed a set of Smith Brothers Pushrods in this engine. These nonadjustable pushrods are manufactured using heat-treated seamless chrome-moly steel, and they are 3/8 inch in diameter. The intake valve pushrod length is 10.075 inches, and the exhaust valve pushrod length is 11.275 inches.

Refer to Chapter 15 for information about timing chain sets, and refer to Chapter 17 for information regarding timing gear covers. We used a 1957 Chrysler 1730518 stamped steel timing gear cover on the engine described here. Luke's Custom Machine & Design modified the cover by removing the mechanical fuel pump boss. We painted the timing gear cover with RM 79674 purple plum high-gloss polyurethane. Refer to Chapter 16 for information about the aluminum valley cover.

Refer to Chapter 17 for information about the Chrysler 392-ci Hemi cylinder heads, and refer to Chapter 15 for information describing the preparation of the cylinder heads. Because this is a blown engine, install a Milodon 80215 cylinder head stud kit. The cylinder head bolt holes in the early Chrysler Hemi engine blocks are blind holes, which will prevent water leaks. Install the cylinder head bolts, or studs, using anti-seize compound.

Hot Heads Research & Racing has introduced its cast 356 T-6 aluminum, CNC-machined hemispherical combustion

An Engle Racing Cams RK-48 solid (mechanical) lifter roller camshaft for the Chrysler 392-ci Hemi engine. This camshaft has upper midrange and top-end power and is more a racing camshaft than a street performance camshaft.

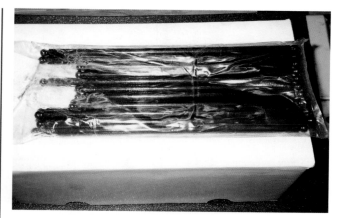

This set of Smith Brothers Pushrods will be installed in the engine described in this chapter.

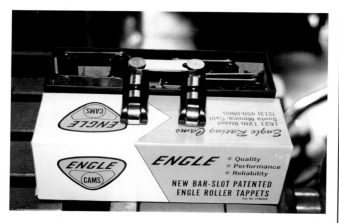

A set of the Engle Racing Cams 658 solid (mechanical) roller lifters.

chamber cylinder heads for the early Chrysler Hemi engines. Each cylinder head weighs 35 pounds, which is about half of what a cast-iron early Chrysler Hemi cylinder head weighs. These cylinder heads have raised intake ports, improved rectangular shape exhaust ports, large pushrod holes, 5/8-inch-thick decks, hardened exhaust valve seat inserts, bronze valve guides, stainless-steel 2.0625-inch head diameter by 11/32-inch stem diameter intake valves, stainless-steel 1.80-inch head diameter by 11/32-inch stem diameter exhaust valves, and they have the spark plug tube oil seals installed. These high-quality cylinder heads are very well designed. The current retail price for a pair of Hot Heads Research & Racing WJ921 aluminum cylinder heads (bare) for a street performance Chrysler 392-ci Hemi engine is $2,495. The WJ922 fully assembled cylinder heads retail at $2,995.

Install a pair of SCE (Specialty Component Engineering) 067064 copper head gaskets (0.042-inch thickness). Use Permatex copper spray-a-gasket when installing copper cylinder head gaskets. These cylinder head gaskets are available at the current retail price of $67 for a pair. Caution: If an engine equipped with copper cylinder head gaskets will be left sitting for any lengthy period of time, drain the water from the engine block. Otherwise, the water will start corroding the copper.

Install the Federal Mogul 240736 spark plug tube oil seals in the cylinder heads along with a set of Hot Heads Research & Racing 40044 bronze intake valve guides and 40046 bronze exhaust valve guides (11/32-inch stem diameter). Install a set of Hot Heads Research & Racing 21218 machined aluminum adjustable roller rocker arm assemblies. With these rocker arm assemblies and the 3/8-inch-diameter pushrods, you must have the intake valve pushrod holes in the cast-iron cylinder heads opened up for pushrod clearance. Luke's Custom Machine & Design fabricated bronze intake valve pushrod sleeves for the cylinder heads that were pressed in with the use of a hydraulic press. Refer to Chapter 16 for information about stainless-steel valves.

Install a set of K-Motion K-900 dual valve springs with damper to work with the high lift of the camshaft and the considerable amount of blower boost. These valve springs are manufactured using H-11 tool steel and have an installed height of: 225 pounds at 1.85 inches valves closed; 625 pounds at 1.150 inches valves open; 1.550-inch o.d. and 1.120-inch/0.070-inch i.d.; coil bind: 1.090 inches. Install new Manley Performance Parts 23635 heat-treated valve spring retainers (10-degree, 11/32-inch stem diameter) with new Manley Performance Parts 13194 heat-treated valve stem locks (10-degree, 11/32-inch stem diameter) and new Manley Performance Parts 42104 heat-treated lash caps (11/32-inch stem diameter, 0.250-inch tip). The current retail price for the valve springs, valve spring retainers, valve stem locks, and the lash caps is $390. Also install Enginetech S2927 viton positive seal valve stem seals.

A Donovan Engineering single idler gear drive, complete with timing gear cover for a Chrysler 392-ci Hemi engine. This is considered a race item, but it could be used in a street performance engine.

A rare Delta cast-aluminum timing gear cover for a Chrysler 392-ci Hemi engine. The upper hole is intended for a mechanical fuel injection pump.

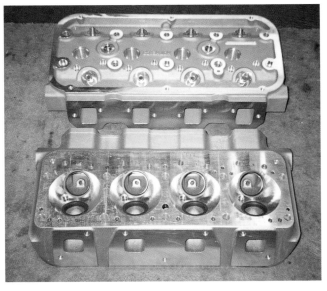

A pair of Hot Heads Research & Racing WJ921 bare aluminum Chrysler Hemi cylinder heads.

A 1958 Chrysler 1731528-1 cast-iron cylinder head that has been fully ported and polished, the combustion chambers polished and cc'd, surfaced, receiver groove O-ringed, and the Hot Heads Research & Racing bronze valve guides installed.

The intake pushrod holes for this Chrysler 392-ci Hemi cylinder head are being opened up on a milling machine at Luke's Custom Machine & Design in order to install oversize bronze pushrod sleeves.

As previously mentioned, install a pair of the Hot Heads Research & Racing 21218 adjustable roller rocker arm assemblies. The stands and rocker arms are machined from billet aluminum 1.50-ratio rocker arms, the chrome-moly thick wall shafts are hard chromed and centerless ground, the rocker arms are fitted with hardened rollers and pins, bronze bushings are pressed into the rocker arms and honed, the adjusters are the 426 ball type utilizing 12-point locking nuts, and aluminum clamps secure the rocker arms in exact alignment. The rocker arms are anodized a purple color, which will match perfectly with the exterior of this engine. The current retail price for a pair of the Hot Heads Research & Racing 21218 roller rocker arm assemblies is $1,850.

BMS (Bob's Machine Shop—see Appendix B—Resources) also manufactures machined aluminum roller rocker arms and stands for the early Chrysler Hemi engines. The complete rocker arm assemblies are top-quality items and BMS prices are competitive.

Install a pair of Hot Heads Research & Racing 21502 cast-aluminum valve covers. These quality valve covers already have the spark plug tube oil seals installed. The current retail price for a pair of these unpolished valve covers is $325, or $450 for the polished version.

In order to relieve the crankcase pressure, Luke's Custom Machine & Design fabricated a fantastic-looking pair of polished-aluminum valve cover breathers. A valve cover breather was mounted on the top front of each valve cover.

Intake System

We installed a vintage Cragar CS-1 polished-aluminum blower intake manifold on the engine. This intake manifold has a pop-off valve (backfire valve) on the front.

It was mentioned at the beginning of this chapter that the owner eventually installed an electronic fuel injection system. The model installed was the Blower Drive Service 56016K bugcatcher electronic fuel injection system for street performance use. This system is designed for engines operating on gasoline and producing 700 to 1,000 horsepower with a GMC 6-71 or GMC 8-71 blower. The system consists of an ECU (electronic control unit), TPI (throttle position sensor), two bar MAP (manifold absolute pressure) sensor, air temperature sensor, coolant temperature sensor, 16- by 30-pound nozzles, polished modified bugcatcher throttle body, 16-nozzle injector plate with IAC (idle air control) motor and hardware, fuel pressure regulator, two electric high-pressure and high-volume fuel pumps, fuel filter, main and injector wiring harness, and the complete installation instructions and diagrams. The computer is preprogrammed with an applicable fuel map. Blower Drive Service recommends the addition of the 5300C air filter, the 56800 user interface module, and the 56801 CalMap software. The current retail price for the Blower Drive Service 56016K bugcatcher electronic fuel injection system is $5,625.

Luke Balogh converted a Hilborn four-port mechanical fuel injection housing into an electronic fuel injection unit for his own blown Chrysler 392-ci Hemi engine. Luke fabricated the butterflies for the Hilborn housing, the injector nozzle stands, the fuel rails, the linkage, and everything else, except the electronics. The system performs exceptionally well. It took a few hundred hours of labor to produce this electronic fuel injection system and, unfortunately, I doubt another one will ever be made.

We installed a Luke's Custom Machine & Design GMC 6-71 blower on the engine. Refer to Chapter 6 for information about the GMC 6-71 blower. This blower has the later model GM 5114442 die-cast front cover and the GM 5122363 die-cast bearing plates installed. Refer to Chapters 6 and 16 for information regarding blower snouts.

Install a Blower Drive Service 6858 aluminum crankshaft blower pulley (8 millimeters by 56 teeth by 3.5 inches wide) and a 6852 aluminum blower snout pulley (8 millimeters by 52 teeth by 3.5 inches wide). Also install a Jason 1440-8M85 blower belt (8 millimeters by 56.69 inches long by 3.35 inches wide). The current retail price for the aluminum blower pulleys and the blower belt is $300. This combination results in an overdrive of 11.5 percent and an estimated boost of 15.5 pounds.

Install an MSD 8544 Pro-Billet distributor in the Chrysler 392-ci Hemi engine. This distributor will operate through 10,000 rpm. Use the Chrysler 1732826 oil pump intermediate driveshaft (6.345-inch length) with that distributor. The current retail price for the MSD 8544 Pro-Billet distributor is $370. Refer to Chapter 7 for information about ignition coils and ignition controls.

The Mallory 3733701 Unilite electronic distributor and the Mallory 5033701 magnetic breakerless distributor are available for the Chrysler 392-ci Hemi engine. Use the Chrysler 1732826 oil pump intermediate driveshaft (6.345-inch length) with these distributors. The current retail price for each of these two Mallory distributors is $290. The Hot Heads Research & Racing 29010 machined aluminum distributor clamp is a nice addition to any early Chrysler Hemi engine, and it is available at the current retail price of $25. Refer to Chapter 15 for information about spark plug tubes, spark plugs, firing order, spark plug wires, and spark plug wire boot kits. Refer to Chapter 17 for information regarding starting motors. Refer to Chapter 7 for information about alternators.

Because a steel billet roller camshaft was installed in this engine, we used a PAW HEM-5328 bronze oil pump intermediate driveshaft gear. The current retail price for this item is $60.

We mounted a Sankyo KC-1 polished air conditioning compressor on the engine using a stainless-steel bracket and brace fabricated by Luke's Custom Machine & Design.

Cooling System

We installed a Hot Heads Research & Racing 20701 aluminum water pump adapter set on the engine. In order to clear the pop-off valve (backfire valve) at the front of the blower intake manifold, install a Hot Heads Research & Racing 21401 aluminum water passage and crossover manifold with thermostat housing. This water passage crossover manifold has a section of stainless-steel hose connecting the two cylinder heads and is designed for a Chrysler 392-ci Hemi engine with Chrysler 392-ci Hemi cylinder heads. The current retail price for this item is

A Hot Heads Research & Racing 21218 aluminum adjustable roller rocker arm assembly installed. The K-Motion K-900 valve springs can be seen as well. The cylinder head has been painted with Glyptal G-1228A medium-gray gloss enamel.

$140. The Hot Heads Research & Racing 21403 water passage crossover manifold is designed for the Chrysler 392-ci Hemi engine with Chrysler 354-ci Hemi cylinder heads. The current retail price for that item is $140. Refer to Chapter 15 for information about water pumps and water pump pulleys.

Engine Summary

Note: The electronic fuel injection system was not installed when this engine was completed. It was added later. Exhaust headers are not listed in this engine summary because a custom set will have to be fabricated.

Engine Block

• 1957 Chrysler Imperial 392-ci engine block; serial number prefix: CE57; casting number 1878729; casting date: J316 (October 31, 1956); stock bore: 4.00 inches; stock stroke: 3.906 inches; two-bolt main bearing caps; 9.25:1 compression ratio; 325 horsepower at 4,600 rpm and 430 ft-lb torque at 2,800 rpm; engine block weight (bare): 209 pounds; $500

• Engine block hot tanked; engine block and main bearing caps and bolts Magnafluxed, main bearing caps and bolts shot peened, all threads retapped, cylinder head bolt holes chamfered, valve lifter bosses deglazed allowing for 0.002-inch valve lifter clearance, and engine block Redi-Stripped; Dorman 568-010 quick-seal copper freeze plugs (1 5/8-inch diameter), Luke's Custom Machine & Design brass rear camshaft boss plug (1.76-inch diameter), stainless-steel oil gallery line plugs, Weatherhead 3152-4 polished-brass water jacket drain plugs (1/4-inch NPT) installed using Permatex aviation form-a-gasket; valve lifter gallery

A set of BMS (Bob's Machine Shop) standard-ratio (1.50) machined billet aluminum roller rocker arms and stands for a Chrysler 392-ci Hemi engine.

ground smooth and painted with Glyptal G-1228A medium-grey gloss enamel; exterior surface of engine block sanded, detailed, and painted with RM 79674 purple plum high-gloss polyurethane; $520.54

• Engine block bored 0.030-inch oversize and honed and deglazed using torque plate and Sunnen 800 series 400-grit stones, final bore: 4.030 inches; piston-to-bore clearance: 0.008 inch, measured below bottom of wrist pin perpendicular to wrist pin; $125

• Milodon 11350 splayed four-bolt main bearing caps and Luke's Custom Machine & Design 1045 steel main bearing cap support bridges (4 5/8-inch length by 1-inch width by 3/4-inch height) installed with aircraft-quality main bearing cap bolts, 180,000 psi; $513

• Engine block align bored and honed; $200

• Engine block parallel decked to 0.010-inch average below deck; $115

• Engine block O-ringed using 0.035-inch-diameter stainless-steel wire; $100

Engine block total: $2,073.54

Crankshaft

• 1957 Chrysler 1737919, forged steel crankshaft, casting number 1673755; crankshaft heat treated, shot peened, and Magnafluxed; main bearing journal diameter: 2.687 inches, and connecting rod journal diameter: 2.375 inches; crankshaft weight: 70 pounds; $350

• Crankshaft aligned, oil holes chamfered, journals polished, and crankshaft balanced; $120

• Federal Mogul 4009M main bearings (standard size) installed allowing for 0.002-inch crankshaft clearance and 0.005-inch end play; main bearing cap bolts installed using molykote and torqued to 85 ft-lb; $215

• Luke's Custom Machine & Design polished-aluminum double-groove crankshaft pulley (6 1/2-inch o.d.) installed with Chrysler 152191 Woodruff key and Chrysler 1731525 crankshaft bolt and 1324264 washer using Loctite and torqued to 85 ft-lb; Chrysler 1618686 oil slinger glass beaded and painted with Glyptal G-1228A medium-grey gloss enamel; $275

Crankshaft total: $960

Connecting Rods and Pistons

• Cunningham custom cross-grain flow, pure 4340 chrome-moly steel "H-I" beam connecting rods; full-floating wrist pin bushings installed allowing for 0.0015-inch wrist pin clearance; Cunningham AISI H-11 tool steel, 12-point connecting rod cap screw bolts (7/16-inch diameter, 296,000 psi); connecting rod length: 6.950 inches (center to center); connecting rod weight: 806 grams each; connecting rod ratio: 1.78 (with 3.906-inch stroke); $1,300

• Clevite 77 CB-1213M connecting rod bearings (standard size) installed allowing for 0.002-inch connecting rod clearance and 0.010-inch side clearance per pair of connecting rods; connecting rod cap screw bolts installed using 80W90 gear oil and torqued to 80 ft-lb, allowing for 0.006-inch stretch; $175

• Ross Racing Pistons forged 2618 T-61 aluminum blower pistons (0.030-inch oversize) with 8.0:1 compression ratio; piston weight: 597 grams each; Ross Racing Pistons 984-01-29 heat-treated and casehardened 4340 chrome-moly steel straight-wall wrist pins installed; wrist pin length: 2.930 inches; wrist pin diameter: 0.984 inch; wrist pin weight: 147 grams each; Ross Racing Pistons 4004-E double Spiro-Lox wrist pin retainers installed; piston grooves: top compression ring groove width: 5/32 inch; second compression ring groove width: 5/32 inch; oil ring groove width: 3/16 inch; Hastings 5508 Power Flex precision racing plasma-moly-coated top compression ring piston ring set installed within manufacturer's recommended arc; top compression ring gap: 0.020 inch; second compression ring gap: 0.024 inch; oil ring gap: 0.018 inch; intake-valve-to-piston clearance: 0.160 inch, and exhaust-valve-to-piston clearance: 0.155 inch (with gasket); new displacement: 398.6 ci (6.5 liters); $760

• Complete V-8 engine balance; Fel-Pro FS7908PT-4 complete gasket set installed; $325

Connecting rods and pistons total: $2,560

Lubrication System

• Hot Heads Research & Racing 21910 high-volume oil pump (for small-block Chrysler 340-ci engine) with attached rear sump oil pump pickup screen installed; 1957 Chrysler 1408853 rear main bearing cap dowel installed; 1957 Chrysler 1732826 oil

A pair of Hot Heads Research & Racing 21502 cast-aluminum valve covers for a Chrysler 392-ci Hemi engine.

The Cragar 503 magnesium blower intake manifold for the early Chrysler Hemi engines shown in Chapter 6. The intake manifold has now been glass beaded and coated with Eastwood Company 10200Z diamond-clear gloss finish.

pump intermediate driveshaft (6.345-inch length) installed with PAW 5328 bronze oil pump intermediate driveshaft gear and Chrysler 1324281 oil pump intermediate driveshaft bushing; PAW HEM-5350 oil diverter valve installed; $264

• Hot Heads Research & Racing 21804 full sump, stamped steel, drag race oil pan, with two trap doors, louvered windage tray, and crankshaft scraper installed; capacity: 8 quarts oil; oil pan installed with polished stainless-steel bolts, lockwashers, and AN flat washers using Loctite and torqued to 15 ft-lb; oil pan gaskets and seals installed using silicone sealant; Hot Heads Research & Racing 20101 polished-aluminum vertical oil filter adapter installed with stainless-steel socket head bolts using Loctite and torqued to 20 ft-lb; oil filter adapter gasket installed using silicone sealant; Fram PH-8A oil filter installed; engine lubricated with 8 quarts Pennzoil HD-30-weight motor oil; oil pan painted with RM 79674 purple plum high-gloss polyurethane; Hot Heads Research & Racing 21955 chrome angled dip stick and dip stick tube installed; $518.11

Lubrication system total: $782.11

Camshaft and Cylinder Heads

• Clevite 77 SH-313S camshaft bearings installed with 0.002-inch camshaft clearance and 0.002-inch end play; No. 1 bearing: SH-313, housing bore: 2.1295 to 2.1305 inches; No. 2, 3, and 4 bearing: SH-314, housing bore: 2.1295 to 2.1305 inches; No. 5 bearing: SH-315, housing bore: 1.5670 to 1.5680 inches; camshaft journal diameter: 2.00 inches; $55

• Engle Racing Cams RK-48 solid (mechanical) roller steel billet camshaft with advertised duration: 291 degrees intake and exhaust; duration at 0.050-inch lift: 253 degrees intake and exhaust; lobe separation angle: 112 degrees; net valve lift

(with 1.50 ratio rocker arms): 0.591 inch intake and 0.589 inch exhaust; valve lash (hot): 0.018 inch intake and 0.020 inch exhaust; camshaft degreed; $500

• Chrysler 1634267 camshaft thrust plate installed with Grade 8 bolts and lock washers using Loctite and torqued to 25 ft-lb; Chrysler 1618717 camshaft sprocket spacer, Chrysler 106751 Woodruff key, and Chrysler 1328644 oil trough installed; Hot Heads Research & Racing 20200 camshaft bolt and washer kit installed; $60

• Engle Racing Cams 658 solid (mechanical) heat-treated roller lifters, lightweight, bar-slot blade (0.903-inch diameter, stock pushrod seat height) installed; Smith Brothers Pushrods heat-treated 4130 seamless chrome-moly steel nonadjustable pushrods (3/8-inch diameter by 0.083-inch wall) installed; intake valve pushrod length: 10.075 inches, and exhaust valve pushrod length: 11.275 inches; $885

• Cloyes 92103 true roller timing chain set with heat-treated sprockets and multi-keyway crankshaft sprocket installed; 1957 Chrysler 1730518 stamped steel timing gear cover (with mechanical fuel pump boss removed) installed with polished stainless-steel bolts and lockwashers using Loctite and torqued to 15 ft-lb; timing gear cover gasket installed using silicone sealant; timing gear cover painted with RM 79674 purple plum high-gloss polyurethane; $100

• Luke's Custom Machine & Design polished-aluminum valley cover installed with polished stainless-steel bolts, lockwashers, and AN flat washers using Loctite and torqued to 15 ft-lb; valley cover gasket installed using silicone sealant; Mr. Gasket 2060 chrome oil filler/crankcase breather cap installed; $160

An Edelbrock B-15 (model 2205) GMC 6-71 blower intake manifold for the 354- and 392-ci Chrysler Hemi engines. It has four internal pop-off valves.

Luke Balogh's blown Chrysler 392-ci Hemi engine that he installed in his daily-driven 1934 Ford five-window coupe. He fabricated the electronic fuel injection using a Hilborn four-port mechanical fuel injection housing as the base for the system.

• 1958 Chrysler 1737809 (casting number 1731528-1) cast-iron hemispherical combustion chamber cylinder heads; cylinder head weight: 66 pounds each; $300

• Cylinder heads hot tanked and Redi-Stripped; intake and exhaust ports fully ported and polished and gasket matched; combustion chambers polished and cc'd; surfaced; receiver groove O-ringed; Hot Heads Research & Racing 40044 bronze intake valve guides and 40046 bronze exhaust valve guides (11/32-inch stem diameter) installed; Federal Mogul 240736 spark plug tube oil seals installed; intake valve pushrod holes opened up and bronze pushrod sleeves installed; Serdi-machined multi-angle blueprint valve grind performed; area beneath valve covers painted with Glyptal G-1228A medium-grey gloss enamel; exterior surface of cylinder heads sanded, detailed, and painted with RM 79674 purple plum high-gloss polyurethane; SCE (Specialty Component Engineering) 067064 copper cylinder head gaskets (0.042-inch thickness) installed using Permatex copper spray-a-gasket; $1,267

• Hot Heads Research & Racing 40016 stainless-steel intake valves (2.125-inch head diameter by 11/32-inch stem diameter by 5.23-inch length overall), undercut stems at head, hardened tips, swirl polished, installed; weight: 141 grams each; Hot Heads Research & Racing 40026 stainless-steel exhaust valves (1.945-inch head diameter by 11/32-inch stem diameter by 5.23-inch length overall), undercut stems at head, hardened tips, swirl polished, installed; weight: 112 grams each; Serdi-machined multi-angle blueprint valve grind performed; Enginetech S2927 viton positive seal valve stem seals installed; $246

• K-Motion K-900 dual valve springs with damper, H-11 tool steel; installed height: 225 pounds at 1.85 inches valves closed, and 625 pounds at 1.15 inches valves open; 1.550-inch o.d. and 1.120-inch/0.070-inch i.d.; coil bind: 1.090 inch; Manley Performance Parts 23635-16 valve spring retainers, heat-treated 4140 chrome-moly steel (11/32-inch stem diameter, 10-degree, standard height, black oxide finish), Manley Performance Parts 13194 valve stem locks, machined 4140 heat-treated chrome-moly steel (11/32-inch stem diameter, 10-degree, standard height, black oxide finish), and Manley Performance Parts 42104 heat-treated steel lash caps (11/32-inch stem diameter, 0.250-inch tip, black oxide finish) installed; $390

• Hot Heads Research & Racing 21218 machined aluminum adjustable roller rocker arm assemblies, purple anodized, installed; rocker arm ratio: 1.50; cylinder heads and rocker arm assemblies installed with Milodon 80215 premium cylinder head stud kit (aircraft-quality 8740 chrome-moly steel, 180,000 psi, 4130 hardened steel parallel ground washers and nuts) using anti-seize compound and torqued to 85 ft-lb; $1,980

• Hot Heads Research & Racing 21502 polished cast-aluminum finned valve covers installed with Papco 264-016 engine studs (5/16 inch by 1 3/4-inch length), polished stainless-steel acorn nuts, lockwashers, and AN flat washers using anti-seize compound and torqued to 15 ft-lb; valve cover gaskets installed using silicone sealant; Luke's Custom Machine & Design polished-aluminum valve cover breathers installed with stainless-steel bolts and lockwashers using Loctite; $750

Camshaft and cylinder heads total: $6,693

Intake System

- Cragar CS-1 polished-aluminum blower intake manifold installed with polished stainless-steel socket bolts and AN flat washers using Loctite and torqued to 25 ft-lb; intake manifold gaskets installed using silicone sealant; $240

- GM 5138725 polished-aluminum large bore die-cast supercharger (blower) case (model 6-71), GM 5122363 polished die-cast front and rear bearing plates, GM 5114442 polished die-cast front cover, Blower Drive Service 671SL bearing seals (5205HD front bearings, 62052RS rear bearings) installed; Blower Drive Service 671-GK complete gasket set installed using Permatex aviation form-a-gasket; Luke's Custom Machine & Design bearing support rings and polished-aluminum rear bearing caps installed with polished stainless-steel bolts and lockwashers using anti-seize compound; rotors double-pinned and clearanced; Blower Drive Service 555 pressure relief valve and 556 oil sight gauge installed; stainless-steel oil filler and oil drain plugs (3/8-inch NPT) installed using pipe thread sealant; blower assembled with polished stainless-steel socket head bolts, lockwashers, and AN flat washers using Permatex aviation form-a-gasket; Armstrong N-8090 blower-to-intake-manifold gasket installed using anti-seize compound; Mooneyham 10884 anodized aluminum blower stud kit installed with polished stainless-steel acorn nuts and AN flat washers using anti-seize compound; $1,368.95

- Luke's Custom Machine & Design LS3000 polished 6061 T-6 aluminum medium blower snout with LS3300 blower snout shaft, and LS4100 gear coupler installed with polished stainless-steel socket head bolts and lockwashers using Permatex aviation form-a-gasket; $385

- Blower Drive Service 6858 polished T-6 aluminum crankshaft blower pulley (8 millimeters by 56 teeth by 3.5 inches wide) and 6852 polished T-6 aluminum blower snout pulley (8 millimeters by 52 teeth by 3.5 inches wide) installed with polished stainless-steel socket head bolts, lockwashers, and AN flat washers using anti-seize compound; Jason 1440-8M85 blower belt (8-millimeter pitch by 56.69-inch length by 3.35-inch width) installed; blower drive ratio: 11.5 percent overdrive; blower boost: 15.5 pounds (estimated); $300

- Luke's Custom Machine & Design polished-aluminum idler pulley bracket (1/2-inch thickness) installed with polished-aluminum idler pulley and 4140 chrome-moly steel stand off; $404.88

- Blower Drive Service 56016K bugcatcher complete electronic fuel injection system installed; $5,625

Intake system total: $8,323.83

Ignition System

- MSD 8544 Pro-Billet maintenance-free magnetic pickup distributor 6061 T-6 aluminum housing installed with Hot Heads Research & Racing 29010 machined aluminum distributor clamp and polished stainless-steel socket head bolt and lockwasher using

The Luke's Custom Machine & Design LS3000 polished medium blower snout and an idler pulley with the idler pulley bracket. This GMC 6-71 blower setup is mounted on a Chrysler 392-ci Hemi engine.

anti-seize compound; MSD 8200 Blaster 2 chrome ignition coil (45,000 volts) installed with Mr. Gasket 9777 chrome ignition coil bracket; MSD 6AL (model 6420) ignition control box with rpm-limiter modules installed; $635.95

- Chrysler 1737379 aluminum spark plug tubes installed; NGK BP6ES resistor-type 18-millimeter spark plugs installed with 0.050-inch gap and torqued to 25 ft-lb; Taylor/Vertex 35071 Pro Series black 8-millimeter high-performance spark plug wire, Spiro-Pro Kelvar resistor core, installed with Mopar Performance (Chrysler Corporation) 4120808 Hemi spark plug tube and insulator kits, Standard ST113 spark plug terminals, Standard TN9 distributor cap nipples, Standard ST26 distributor cap terminals, and Spectre 4245 chrome/plastic spark plug wire separators; $191.28

- Powermaster 17509 chrome Chrysler alternator (externally regulated, 75 amps) installed with Luke's Custom Machine & Design polished stainless-steel adjusting brace and mounting bracket using polished stainless-steel bolts, lockwashers, and flat washers; $225.62

- Mopar Performance (Chrysler Corporation) P5249644 lightweight starting motor installed; Gates 11A1145 crankshaft/water pump/alternator v-belt (7/16 inch by 45-inch length) installed; $155.67

- Sankyo KC-1 polished air conditioning compressor installed with Luke's Custom Machine & Design polished stainless-steel mounting bracket and adjustment brace using heim joints and polished stainless-steel bolts, lockwashers, AN flat washers, and acorn nuts; Gates 11A1040 air conditioning compressor v-belt (7/16 inch by 41-inch length) installed; Luke's Custom Machine & Design polished T-6 aluminum air conditioning compressor pulley installed; $765

Ignition system total: $1,973.52

Luke's Custom Machine & Design fabricated this complete GMC 6-71 blower drive kit with water pump and alternator bracket for an early Chrysler Hemi engine.

Luke's Custom Machine & Design fabricated the crankshaft pulley and the alternator bracket for the early Chrysler Hemi engines. The crankshaft pulley has degree marks on the edge, and it is designed to accept a blower pulley.

The completed blown Chrysler 392-ci Hemi engine. Unfortunately, the electronic fuel injection system was not installed for this photograph.

The blown Chrysler 392-ci Hemi engine was initially started with a single four-barrel Holley carburetor for ease of tuning.

Cooling System

• Hot Heads Research & Racing 20701 polished-aluminum water pump adapter set installed with stainless-steel socket head bolts using Loctite and torqued to 25 ft-lb; water pump adapter gaskets installed using silicone sealant; Weiand 8212 action-plus polished-aluminum big-block Chevrolet short-style water pump installed with polished stainless-steel bolts and lockwashers using anti-seize compound and torqued to 25 ft-lb; water pump gaskets installed using silicone sealant; Trans-Dapt 9478 polished T-6 aluminum single-groove (6-inch-diameter) water pump pulley installed with polished stainless steel socket head countersunk bolts using Loctite and torqued to 25 ft-lb; $328

• Hot Heads Research & Racing 21401 polished-aluminum/stainless-steel hose water passage crossover manifold installed with polished stainless-steel bolts and lockwashers using Loctite and torqued to 25 ft-lb; water passage crossover manifold gaskets installed using silicone sealant; Robert Shaw 330-160 extra performance balanced 160-degree (Fahrenheit) thermostat installed with polished stainless-steel socket head bolts and lockwashers using anti-seize compound and torqued to 20 ft-lb; $203

Cooling system total: $531

Labor

• Labor for checking clearances, gapping piston rings, degree camshaft, valvetrain assembly, blower setup, detailing, trial engine assembly, final engine assembly, and initial engine start-up; $1,200

Labor total: $1,200

Engine Grand Total: $25,097 (U.S.)

Note: The estimated output of this engine is 831 horsepower at 8,000 rpm and 630 ft-lb torque at 6,000 rpm (see Appendix A—Dyno Print-Outs).

APPENDIX A
DYNO PRINT-OUTS

1970 Cadillac 500-ci Engine

Luke's Custom Machine & Design built this 1970 Cadillac 500-ci V-8 engine. It will be installed in Luke Balogh's 1939 Ford C.O.E. Truck (cab over engine).

CALCULATED POWER AND ENGINE PRESSURES

Engine RPM	Power (Fly)	Torque (Fly)	Int Man Pressure	Vol Eff %	IMEP Pressure	FMEP Pressure	BMEP Pressure
2000	197	516	14.65	75.8	204.9	18.7	157.8
2500	246	517	14.61	77.6	197.5	20.5	158.0
3000	287	502	14.57	78.2	190.6	22.6	153.4
3500	325	487	14.51	80.4	184.2	24.7	149.0
4000	345	453	14.44	81.2	174.1	27.1	138.7
4500	335	391	14.37	78.1	156.5	29.6	119.7
5000	297	312	14.32	72.2	133.4	32.3	95.4
5500	246	235	14.31	66.0	111.4	35.2	71.9
6000	181	158	14.31	59.3	89.6	38.2	48.5
6500	114	92	14.33	53.8	71.3	41.4	28.2
7000	30	23	14.35	48.5	52.2	44.8	7.0
7500	0	0	14.37	43.9	36.4	48.3	-11.2
8000	0	0	14.39	40.0	21.7	52.0	-28.6
8500	0	0	14.41	36.1	8.8	55.9	-44.4
9000	0	0	14.44	32.9	-1.9	59.9	-58.3
9500	0	0	14.46	29.7	-11.7	64.1	-71.5
10000	0	0	14.48	27.0	-19.1	68.5	-82.7
10500	0	0	14.50	24.5	-25.8	73.1	-93.3
11000	0	0	14.52	21.9	-32.1	77.8	-103.6

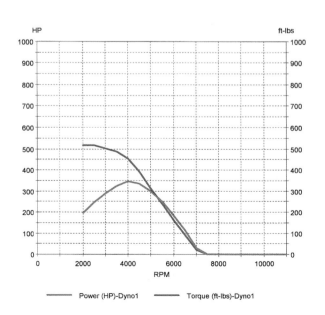

SHORT BLOCK

Block: CADILLAC.	Bore: 4.300 in	Stroke: 4.304 in
Cylinders: 8	Cyl Vol: 1024.2 cc	Total Vol: 500.0 ci

CYLINDER HEADS

Cylinder Heads:	Wedge/Stock Ports And Valves	
Air Flow File:	***	
Intake Valves:	1	Exhaust Valves: 1
Intake Valve:	2.000 in	Exhaust Valve: 1.625 in

COMPRESSION

Compression Ratio: 10.00	Combustion Space: 113.8 cc

INDUCTION

Induction Flow:	800.0 cfm @ 1.5 inHg	Fuel: Gasoline
Manifold Type:	Dual-Plane Manifold	N20: 0.0 lbs/min

Blower: None		Intercooler: *** %
Flow: *** cfm	Pressure Ratio: ***	Boost Limit: *** psi
Speed: *** rpm	Belt Gear Ratio: ***	Surge Flow: *** cfm
Eff: *** %	Internal Gear Ratio: ***	

EXHAUST

Exhaust System: Small-Tube Headers With Mufflers

CAMSHAFT

Camshaft Type:	CLEVITE.	Cam File: ***
Lifter:	Hyd.	Lobe Center: 109.5
Cam Specs @:	0.050-Lift	Valve Overlap: 5.0
Int Lift@Valve:	0.505 in	Int Duration: 220.0
Exh Lift@Valve:	0.512 in	Exh Duration: 228.0
Nominal Timing		Timing@ Adv(+)/Ret(-): 0.0

IVO (BTDC): 1.0	IVC (ABDC): 39.0	IVO: 1.0	IVC: 39.0
EVO (BBDC): 44.0	EVC (ATDC): 4.0	EVO: 44.0	EVC: 4.0
ICA (ATDC): 109.0	ECA (BTDC): 110.0	ICA: 109.0	ECA: 110.0

DYNO PRINT-OUTS

1967 Corvette 327-ci Engine (L79 Clone)

High Performance Engines and Luke's Custom Machine & Design built this engine to install in a 1967 Corvette convertible.

CALCULATED POWER AND ENGINE PRESSURES

Engine RPM	Power (Fly)	Torque (Fly)	Int Man Pressure	Vol Eff %	IMEP Pressure	FMEP Pressure	BMEP Pressure
2000	117	307	14.66	68.7	183.9	17.0	141.4
2500	152	320	14.64	71.6	183.4	18.3	147.5
3000	194	340	14.61	76.4	191.3	19.6	156.8
3500	235	352	14.55	80.6	194.9	21.1	162.5
4000	273	358	14.49	83.7	197.6	22.6	165.1
4500	306	357	14.41	85.5	198.8	24.3	164.7
5000	332	349	14.33	86.4	196.5	26.0	160.8
5500	347	331	14.24	86.1	189.8	27.9	152.8
6000	351	307	14.16	84.4	180.0	29.8	141.7
6500	339	274	14.09	81.1	165.7	31.8	126.3
7000	320	240	14.04	77.7	151.1	33.9	110.6
7500	299	209	14.01	74.3	138.4	36.2	96.5
8000	268	176	13.98	70.9	124.3	38.5	81.0
8500	232	144	13.96	67.0	111.0	40.9	66.2
9000	191	111	13.96	63.5	97.8	43.4	51.4
9500	144	80	13.96	59.8	85.0	46.0	36.8
10000	98	51	13.97	56.5	73.7	48.7	23.6
10500	42	21	13.98	53.3	61.8	51.5	9.7
11000	0	0	14.00	49.8	50.3	54.4	-3.8

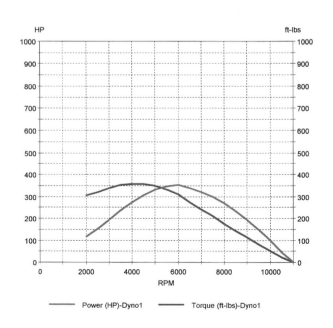

——— Power (HP)-Dyno1   ——— Torque (ft-lbs)-Dyno1

DYNO PRINT-OUTS

SHORT BLOCK

Block: CHEVROLET.	Bore: 4.030 in	Stroke: 3.250 in
Cylinders: 8	Cyl Vol: 679.3 cc	Total Vol: 331.6 ci

CYLINDER HEADS

Cylinder Heads:	Wedge/Pocket Porting, Large Valves	
Air Flow File:	***	
Intake Valves:	1	Exhaust Valves: 1
Intake Valve:	2.020 in	Exhaust Valve: 1.600 in

COMPRESSION

Compression Ratio: 11.00	Combustion Space: 67.9 cc

INDUCTION

Induction Flow: 585.0 cfm @ 1.5 inHg		Fuel: Gasoline
Manifold Type: Dual-Plane Manifold		N20: 0.0 lbs/min

Blower: None		Intercooler:	*** %
Flow: *** cfm	Pressure Ratio: ***	Boost Limit:	*** psi
Speed: *** rpm	Belt Gear Ratio: ***	Surge Flow:	*** cfm
Eff: *** %	Internal Gear Ratio: ***		

EXHAUST

Exhaust System: H.P. Manifolds And Mufflers

CAMSHAFT

Camshaft Type:	C.C. #122102.	Cam File: ***	
Lifter:	Hyd.	Lobe Center:	110.0
Cam Specs @:	0.050-Lift	Valve Overlap:	-2.0
Int Lift@Valve:	0.454 in	Int Duration:	218.0
Exh Lift@Valve:	0.454 in	Exh Duration:	218.0
Nominal Timing		Timing@ Adv(+)/Ret(-):	0.0

IVO (BTDC):	-1.0	IVC (ABDC):	39.0	IVO:	-1.0	IVC:	39.0
EVO (BBDC):	39.0	EVC (ATDC):	-1.0	EVO:	39.0	EVC:	-1.0
ICA (ATDC):	110.0	ECA (BTDC):	110.0	ICA:	110.0	ECA:	110.0

1970 Corvette 355-ci Engine (LT-1 Clone)

My 1923 Ford Model T Roadster Pickup with the Corvette LT-1 clone engine installed.

CALCULATED POWER AND ENGINE PRESSURES

Engine RPM	Power (Fly)	Torque (Fly)	Int Man Pressure	Vol Eff %	IMEP Pressure	FMEP Pressure	BMEP Pressure
2000	118	310	14.69	70.1	174.7	17.4	133.3
2500	158	332	14.69	73.7	178.5	18.8	142.6
3000	200	350	14.68	77.2	184.9	20.3	150.4
3500	255	382	14.67	84.4	197.6	21.9	164.2
4000	313	411	14.65	91.4	211.1	23.6	176.9
4500	371	433	14.62	96.7	222.7	25.4	186.2
5000	420	441	14.59	100.4	228.2	27.3	189.5
5500	453	432	14.56	102.0	226.4	29.4	185.8
6000	472	413	14.52	101.7	220.0	31.5	177.8
6500	468	378	14.49	98.9	206.1	33.8	162.5
7000	456	342	14.47	96.3	192.2	36.2	147.2
7500	443	310	14.45	93.0	180.1	38.7	133.4
8000	404	265	14.44	88.9	162.2	41.3	114.1
8500	359	222	14.43	83.3	145.1	44.0	95.4
9000	315	184	14.43	79.6	130.6	46.8	79.1
9500	263	146	14.43	75.4	116.1	49.7	62.6
10000	215	113	14.43	71.6	104.2	52.7	48.6
10500	142	71	14.43	67.1	88.2	55.9	30.5
11000	77	37	14.44	63.2	75.9	59.1	15.8

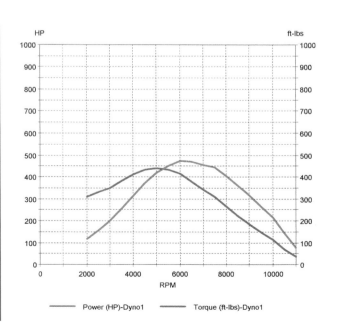

SHORT BLOCK

Block: CHEVROLET.	Bore: 4.030 in	Stroke: 3.484 in
Cylinders: 8	Cyl Vol: 728.2 cc	Total Vol: 355.5 ci

CYLINDER HEADS

Cylinder Heads: Wedge/Fully Ported, Large Valves

Air Flow File: ***

Intake Valves: 1	Exhaust Valves: 1
Intake Valve: 2.020 in	Exhaust Valve: 1.600 in

COMPRESSION

Compression Ratio: 9.72	Combustion Space: 83.5 cc

INDUCTION

Induction Flow: 1300.0 cfm @ 1.5 inHg	Fuel: Gasoline
Manifold Type: Tunnel-Ram Manifold	N20: 0.0 lbs/min

Blower: None		Intercooler: *** %
Flow: *** cfm	Pressure Ratio: ***	Boost Limit: *** psi
Speed: *** rpm	Belt Gear Ratio: ***	Surge Flow: *** cfm
Eff: *** %	Internal Gear Ratio: ***	

EXHAUST

Exhaust System: Small-Tube Headers With Mufflers

CAMSHAFT

Camshaft Type: GM #3927140.	Cam File: ***	
Lifter: Solid	Lobe Center:	112.0
Cam Specs @: 0.050-Lift	Valve Overlap:	24.5
Int Lift@Valve: 0.475 in	Int Duration:	243.0
Exh Lift@Valve: 0.495 in	Exh Duration:	254.0
Nominal Timing	Timing@ Adv(+)/Ret(-):	0.0

IVO (BTDC): 13.5	IVC (ABDC): 49.5	IVO: 13.5	IVC: 49.5
EVO (BBDC): 63.0	EVC (ATDC): 11.0	EVO: 63.0	EVC: 11.0
ICA (ATDC): 108.0	ECA (BTDC): 116.0	ICA: 108.0	ECA: 116.0

1970 Corvette 454-ci Engine (LS7 Clone)

My 1969 Corvette coupe. The LS7 clone was the first engine I installed.

CALCULATED POWER AND ENGINE PRESSURES

Engine RPM	Power (Fly)	Torque (Fly)	Int Man Pressure	Vol Eff %	IMEP Pressure	FMEP Pressure	BMEP Pressure
2000	175	459	14.68	77.5	200.6	18.2	154.6
2500	230	483	14.67	80.5	201.9	19.9	162.5
3000	282	494	14.65	82.8	203.8	21.7	166.3
3500	343	514	14.62	87.5	208.8	23.6	173.1
4000	402	528	14.59	91.3	214.1	25.7	177.7
4500	457	533	14.55	93.5	218.2	28.0	179.4
5000	497	522	14.50	94.4	216.7	30.4	175.8
5500	521	497	14.46	94.0	210.4	32.9	167.4
6000	515	451	14.41	90.4	196.5	35.6	151.8
6500	490	396	14.39	86.1	179.7	38.5	133.3
7000	452	339	14.37	81.7	162.5	41.4	114.2
7500	412	288	14.36	76.9	147.5	44.6	97.1
8000	348	228	14.36	72.1	129.3	47.8	76.9
8500	289	178	14.36	67.4	115.0	51.3	60.1
9000	210	123	14.37	62.5	98.6	54.8	41.3
9500	133	74	14.38	58.2	84.8	58.5	24.8
10000	53	28	14.39	54.2	72.3	62.4	9.3
10500	0	0	14.41	50.3	58.9	66.4	-7.0
11000	0	0	14.42	46.4	47.1	70.5	-22.1

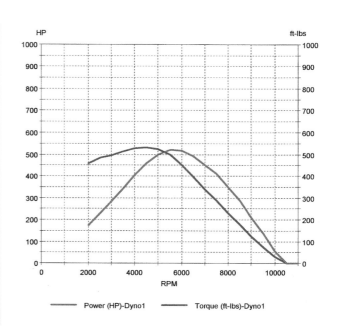

Power (HP)-Dyno1   Torque (ft-lbs)-Dyno1

DYNO PRINT-OUTS

185

SHORT BLOCK

Block: CHEVROLET.	Bore: 4.251 in	Stroke: 4.000 in
Cylinders: 8	Cyl Vol: 930.3 cc	Total Vol: 454.2 ci

CYLINDER HEADS

Cylinder Heads:	Canted/Rectangular Ports, Fully Ported
Air Flow File:	***
Intake Valves: 1	Exhaust Valves: 1
Intake Valve: 2.190 in	Exhaust Valve: 1.880 in

COMPRESSION

Compression Ratio: 9.00	Combustion Space: 116.3 cc

INDUCTION

Induction Flow: 1200.0 cfm @ 1.5 inHg	Fuel: Gasoline
Manifold Type: Dual-Plane Manifold	N20: 0.0 lbs/min

Blower: None		Intercooler: *** %
Flow: *** cfm	Pressure Ratio: ***	Boost Limit: *** psi
Speed: *** rpm	Belt Gear Ratio: ***	Surge Flow: *** cfm
Eff: *** %	Internal Gear Ratio: ***	

EXHAUST

Exhaust System: Large-Tube Headers With Mufflers

CAMSHAFT

Camshaft Type:	CROWER #01321.	Cam File: ***
Lifter:	Solid	Lobe Center: 114.0
Cam Specs @:	0.050-Lift	Valve Overlap: 17.0
Int Lift@Valve:	0.501 in	Int Duration: 244.0
Exh Lift@Valve:	0.513 in	Exh Duration: 246.0
Nominal Timing		Timing@ Adv(+)/Ret(-): 0.0

IVO (BTDC):	12.0	IVC (ABDC):	52.0	IVO: 12.0	IVC: 52.0
EVO (BBDC):	61.0	EVC (ATDC):	5.0	EVO: 61.0	EVC: 5.0
ICA (ATDC):	110.0	ECA (BTDC):	118.0	ICA: 110.0	ECA: 118.0

Chevrolet 492-ci Engine

The second engine I installed in my 1969 Corvette coupe. It is a very strong street performance engine.

CALCULATED POWER AND ENGINE PRESSURES

Engine RPM	Power (Fly)	Torque (Fly)	Int Man Pressure	Vol Eff %	IMEP Pressure	FMEP Pressure	BMEP Pressure
2000	189	496	14.67	72.7	200.6	18.6	154.3
2500	250	525	14.65	76.4	203.5	20.4	163.5
3000	317	554	14.62	80.8	211.2	22.4	172.4
3500	394	591	14.58	87.0	221.2	24.5	183.8
4000	469	616	14.51	91.9	229.9	26.9	191.6
4500	545	635	14.43	96.0	238.9	29.3	197.7
5000	602	632	14.34	98.0	240.6	32.0	196.8
5500	635	606	14.25	97.9	234.7	34.8	188.6
6000	647	566	14.16	96.1	224.4	37.7	176.1
6500	631	510	14.09	92.6	209.0	40.9	158.6
7000	581	436	14.04	87.2	188.0	44.2	135.7
7500	537	376	14.03	82.4	171.6	47.6	117.0
8000	476	313	14.02	78.2	154.4	51.3	97.3
8500	397	245	14.01	72.4	135.9	55.0	76.3
9000	318	186	14.04	68.0	120.2	59.0	57.7
9500	226	125	14.05	63.4	104.4	63.1	38.9
10000	141	74	14.07	59.4	91.7	67.4	23.0
10500	28	14	14.09	55.2	76.4	71.8	4.3
11000	0	0	14.12	51.2	63.7	76.5	-12.0

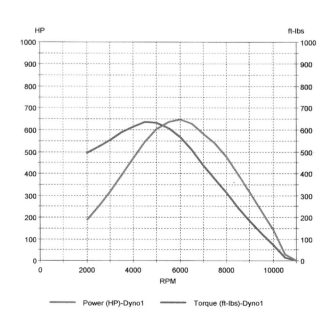

Power (HP)-Dyno1   Torque (ft-lbs)-Dyno1

SHORT BLOCK

Block: CHEVROLET.	Bore: 4.290 in	Stroke: 4.250 in
Cylinders: 8	Cyl Vol: 1006.7 cc	Total Vol: 491.5 ci

CYLINDER HEADS

Cylinder Heads:	Canted/Rectangular Ports, Fully Ported	
Air Flow File:	***	
Intake Valves:	1	Exhaust Valves: 1
Intake Valve:	2.250 in	Exhaust Valve: 1.900 in

COMPRESSION

Compression Ratio: 10.00	Combustion Space: 111.9 cc

INDUCTION

Induction Flow:	990.0 cfm @ 1.5 inHg	Fuel: Gasoline
Manifold Type:	Single-Plane Manifold	N20: 0.0 lbs/min

Blower: None			Intercooler: *** %
Flow: *** cfm	Pressure Ratio: ***		Boost Limit: *** psi
Speed: *** rpm	Belt Gear Ratio: ***		Surge Flow: *** cfm
Eff: *** %	Internal Gear Ratio: ***		

EXHAUST

Exhaust System: Large-Tube Headers With Mufflers

CAMSHAFT

Camshaft Type:	CROWER #01476.	Cam File: ***	
Lifter:	Roller	Lobe Center:	112.0
Cam Specs @:	0.050-Lift	Valve Overlap:	29.0
Int Lift@Valve:	0.559 in	Int Duration:	252.0
Exh Lift@Valve:	0.550 in	Exh Duration:	254.0
Nominal Timing		Timing@ Adv(+)/Ret(-):	0.0

IVO (BTDC):	18.0	IVC (ABDC):	54.0	IVO:	18.0	IVC:	54.0
EVO (BBDC):	63.0	EVC (ATDC):	11.0	EVO:	63.0	EVC:	11.0
ICA (ATDC):	108.0	ECA (BTDC):	116.0	ICA:	108.0	ECA:	116.0

DYNO PRINT-OUTS

Blown Keith Black 541-ci Engine

My 1972 Corvette coupe with the blown Keith Black engine installed. This is an amazing street performance engine.

CALCULATED POWER AND ENGINE PRESSURES

Engine RPM	Power (Fly)	Torque (Fly)	Int Man Pressure	Vol Eff %	IMEP Pressure	FMEP Pressure	BMEP Pressure
2000	274	718	16.67	90.6	258.3	18.6	203.1
2500	365	767	17.91	97.9	263.4	20.4	217.0
3000	454	794	19.15	104.5	268.3	22.4	224.6
3500	534	801	20.38	109.7	267.1	24.5	226.6
4000	610	801	21.60	113.9	266.9	26.9	226.4
4500	681	795	22.83	117.0	267.6	29.3	224.8
5000	731	767	24.04	118.5	262.0	32.0	217.0
5500	753	719	25.26	118.3	250.3	34.8	203.3
6000	731	640	25.96	114.2	229.6	37.7	181.0
6500	689	557	25.94	107.9	207.8	40.9	157.5
7000	628	471	25.93	100.6	185.3	44.2	133.1
7500	581	407	25.93	94.3	169.6	47.6	115.0
8000	535	351	25.93	89.5	156.5	51.3	99.2
8500	449	277	25.93	82.8	138.1	55.0	78.4
9000	408	238	25.94	79.0	130.4	59.0	67.4
9500	317	175	25.94	73.5	115.7	63.1	49.6
10000	254	134	25.95	69.3	107.4	67.4	37.8
10500	192	96	25.95	66.4	100.7	71.8	27.2
11000	77	37	25.95	61.6	87.5	76.5	10.4

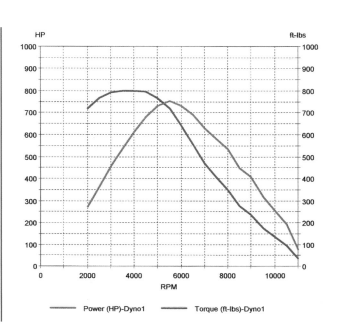

SHORT BLOCK

Block: KEITH BLACK.	Bore: 4.500 in	Stroke: 4.250 in
Cylinders: 8	Cyl Vol: 1107.7 cc	Total Vol: 540.7 ci

CYLINDER HEADS

Cylinder Heads:	Canted/Rectangular Ports, Fully Ported	
Air Flow File:	***	
Intake Valves: 1	Exhaust Valves:	1
Intake Valve: 2.250 in	Exhaust Valve:	1.880 in

COMPRESSION

Compression Ratio: 8.00	Combustion Space: 158.2 cc

INDUCTION

Induction Flow: 1990.0 cfm @ 1.5 inHg		Fuel: Gasoline
Manifold Type: Forced Induction		N20: 0.0 lbs/min

Blower: Roots- Weiand 671			Intercooler: *** %
Flow: 411.0 cfm	Pressure Ratio:	***	Boost Limit: 11.5 psi
Speed: *** rpm	Belt Gear Ratio:	1.24	Surge Flow: *** cfm
Eff: 55.0 %	Internal Gear Ratio:	***	

EXHAUST

Exhaust System: Forced Induction Exhaust

CAMSHAFT

Camshaft Type: CROWER #01404.	Cam File: ***
Lifter: Roller	Lobe Center: 110.0
Cam Specs @: 0.050-Lift	Valve Overlap: 20.5
Int Lift@Valve: 0.586 in	Int Duration: 236.0
Exh Lift@Valve: 0.612 in	Exh Duration: 245.0
Nominal Timing	Timing@ Adv(+)/Ret(-): 0.0

IVO (BTDC): 12.0	IVC (ABDC): 44.0	IVO: 12.0	IVC: 44.0
EVO (BBDC): 56.5	EVC (ATDC): 8.5	EVO: 56.5	EVC: 8.5
ICA (ATDC): 106.0	ECA (BTDC): 114.0	ICA: 106.0	ECA: 114.0

1956 Chrysler 354-ci Hemi Engine

The right side of the completed 1956 Chrysler 354-ci Hemi engine.

CALCULATED POWER AND ENGINE PRESSURES

Engine RPM	Power (Fly)	Torque (Fly)	Int Man Pressure	Vol Eff %	IMEP Pressure	FMEP Pressure	BMEP Pressure
2000	150	393	14.66	75.8	215.3	17.6	167.5
2500	192	403	14.62	78.3	211.7	19.1	172.0
3000	236	413	14.57	80.6	213.5	20.6	176.1
3500	282	423	14.52	84.0	215.6	22.3	180.6
4000	325	427	14.44	86.2	217.2	24.2	182.2
4500	364	425	14.36	87.2	218.1	26.1	181.1
5000	392	412	14.27	87.1	214.4	28.1	175.7
5500	405	387	14.18	85.5	205.2	30.3	165.0
6000	404	354	14.10	82.6	192.5	32.6	150.8
6500	383	309	14.05	78.1	174.9	35.0	132.0
7000	354	265	14.02	73.6	157.6	37.6	113.2
7500	321	224	14.01	69.0	141.7	40.2	95.7
8000	277	182	14.01	64.7	125.2	43.0	77.6
8500	231	143	14.01	60.3	110.5	45.9	61.0
9000	179	104	14.03	56.2	96.0	48.9	44.4
9500	122	67	14.06	52.2	82.4	52.0	28.7
10000	64	34	14.08	48.6	70.5	55.3	14.4
10500	0	0	14.11	45.0	57.7	58.6	-0.9
11000	0	0	14.14	41.7	47.0	62.1	-14.3

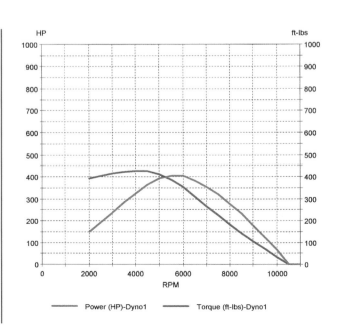

Power (HP)-Dyno1   Torque (ft-lbs)-Dyno1

SHORT BLOCK

Block: CHRYSLER "HEMI".	Bore: 3.968 in	Stroke: 3.625 in
Cylinders: 8	Cyl Vol: 734.6 cc	Total Vol: 358.6 ci

CYLINDER HEADS

Cylinder Heads:	Canted/Rectangular Ports, Fully Ported	
Air Flow File:	***	
Intake Valves:	1	Exhaust Valves: 1
Intake Valve:	1.940 in	Exhaust Valve: 1.750 in

COMPRESSION

Compression Ratio: 9.00	Combustion Space: 91.8 cc

INDUCTION

Induction Flow: 600.0 cfm @ 1.5 inHg		Fuel: Gasoline
Manifold Type: Dual-Plane Manifold		N20: 0.0 lbs/min

Blower: None			Intercooler: *** %
Flow: *** cfm	Pressure Ratio:	***	Boost Limit: *** psi
Speed: *** rpm	Belt Gear Ratio:	***	Surge Flow: *** cfm
Eff: *** %	Internal Gear Ratio:	***	

EXHAUST

Exhaust System: Large-Tube Headers With Mufflers

CAMSHAFT

Camshaft Type:	SHADBOLT.	Cam File: ***	
Lifter:	Solid	Lobe Center:	110.0
Cam Specs @:	0.050-Lift	Valve Overlap:	10.0
Int Lift@Valve:	0.458 in	Int Duration:	230.0
Exh Lift@Valve:	0.457 in	Exh Duration:	230.0
Nominal Timing		Timing@ Adv(+)/Ret(-):	0.0

IVO (BTDC):	9.0	IVC (ABDC):	41.0	IVO: 9.0		IVC: 41.0
EVO (BBDC):	49.0	EVC (ATDC):	1.0	EVO: 49.0		EVC: 1.0
ICA (ATDC):	106.0	ECA (BTDC):	114.0	ICA: 106.0		ECA: 114.0

Blown 1958 Dodge Truck 354-ci Hemi Engine

A right-side photograph of the completed 1958 Dodge Truck 354-ci Hemi engine installed in the owner's 1932 Ford Model B five-window coupe. The engine looks great even though there is still a lot of work to be done to the original metal body.

CALCULATED POWER AND ENGINE PRESSURES

Engine RPM	Power (Fly)	Torque (Fly)	Int Man Pressure	Vol Eff %	IMEP Pressure	FMEP Pressure	BMEP Pressure
2000	161	423	14.89	81.6	230.0	17.6	180.0
2500	218	457	15.69	88.7	236.7	19.1	194.3
3000	274	480	16.48	94.7	244.2	20.7	204.2
3500	328	491	17.27	99.5	246.0	22.4	209.0
4000	378	496	18.05	102.8	247.9	24.2	211.0
4500	431	503	18.82	105.7	253.0	26.1	214.0
5000	477	500	19.54	107.4	253.8	28.2	212.8
5500	500	477	19.50	105.7	245.5	30.4	203.0
6000	516	452	19.47	103.1	236.4	32.7	192.2
6500	528	427	19.44	100.8	227.5	35.1	181.5
7000	522	392	19.42	97.3	214.2	37.7	166.6
7500	513	359	19.40	93.3	202.2	40.3	152.7
8000	497	326	19.38	90.0	190.1	43.1	138.7
8500	468	289	19.37	85.4	176.3	46.0	123.0
9000	436	254	19.36	81.2	163.8	49.0	108.2
9500	397	219	19.36	76.9	151.0	52.2	93.2
10000	362	190	19.36	73.1	141.2	55.5	80.9
10500	311	155	19.36	68.9	128.9	58.8	66.1
11000	260	124	19.37	65.0	118.3	62.4	52.8

SHORT BLOCK

Block: CHRYSLER HEMI.	Bore: 3.968 in	Stroke: 3.635 in
Cylinders: 8	Cyl Vol: 736.6 cc	Total Vol: 359.6 ci

CYLINDER HEADS

Cylinder Heads: Canted/Rectangular Ports, Fully Ported

Air Flow File: ***

Intake Valves: 1	Exhaust Valves: 1
Intake Valve: 2.125 in	Exhaust Valve: 1.945 in

COMPRESSION

Compression Ratio: 8.00   Combustion Space: 105.2 cc

INDUCTION

Induction Flow: 1200.0 cfm @ 1.5 inHg	Fuel: Gasoline
Manifold Type: Forced Induction	N20: 0.0 lbs/min

Blower: Roots- Weiand 671		Intercooler: *** %
Flow: 411.0 cfm	Pressure Ratio: ***	Boost Limit: 5.0 psi
Speed: *** rpm	Belt Gear Ratio: 0.80	Surge Flow: *** cfm
Eff: 55.0 %	Internal Gear Ratio: ***	

EXHAUST

Exhaust System: Forced Induction Exhaust

CAMSHAFT

Camshaft Type:	CROWER BLOWER.	Cam File: ***
Lifter:	Solid	Lobe Center:	112.0
Cam Specs @:	0.050-Lift	Valve Overlap:	0.0
Int Lift@Valve:	0.452 in	Int Duration:	224.0
Exh Lift@Valve:	0.450 in	Exh Duration:	224.0
Nominal Timing		Timing@ Adv(+)/Ret(-):	0.0

IVO (BTDC):	4.0	IVC (ABDC):	40.0	IVO:	4.0	IVC:	40.0
EVO (BBDC):	48.0	EVC (ATDC):	-4.0	EVO:	48.0	EVC:	-4.0
ICA (ATDC):	108.0	ECA (BTDC):	116.0	ICA:	108.0	ECA:	116.0

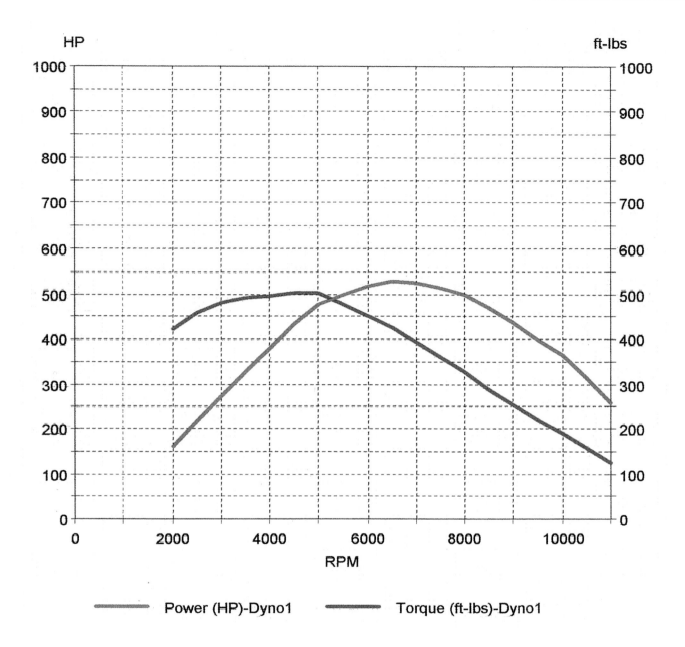

HP ft-lbs

——— Power (HP)-Dyno1   ——— Torque (ft-lbs)-Dyno1

1957 Chrysler 392-ci Hemi Engine

The completed Chrysler 392-ci Hemi engine ready to be installed in the owner's 1950 Ford two-door coupe.

CALCULATED POWER AND ENGINE PRESSURES

Engine RPM	Power (Fly)	Torque (Fly)	Int Man Pressure	Vol Eff %	IMEP Pressure	FMEP Pressure	BMEP Pressure
2000	166	437	16.30	80.1	215.7	18.0	167.5
2500	233	489	17.45	88.8	229.8	19.7	187.6
3000	298	522	18.59	96.3	240.7	21.4	200.3
3500	369	553	19.73	104.2	250.6	23.3	212.4
4000	442	581	20.85	111.3	261.6	25.3	222.8
4500	520	607	21.95	117.3	274.2	27.5	232.8
5000	593	623	23.05	122.5	283.0	29.8	238.9
5500	659	629	24.14	127.0	288.2	32.3	241.5
6000	720	630	25.21	130.6	291.2	34.9	241.9
6500	769	621	26.28	133.4	290.1	37.6	238.2
7000	804	603	27.33	136.0	285.7	40.4	231.3
7500	825	577	28.38	136.2	278.3	43.5	221.6
8000	831	545	29.37	136.8	268.4	46.6	209.2
8500	778	480	29.25	130.5	245.3	49.9	184.4
9000	763	445	29.24	126.7	234.4	53.3	170.9
9500	716	396	29.19	121.5	217.9	56.9	151.9
10000	690	362	29.17	117.4	207.9	60.6	139.0
10500	638	319	29.14	112.6	194.2	64.4	122.5
11000	574	274	29.13	107.2	179.9	68.4	105.2

DYNO PRINT-OUTS

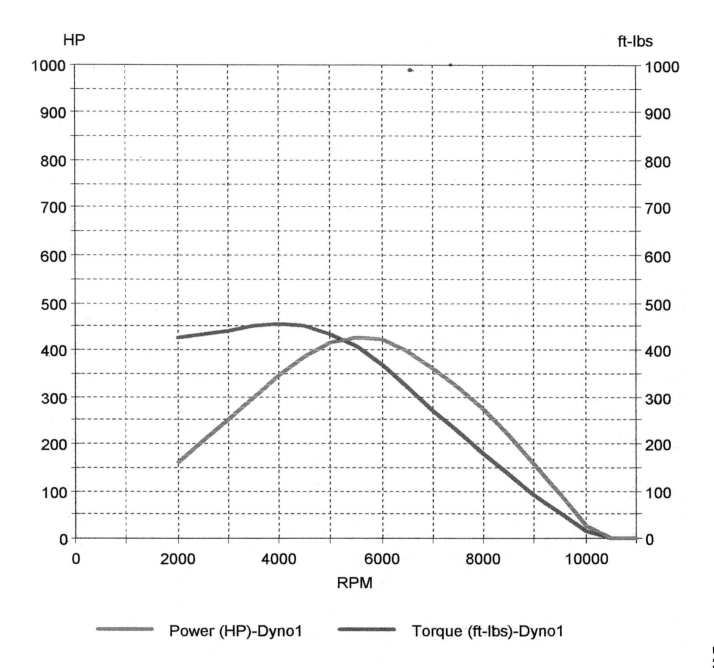

HP

ft-lbs

Power (HP)-Dyno1   Torque (ft-lbs)-Dyno1

SHORT BLOCK

Block: CHRYSLER HEMI.	Bore: 4.040 in	Stroke: 3.906 in
Cylinders: 8	Cyl Vol: 820.5 cc	Total Vol: 400.6 ci

CYLINDER HEADS

Cylinder Heads:	Canted/Rectangular Ports, Fully Ported		
Air Flow File:	***		
Intake Valves:	1	Exhaust Valves:	1
Intake Valve:	2.000 in	Exhaust Valve:	1.938 in

COMPRESSION

Compression Ratio: 9.25	Combustion Space: 99.5 cc

INDUCTION

Induction Flow:	750.0 cfm @ 1.5 inHg	Fuel: Gasoline
Manifold Type:	Dual-Plane Manifold	N20: 0.0 lbs/min

Blower: None				Intercooler: *** %
Flow: *** cfm	Pressure Ratio:	***	Boost Limit: *** psi
Speed: *** rpm	Belt Gear Ratio:	***	Surge Flow: *** cfm
Eff: *** %	Internal Gear Ratio:	***	

EXHAUST

Exhaust System:	Large-Tube Headers With Mufflers

CAMSHAFT

Camshaft Type:	SCHNEIDER #270-H.	Cam File: ***
Lifter:	Hyd.	Lobe Center:	112.0
Cam Specs @:	0.050-Lift	Valve Overlap:	-10.0
Int Lift@Valve:	0.443 in	Int Duration:	214.0
Exh Lift@Valve:	0.443 in	Exh Duration:	214.0
Nominal Timing		Timing@ Adv(+)/Ret(-):	0.0

IVO (BTDC):	-5.0	IVC (ABDC):	39.0	IVO: -5.0		IVC: 39.0
EVO (BBDC):	39.0	EVC (ATDC):	-5.0	EVO: 39.0		EVC: -5.0
ICA (ATDC):	112.0	ECA (BTDC):	112.0	ICA: 112.0		ECA: 112.0

Blown 1957 Chrysler 392-ci Hemi Engine

This blown Chrysler 392-ci Hemi engine is waiting for the owner to take delivery and install it in a 1934 Dodge Truck.

CALCULATED POWER AND ENGINE PRESSURES

Engine RPM	Power (Fly)	Torque (Fly)	Int Man Pressure	Vol Eff %	IMEP Pressure	FMEP Pressure	BMEP Pressure
2000	117	307	14.66	68.7	183.9	17.0	141.4
2500	152	320	14.64	71.6	183.4	18.3	147.5
3000	194	340	14.61	76.4	191.3	19.6	156.8
3500	235	352	14.55	80.6	194.9	21.1	162.5
4000	273	358	14.49	83.7	197.6	22.6	165.1
4500	306	357	14.41	85.5	198.8	24.3	164.7
5000	332	349	14.33	86.4	196.5	26.0	160.8
5500	347	331	14.24	86.1	189.8	27.9	152.8
6000	351	307	14.16	84.4	180.0	29.8	141.7
6500	339	274	14.09	81.1	165.7	31.8	126.3
7000	320	240	14.04	77.7	151.1	33.9	110.6
7500	299	209	14.01	74.3	138.4	36.2	96.5
8000	268	176	13.98	70.9	124.3	38.5	81.0
8500	232	144	13.96	67.0	111.0	40.9	66.2
9000	191	111	13.96	63.5	97.8	43.4	51.4
9500	144	80	13.96	59.8	85.0	46.0	36.8
10000	98	51	13.97	56.5	73.7	48.7	23.6
10500	42	21	13.98	53.3	61.8	51.5	9.7
11000	0	0	14.00	49.8	50.3	54.4	-3.8

DYNO PRINT-OUTS

SHORT BLOCK

Block: CHRYSLER HEMI.	Bore: 4.030 in	Stroke: 3.906 in
Cylinders: 8	Cyl Vol: 816.5 cc	Total Vol: 398.6 ci

CYLINDER HEADS

Cylinder Heads: Canted/Rectangular Ports, Fully Ported

Air Flow File: ***

Intake Valves: 1	Exhaust Valves: 1
Intake Valve: 2.125 in	Exhaust Valve: 1.945 in

COMPRESSION

Compression Ratio: 8.00	Combustion Space: 116.6 cc

INDUCTION

Induction Flow: 1200.0 cfm @ 1.5 inHg	Fuel: Gasoline
Manifold Type: Forced Induction	N20: 0.0 lbs/min

Blower: Roots- Weiand 671	Intercooler: *** %
Flow: 411.0 cfm	Pressure Ratio: ***	Boost Limit: 15.5 psi
Speed: *** rpm	Belt Gear Ratio: 1.15	Surge Flow: *** cfm
Eff: 55.0 %	Internal Gear Ratio: ***

EXHAUST

Exhaust System: Forced Induction Exhaust

CAMSHAFT

Camshaft Type: ENGLE #RK-48	Cam File: ***
Lifter: Roller	Lobe Center: 112.0
Cam Specs @: 0.050-Lift	Valve Overlap: 29.0
Int Lift@Valve: 0.591 in	Int Duration: 253.0
Exh Lift@Valve: 0.589 in	Exh Duration: 253.0
Nominal Timing	Timing@ Adv(+)/Ret(-): 0.0

IVO (BTDC): 17.0	IVC (ABDC): 56.0	IVO: 17.0	IVC: 56.0
EVO (BBDC): 61.0	EVC (ATDC): 12.0	EVO: 61.0	EVC: 12.0
ICA (ATDC): 109.5	ECA (BTDC): 114.5	ICA: 109.5	ECA: 114.5

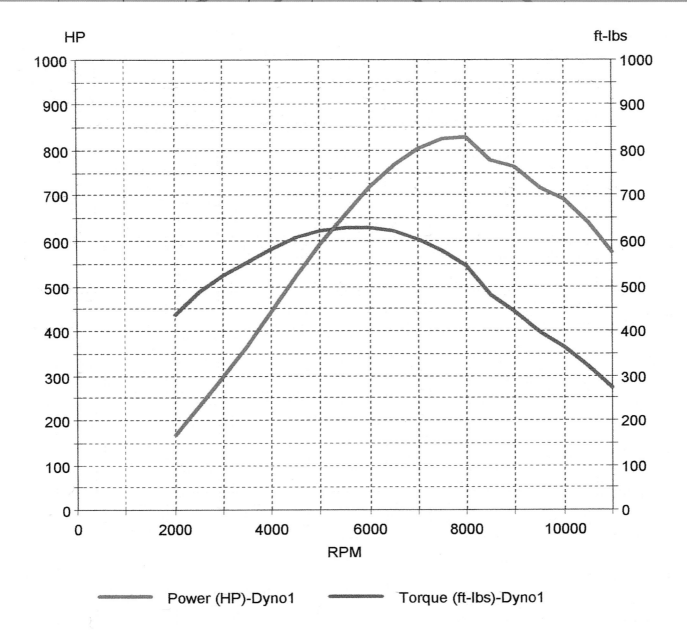

HP   ft-lbs

RPM

━━━ Power (HP)-Dyno1   ━━━ Torque (ft-lbs)-Dyno1

APPENDIX B
RESOURCES

Here is a list, in alphabetical order, of the parties and parts sources I believe are important to know when building a street performance engine. I have given a brief explanation for companies that I presently contact on a regular basis. I have had positive dealings with these companies. I have not received any financial or commercial considerations for mentioning these companies, even though I have frequently hinted that anonymous cash donations and kegs of German Pilsner beer are always welcome!

There are hundreds of speed equipment manufacturers and engine building shops throughout North America. It was not my intention to write a speed equipment directory, and there is not space left in the book to do so.

Parts Sources
Keith Black Racing Engine
11120 Scott Avenue
South Gate, CA 90280-7494
Phone: (562) 869-1518
Fax: (562) 869-2544
Website: www.keithblack.com

Blower Drive Service
12140 E. Washington Boulevard
Whittier, CA 90606
Phone: (562) 693-4302
Fax: (562) 696-7091
Website: www.blowerdriveservice.com

BMS (Bob's Machine Shop), Inc.
4354 South 00 E.W.
Kokomo, IN 46902
Phone: (765) 453-3665

Cad Company (Flashcraft, Inc.)
Formerly: Cadillac Motorsports Development
8333 Jefferson Street N.E.
Albuquerque, NM 87113
Phone: (505) 823-9340
Fax: (505) 797-0627
Website: www.cad500parts.com

Crower Cams & Equipment Company, Inc.
Jerry MacLaughlin of Crower Cams & Equipment Company's technical department has been of the greatest assistance with his recommendations for specific camshafts for particular engines. The products he has suggested have always worked superbly and the quality of the components is outstanding.
3333 Main Street
Chula Vista, CA 91911-5899
Phone: (619) 661-6477
Fax: (619) 661-6466
Website: www.crower.com

Cunningham Rods
550 West 172 Street
Gardena, CA 90248
Phone: (310) 538-0605
Fax: (310) 538-0695
Website: www.cunninghamrods.com
Email: staff@cunninghamrods.com

Edelbrock Corporation
2700 California Street
Torrance, CA 90503
Phone: (310) 781-2222
Fax: (310) 320-1187
Website: www.edelbrock.com

Egge Parts House
11707 Slauson Avenue
Santa Fe Springs, CA 90670
Toll free: 800-886-3443
Phone: (562) 945-3419
Fax: (562) 693-1635
Website: www.egge.com
Email: info@egge.com

Engle Racing Cams, Inc.
1621 12th Street
Santa Monica, CA 90404
Phone: (310) 450-0806
Fax: (310) 452-3753
Website: www.englecams.com

Hedman Street Hedders

16410 Manning Way
Cerritos, CA 90703
Phone: (562) 921-0404
Fax: (562) 921-7515
Website: www.hedman.com
Email: techsupport@hedman.com

High Performance Engines, Ltd.

High Performance Engines is located in Burnaby, British Columbia, Canada, and was founded by Bud Child almost 40 years ago. Bud is now retired and only works eight hours a day, six days a week at the shop! His son, Dave, has taken over the ownership and operation of the business with a dedication to the same high standards Bud practiced.

The machining and engine assembly at High Performance Engines is superb and reasonably priced. This shop builds engines for customers from all over North America, and many of those engines have become record-holding drag race and drag boat winners.

Once again, I would like to thank Dave Child for allowing me access to his shop in order to photograph the engine machining procedures featured in this book. I would also like to thank Dave Cummings, the parts manager of High Performance Engines, for providing me with many of the current part numbers and the availability of those parts.

4329 Buchanan Street
Burnaby, BC V5C 3X7
Canada
Phone: (604) 299-6131
Fax: (604) 299-6017

Hot Heads Research & Racing, Inc.

276 Walker's Hollow Trail
Lowgap, NC 27024
Phone: (336) 352-4866
Fax: (336) 352-3892
Website: www.hotHemiheads.com
Email: info@hotHemiheads.com

J & M Autobody & Paint Ltd.

J & M Autobody & Paint (formerly J & M Enterprises Ltd.) started out over 30 years ago with the restoration of Corvettes. Jerry Olsen and Larry Woida are the founders and owners of that fine establishment. They have been spraying every type of paint imaginable on cars, automobile frames, engines, boats, and helicopters for decades. If the best paint job is a priority, go and see these people.

1764 Powell Street
Vancouver, BC V5L 1H7 Canada
Phone: (604) 254-5505
Fax: (604) 254-4114

Jet Performance Products

17491 Apex Circle
Huntington Beach, CA 92647
Phone: (714) 848-5515
Fax: (714) 847-6290
Website: www.jetchip.com
Email: sales@jetchip.com

Luke's Custom Machine & Design Ltd.

Luke Balogh, owner of Luke's Custom Machine & Design, has operated the business for more than 25 years, although he has been involved in performance engine building and custom automobile building for more than 30 years.

Luke is a true automotive machinist by trade, specializing in lathe and milling machine assignments as well as all types of welding. Luke is renowned for his aluminum designs, fabrication, and welding. He has built a wide variety of engines over the years, but his preference is for the early Chrysler Hemi V-8 engine, the rare Ardun V-8 engine, and the beloved Ford flathead V-8 engine.

1457 Charlotte Road
North Vancouver, BC V7J 1H1
Canada
Phone: (604) 980-8617
Fax: (604) 980-8656

Manley Performance Parts, Inc.

1960 Swarthmore Avenue
Lakewood, NJ 08701
Phone: (732) 905-3366
Fax: (732) 905-3010
Website: www.manleyperformance.com

Mooneyes USA, Inc.

10820 South Norwalk Boulevard
Santa Fe Springs, CA 90670
Phone: (562) 944-6311
Fax: (562) 946-2961
Website: www.mooneyes.com

Pacific Fasteners Ltd.

Pacific Fasteners is one of the best sources for quality stainless-steel bolts, washers, nuts, screws, rods, cotter pins, etc. These people seem to stock everything that is required for an automobile. Bolts can be purchased individually or in bulk quantities, but there is usually a $5 minimum for orders. They will ship FedEx or UPS to just about anywhere.

Pacific Fasteners (U.S.), Inc.
2411 South 200 Street
Seattle, WA 98198
Phone: (206) 824-0416

Fax: (206) 878-1041
Website: www.pacificfasteners.com
Email: pacfast@pacificfasteners.com

Pacific Fasteners Ltd.
3934 East 1 Avenue
Vancouver, BC V5C 5S3
Canada
Phone: (604) 294-9411
Fax: (604) 294-4730

PAW (Performance Automotive Warehouse)

I have purchased parts from PAW in the past, and I found their service to be courteous and prompt. PAW stocks just about every type of speed equipment imaginable for all the popular engines. The company is one of a very few performance centers that offers not only parts for the early Chrysler Hemi engines, but also complete short- and long-block assemblies as well.

21001 Nordhoff Street
Chatsworth, CA 91311
Phone: (818) 678-3000
Fax: (818) 678-3001
Website: www.pawinc.com

Redi-Strip Metal Cleaning Canada Ltd.

Redi-Strip Metal Cleaning Canada has been in business for about 20 years. The company specializes in all types of metal cleaning, from engine blocks to entire automobile body shells. They do excellent work and their prices are reasonable. They also have a separate division for metallic-ceramic-coating exhaust headers and systems.

7961 Vantage Way
Delta, BC V4G 1A6
Canada
Phone: (604) 946-7761
Fax: (604) 946-5936

Ross Racing Pistons

In June 2001, I was in Los Angeles on business and I took that opportunity to visit Ross Racing Pistons and meet Ken Roble, the president. I had been buying all my pistons from Ross Racing Pistons for a number of years, and I thought it was time to meet Ken. Roble has been an avid hot rodder all his life, and he is an extremely talented tool and die maker, responsible for much of the tooling at his company.

I was given the grand tour of the Ross Racing Pistons facilities and was more than suitably impressed. Ross Racing Pistons produces top-quality pistons using state-of-the-art CNC machining technology. The result is one of the best pistons available at an affordable price. Ross Racing Pistons can custom build just about

any type of piston, from lawnmowers to aircraft size. Thank you, Ken, for the great tour!

625 South Douglas
El Segundo, CA 90245
Toll free: 800-392-7677
Tech line: (310) 536-0100
Fax: (310) 536-0333
Website: www.rosspistons.com

RPM Catalog (Dale Wilch's)

Dale Wilch is the owner of RPM Catalog in Kansas City, Kansas. He has been selling used speed equipment for years. Dale always has some interesting vintage parts for sale, and he frequently sells these items on eBay. I have purchased items from him in the past and found his service to be courteous, efficient, and prompt. His prices are competitive.

Dale Wilch
RPM Catalog
P.O. Box 12301
Kansas City, KS 66112
Phone: (913) 788-3219
Fax: (913) 788-9682
Website: www.rpmcat.com

Sanderson Headers
517 Railroad Avenue
South San Francisco, CA 94080
Phone: (650) 583-6617
Fax: (650) 583-8475
Website: www.sandersonheaders.com
Email: sales@sandersonheaders.com

Scat Enterprises, Inc.
1400 Kingsdale Avenue
Redondo Beach, CA 90278
Phone: (310) 370-5501
Fax: (310) 214-2285
Website: www.scatenterprises.com

Schneider Racing Cams, Inc.
1235 Cushman Avenue
San Diego, CA 92110
Phone: (619) 297-0227
Fax: (619) 297-0577
Website: www.schneidercams.com

Smith Brothers Pushrods
1320 S.E. Armour Road, #A-1
Bend, OR 97702
Toll free: 800-367-1533

RESOURCES

Phone: (541) 388-8188
Fax: (541) 389-8840
Website: www.pushrods.net
Email: smithbros@bendcable.com

Summit Racing Equipment
P.O. Box 909
Akron, OH 44309-0909
Toll free: 800-230-3030
Fax: (330) 630-5333
Website: www.summitracing.com

Titan Speed Engineering, Inc.
13001 Tree Ranch Road
Ojai, CA 93023
Phone: (805) 525-8660
Fax: (805) 933-1028

Website: www.titanspeed.com
Email: info@titanspeed.com

Wilkinson's Automobilia
Wilkinson's Automobilia is one of the finest sources of vintage and current automotive books, shop manuals, chassis manuals, and hot rod magazines. Some of the publications they have in stock date back to the early part of the twentieth century. They seem to stock just about everything. These people are extremely helpful and friendly.

2531 Ontario Street
Vancouver, BC V5T 2X7
Canada
Phone: (604) 873-6242
Fax: (604) 873-6259
Website: www.eautomobilia.com
Email: info@wilkinsonsauto.com

INDEX

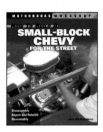

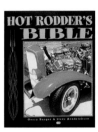

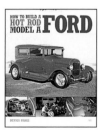
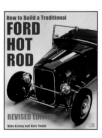